standard catalog of®

GERMAN
MILITARY
VEHICLES

MW00562908

DAVID DOYLE

©2005 David Doyle

Published by

kp books

An imprint of F+W Publications, Inc.

700 East State Street • Iola, WI 54990-0001
715-445-2214 • 888-457-2873

Our toll-free number to place an order or obtain
a free catalog is (800) 258-0929.

Library of Congress Catalog Number: 2004115354

ISBN: 0-87349-783-x

Designed by Jamie Griffin

Edited by Brian Earnest

Printed in United States of America

Cover photo: Panzer III Ausf. L, owned by Kevin Wheatcroft. (Simon Thomson photo)
Back cover photo: Sd. Kfz. 10 halftrack and Nebelwerfer 41 six-tube rocket launcher.
(Simon Thomson photo

Dedication

This book is dedicated to the hundreds of Signal Corps photographers and Kriegsberichters without whose work, this and many other books, would not have been possible.

Acknowledgments

This book is about the vehicles and equipment used by the German soldier during WWII. It is not a celebration of the soldiers', or their leaders' political ideology, nor the motivation for the creation of this equipment.

Much of the material contained herein has had an interesting lifecycle. Manufacturers took photographs of newly created equipment. The pride in their craftsmanship is evident in the pristine appearance of the equipment. The dramatic poses of the vehicles so often captured on film were often not so much a reflection of national pride, as a reflection of craftsmen's pride.

Soldier-photographers on both sides—Allied combat photographers (typified by the U.S. Signal Corps photographers) and the German Kriegsberichters—captured on film these vehicles in use, and under repair. But once the "new" of the product was gone, and once the war ended, these photographs and related documents often became so much clutter. Factories closed, firms merged, and the secret weapons of the past became common. Photographs, negatives and documents by the thousand were discarded and destroyed.

A book like this is the result of the efforts of dozens of people, hundreds perhaps. Though my name appears solely on the cover of this work, and other books may be attributed to two or three authors, these distinctions are not entirely accurate. Much of the material that we have today was collected and preserved by a handful of enthusiasts, who made a point of being at the right places, at the right time, and took it upon themselves to gather and preserve this material. Col. Robert Icks, Richard Hunnicutt, Fred Crismon, G.B. Jarrett, Armin Sohns, Charles Kliment, and Walter Spielberger all compiled vast amounts of information, and have openly shared this material with the world through their publications. Not only that, they have willingly shared this material with this and other researchers either through direct loan, or through the donation of the private archives to public archives both here and abroad.

No less important are the staffs of the various archives now housing these and other collections. Usually working under less-than-ideal and underfinanced conditions, these curators and archivists toil on--largely as a labor of love--cataloging and preserving these documents and photographs for future generations. Candace Fuller and Charles Lemons at the Patton Museum, Ft. Knox, Kentucky, are two of these preservationists. They gave willingly of their time and energies helping compile this work, and their contribution cannot be overstated. Ann Bos at the U.S. Army Tank–Automotive and Armaments Command likewise was a great help, as was the staff at the Military History Institute, Carlisle Barracks, and the Ordnance Museum, Aberdeen Proving Ground, Maryland, and of course, the U.S. National Archives.

Also invaluable were the new generation of photo and document preservationist/collector. These individuals often gather material from a previously ignored source – the individual soldier. Stefan De Meyer has amassed a huge collection of images, and graciously lent me as many as I needed. So, too, Patrick Stansell of *Military Miniatures in Review*, who, along with Stefan, proofread, corrected and suggested changes in the text. Mike Harpe and Christian Ankerstjerne filled missing holes in the manuscript with images from their personal collections. BMW generously supplied photos and technical information regarding its military production. Noted motorcycle collector John Lacko spent hours sharing his knowledge with me. Karl Dietrick located and forwarded many documents to me, and Simon Thomson generously supplied the cover photos.

My editor, Brian Earnest, graciously endured seemingly unending rewrites as more and more material was uncovered, yet somehow kept the project moving forward. My friend John Adams-Graf kept me focused on the big picture when I started going too far astray, or going too deep into a specific area. Heaven will hold a special place for friends and professionals like John.

Also a special "thank you" to my friends and family, who suffered through two years of neglect or irritability as I worked 12 or more hours per day, six or more days a week, on this project. You all put up with a lot, and it is appreciated more than I can say.

Introduction   6

Fully tracked Armored Vehicles

Tanks   9

Assault guns   100

Jagdpanzers   128

Recovery vehicles   146

Antiaircraft tanks   153

Self-propelled fully tracked howitzers and mortars   165

Panzerjäger   202

Flammpanzer   244

Fully tracked armored engineer vehicles   261

Fully tracked armored support vehicles   281

Wheeled and semi-tracked armored vehicles

Armored Cars   **290**

Armored Half-tracks   **341**

Softskin Vehicles

Motorcycles   **397**

Pkw – Personenkraftwagen (cars)   **409**

Lkw – Lastkraftwagen (trucks)   **429**

Unarmored halftracks   **456**

Unarmored full-tracked prime movers   **497**

Glossary   **501**
List of Kfz. & Sd.Kfz. Numbers   **507**
Index   **511**

Introduction

The study of Germany's WWII weapons has been an area of interest and fascination for historians, modelers, strategists and collectors since even before the war ended.

The German propaganda machine, mistakes on the part of Allied military intelligence, and the lack of careful research based on original documents together have fueled an almost mythical mystique about much of this equipment. Indeed, to read some accounts it seems almost a miracle that the Allies prevailed. In this volume every effort has been made to present only factual information obtained from original documents, with the goal being to present an impartial view of the equipment described herein.

While Germany's military-industrial complex did foster a number of creative designs, and design elements, some of which were the basis for concepts in use today, many other designs can be considered failures.

The limited manufacturing resources of wartime Germany were scattered over many unproven projects, and continual redesign stymied the actual production of many vehicles.

In this volume you will find described, and in almost every case illustrated with multiple views, every armored vehicle actually put to use by German troops. Similarly, most of the specialized, unarmored, "softskin" vehicles are shown and described as well. Unfortunately, many of the support vehicles did not garner the same level of attention from photographers as their armored brethren, either from the German propaganda ministry or Allied intelligence.

While, of course, the bulk of the material referred to in the preparation of this volume was written in German,

it is recognized that this work will be printed in English. Therefore, most terms are presented in English, especially the less common ones. Books printed for English-speaking audiences are often so littered with German language terms it seems the authors are attempting to showcase their command of that tongue, rather than providing the reader with meaningful information. This can result in the reader spending as much time digging into a German-English dictionary as is spent reading the text itself!

In most cases the vehicles herein are referred to by the terms used by the German military establishment. This, however, does not mean that other terms are "wrong." While the German military did not refer to the Tiger II as a "Royal Tiger," or a Panzerkampfwagen IV as a "Mark IV," both of those terms were used during wartime by the British when referring to these tanks. To say these terms are "wrong" is akin to a Brit telling an American that a device conveying people vertically in a building is not an elevator, but rather a lift. Correct terminology is dependent upon the speaker's perspective. To tell an English-speaking reader that there was six of a given vehicle per Abteilung is often meaningless, whereas saying that the six vehicles per battalion presents a clear picture of the same situation. The most common technical terms are found from time to time throughout the text, in context that is self-explanatory, in hopes this will help the reader to become familiar with them, and even aid them in reading other texts. A glossary is also provided encompassing both English and German technical terms.

This volume is arranged in the following manner. First, fully tracked armored vehicles are presented, grouped by function rather than chassis (tanks, tank destroyers, etc.). This is followed by semi-tracked and wheeled armored vehicles. These are arranged by chassis type. The third

section, unarmored or "soft skin" vehicles, is also arranged by chassis type. The goal is to provide the quickest means for the reader to locate the entry desired. Form follows function closely with most full-tracked armored vehicles. That is, a tank is easily distinguished from an armored bridge layer, while a communications halftrack looks like a personnel carrier to the average eye.

An effort has been made to provide views of each side of each major vehicle variation, with the photos being a mixture of both pristine "factory" photos as well as vehicles in service, or "combat" photos. In some instances this has simply not been possible, either because of a scarcity of photos or because of space considerations. The use of photos of restored or preserved vehicles has been avoided as much as possible. Oftentimes these vehicles show the modifications made during wartime, but also innumerable changes made by captured equipment evaluators, civilian owners and well-meaning but under-funded museum staffs, or those bowing to pressure to present a visually appealing display at the sacrifice of authenticity.

Tabulated technical data has been provided for these vehicles. This is limited to the features that are of interest to most enthusiasts and model builders. Keep in mind that, short of cataloging each individual vehicle, it would be impossible to present a 100-percent complete and accurate record of the German arsenal. Manufacturing variations were commonplace as engineers attempted to both improve

the vehicles and cope with material and component shortages caused by the turning tide of the war. These improvements are often blurred by the first-in, last-out inventory control method used by the assembly firms. Older parts were literally buried under new arriving stocks, resurfacing only when the new stocks were exhausted. This led to an almost infinite number of variations, which were then compounded by field repairs, depot rebuilding and troop modifications.

While an overview has been provided herein of Germany's military motor pool, for additional, detailed reading on specific vehicle types many specialized titles exist. The Allied-Axis series from Ampersand Publishing, various authors; Walter Spielberger, the dean of German armor's Militärfahrzeuge series; Charles Kliment's various works on Czechoslovak-built vehicles; and Hilary Doyle and Tom Jentz's Panzer Tracts series are especially recommended. Rheinhard Frank's books on soft skin vehicles are also worthwhile additions to this list.

FULLY TRACKED
ARMORED VEHICLES

The Panzer I series

Panzerkampfwagen I Ausf. A ohne Aufbau

The Treaty of Versailles, which ended World War I, was intended to prevent the re-arming of Germany, and so banned Germany's production or ownership of armored fighting vehicles. For this reason ,when the production contracts were awarded to Krupp-Gruson, MAN, Daimler-Benz, Henschel and MAN for 3 vehicles each, the vehicles were referred to as Landwirtschaftlicher Schlepper, or "agricultural tractor." Regardless of the manufacturer, the vehicles were all produced to the Krupp design, and were utilized as training vehicles to provide trainees experience with tracklaying vehicles.

The suspension system of the production Panzer I A was based on a Carden-Loyd design, with the lead road wheel using a coil spring and hydraulic shock absorber. The remaining four road wheels on each side were mounted in pairs on leaf springs, which were supported by an external girder.

The light weight, light armament, light armor and small size were a far cry from the fearsome Panther and Tiger tanks Germany would field less than a decade later.

Panzer I A (Sd Kfz 101)

The Panzer I Ausf. A was the first tank mass produced for WWII-era German Army. Production began in October 1934 and continued into 1936, by which time 1,190 had been produced by five firms. The initial order for 135 had been with Krupp, but additional

The Panzerkampfwagen I was the first tank Germany developed after WWI. The design was done clandestinely because of postwar prohibitions against Germany rearming.

contracts for three each were awarded to Daimler-Benz, MAN, Henschel and Krupp-Gruson, bringing the total of the first run to 150 units. The Panzer I A was initially designated MG Panzerwagen (armored machine gun carrier), but was soon renamed.

The Panzer I Ausf. A was built on the same suspension used on the Panzerkampfwagen I Ausf. A ohne Aufbau, with some modification of the superstructure. The fighting compartment was extended over the tracks, and a turret was mounted on top of it, offset to the right. The turret was armed with dual co-axial 7.92mm MG13 machine guns. The two-man crew consisted of the commander, who rode in the turret, and the driver, who rode in the hull.

The Panzer I A was withdrawn from combat service during 1941.

Panzer I B (Sd Kfz 101)

The Panzer I Ausf. A was an underpowered vehicle, and its engine was susceptible to overheating. Therefore, it was decided to adapt the chassis that had been developed for the kI Pz Bef Wg for use in an improved model. The new version was longer than that of the previous models, but retained the two-man crew. The new version was designated the Panzer I B (Sd Kfz 101) and could be distinguished by its five road wheels and separate rear idler (vs. the Ausf. A's four road wheels, and rear idler that doubled as a road wheel as well). The Panzer I B had four return rollers. Like the Ausf. A, the suspension of the Ausf. B was patterned after that of the Carden-Loyd carrier.

The Panzer I Ausf. B (Sd Kfz 101) was built by four of the five firms that had built the Ausf. A — the exception

Four road wheels and three return rollers distinguish the Panzerkampfwagen I Ausf. A from the later Ausf. B.

Though missing from this example, the Panzerkampfwagen Ausf. A was armed with two 7.92 mm M.G. 13k machine guns.

The Ausf. A would see combat in cold climates as Germany pushed in to Poland, Belgium, and Czechoslovakia.

Some of the Ausf. A tanks were also especially modified to operate in the tropical conditions of North Africa.

The Panzerkampfwagen I Ausf. B added a fifth roadwheel and fourth return roller. This captured example was photographed on display at Aberdeen Proving Ground in April 1947.
Ordnance Museum, Aberdeen Proving Ground.

being Rheinmetall. Production was underway in August 1936 and continued through May 1937, with production totaling 399 tanks. The Panzer I B was used as a tank from 1936 until June 1941, however, it continued to serve as a command vehicle for certain tank-hunter units into 1943.

Panzer I C

Ausf. C development began in September 1939. The goal was to develop a light airborne reconnaissance vehicle. Only 40 of these vehicles were produced, all by

Patton Museum, Fort Knox, KY

Here is an Ausf. A (in the background) and an Ausf. B (foreground) loaded for rail transport. The revised exhaust system is clearly visible.

Patton Museum, Fort Knox, KY

The Panzerkampfwagen I's twin 7.92mm MG13 machine guns were effective against infantry, but soon were outmatched when pitted against other armored vehicles.

This example, evaluated at Aberdeen Proving Ground in 1942, is missing much of its engine compartment. Nevertheless the suspension is shown to good advantage.

The Panzerkampfwagen I C had a radically different appearance due to its torsion bar suspension and overlapping road wheels.

The Pz. Kpfw. I C was armed with one 7.92 MG34 and one EW141 MG. It was intended for fast reconnaissance work.

Locomotivenfabrik Krauss-Maffei AG, with turrets and superstructures designed by Daimler-Benz. The Panzer I Ausf. C was a totally different vehicle from the Ausf. A and B. Rather than the Carden-Loyd suspension used previously, the Ausf. C ran on a torsion-bar suspension with interleaved road wheels known as geschachteltes Laufwerk.

The Ausf. C was armed with a 2cm EW141 machine gun and a coaxially mounted 7.92mm MG34.

Two of these vehicles were tested in Russia during 1943. The remainder were held in reserve until the invasion in Normandy.

Walter J. Spielberger

The power plant was also upgraded, allowing it to reach a top speed in excess of 65 kilometers per hour.

Panzer I F

The Panzer Ausf. F was designed to be an infantry assault tank, and had increased armor protection. Design work on the Ausf. F chassis and superstructure was done by Locomotivenfabrik Krauss-Maffei AG, with a Daimler-Benz designed turret. The Ausf. F featured the geschachteltes Laufwerk interleaved wheels similar to the type used on German half-tracks and heavy tanks.

Development of the Ausf. F had begun in 1939, but the limited production run of 30 vehicles wasn't begun until April 1942, and was concluded by December of the same year. Like all the Panzer I series vehicles, this tank was armed with twin MG34 machine guns to suit its role as an infantry assault tank. It saw considerable service with the SS police units.

A final unusual version of the Panzerkampfwagen I family was the Panzerkampfwagen I Ausf. F. This little tank had exceptionally heavy armor, and broader track to support the increased weight.

Walter J. Spielberger

Kleiner Panzerbefehlswagen (Sd Kfz 265)

During the early stages of the war radio communication, neither small transmitters nor large tanks were very advanced, even though they were considered crucial to the successful use of armor. Therefore, special command vehicles were constructed in order to house these transmitters and transport the field commanders into the fray while still offering some degree of protection.

Rather than the normal turret, an extended superstructure was mounted on top of modified Panzerkampfwagen I Ausf. B. Ihe transmitter, receiver and an MG 34 were all inside this fixed "turret." Production of these vehicles began in mid-1936. The Kleiner Panzerbefehlswagen was built new by Daimler-Benz utilizing chassis built by Daimler-Benz, Henschel and Grusonwerk. Rather than being converted battle tanks, these were built specifically for this purpose. Ultimately, 184 were produced. As two-way radio communications became standard in combat tanks the Kleiner Panzerbefehlswagen was transferred to artillery units for use as fire control centers, and for use by forward observers.

Panzerkampfwagen I Ausf. A

Length	4.02 m	Communications	Fu 2
Width	2.06 m		
Height	1.72 m	Weapon, main	2 x 7.92 MG 13k
Weight	5.4 tons	Ammo stowage, main	2,250 rnds
Fuel capacity	140 liters		
Maximum speed	37.5 km/hr (23.25 mph)	Engine make	Krupp
Range, on road	140 km (86.9 miles)	Engine configuration	four-cylinder, air-cooled
Range, cross country	93 km (57.66 miles)	Engine displacement	3.5 liter
Crew	2	Engine horsepower	60 @ 2500 rpm

Panzerkampfwagen I Ausf. B

Length	4.42 m	Weapon, main	2 x 7.92 MG 13k
Width	2.06 m		
Height	1.72 m	Ammo stowage, main	2,250 rnds
Weight	5.8 tons		
Fuel capacity	146 liters	Engine make	Maybach
Maximum speed	40 km/hr (24.8 mph)	Engine model	NL 38 Tr
Range, on road	170 km (105.4 miles)	Engine configuration	six-cylinder, liquid cooled
Range, cross country	115 km (71.3 miles)	Engine displacement	3.8 liter
Crew	2	Engine horsepower	100 @ 3000 rpm
Communications	Fu 2		

Panzerkampfwagen I Ausf. C

Length	4.195 m	Weapon, main	1 x 7.92 MG 34, 1 x 7.92mm EW 141
Width	1.92 m		
Height	1.945 m		
Weight	8 tons	Ammo stowage, main	2100 rnds
Fuel capacity	170 liters	Engine make	Maybach
Maximum speed	79 km/hr (48.98 mph)	Engine configuration	six-cylinder, liquid cooled
Range, on road	300 km (1,860 miles)		
Range, cross country	190 km (117.8 miles)	Engine displacement	4.678 liter
Crew	2	Engine horsepower	150 @ 3800 rpm
Communications	Fu.Spr.Ger. A		

Panzerkampfwagen I Ausf. F

Length	4.375 m	Weapon, main	2 x 7.92 MG 34
Width	2.64 m		
Height	2.05 m	Ammo stowage, main	5100 rnds
Weight	21 tons		
Fuel capacity	180 liters	Engine make	Maybach
Maximum speed	25 km/hr (15.5 mph)	Engine model	HL 45 P
Range, on road	150 km (93 miles)	Engine configuration	six-cylinder, liquid cooled
Range, cross country	110 km (68.2 miles)	Engine displacement	4.678 liter
Crew	2	Engine horsepower	150 @ 3800 rpm
Communications	Fu. 2		

Military History Institute, Carlisle Barracks, PA.

Of course the change in power plant brought about a redesign of the Ausf. C hull rear.

Only a few of these Ausf. F vehicles actually saw combat, and the bulk of the planned production was cancelled. The vehicles were armed with twin MG 34 machine guns.

Walter J. Spielberger

The Kleiner Panzerbefehlswagen, built as an armored observation vehicle, did not have a rotating turret. Rather, its enlarged, fixed superstructure housed a radio transmitter, in addition to the receiver as carried in a standard Panzerkampfwagen I.

Patton Museum, Fort Knox, KY

Patton Museum, Fort Knox, KY

The only armament carried by the Kleiner Panzerbefehlswagen was a ball-mounted MG 34 on the face of the superstructure. After being phased out in tank units, these unusual vehicles continued to be used as observation vehicles by the artillery and armored ambulances.

Panzerkampfwagen II

The Panzerkampfwagen II was intended to supplement forces equipped with the Panzerkampfwagen I by providing them with a more heavily armed tank. The Panzerkampfwagen II was armed with a 20mm KwK in addition to a machine gun. The classification of the various versions of the Panzerkampfwagen II, using upper and lower case letters, is somewhat confusing.

The earliest models of the Panzer II, the Ausf. a/1, a/2 and a/3, the earliest appearing in 1936, even resembled the Panzerkampfwagen I, particularly in the suspension area. These three versions were essentially a preproduction series, with very low numbers.

The next version was the Panzerkampfwagen II Ausf. B, which was introduced in February, 1937. Again, relatively low numbers were produced, with most of the improvements being internal, however, the vehicle did have wider tracks than its predecessor.

The Panzerkampfwagen II Ausf, c, differed radically from the earlier ausfürung. The three variants of the Ausf. c, the A, B and C, each had five large road wheels rather than six smaller road wheels, and the front of the hull was rounded.

With the introduction of next version the following month, the Ausf c, the Panzerkampfwagen II had taken the form in which it is most often remembered. The Panzer I-style suspension with six small road wheels was discarded and replaced with a system employing five

The suspension of the Panzerkampfwagen II Ausf. a/1, a/2, a/3 and b was reminscent of the Panzerkampfwagen I in construction. However, beyond this similarity there was little in common between the two vehicles. These early models of the Panzerkampfwagen II were produced in very limited numbers beginning in 1936.

The detail of the new type suspension system and hull front can be seen clearly in this factory photo of a Panzer II-based bridgelayer. The Ausf. c was the most widely produced version of the Panzerkampfwagen II.

Automotively, the Panzerkampfwagen II was reasonably successful, and even after it was phased out of service as a combat tank in 1943 the chassis was used for self-propelled guns and other vehicles.

As built the Panzerkampfwagen II had a split hatch in the turret roof for the commander. It is seen here in the open position. Due to limited visibility, in late 1940 a modification was authorized which installed a cupola with eight periscopes.

A major area of complaint was insufficient armor protection. This was addressed by bolting additional 20 mm-thick armor plates on the faces of the hull, turret and superstructure. These additional armor plates masked the rounded shape of the transmission housing.

large road wheels. The Ausf. c was produced in three sub-variants, A through C, which differed in detail. However, the armor of the Panzerkampfwagen II was found to be insufficient, and additional armor plates were retrofitted to the vehicles, increasing the number of different looking vehicles even more. The Ausf. c was the first version of the Panzerkampfwagen II to be truly mass-produced, with more than 1,000 delivered.

The chassis of the Panzerkampfwagen II Ausf. D and Ausf. E were unlike their predecessors. In fact, the only major area that looked the same was the turret. These tanks used a torsion bar suspension system with double road wheels. Less than 50 were built, and they were later converted to flame throwers.

The Panzerkampfwagen II Ausf. F was similar to the Ausf. c, but with some improvements. The rounded hull front was replaced with a flat-paneled one, and the front of the superstructure was redesigned. The bulk of the Panzerkampfwagen II Ausf. F chassis production was diverted for use building self-propelled antitank guns, resulting in only about 500 being completed as gun tanks by the time production ceased at the end of 1942.

Many attempts were made through the years to produce a Panzerkampfwagen II specifically for use in fast reconnaissance. None of these projects resulted in mass-produced vehicles, despite considerable effort and bold projections.

The VK 901, designated the Ausf. G, was an improved Ausf. D and was the intended replacement for the Ausf. F. From April of 1941 through February 1942 M.A.N.

This close up view of the turret reveals the conical armor bolts used to secure the supplemental armor. Almost out of the frame is the retrofitted cupola with periscopes as well.

Military History Institute, Carlisle Barracks, PA

produced a dozen of these as trial vehicles, although plans had been laid for them years before. In a departure from earlier practice, the Ausf. G was armed with an EW141 2.0 cm heavy machine gun with a coaxial 7.92mm MG34 machine gun. In January of 1942, the Ausf. G were rearmed with heavier 5.0 cm Pak 38 L/60 main guns and were shipped to the Russian Front for troop testing. The significant delays in fielding the trial vehicles led to an overall loss of interest, with more emphasis shifted to later models.

The Ausf. H was, naturally enough, the successor to the Ausf. G. Also known as the VK 903, the Ausf. H had heavier armor than the earlier model. Armament reverted to the 2.0 cm Kw.K. 38 L/55 cannon and 7.92mm MG34 machine gun. The Ausf. H was also intended to utilize the transmission from the Panzerkampfwagen 38(t). Despite ambitious production plans, the Ausf. H never advanced beyond the prototype stage.

The companion vehicle for the Ausf. H was to have been the Ausf. M. This vehicle was initially planned with

Even with the additional armor, spare track sections were stowed in areas believed to be vulnerable to act as even more protection as seen on this vehicle captured in North Africa.

Patton Museum, Fort Knox, KY

The Panzerkampfwagen II Ausf. c had a considerably more modern appearance than did Germany's earlier tanks, even though only 3 years had passed since the Panzerkampfwagen I had been introduced. This captured vehicle has had its 20 cm KwK L/55 removed.

The upper left side of the engine compartment was flat, while the right side sloped upward toward the turret ring. A pair of spare road wheels can be seen stowed on the left side.

The main weapon and most of the external stowage has been removed from this captured Panzerkampfwagen I, affording a clear view of the superstructure and turret configuration. Note the layout of the cooling air intakes and exhausts.

While the Panzerkampfwagen II had been used as a combat tank during the invasion of Poland, by the time of the African campaign the Panzerkampfwagen II had been relegated primarily to a reconnaissance role. The small size of this Ausf. c can be judged by the crewman riding on the turret.

a 5.0 cm Kw.K. 39/1 cannon, but the trial vehicle instead carried the 2.0 cm Kw.K. 38 L/55 main gun. Its builder's designation was VK1301.

The VK 1601, or Ausf. J, was produced in larger numbers than many of these other trial vehicles. Twenty-two of these vehicles, armed with 2.0 cm Kw.K. 38 L/55 cannon and 7.92mm MG34 machine gun, were produced. The Ausf. J was better protected than were the G, H or even M, with plating up to 80mm thick in places. Thirty-millimeter plate was the maximum found on more common models.

Also unlike most of these unusual Panzerkampfwagen II vehicles, the Ausf. J actually saw combat. The Twelfth Panzer Division, operating on the Eastern Front, received seven of the vehicles during 1943. One of these later had its turret removed in the field, and a boom retrofitted. It served with the 116th Panzer Division's Panzer Werkstatt Kompanie (Tank Repair Company).

Probably the most widely known of the advanced Panzerkampfwagen II was the Panzerspähwagen II Ausf. L, also known as the Luchs (Lynx). The Luchs, or VK 1303, was an improvement on the VK 1301, with the objective being increased speed. Although 500 of these vehicles were originally ordered, the contracts were changed to reduce total production to 100 combat-worthy vehicles. The Sd.Kfz. number assigned was 123.

Deliveries of the new vehicles began by M.A.N. in September 1942 and continued through January 1944.

Despite earlier plans to arm some of the vehicles with 5.0 cm cannon, ultimately all of them mounted the 2.0 cm Kw.K.38.

Initially, a triple-radius steering unit was installed, but on later production a clutch brake steering unit was used instead. The ZF Aphon SSG48 gearbox was used in all of the Luchs.

While two companies were outfitted with the Luchs, the remainder of the vehicles were parceled out in small numbers to a handful of reconnaissance units on both fronts.

While the Panzerkampfwagen II had a solid automotive design, its armor and armament were quickly outpaced, rendering the vehicle obsolete early in the war, regardless of form.

Patton Museum, Fort Knox, KY

The commander of this Panzerkampfwagen II Ausf. F watches a German observation plane pass by. The Ausf. F had a revised front plate on the superstructure, which included a dummy vision port seen here to the left of the real driver's vision port. Its function was to draw fire from the relatively vulnerable actual vision port.

Patton Museum, Fort Knox, KY

A pair of Panzerkampfwagen II of the famed Afrika Korps prepare to move out. The commander was the only member of the three-man crew to have reasonable visibility from the small vehicle. Notice the extra rack added to the fender which is holding extra 5 gallon water cans. While gas was essential for the tank, water was even more important for the crew in the heat of the North African day.

Pz Kpfw II Ausf a/1, a/2 und a/3 (Sd Kfz 121)

Length	4.38 m	Weapon, coaxial	7.92mm MG 34
Width	2.14 m	Ammo stowage, main	180 rnds
Height	1.95 m		
Weight	7.6 tons	Ammo stowage, secondary	2,250 rnds
Fuel capacity	170 liters		
Maximum speed	40 km/hr (24.8 mph)	Engine make	Maybach
Range, on road	190 km (117.8 miles)	Engine model	HL57TR
		Engine configuration	straight six-cylinder
Crew	3		
Communications	FuG 5	Engine displacement	5.7 liter
Weapon, main	2 cm Kw.K. 40 L/55	Engine horsepower	130 @ 2600 rpm

Pz Kpfw II Ausf b (Sd Kfz 121)

Length	4.76 m	Weapon, coaxial	7.92mm MG 34
Width	2.14 m	Ammo stowage, main	180 rnds
Height	1.96 m		
Weight	7.9 tons	Ammo stowage, secondary	2,250 rnds
Fuel capacity	170 liters		
Maximum speed	40 km/hr (24.8 mph)	Engine make	Maybach
Range, on road	190 km (117.8 miles)	Engine model	HL57TR
		Engine configuration	straight six-cylinder
Crew	3		
Communications	FuG 5	Engine displacement	5.7 liter
Weapon, main	2 cm Kw.K. 40 L/55	Engine horsepower	130 @ 2600 rpm

Pz Kpfw II Ausf c, A, B und C (Sd Kfz 121)

Length	4.81 m	Weapon, coaxial	7.92mm MG 34
Width	2.22	Ammo stowage, main	180 rnds
Height	1.99		
Weight	8.9 tons	Ammo stowage, secondary	2,250 rnds
Fuel capacity	170 liters		
Maximum speed	40 km/hr (24.8 mph)	Engine make	Maybach
Range, on road	200 km (124 miles)	Engine model	HL62TR
		Engine configuration	straight six-cylinder
Crew	3		
Communications	FuG 5	Engine displacement	6.2 liter
Weapon, main	2 cm Kw.K. 40 L/55	Engine horsepower	140 @ 2600 rpm

Pz Kpfw II Ausf D und E (Sd Kfz 121)

Length	4.65 m	Weapon, coaxial	7.92mm MG 34
Width	2.30 m	Ammo stowage, main	180 rnds
Height	2.06 m		
Weight	10.0 tons	Ammo stowage, secondary	2,250 rnds
Fuel capacity	200 liters		
Maximum speed	55 km/hr (34.1 mph)	Engine make	Maybach
Range, on road	200 km (124 miles)	Engine model	HL62TR
		Engine configuration	straight six-cylinder
Crew	3		
Communications	FuG 5	Engine displacement	6.2 liter
Weapon, main	2 cm Kw.K. 40 L/55	Engine horsepower	140 @ 2600 rpm

The Ausf. F also had a new hull front fabricated from flat armor plate, rather than the rounded front with additional flat armor grafted on as was the case with the Ausf. c. This captured Panzerkampfwagen II Ausf. F was photographed at Aberdeen Proving Ground in April 1947, shortly after it had been sectionalized to allow visitors to see its interior. This proved to be a bad idea when the collection was moved outdoors.

Ordnance Museum, Aberdeen Proving Ground

Scarcely resembling the conventional Panzerkampfwagen II, the Ausf. L retained the armament of the Ausf. c, but had all-new hull, suspension and turret. It was intended as a high-speed reconnaissance vehicle.

Military History Institute, Carlisle Barracks, PA

Panzerkampfwagen II, Ausf. J

Weight	18 tons	Weapon, coaxial	7.92mm MG34
Maximum speed	31 km/hr	Engine make	Maybach
Crew	3	Engine model	HL45P
Communications	Fu 12, Fu.Spr.Ger. f, Intercom	Engine configuration	inline six, liquid cooled
		Engine displacement	4.5 liters
Weapon, main	2.0 cm Kw.K.38 L/55	Engine horsepower	150 @ 3800 rpm

Pz Kpfw II Ausf F (Sd Kfz 121)

Length	4.81 m	Weapon, coaxial	7.92mm MG 34
Width	2.28 m	Ammo stowage, main	180 rnds
Height	2.15 m		
Weight	9.5 tons	Ammo stowage, secondary	2,250 rnds
Fuel capacity	170 liters		
Maximum speed	40 km/hr	Engine make	Maybach
Range, on road	200 km	Engine model	HL62TR
Crew	3	Engine configuration	straight six-cylinder
Communications	FuG 5	Engine displacement	6.2 liter
Weapon, main	2 cm Kw.K. 40 L/55	Engine horsepower	140 @ 2600 rpm

Patton Museum, Fort Knox, KY

A heavier-armed version of the Ausf. L had been planned, but was never placed into production. All 100 produced mounted the 2.0 cm cannon as seen here. There is no angle from which the Ausf. L resembles the classic Panzer II.

Panzerspähwagen II Sd.Kfz. 123

Length	4.63 m	Weapon, main	2.0 cm Kw.K.38
Width	2.48 m	Weapon, coaxial	7.92mm MG34
Height	2.21 m		
Weight	11.8 tons	Ammo stowage, main	320 rnds
Fuel capacity	235 liters	Ammo stowage, secondary	2,250 rnds
Maximum speed	60 km/hr (37.2 mph)		
Range, on road	260 km (161.2 miles)	Engine make	Maybach
Range, cross country	155 km (96.1 miles)	Engine model	HL66P
Crew	4	Engine configuration	inline six, liquid cooled
Communications	Fu 12, Fu.Spr.Ger. f, Intercom	Engine displacement	6.6 liters
		Engine horsepower	180 @ 3200 rpm

Panzerkampfwagen 35(t) and 38(t)

In September 1938, Hitler's Germany seized the Sudetenland region of Czecho-Slovakia (the name becoming officially hyphenated earlier that year) claiming the move was an effort to protect people of German ancestry. Interestingly, this portion of Czecho-Slovakia was given to Hitler not by Czecho-Slovakia, but by Britain's Neville Chamberlain with the assistance of France.

In 1939, after persuading the Czecho-Slovakian government to cede more territory to Hungary and Poland, and the Slovakia region being granted independence, Hitler occupied the Czech region. It could be considered that Hitler wanted not only the real estate and raw materials, but also the many fine, advanced, armament manufacturing facilities in the region. Not only were the manufacturing facilities secured, but also some very advanced armament designs as well.

Patton Museum, Fort Knox, KY

This photo, though heavily retouched, shows what the LT vz.35 looked like when delivered to the Czech Army. The many rivets, visible in this photo, were the primary weakness in the tank's armor protection.

Charles Kliment.

The Škoda-designed LT vz.35, built originally for the Czech Army, was taken over by the Wehrmacht who classified it as the Panzerkampfwagen 35(t). When used is France, as seen here, it performed well, however, Russian winters proved problematic for the machine.

Moderate winters were not an obstacle to the Panzerkampfwagen 35(t), but in the frigid conditions encountered in Russia the air-operated transmission proved troublesome.

Among these were the Škoda LT vz.35 and the Ceskomoravska Kolben Danek (ČKD) LT vz.38, known in German service as Panzerkampfwagen 35(t) and 38(t), respectively.

These vehicles were the equal of their German counterparts, and were in many ways superior to them. The armor and armament of the LT vz.35 light tank exceeded not only that of the German Panzerkampfwagen II, but the Panzerkampfwagen III as well! The LT vz.38 had even heavier armor than the LT vz. 35.

The primary shortcoming of the vehicles was their riveted construction, although this was less of a factor in the LT vz.38 than with the LT vz.35, which was essentially covered in rivets. Were impacting rounds to shear off the

The (CKD) LT vz.38 was standardized by the German Army as the Panzerkampfwagen 38(t). Shown here is an Ausf. A of the 35rd Leichte Division. Identifying the various Ausführungen of the 38(t) is not always simple, as many vehicles were repaired, often by the factory, with parts of newer machines. The Ausf. A had six bolts on either side of the turret front plate.

Panzerkampfwagen 35(t) roll into Poland as part of the 11th Panzer Regiment in September 1939. The exhaust muffler is alongside the engine compartment and the rear of the hull is relatively free of interruptions.

After Germany overran Czecho-Slovakian, CKD became known as Böhmisch-Mährische Maschinenfabrik AG, or BMM, but production of the LT vz. 38 continued. Here a group of Ausf. G are shown awaiting delivery at the BMM plant.

The compact size of the Panzerkampfwagen 38(t) made for cramped working conditions for the crew, but also presented a small target for opposing tanks. This Ausf. G shows that models characteristic lack of bolts on the lower front hull plate and turret bolt pattern. The superstructure front plate with two vision ports on this model have very few bolts as well.

The straight driver's plate on this 38 (t) of the 7th Panzer Division is one of the clues that it is the Ausf. G variant. This tank, photographed in Russia in 1941, is not likely to have lasted long against the powerful Red Army tanks it soon encountered.

head of rivet, its shank could ricochet inside the tank, inflicting casualties upon both crew and equipment.

The LT vz.35, nee Panzerkampfwagen 35 (t), though designed by Škoda, was also produced in equal quantities by ČKD. Regardless of manufacturer, they were armed with the Škoda A3 3.7 cm gun mounted in the manually traversed turret. Also in the turret was a ZB vz. 35 heavy machine gun mounted coaxially with the main gun. A second ZB vz. 35 heavy machine gun was ball mounted

This Panzerkampfwagen 38(t) was used by the Slovak Army. An Ausf. E or F, this vehicle was
knocked out near Tegart during the Slovak uprising against Germany in 1944.

in the front of the hull superstructure as well. In later
production, a ZB vz. 37 heavy machine gun was used
instead of the ZB vz. 35 heavy machine gun. This later
weapon was retrofitted to earlier vehicles as well.

The transmission of the LT vz. 35 was pneumatically
shifted, so it functioned almost flawlessly in the Czech,
German and French climates, but often failed to perform
in the harsh conditions of Russian winter. Many vehicles
were lost due to this problem.

The total production of the LT vz.35 was 298 for
the Czechoslovak army, 126 for Romania and 10 for
Afghanistan (those vehicles were later given to Bulgaria).
After the German occupation, neither Škoda nor ČKD
(BMM) manufactured any new LT vz.35 tanks.

Teething problems with the LT vz.35, which was
hurried into production, caused the Czech Army to
look for a replacement even while LT vz.35 production
continued.

The vehicle settled on was the ČKD-designed LT
vz.38. In contrast to the small road wheels used by the
LT vz.35, the LT vz.38 had four large road wheels on

each side. These were mounted in tandem pairs on wheel
carriers with leaf spring suspensions.

The hull and turret were of riveted construction,
but with fewer joints and rivets than on the LT vz.35,
increasing crew safety.

The tank carried a new Škoda 3.7 cm gun designated
by the military as Uvvz.38 and mounted in the manually
traversed turret. Also in the turret was a ZB vz. 37 heavy
machine gun mounted coaxially with the main gun in a
ball mount. Another ZB vz. 37 heavy machine gun was
installed in the front of the hull by a ball mount.

The first 15 vehicles from the initial order of 150
tanks were produced in 1938 for the Czech government,
which capitulated to Nazi occupation prior to delivery of
the vehicles. The German Army instead bought those 150,
classified them Panzerkampfwagen 38 (t), and ordered
even more. When production ended in 1942, more
than 1,400 had been built as gun tanks, and the chassis
continued to be produced for other uses, primarily self-
propelled guns.

Panzerkampfwagen 35(t)

Length	4.9 m	Weapon, secondary	2 x 7.92mm MG 34 or MG 35/37(t)
Width	2.1 m		
Height	2.35 m	Ammo stowage, main	72 to 90 rnds
Weight	5 tons		
Maximum speed	35 km/hr (21.7 mph)	Ammo stowage, secondary	1,800 to 2,550 rnds
Range, on road	190 km (117.8 miles)	Engine make	Skoda
Range, cross country	120 km (74.4 miles)	Engine model	T 11
Crew	4	Engine configuration	six-cylinder
Weapon, main	37mm KwK 34(t) L/40	Engine displacement	8.52 liters
		Engine horsepower	120

Panzerkampfwagen 38(t) Ausf. A

Length	4.60 m	Weapon, secondary	2 x 7.92mm MG 37(t)
Width	2.12 m		
Height	2.40 m	Ammo stowage, main	72 rnds
Weight	5 tons		
Fuel capacity	220 liters	Ammo stowage, secondary	2,400 rnds
Maximum speed	42 km/hr (26.04 mph)		
Range, on road	250 km (155 miles)	Engine make	Praga
		Engine model	EPA
Range, cross country	160 km (99.2 miles)	Engine configuration	six-cylinder
Crew	4	Engine displacement	7.75 liters
Weapon, main	37mm KwK 38(t) L/47.8	Engine horsepower	125

Panzerkampfwagen 38(t) Ausf. G

Length	4.61 m	Weapon, secondary	2 x 7.92mm MG37(t)
Width	2.14 m		
Height	2.40 m	Ammo stowage, main	72 rnds
Weight	5 tons		
Maximum Speed	42 km/h (26.04 mph)	Ammo stowage, secondary	2,400 rnds
Range, on road	250 km (155 miles)	Engine make	Praga
		Engine model	EPA
Range, cross country	160 km (99.2 miles)	Engine configuration	six-cylinder
Crew	4	Engine displacement	7.75 liters
Weapon, main	37mm KwK 38(t) L/47.8	Engine horsepower	125 @ 2200 rpm

An LT vz.38, or TNHPS to use its CKD model number, was demonstrated to England in March 1939 in hopes of gaining export sales. While the sales campaign was not successful, it was documented in this clear photo.

Patton Museum, Fort Knox, KY

Some Panzerkampfwagen 38(t) were converted for use a Panzerbefelswagen. In the foreground of this photograph taken during the invasion of France in 1940 is an Ausf. B that has been so outfitted. Seven of these vehicles were assigned to each panzer division.

Patton Museum, Fort Knox, KY

Panzerkampfwagen III

The German armored strategy of the mid-1930s envisioned two types of tanks carrying the offensive forward. One of these was to be armed with a fairly heavy weapon for dispatching enemy fortifications at range. The Panzerkampfwagen IV filled this role. The other tank type, more numerous at the ratio of three companies to one, was to be armed with cannon firing armor-piercing rounds for use against enemy armor, and machine guns for use against infantry. The tank that was designed to meet these criteria was the Panzerkampfwagen III.

During 1934, the Waffenamt issued development contracts for Panzerkampfwagen III, code named ZugfuhrerWagen (ZW), or platoon leader's vehicle. Design proposals were solicited from Krupp AG (Essen), Daimler-Benz AG (Berlin-Marienfelde), MAN (Nurnberg), and Rheinmetall-Borsig (Berlin). The latter firm designed the turret, while Krupp and Daimler-Benz offered complete vehicle designs.

In the interest of standardizing weapons and ammunition with those already in service, the new tank was to be armed with a 3.7 cm main gun. However, the Inspector for Mechanized Troops foresaw that this would be inadequate and insisted that the new tank incorporate a turret ring large enough to permit the installation of a heavier cannon.

A crew of five men would operate the new tank: a commander, gunner and loader all in the turret, and the driver and radio operator in the hull front. An intercom was provided for easy communication between crewmembers.

After comparative trials of both the Daimler-Benz and Krupp prototypes at Kummersdorf and Ulm, a decision was reached; In early 1936, the Daimler-Benz design was ordered into production.

The Panzerkampfwagen III had what has come to be viewed as the traditional German tank styling, with a boxy superstructure housing the engine at the rear, gearbox at

The Panzerkampfwagen III, initially produced as the Ausf. A shown here, was to be Germany's first-line tank for first half of the war.

The Panzerkampfwagen III Ausf. A could be distinguished by the five large road wheels on each side.

With only 10 of the Ausf. A Panzerkampfwagen III constructed photographs of them in combat service are difficult to locate. A photographer snapped this one during the invasion of Poland.

In addition to Daimler-Benz, Krupp offered a design for what was to become the Panzerkampfwagen III. Shown here is Krupp's unsuccessful prototype.

The Ausf. D, like the Ausf. B and C, had eight pairs of road wheels on each side, rather than the six normally associated with the Panzerkampfwagen III.

The angle-set leading spring of the Panzerkampfwagen III Ausf. D can be clearly seen here as the tank speeds past a halftrack.

This Ausf. D, employed in the Polish campaign, shows of the new-style commander's cupola introduced with this model. The intricate leaf-spring suspension can also be plainly seen.

the front with driver and radio operator just behind it, and the turret essentially centered.

Ten of the 1-Serie ZW, the Panzerkampfwagen III Ausf. A, were built and used for troop trials. The Ausf.

A featured five large road wheels on each side utilizing coil spring suspension. Troop trials revealed that the suspension was not up to the task of carrying the 15-plus-ton tank through rugged terrain. Nevertheless, these vehicles were employed during the Polish Campaign with the 1st Panzer Division. This led to a redesign of the suspension for the next series and the withdrawal of the Ausf. A from combat use.

In an attempt to remedy the suspension problems, a new series was produced that eliminated the five road wheels and their coil springs in favor of eight road wheels mounted on leaf springs. The first two wheel stations were mounted at one end of a leaf spring assembly, and the second two wheel stations were mounted at the other. This arrangement was duplicated further to the rear with the fifth-sixth and seventh-eighth wheel stations being mounted at either end of a second leaf spring assembly. Known as the 2-Serie, or Ausf. B, 12 of these vehicles

were produced for trials. The remainder of the tank was essentially unchanged from the previous model.

While the leaf spring suspension introduced with the Ausf. B was an improvement over the coil springs fitted to the Ausf. A, there was still room for improvement. This led to the production of the Ausf. C. On the Ausf. C three sets of leaf springs were utilized. The first two wheel stations were mounted on one spring, the last two were mounted on another, and the fourth wheel stations in the middle were mounted on a third, longer leaf spring.

In June of 1937, Daimler-Benz improved the suspension yet again, introducing its 3a-Serie, also known

Walter J. Spielberger

The ZW 38 chassis in the background introduced torsion bar suspension to the Panzerkampfwagen III. Beginning with the Ausf. E, this was the suspension used for the remainder of the series. An Ausf. D chassis, with the older style leaf spring suspension, is in the foreground for comparison.

Patton Museum, Fort Knox, KY

The classic form of the Panzerkampfwagen III was defined by the Ausf. E. Its six paired road wheels per side would remain for the balance of the type's production, but the Ausf. E's short, slender cannon would soon give way to heavier armament.

Patton Museum, Fort Knox, KY

The radio operator's bow-mounted MG 34 is visible here. Weapons such is this are critical for a tank's survival against infantry.

A Panzerkampfwagen III Ausf. E moves out cross-country. Notice the escape hatch in the side of the hull and the foldable radio antenna.

as the Panzerkampfwagen III Ausf C. Fifteen vehicles were produced in this series and, like the earlier models, they were employed in the invasion of Poland.

In January 1938, yet another variation of the Panzerkampfwagen III was introduced. The 3b-Serie, or Ausf. D, had increased armor protection, with 30mm plating replacing the 14.5mm previously used. A different transmission was used. Instead of the five-speed ZF SFG 75 used in previous Panzerkampfwagen III, a six-speed ZF SSG was installed. Once again, the suspension was changed, differing from the Ausf. C in that the leaf spring assemblies supporting the first and last pairs of road wheel stations were mounted at an angle. A cast commander's cupola was installed on the turret in lieu of the fabricated steel cupola of the earlier models. As with the Ausf. C, 15 of the Ausf. D were built.

By December 1938, the running gear for the Panzerkampfwagen III had been revamped yet again. This time the design featured six road wheels on each side, mounted on a torsion bar suspension. With this version, the Ausf. E, the Panzerkampfwagen III had finally taken the form in which it is most often remembered. With this version, more assembly plants became involved in order to meet the increasing demand. In addition to Daimler-Benz, Henschel and M.A.N. began producing the Panzerkampfwagen III.

The first five ausfürung were all powered by the Maybach HL 108 TR engine. For armament they carried the 3.7 cm KwK 35/36 L/46.5 gun and three 7.92mm MG 34 machine guns. One machine gun was mounted in the hull, and the other two were mounted to the right of the main gun.

By September of 1939, it was time yet again to improve the design, which was designated Ausf. F. Externally, the most noticeable change was the addition of brake cooling air intakes on the top of the glacis. Internally, an upgraded Maybach HL120TRM engine was installed. This magneto-ignition engine had a higher horsepower rating than the earlier HL 108 TR, which allowed it to better cope with the ever-increasing weight of the tank. A Maybach Variorex 10-speed transmission transferred power to the tracks.

The manufacturing pool broadened again with the Ausf. F, with Alkett and FAMO joining Daimler-Benz, Henschel, and M.A.N. in producing more than 400 of these tanks. The first 335 were assembled, as were all the previous ausführung, with a 3.7 cm Kw.K. 35/36 L/46.5 gun and three 7.92mm MG 34 machine guns as armament.

However, combat experience was proving that the 3.7 cm cannon was inadequate against enemy armored

As originally built the Panzerkampfwagen III Ausf. G retained the 3.7 cm armament and internal mantlet of its predecessors. Later many vehicles, such as this one, were rearmed with a 5.0 cm gun mounted with an external mantlet. Notice how the top of the turret begins wrapping around the rear almost at the side door hinge.

vehicles. Therefore, the decision was made to begin fitting 5.0 cm cannon to the Panzerkampfwagen III. These tanks, armed with the 5.0 cm Kw.K 38 L/42, also had external mantlets and a single coaxially mounted MG 34. About 100 of these up-armed tanks were built.

Beginning in August of 1940 and continuing into 1942, a program was conducted to rearm the early Ausf. F and the earlier Ausf. E tanks with a 5.0 cm KwK 38 L/42 gun. Concurrent with the rearming, 30mm supplemental armor plates were added to the front and rear of the hull and the superstructure front.

Beginning in April of 1940, production of the Panzerkampfwagen III switched to the Ausf. G. About 600 of this model, produced by Alkett, Daimler-Benz, FAMO, Henschel, M.A.N., MNH and Wegmann, would ultimately be built. Strangely, the first few produced were armed with the obsolete 3.7 cm Kw.K. 35/36 L/46.5 gun mounted in an internal mantlet, but the bulk of the production carried the more powerful 5.0 cm Kw. K 38 L/42. Construction of the Ausf. G ceased in February of 1941.

This mired tank, about to be towed out by two others, shows the engine deck of the Ausf. E and the two-piece turret hatches that were new to this model.

This factory photo of an Ausf. F shows the vehicle in its as-delivered form. Troops invariably will cover every available inch of the vehicle with a variety of gear as the interior was too crowded for anything but essentials.

The Ausf. F was very similar to the Ausf. E externally. The scoop-like air intakes added to the glacis are the easiest way to distinguish them. These admitted cooling air for the brakes and final drive.

Two mufflers were mounted on the rear of the hull of the Ausf. F, with a N.K.A.V. smoke candle rack installed above the right muffler. Also clear here are the plugs for the two pistol ports in the rear of the turret.

The turret was redesigned, with its sides growing longer. As a result of this, the base of the commander's cupola no longer protruded from the rear of the turret. The armor thickness at the rear of the hull was increased on this model as well, and an improved driver's visor was installed.

By October 1940, a new model was entering production concurrently with the Ausf. G. The Ausf. H, which was in production until 1941. Alkett, Henschel, MAN, MNH, MIAG and Wegmann manufactured the Ausf. H. Thirty millimeter-thick supplemental armor plates were bolted on in an effort to increase protection from increasingly efficient enemy antitank guns.

The somewhat troublesome 10-speed Variorex transmission was replaced in this model with a six-speed Maybach SSG 77 gearbox. New sprockets and idler wheels were also featured on the new model.

The Panzerkampfwagen III, like most armored vehicles, was somewhat cramped inside. Therefore, external stowage such as the boxes on the rear deck that these men are closing was commonplace. Later versions included a small stowage bin permanently mounted on the rear of the turret.

As heavier enemy tanks were encountered, it was decided that the Panzerkampfwagen III should be armed with the 5.0 cm Kw.K 38 L/42. A limited number of the Ausf. F were so equipped from the factory, and may others were converted to the new configuration, which also included installing an external mantlets and a single coaxially mounted MG 34. The particular tank shown here had previously been equipped for submerged operation, and some of that gear is still evident.

As built, the armament of the Ausf. H was (as it was on the bulk of the Ausf. G) the 5.0 cm Kw.K. 38 L/42. However, during 1942/43, many of the Ausf. H were rearmed with 5.0 cm Kw.K. 39 L/60 gun.

It became apparent that the existing Panzerkampfwagen III designs were inadequately armored for the modern battlefield. As a result, a complete redesign of the vehicle was undertaken in order to upgrade its protection. The result of this effort was the Panzerkampfwagen III Ausf. J.

The bulk of the Panzerkampfwagen Ausf. G were armed with the 5.0 cm cannon like the tank in the background, however a small number were built with the 3.7 cm gun like the ones in the foreground. Evenly spaced return rollers and an improved visor were identifying features of the Ausf. G.

Patton Museum, Fort Knox, KY

The Ausf. H had additional 30 mm-thick armor plates bolted to the hull front to increase protection. The tank, serving in North Africa, has had a field-made rack added to its right fender to hold additional water cans, a critical commodity in this climate.

Patton Museum, Fort Knox, KY

Dust and sand boils off of this Afrika Korps Ausf. H as it passes at speed. The clouds of dust were the enemy of both Germany and the Allies, providing easy spotting for the enemy and creating maintenance nightmares.

Patton Museum, Fort Knox, KY

This builder's photo shows the 5.0 cm Kw.K. 38 L/42 main gun installed on the Ausf. H at the factory. Combat experience lead to the up arming of many of these tanks to the longer 5.0 cm Kw.K. 39 L/60 gun during 1942/43.

Entering production in March of 1941, the Ausf. J was designated as both the last Sd.Kfz.141 and first Sd.Kfz.141/1 Panzerkampfwagen III tank. Alkett, Daimler-Benz, Henschel, M.A.N. MNH, MIAG and Wegmann all were contracted in an effort to fill orders for 2,700 of these vehicles. By July of 1942, 2,616 had been built.

In addition to improvements in the armor, the Ausf. J incorporated a new driver's visor (Fahrersehklappe 50) and ballmount (Kugelblende 50) for the hull 7.92mm MG 34 machine gun. Beginning in April of 1942, 20mm spaced armor began to be added to the gun mantlet, as well as the superstructure front. The first 1,549 vehicles produced were armed with a 5.0 cm KwK 38 L/42 gun and two MG 34 machine guns. These would be the last

Patton Museum, Fort Knox, KY

The bolts holding the additional armor plates to the hull and superstructure fronts of the Ausf. H are plainly evident in this view, as is the palm tree-swastika emblem of Rommel's famed Afrika Korps.

vehicles designated as PzKpfw III Ausf J / Sd.Kfz.141. The 1067 vehicles produced from December of 1941 to July of 1942, armed with 5.0 cm KwK 39 L/60 and two

The Panzerkampfwagen III Ausf. J saw the introduction of the hemispherical ball mount, known as the Kugelblende 50, to the series. This would be used on all later models as well.

The uneven return roller spacing, introduced with the Ausf. H, was carried over onto the Ausf. J as well. The Ausf. J was also the last ausfrüng that had turret side ports on every vehicle.

The armor of the hull was strengthened to 50 mm on the Ausf. J, negating the need for the additional bolted-on armor plate that had characterized the Ausf. H. The driver's vision port was improved yet again with this series.

Part of the right fender is missing on the example of the early Ausf. J being hauled in by the British for evaluation. This example, like the other 1548 Panzerkampfwagen III Ausf. J produced before December 1941 was armed with the short 5.0 cm KwK 38 L/42 gun.

MG 34 machine guns, were designated as PzKpfw III Ausf J / Sd.Kfz.141/1. The long-barreled versions were known to the British fighting them in North Africa as the "Mark III Special."

Improvements to the gun mount and turret armor resulted in a tank known as the Panzerkampfwagen III, Ausf. L being produced. Starting in June of 1942, Alkett, Daimler-Benz, Henschell, M.A.N., MIAG, MNH, and Wegmann combined to produce 653 of these tanks. Like the Ausf. J, the Ausf. L was armed with a 5.0 cm KwK 39 L/60 gun and two 7.92mm MG 34 machine guns. The bulk of the production lacked hull side escape hatches, as well as loader's front visor and turret side ports. Tanks supplied to the Afrika Korps were equipped with additional air filters, improved oil filters and a different cooling fan reduction

ratio. This sub-variant was known as the Ausf. L (Tp). For the first time, the Panzerkampfwagen III was equipped to defend itself against aerial attacks with the mounting an anti-aircraft machine gun mount (Fliegerbeschussgerat 41/42) on the commander's cupola. This mount was also retrofitted to older tanks.

By October of 1942, production of the Ausf. M was underway. Two hundred-fifty of these ultimately were produced by M.A.N., MIAG, MNH, and Wegman before production of this model ceased in February 1943. The Ausf. M was equipped to make hard-bottom water crossings approximately 1.3 meters deep—a half-meter increase over previous models. The Ausf. M was equipped with a 90mm three-tube NbK discharger mounted well forward on each side of the turret. Like the Ausf. J and

Ausf. L, the Ausf. M was armed with a 5.0 cm Kw.K. 39 L/60 gun and two 7.92mm MG 34 machine guns, one in the bow, the other coaxial with the main gun. Armored skirts, known as schürzen, began to be hung from the sides of the hull beginning in March 1943. Similar armor was also suspended from the turret sides.

Dismayed by the superiority of Soviet tanks being encountered, Hitler decried the Panzerkampfwagen III as an inferior vehicle and ordered production halted, allowing the facilities to convert fully to Sturmgeschütz

Beneath the relatively plain engine deck lay the reliable Maybach HL120TRM V-12 gasoline engine. The raised armored covers are "tropical vents" used to protect the enlarged cooling openings required by the African climate.

Patton Museum, Fort Knox, KY

Known to the British as the "Mark III Special," the final 1056 vehicles carried the 5.0 cm KwK 39 L/60, which was considerably more effective than the shorter weapon.

Patton Museum, Fort Knox, KY

With the introduction of the longer gun, the Panzerkampfwagen III's Sd.Kfz. number changed from 141, the number it had carried from the beginning, to 141/1.

Patton Museum, Fort Knox, KY

production. The final version built, the Ausf. N, was in production from June of 1942 through August of 1943 at Henschel, M.A.N., MIAG, MNH, and Wegmann.

The Ausf. N was armed with the short 7.5 cm Kw.K. 37 L/24, which had been removed from PzKpfw. IV Ausf. A to F1 tanks, which were then being rearmed with longer 7.5 cm guns. The two MG 34 machine guns were retained. These vehicles were intended to work in the close support role. A total of 663 Ausf. N were produced using chassis types intended for Ausf. J (3), L (447) and M (213). Due to weight considerations, these were produced without spaced armor on the mantlet. The number of main gun

rounds carried varied depending upon what chassis was used as the basis for the tank. Tanks built on the Ausf. L chassis carried 56 rounds of 7.5 cm ammunition, while those on the Ausf. M had stowage for 64 rounds.

Later production vehicles used a one-piece commander's cupola hatch, rather than the earlier two-piece, while the very last vehicles utilized cupola taken over from Panzerkampfwagen IV, Ausf. G.

After March 1943, like the other tanks in this series, these vehicles were shipped with schürzen installed, as well as having Zimmerit anti-magnetic mine paste applied.

The earliest of the Panzerkampfwagen III Ausf. L had the hull side escape hatches as well as turret side vision ports. However they were phased out quickly. This example being evaluated at Aberdeen Proving Ground lacks the turret visors, but retains the escape hatches.
Ordnance Museum, Aberdeen Proving Ground, MD

Supplemental armor was added to the mantlet of many of Ausf. L vehicles, including the example shown here. Note the abundance of spare road wheels and track stowed on the vehicle.
Patton Museum, Fort Knox, KY

Bryce Sunderlin collection.

U.S. troops using a Diamond T 4-ton wrecker recover an abandoned Panzerkampfwagen III Ausf. L. The compact size of the tank is apparent in this comparison.

Ordnance Museum, Aberdeen Proving Ground, MD

This Ausf. L was photographed while undergoing tests in Maryland. Captured enemy ordnance was evaluated not only looking for innovations, but also to discover weaknesses that could be exploited by Allied forces.

The headlights on the Ausf. M were the removable type, and were mounted on the fenders rather than on the glacis. Schürzen was commonly found on the Ausf. M as well as spaced armor for the turret. This was the Panzer in its finest form.

This illustration from the operator's manual of the Ausf. M displays both the exhaust arrangement and the relocated headlamps.

Patton Museum, Fort Knox, KY

Faced with ever better-armored opposition, the 5.0 cm cannon was outclassed by 1943, resulting in the Panzerkampfwagen III Ausf. M being the last Panzer III so armed.

Even with the addition of schürzen, the armor of the Panzerkampfwagen III was not up to the mid-1940s opposition. That, coupled with its inadequate weaponry, led to production ceasing in August 1943.

The Panzerkampfwagen III, Ausf. N was created by installing the 7.5 cm Kw.K. 37 L/24 into chassis originally intended to be Ausf. J, L, or M. These guns became available when they were removed from early Panzerkampfwagen IV as that series was rearmed with longer weapons.

The Ausf. N retained the chassis characteristics of the base vehicle, but the entire gun, mount and mantlet were replaced. Notice how the hardened armor shattered when hit on this destroyed vehicle.

The 7.5 cm cannon had greater destructive ability, even with its short barrel, than did the 5.0 cm gun it replaced. That what was obsolete for a Panzer IV became an improvement for the Panzer III is testament to the different roles played by these tanks.

This Panzerkampfwagen III Ausf. N was photographed while on display at Aberdeen Proving Ground shortly after the war. The stubby barrel of the 7.5 cm gun provides a ready means of positive identification of this version of the Panzer III.

Both the ball-mount machinegun in the hull and all the normal Panzer III armament in the turret were removed during the Beobachtung conversion to Panzerbeobachtungswagen. Instead a dummy main gun was installed on the turret along with a ball mount machine gun in the faux mantlet.

Panzerbeobachtungswagen III

Two hundred sixty two Panzerkampfwagen III tanks were rebuilt into artillery observation vehicles, or Artillerie-Panzerbeobachtungswagen III between February 1943 and April 1944. The idea was to provide a means to insert forward artillery observers in panzer formations that would both protect the crew and disguise their purpose.

The conversion entailed removing the main gun and mantlet, substituting a slightly thicker fixed plate in its place. In that fixed plate a MG 34 machine gun with ball mount in the center was installed. Just to its right a dummy main gun was welded. The turret roof was pierced to allow a TBF2 artillery observation periscope to be extended. Provisions for additional periscopes were made in the commander's cupola as well.

In the hull, the ball-mounted machine gun was eliminated to open up internal space for additional radio equipment consisting of Fu 8, Fu 4, Funksprechgerät f, and a dismountable Tornisterfunkgerät. A pistol port replaced the hull ball mount, allowing a modicum of protection during desperate times.

The Panzerbeobachtungswagen III were issued to forward observers with Hummel and Wespe batteries and served throughout the war.

Ordnance Museum, Aberdeen Proving Ground, Md.

Panzerkampfwagen III Ausf. E, F and G all were used as basis for constructing Panzerbeobachtungswagen III. Rather than building the observation vehicles new from the ground up, older tanks were converted in the course of their rebuilding after extensive use or damage in the field.

The objective of the Panzerbeobachtungswagen III design was to conceal the artillery forward observers within Panzer formations. This allowed the to direct the fire of the gun batteries without themselves becoming primary targets.

Patton Museum, Fort Knox, KY

Panzerbefehlswagen III

Command tanks were also built on the Panzerkampfwagen III chassis by Daimler-Benz. Known as Panzerbefehlswagen III, these vehicles were produced from June 1938 through February 1943 in the Ausf D1 (30), Ausf E (45) and Ausf H (175) (Sd.Kfz.266-268) versions. Filling the interiors of these tanks was additional communications equipment that allowed them to serve in the command role. This required the deletion of the main gun and ammunition, with a dummy weapon mounted instead.

Beginning in August of 1942, a new form of command tank was also created, both as new production and by retrofitting. Known as the Panzerbefehlswagen III mit 5cm KwK L/42 / Sd.Kfz.141, these vehicles retained their 5.0 cm main gun, but gave up part of their ammunition stowage and hull machine gun to provide room for the additional radio equipment.

An usual version of the Panzerkampfwagen III that never advanced beyond the trial stage was based upon the Ausf. N. Three prototypes of this vehicle, which was equipped to operate on railroad track, were produced in October of 1943. With a maximum on-rail speed of 100 km/hr (62 mph), it was hoped these could be employed to protect railway lines on the Russian front. But like many experiments, the project foundered

During wartime there existed a need to place commanders on the front line of the action, yet keep them in communication with their subordinates. The Panzerbefehlswagen was intended to do just that. Modified combat tanks, such as this Ausf. D, were used in this capacity.

The turret was fixed in place, and a dummy main weapon installed. The space normally occupied by ammunition taken up with radio equipment. This required additional antenna, including the large frame antenna on the engine deck.

Panzerkampfwagen III Ausf. E were also converted to Panzerbefehlswagens. The dummy guns were quite convincing looking, but the myriad of radio antenna clearly signals this Afrika Korps vehicle's purpose.

The number of men in the crew remained the same whether a gun tank or command tank. The additional radio equipment being operated "extra" crewman.

Far removed from the desert, a Panzerbefehlswagen based on the Panzerkampfwagen III Ausf. H leads a column of gun tanks. The blanked-out hull ball mount is visible in this view, only the 7.92 mm MG34 in the former turret armed the command vehicles.

Panzerkampfwagen III als Tauchpanzer

Produced in large quantities, the Panzerkampfwagen III als Tauchpanzer was developed in preparation of the invasion of England, dubbed operation Sea Lion. The Tauchpanzer was a Panzerkampfwagen III (various Ausf. were converted) equipped for submerged operation at depths up to 15 meters. After Sea Lion was scrapped, the Tauchpanzer units were used for river crossings in the East.

Like the Ausf. N, the Panzerkampfwagen III als Tauchpanzer was not constructed new for this purpose, rather existing tanks of various ausführung were modified for submerged use.

Panzerkampfwagen III Ausf. A

Length	5.69 m	Weapon, coaxial	2 x 7.92mm MG 34
Width	2.81 m	Weapon, ball mounted	7.92mm MG 34
Height	2.34 m		
Weight	15.4 tons	Ammo stowage, main	120 rnds
Fuel capacity	300 liters		
Maximum speed	32 km/hr (19.84 mph)	Ammo stowage, secondary	4,425 rnds
Range, on road	165 km (102.3 miles)	Engine make	Maybach
Range, cross country	95 km (58.9 miles)	Engine model	HL108TR
Crew	5	Engine configuration	V-12 liquid cooled
Communications	Fu. G. 5	Engine displacement	10.8 liters
Weapon, main	3.7 cm Kw.K. L45	Engine horsepower	250 @ 3000 rpm

Panzerkampfwagen III Ausf. B

Length	6.00 m	Weapon, coaxial	2 x 7.92mm MG 34
Width	2.87 m	Weapon, ball mounted	7.92mm MG 34
Height	2.45 m		
Weight	15.9 tons	Ammo stowage, main	120 rnds
Fuel capacity	300 liters		
Maximum speed	35 km/hr (21.7 mph)	Ammo stowage, secondary	4,425 rnds
Range, on road	165 km (102.3 miles)	Engine make	Maybach
Range, cross country	95 km (58.9 miles)	Engine model	HL108TR
Crew	5	Engine configuration	V-12 liquid cooled
Communications	Fu. G. 5	Engine displacement	10.8 liters
Weapon, main	3.7 cm Kw.K. L45	Engine horsepower	250 @ 3000 rpm

Intended to play a key role in Operation Sea Lion, the planned invasion of England. When that operation was cancelled, the vehicles were transferred to the Eastern Front and used for river crossing.

The large hose wrapped around this Tauchpanzer was its snorkel. Check valves prevented water from entering the exhaust during submerged operation.

Panzerkampfwagen III Ausf. C

Length	5.69 m	Weapon, coaxial	2 x 7.92mm MG 34
Width	2.81 m	Weapon, ball mounted	7.92mm MG 34
Height	2.34 m		
Weight	15.9 tons	Ammo stowage, main	120 rnds
Fuel capacity	300 liters	Ammo stowage, secondary	4,425 rnds
Maximum speed	35 km/hr (21.7 mph)		
Range, on road	165 km (102.3 miles)	Engine make	Maybach
		Engine model	HL108TR
Range, cross country	95 km (58.9 miles)	Engine configuration	V-12 liquid cooled
Crew	5		
Communications	Fu. G. 5	Engine displacement	10.8 liters
Weapon, main	3.7 cm Kw.K. L45	Engine horsepower	250 @ 3000 rpm

Panzerkampfwagen III Ausf. D

Length	5.92 m	Weapon, coaxial	2 x 7.92mm MG 34
Width	2.87 m	Weapon, ball mounted	7.92mm MG 34
Height	2.45 m		
Weight	15.9 tons	Ammo stowage, main	120 rnds
Fuel capacity	300 liters	Ammo stowage, secondary	4,425 rnds
Maximum speed	35 km/hr (21.7 mph)		
Range, on road	165 km (102.3 miles)	Engine make	Maybach
		Engine model	HL108TR
Range, cross country	95 km (58.9 miles)	Engine configuration	V-12 liquid cooled
Crew	5		
Communications	Fu. G. 5	Engine displacement	10.8 liters
Weapon, main	3.7 cm Kw.K. L45	Engine horsepower	250 @ 3000 rpm

Panzerkampfwagen III Ausf. E

Length	5.38 m	Weapon, coaxial	2 x 7.92mm MG 34
Width	2.91 m	Weapon, ball mounted	7.92mm MG 34
Height	2.44 m		
Weight	19.5 tons	Ammo stowage, main	120 rnds
Fuel capacity	320 liters	Ammo stowage, secondary	3,600 rnds
Maximum speed	40 km/hr (24.8 mph)		
Range, on road	165 km (102.3 miles)	Engine make	Maybach
		Engine model	HL 120 TRM
Range, cross country	95 km (58.9 miles)	Engine configuration	V-12, liquid cooled
Crew	5		
Communications	Fu. G. 5	Engine displacement	11.9 liters
Weapon, main	3.7 cm Kw.K. L/45	Engine horsepower	265 @ 2600 rpm

Panzerkampfwagen III Ausf. F as designed

Length	5.38 m	Weapon, coaxial	2 x 7.92mm MG 34
Width	2.91 m	Weapon, ball mounted	7.92mm MG 34
Height	2.44 m		
Weight	15.9 tons	Ammo stowage, main	120 rnds
Fuel capacity	320 liters	Ammo stowage, secondary	4,450 rnds
Maximum speed	40 km/hr (24.8 mph)		
Range, on road	165 km (102.3 miles)	Engine make	Maybach
		Engine model	HL 120 TRM
Range, cross country	95 km (58.9 miles)	Engine configuration	V-12, liquid cooled
Crew	5		
Communications	Fu. G. 5	Engine displacement	11.9 liters
Weapon, main	3.7 cm Kw.K. L/45	Engine horsepower	265 @ 2600 rpm

Rubberized canvas sealed the gun mantlet, hull machine gun mount and commanders cupola during underwater maneuvers.

Patton Museum, Fort Knox, KY

Panzerkampfwagen III Ausf. G with 5.0 cm gun

Length	5.38 m	Weapon, coaxial	7.92mm MG 34
Width	2.91 m		
Height	2.44 m	Weapon, ball mounted	7.92mm MG 34
Weight	19.8 tons		
Fuel capacity	300 liters	Ammo stowage, main	99 rnds
Maximum speed	40 km/hr (24.8 mph)	Ammo stowage, secondary	3,750 rnds
Range, on road	165 km (102.3 miles)		
Range, cross country	95 km (58.9 miles)	Engine make	Maybach
		Engine model	HL 120 TRM
Crew	5	Engine configuration	V-12, liquid cooled
Communica-tions	Fu. G. 5	Engine displacement	11.9 liters
Weapon, main	5.0 cm Kw.K.39 L/42	Engine horsepower	265 @ 2600 rpm

Panzerkampfwagen III Ausf. H

Length	5.52 m	Weapon, coaxial	7.92mm MG 34
Width	2.95 m		
Height	2.50 m	Weapon, ball mounted	7.92mm MG 34
Weight	21.8 tons		
Fuel capacity	320 liters	Ammo stowage, main	99 rnds
Maximum speed	40 km/hr (24.8 mph)	Ammo stowage, secondary	3,750 rnds
Range, on road	165 km (102.3 miles)		
Range, cross country	95 km (58.9 miles)	Engine make	Maybach
		Engine model	HL 120 TRM
Crew	5	Engine configuration	V-12, liquid cooled
Communica-tions	Fu. G. 5	Engine displacement	11.9 liters
Weapon, main	5.0 cm Kw.K.39 L/42	Engine horsepower	265 @ 2600 rpm

Though scarcely submerged in this view, the Tauchpanzer was designed to operate in depths up to 15 meters.

Panzerkampfwagen III Ausf. L

Length	6.41 m	Weapon, coaxial	7.92mm MG 34
Width	2.95 m	Weapon, ball mounted	7.92mm MG 34
Height	2.50 m		
Weight	21.3 tons	Ammo stowage, main	78 rnds
Fuel capacity	320 liters	Ammo stowage, secondary	4,950 rnds
Maximum speed	40 km/hr (24.8 mph)		
Range, on road	155 km (96.1 miles)	Engine make	Maybach
		Engine model	HL 120 TRM
Range, cross country	95 km (58.9 miles)	Engine configuration	V-12, liquid cooled
Crew	5		
Communications	Fu. G. 5	Engine displacement	11.9 liters
Weapon, main	5.0 cm Kw.K.39 L/60	Engine horsepower	265 @ 2600 rpm

Panzerkampfwagen III Ausf. N

Length	5.65 m	Weapon, coaxial	7.92mm MG 34
Width	3.41 m (w/ schürzen)	Weapon, ball mounted	7.92mm MG 34
Height	2.50 m		
Weight	23 tons	Ammo stowage, main	64 rnds
Fuel capacity	320 liters	Ammo stowage, secondary	3,450 rnds
Maximum speed	40 km/hr (24.8 mph)		
Range, on road	155 km (102.3 miles)	Engine make	Maybach
		Engine model	HL 120 TRM
Range, cross country	95 km (58.9 miles)	Engine configuration	V-12, liquid cooled
Crew	5		
Communications	Fu. G. 5	Engine displacement	11.9 liters
Weapon, main	7.5 cm Kw.K. L/24	Engine horsepower	265 @ 2600 rpm

Panzerkampfwagen III Ausf. J as initially produced

Length	5.56 m	Weapon, coaxial	7.92mm MG 34
Width	2.95 m	Weapon, ball mounted	7.92mm MG 34
Height	2.50 m		
Weight	21.5 tons	Ammo stowage, main	99 rnds
Fuel capacity	320 liters	Ammo stowage, secondary	3,750 rnds
Maximum speed	40 km/hr (24.8 mph)		
Range, on road	145 km (89.9 miles)	Engine make	Maybach
		Engine model	HL 120 TRM
Range, cross country	85 km (52.7 miles)	Engine configuration	V-12, liquid cooled
Crew	5		
Communications	Fu. G. 5	Engine displacement	11.9 liters
Weapon, main	5.0 cm Kw.K.39 L/42	Engine horsepower	265 @ 2600 rpm

Panzerkampfwagen III Ausf. M

Length	6.41 m	Weapon, coaxial	7.92mm MG 34
Width	3.41 m (w/ schürzen)	Weapon, ball mounted	7.92mm MG 34
Height	2.50 m		
Weight	21.3 tons	Ammo stowage, main	84 rnds
Fuel capacity	320 liters	Ammo stowage, secondary	3800 rnds
Maximum speed	40 km/hr (24.8 mph)		
Range, on road	155 km (102.3 miles)	Engine make	Maybach
		Engine model	HL 120 TRM
Range, cross country	95 km (58.9 miles)	Engine configuration	V-12, liquid cooled
Crew	5		
Communications	Fu. G. 5	Engine displacement	11.9 liters
Weapon, main	5.0 cm Kw.K.39 L/60	Engine horsepower	265 @ 2600 rpm

Panzerbeobachtungswagen III

Length	5.52 m	Communications	Fu. 8, Fu 4, Fu.Spr.Ger.f
Width	2.95 m	Weapon, main	7.92mm MG 34
Height	2.50 m		
Weight	23 tons	Engine make	Maybach
Fuel capacity	310 liters	Engine model	HL 120 TRM
Maximum speed	40 km/hr (24.8 mph)	Engine configuration	V-12, liquid cooled
Range, on road	155 km (102.3 miles)		
Range, cross country	95 km (58.9 miles)	Engine displacement	11.9 liters
		Engine horsepower	265 @ 2600 rpm
Crew	5		

The Panzer IV

When the German military envisioned its armored force, it anticipated that each regiment would include two companies of heavy tanks armed with comparatively large weapons. The Panzerkampfwagen IV was to be this tank. Its 75mm L/24 howitzer was intended to knock out enemy antitank weapons and fortifications from long ranges, allowing the lighter Panzer IIs and IIIs to move about the battlefield at will.

The Panzer IV design bore a strong resemblance to the earlier Krupp-designed VK2001/K. The Herreswaffenamt had wanted a torsion bar suspension featuring interleaved road wheels, but Krupp engineers strongly objected, in the end prevailing with eight paired road wheels on each side on four leaf springs per side. One pair was mounted on each end of each leaf spring. Krupp felt this system had many advantages, both in design and in maintenance, over the torsion bar suspension.

The turret of the Mark IV was not centered on the tank, but was offset 2 5/8 inches to the left of the hull centerline, and the engine was offset 6 inches to the right. This arrangement allowed the driveshaft to extend to the front-mounted transmission without interfering with the electrical supply serving the turret.

The Panzerkampfwagen IV Ausf. A was the first in this series, which would be the only series of tanks that would remain in production throughout WWII in Germany. Though its design was constantly improved, the basic form remained the same as this one.

Patton Museum, Fort Knox, KY

The Ausf. A, and the next five models, was armed with the 7.5 cm Kw.K. L/24 main gun. On the Ausf. A an internal mantlet was used joining the gun and turret.

Patton Museum, Fort Knox, KY

On the staggered hull front plate was mounted a ball mount for a MG 34 and a driver's visor adapted from a Panzerkampfwagen II. In this view the turret has been traversed almost to the rear.

Patton Museum, Fort Knox, KY

The superstructure of the Ausf. A was wider than those on succeeding ausfuehrung, which resulted in a narrow fender. Note the large muffler which stretches almost completely across the rear of the tank.

Patton Museum, Fort Knox, KY

Panzerkampfwagen IV Ausf. A

The first of the new family to go into production was the Ausführung A. The contract for the 35 Ausf. A was issued to Krupp in December 1936. The first of these were completed in November of the following year, with production being completed in June 1938.

The Panzer IV Ausf. A was powered by the Maybach HL 108 TR V-12 gasoline engine and drove the tank through a five-speed ZF SSG 75 transmission.

Even with such a small production run, there were variations within the series. Ammunition stowage for the main gun was reduced in December 1937 to 122 rounds (versus the 140 rounds previously carried). The external antiaircraft machine gun was deleted beginning with the February 1938 production as well. The final five Ausf. A's were built on Ausf. B hulls having heavier 30mm front plates.

The Ausf. A's were fitted with various upgrades during their service life. Among these were the addition of smoke candle launchers on the rear of the hull from August 1938, and the adding of Notek and convoy lights beginning in Spring 1940. Beginning in February 1941, additional 30mm armor plates were added to hull front, this was followed in March by the addition of a stowage box on the rear of the turret for crew gear.

Panzerkampfwagen IV, Ausf. A

Length	5.92 m	Weapon, coaxial	7.92mm MG 34
Width	2.83 m	Weapon, ball mounted	7.92mm MG 34
Height	2.68 m		
Weight	18 tons	Ammo stowage, main	122 rnds
Fuel capacity	470 liters		
Maximum speed	32.4 km/h (19.84 mph)	Ammo stowage, secondary	3,000 rnds
Range, on road	210 km (130.2 miles)	Engine make	Maybach
Range, cross country	130 km (80.6 miles)	Engine model	HL 108 TR
Crew	5	Engine configuration	V-12, liquid cooled
Communications	Fu 6 and Fu 2, intercom	Engine displacement	10.8 liters
Weapon, main	7.5 cm Kw.K L/24	Engine horsepower	230 @ 2600 rpm

The Panzerkampfwagen IV Ausf. A had previously been deployed during the occupation of Sudetenland. Virtually every hatch and visor on the tank is open in this view.

Walter J. Spielberger

The Panzerkampfwagen IV first drew blood during the invasion of Poland in 1939. The white cross was a marking used during that campaign. In this photo we can clearly see the mounting bosses for the four leaf spring suspension assemblies on each side of the Panzerkampfwagen IV.

Among the lessons learned in Poland was that the Panzerkampfwagen IV, though intended to knock out antitank guns, was itself vulnerable to the better antitank weapons fielded by the Polish Army. The design intention was that the relatively heavy Panzerkampfwagen IV would reckon with serious threats such as antitank guns and fortifications, and the lighter Panzerkampfwagen I and II would operate in tandem with the infantry.

Although the commander's cupola protruded from the rear of the turret rig on both the Ausf. A and the Ausf. B, the shape and height of the Ausf. A's cupola was distinctive.

Panzerkampfwagen IV Ausf. B

The second series of the Panzer IV was the Ausf. B. The contract for these 42 vehicles was awarded by October 1937. The Ausf. B improved on the previous model in the following areas: increased frontal armor protection, a more powerful Maybach HL 120 TR engine, and installation of a six-speed SSG 76 transmission.

Ammunition stowage was again reduced, and the width of the superstructure reduced, in an effort to maintain constant vehicle weight in spite of the thicker armor. The front superstructure plate of the Ausf B was straight, whereas the Ausf. A had a staggered front plate. On the left side of the front plate was a sliding driver's visor, and on the right a pistol port and visor replaced the ball-mounted machine gun.

A new commander's cupola was introduced, and a cone-shape covered was added to left signal port on the turret roof. The machine gun ports on the rear of the turret were replaced with pistol ports, and pistol ports were added to the turret hatches as well.

One of the 42 Panzerkampfwagen IV Ausf. B demonstrates its fording abilities. The superstructure of the Ausf. B was narrower than that on the Ausf. A in an effort to offset the weight increase due to increased armor thickness. This resulted in more of the fender eing exposed amidships.

Production of the Ausf. B ran from May through October 1938, during which time 42 machines were built. Even with such a small production run, there were numerous major variations. The last 30 produced utilized

A side-by-side comparison is offered by this view, with the Ausf. B on the right, and the Ausf. A on the left of the photo. Notice the flat front of the Ausf. B superstructure contrasted to the offset front on the Ausf. A, as well as the difference in driver's vision slits.

As it had on the Ausf. A, the commander's cupola of the Ausf. B protruded from the rear of the turret. However, the cupola itself was much different. In this view the one-piece, forward-hinged turret side doors are clearly visible.

Walter J. Spielberger

hulls designed for the Ausf. C, while five of the first dozen Ausf. B's used hulls originally intended for the Ausf. A.

Numerous items were retrofitted to these tanks during their service life, including the ones listed above for the Ausf. A.

Panzerkampfwagen IV, Ausf. B

Length	5.92 m	Weapon, coaxial	7.92mm MG 34
Width	2.83 m	Weapon, ball mounted	—
Height	2.68 m		
Weight	18.5 tons	Ammo stowage, main	80 rnds
Fuel capacity	470 liters		
Maximum speed	42 km/h (26.04 mph)	Ammo stowage, secondary	2,500 rnds
Range, on road	210 km (130.2 miles)		
Range, cross country	130 km (80.6 miles)	Engine make	Maybach
		Engine model	HL 120 TR
Crew	5	Engine configuration	V-12, liquid cooled
Communications	Fu 6 and Fu 2, intercom		
		Engine displacement	11.9 liters
Weapon, main	7.5 cm Kw.K L/24	Engine horsepower	265 @ 2600 rpm

Patton Museum, Fort Knox, KY

The Ausf. B continued to use an internal mantlet. Notice the arc of the upper edge of the opening. The shape of this area changed with the introduction of the Ausf. C.

This oft-reproduced photograph clearly shows the detail of the turret design, and the unusual shape of the turret front vision cover. Notice the hinged forward section of the front fender is missing.

Stowage bins were not originally attached to the rear of the Ausf. B turret, but they were retrofitted beginning in March 1941. Also note the smoke candle discharge rack mounted above the muffler.

The relative stiffness of the Panzerkampfwagen IV's leaf spring suspension is evident by looking at this tank on maneuvers. In this view the flat superstructure front is clear.

The Panzerkampfwagen IV Ausf. C continued the flat-faced superstructure that had been introduced with the Ausf. B. In this view the guide that was mounted beneath the main gun can be seen. This guide deflected the antenna when the turret was rotated.

Panzerkampfwagen IV Ausf. C

The contract for the production of the third series of Panzerkampfwagen IV was awarded to Krupp-Grusonwerk in October 1937. Due to a June 1937 ban on further development of the Panzerkampfwagen IV chassis, very little difference between the Ausf. C and the Ausf. B existed. From this point, the chassis of the Panzerkampfwagen IV would remain essentially unchanged through the end of the war. This standardization went a long way toward getting a large number of the Panzerkampfwagen IV built.

The most apparent change between the Ausf. C and the earlier Ausf. B was in the design of the mantlet. An armored sleeve for the coaxial MG 34 was added.

Although 140 Panzerkampfwagen IV Ausf. C were ordered, only 134 were delivered. The chassis for the remaining four were diverted for use as bridge-laying tanks. Most of the Ausf. C were equipped with the Panzerkampfwagen III commander's cupola and had a rain guard over the driver's visor. Internally, the ignition system of the engine was improved.

Ultimately, three of the chassis which had been set aside for bridge layers were completed as tanks in late 1940. Having an Ausf. C hull, Ausf. C turret, and Ausf. E superstructures, these were somewhat unique.

One the most obvious differences between the Ausf. C and the earlier Ausf. B was the addition of an armored sleeve to protect the barrel of the coaxial machine gun. The rain guard over the driver's visor was present on most of the Ausf. C.

The overall dark gray (Dunklegrau RAL 46) paint scheme of this Ausf. C stands out boldly against the snowy terrain. This is the reason most vehicles received a whitewash coat during winter operations.

Panzerkampfwagen IV, Ausf. C

Length	5.92 m	Weapon, coaxial	7.92mm MG 34
Width	2.83 m	Weapon, ball mounted	—
Height	2.68 m		
Weight	18.5 tons	Ammo stowage, main	80 rnds
Fuel capacity	470 liters		
Maximum speed	42 km/h (26.04 mph)	Ammo stowage, secondary	2500 rnds
Range, on road	210 km (130.2 miles)	Engine make	Maybach
Range, cross country	130 km (80.6 miles)	Engine model	HL 120 TRM
Crew	5	Engine configuration	V-12, liquid cooled
Communications	Fu 5 and Fu 2, intercom	Engine displacement	11.9 liters
Weapon, main	7.5 cm Kw.K L/24	Engine horsepower	265 @ 2600 rpm

The tray that received the antenna when it was pushed over by the pivoting turret is just visible on the side of the superstructure in this photo. Spare road wheels, an often replaced item, have been stowed on the turret side.

Patton Museum, Fort Knox, KY

The turret side doors of the Panzerkampfwagen Ausf. C and Ausf. D had pistol ports, whereas the earlier models did not. The muffler for the auxiliary power unit, as well as the rear fenders, has been knocked off of this tank.

Patton Museum, Fort Knox, KY

Panzerkampfwagen IV Ausf. D

Krupp-Grusonwerk's next contract for Panzer-kampfwagen IV production came in July 1938 when 200 more tanks were ordered. A further 48 were placed on order for the SS just before the end of the same year. These 248 tanks were designated Panzerkampfwagen Ausf. D. Production of the new version began in October 1939 and lasted one full year. Only 232 of the 248 vehicles were completed as gun tanks, the balance being taken over in bridge-layer production.

Improvements associated with the new model included installing thicker (20mm) side armor and face hardening the front of the hull and superstructure. The offset superstructure front was reintroduced, along with a ball-mounted machine gun. An external mantlet was introduced, replacing the internal mantlet previously used with the main gun. The chassis remained relatively unchanged, with only the track center guide height being increased and five bump stops being added to each side.

Beginning with the February production, Notek and convoy lights were installed at the factory, and in July 1940 additional 30mm armor plates were added to the front of the hull and superstructure. The final 68 vehicles, however, had one-piece 50mm armor on the hull front.

Patton Museum, Fort Knox, KY

The external gun mantlet distinguishes the Panzerkampfwagen IV Ausf. D from its predecessors. The small hinges on the brake covers and style of visor provided for the driver distinguish it from its successors.

Patton Museum, Fort Knox, KY

The engine deck of the Ausf. D was relatively clean, as was the top of the turret. Notice the commander's cupola is faired into the rear wall of the turret. When the Ausf. E. debuted, the cupola was no longer faired into the turret rear, rather it was on top of the turret, and a ventilator protruded from the turret roof as well.

National Archives and REcords Administration

This battle-weary Ausf. D has lost its right front fender, as well as the radio operator's hatch. Notice the offset superstructure front and the guard on top of the superstructure surrounding the turret, which was designed to prevent bullet splash from jamming the turret. National Archives and Records Administration photo.

Four dozen of these vehicles were converted to the submersible Tauchpanzer during July and August of 1940. Slightly more than two dozen other tanks were modified for use in North Africa early in 1941. During the course of the war worn or damaged tanks were returned for depot and factory overhaul. At that time any number of more modern components could be retrofitted, resulting in a true jumble of parts being assembled. As a result, the original chassis serial number was required to positively identify a given vehicle's model.

Despite utilizing a leaf-spring suspension that many felt was outmoded, the Panzerkampfwagen IV was relatively mobile, and could cross a fairly wide trench. The side visor, seen here, was originally designed for the Panzerkampfwagen III, which had 30mm side armor. It was used here despite the Panzerkampfwagen IV Ausf. D having only 20mm side armor.

Panzerkampfwagen IV, Ausf. D

Length	5.92 m	Weapon, coaxial	7.92mm MG 34
Width	2.84 m	Weapon, ball mounted	7.92mm MG 34
Height	2.68 m	Ammo stowage, main	80 rnds
Weight	20 tons		
Fuel capacity	470 liters	Ammo stowage, secondary	2,700 rnds
Maximum speed	42 km/h (26.04 mph)		
Range, on road	210 km (130.2 miles)	Engine make	Maybach
		Engine model	HL 120 TRM
Range, cross country	130 km (80.6 miles)	Engine configuration	V-12, liquid cooled
Crew	5		
Communications	Fu 5 and Fu 2, intercom	Engine displacement	11.9 liters
Weapon, main	7.5 cm Kw.K L/24	Engine horsepower	265 @ 2600 rpm

The fender extensions on this Ausf. D have been folded to the rear. These extensions were often lost or damaged during field operations. Extra track sections were often carried, both as repair parts as well to act as supplemental armor.

Photo from the collection of Stefan De Meyer.

Panzerkampfwagen IV Ausf. E

Naturally enough, the successor to the Panzerkampfwagen IV Ausf. D was the Ausf. E and it entered production in October 1940, having been contracted for in July of the previous year. Originally, 223 of the new tanks were ordered from Krupp-Grusonwerk, but by March 1941 this number had been reduced to 206. The order was filled by the end of April 1941. Unlike the previous two contracts, the bulk of these vehicles were completed as conventional tanks, with only four chassis being diverted to bridge layer construction, and the final two vehicles being converted to an experimental interleaved suspension.

Mechanically, the Ausf. E was almost identical to the Ausf. D, with the changes in the road wheel caps and drive sprocket ring being most evident. A new driver's visor adapted from the Panzerkampfwagen III was installed on the front of the superstructure. The superstructure front was reinforced with an additional 30mm-thick armor plate attached to the existing 30mm face-hardened plate. This

A factory-fresh Panzerkampfwagen IV Ausf. E ready for delivery. Thirty millimeter-thick supplemental armor plates were added to the face and sides of the superstructure on these vehicles to counter improving antitank rifles.

Walter J. Spielberger

The Panzerkampfwagen IV Ausf. E was the last Panzer IV to use the one-piece doors in the turret sides. A ventilator, introduced with this model, is visible on the forward part of the turret roof.

Patton Museum, Fort Knox, KY

was a result of encountering superior antitank weapons too late in the production planning to increase the base armor thickness.

Some of the Ausf. E were factory-modified to operate in North Africa and given improved engine cooling. Others were so modified in the field. Other tanks were converted for submerged operation. Beginning in March 1941, stowage bins began to be retrofitted to the rear of the turret.

Seen here firing at night, the Ausf. E's 7.5 cm L/24 main gun would have been more than sufficient through the Polish and French campaign, but was inadequate against the heavier Soviet tank armor.

Walter J. Spielberger

Panzerkampfwagen IV, Ausf. E

Length	5.92 m	Weapon, coaxial	7.92mm MG 34
Width	2.84 m	Weapon, ball mounted	7.92mm MG 34
Height	2.68 m		
Weight	22 tons	Ammo stowage, main	80 rnds
Fuel capacity	470 liters		
Maximum speed	42 km/h (26.04 mph)	Ammo stowage, secondary	3,150 rnds
Range, on road	210 km (130.2 miles)	Engine make	Maybach
Range, cross country	130 km (80.6 miles)	Engine model	HL 120 TRM
		Engine configuration	V-12, liquid cooled
Crew	5		
Communica-tions	Fu 5 and Fu 2, intercom	Engine displacement	11.9 liters
Weapon, main	7.5 cm Kw.K L/24	Engine horsepower	265 @ 2600 rpm

These tanks, loaded for rail transport in North Africa, still show signs of ocean transport, such as the sealed hull machinegun mount.

Walter J. Spielberger

Several changes were made with the introduction of the Ausf. F. A Kugelblende 50 ball mount was provided for the bow machine gun, a new driver's visor, adopted from the Sturmgeschütz was installed, and two-piece turret doors, taken from the Panzerkampfwagen III were used.

Patton Museum, Fort Knox, KY

Panzerkampfwagen IV Ausf. F

While production quantities had gradually increased until the Ausf. D and E orders, which were steady, true mass production began at the Ausf. F. The 128-vehicle order of December 1938 was increased to 500 in November 1939 due to the beginning of the war. Like the previous Panzerkampfwagen IV orders, Krupp-Grusonwerk was the recipient of this contract. However, by the following June orders for a further 100 each had been placed with Vomag and Nibelungenwerke. By January 1941, it was decided that, even with these increases, not enough of the tanks were on order, and Krupp-Grusonwerk received an additional order for 300.

The armor thickness of the front surfaces of the hull, turret and superstructure was increased to 50mm of face hardened armor. The sides were 30mm thick. By the beginning of February 1942 even this was felt inadequate, and additional 20mm-thick spaced armor plates were set in front of the turret and superstructure. The front plate of the superstructure reverted to being straight, with the

offset front plate abandoned for the final time. On the right side a kugelblende 50 machine gun ball mount was installed with its associated MG 34.

National Archives and Records Administration

Shown here during testing at Aberdeen Proving Ground, the flat surface of the Ausf. F superstructure front of this captured example is evident. Previously, the Ausf. B and C had flat superstructure faces, while the others all had offset faces.

On previous models, the muffler had extended almost the full width of hull. However, the muffler of the Ausf. F was markedly shorter. A second, much smaller and flatter muffler was installed to its left for use by the auxiliary generator.

Patton Museum, Fort Knox, KY

The weight of the Panzerkampfwagen IV had been increasing with each successive Ausführung, with a corresponding increase in ground pressure and decrease in mobility. As a result of this, 400mm-wide track (which was actually 380mm wide with 400mm-long track pins) was installed on the Panzerkampfwagen Ausf. F. Of course, this required a change in the drive sprocket, and a return idler made of welded tube replaced the earlier cast unit.

Despite the large numbers ordered, only 393, 64, and 13 of the Panzerkampfwagen Ausf. F were completed by Krupp-Grusonwerk, Vomag and Nibelungenwerke, respectively. The reason for this was the abandoning of the 7.5 cm Kw.K. L/24, which had been the Panzerkampfwagen IV's main weapon from the beginning. Instead, a new long-barreled, high-velocity 7.5 cm Kampfwagen Kanone was to be mounted.

Panzerkampfwagen IV, Ausf. F

Length	5.92 m	Weapon, coaxial	7.92mm MG 34
Width	2.88 m	Weapon, ball mounted	7.92mm MG 34
Height	2.68 m		
Weight	22.3 tons	Ammo stowage, main	80 rnds
Fuel capacity	470 liters	Ammo stowage, secondary	3,150 rnds
Maximum speed	42 km/h (26.04 mph)		
Range, on road	210 km (130.2 miles)	Engine make	Maybach
Range, cross country	130 km (80.6 miles)	Engine model	HL 120 TRM
		Engine configuration	V-12, liquid cooled
Crew	5		
Communications	Fu 5 and Fu 2, intercom	Engine displacement	11.9 liters
Weapon, main	7.5 cm Kw.K L/24	Engine horsepower	265 @ 2600 rpm

The harsh Russian winters led to the development of a coolant heater to aid in starting. This were retrofitted beginning in September 1942. Although this Ausf. F was not equipped with them, special, wider tracks were developed as well for use in snow and ice.

Patton Museum, Fort Knox, KY

The Panzerkampfwagen IV Ausf. G, known as the Panzerkampfwagen IV Ausf. F2 from March 21 through June 5, 1942, was essentially an Ausf. F armed with a longer-barreled cannon. Through April 1943 it mounted the 7.5 cm Kw.K. 40 L/43. At that time it was rearmed again with the even longer L/48. This captured example was returned to Britain for examination.

Patton Museum, Fort Knox, KY

Panzerkampfwagen IV Ausf. G

As the German Army encountered increasingly superior Soviet tanks during its push into Russia, a more potent weapon than the 7.5 cm Kw.K. L/24 became a critical need. The answer was the 7.5 cm Kw.K. L/40. This gun, with its markedly longer barrel and higher muzzle velocity, was installed in the Panzerkampfwagen IV Ausf. F, requiring minor changes to the tank, primarily inside the turret.

From April 1942 until July 1, 1942, the rearmed tank was known by various names, most of them involving "F2" (to distinguish if from the short-gunned F1). However, on that date they were redesignated Panzerkampfwagen IV Ausf. G.

The balance of the Panzerkampfwagen IV Ausf. F orders were modified to specify the new armament, and an additional 1,400 of the Panzerkampfwagen Ausf. G were ordered between June 1941 and February 1942. The Ausf. G was to remain in production through June 1943

Patton Museum, Fort Knox, KY

During the April 1942 production, the visors previously mounted on the turret sides, as well as the visor to the left of the main gun, were eliminated on the Panzerkampfwagen IV Ausf. G.

The two-piece commander's hatch, shown here open, was replaced with a one-piece hatch in February 1943. Through May of 1943 the antenna was mounted on the right side of the hull. To the left of the main muffler, just above a bucket, is the small muffler for the auxiliary generator.

Walter J. Spielberger

The rack for two pair of spare road wheels was added to the right side of the Ausf. G beginning with the June 1942 production. At about the same time spare track links began to be mounted on top of the glacis plate.

Patton Museum, Fort Knox, KY

The very earliest 7.5 cm-armed Panzerkampfwagen IV sported the ball-shaped muzzle brake shown here. Later models used a double baffle muzzle brake. Notice that the right front turret visor is open. This visor was eliminated during the course of Ausf. G production.

Walter J. Spielberger

As the turret spun around, the main gun pushed the antenna over until it lay in the rack seen here on the side of the superstructure. Note crewman peering out of the turret side hatch with binoculars. Stowage in tanks was always at a premium, so many crews fitted extra stowage compartments to their vehicles, such as this one mounted on the top corner of the engine deck.

Walter J. Spielberger

at all three firms: Krupp-Grusonwerk, Nibelungenwerke and Vomag.

As the Panzerkampfwagen Ausf. G was in production for a bit more than a year, it is not surprising that there were some changes made during the run. Among these were the elimination of visors from the turret front and sides during the first month's production, adding provision for carrying spare road wheels and track links in June, and replacing the Notek light with covered headlights

in September. Two attempts at increasing the armor protection were made: 30mm spaced armor was added to the hull front and superstructure intermittently from May 1942 through January 1943, and to all there after, schürzen armored skirts were installed beginning in April 1943.

Zimmerit was not applied to these vehicles at the factory, but beginning in January 1944 it was applied to tanks in the field.

Patton Museum, Fort Knox, KY

This captured Panzerkampfwagen IV Ausf. G was displayed with its engine compartment open, revealing two belt-driven cooling fans. This vehicle is also equipped with the Winterketten, and extended-width track for improved mobility in snow and mud.

Panzerkampfwagen IV, Ausf. G

Length	6.63 m	Weapon, coaxial	7.92mm MG 34
Width	2.88 m	Weapon, ball mounted	7.92mm MG 34
Height	2.68 m		
Weight	23.6 tons	Ammo stowage, main	87 rnds
Fuel capacity	470 liters		
Maximum speed	42 km/h (26.04 mph)	Ammo stowage, secondary	3,150 rnds
Range, on road	210 km (130.2 miles)	Engine make	Maybach
Range, cross country	130 km (80.6 miles)	Engine model	HL 120 TRM
Crew	5	Engine configuration	V-12, liquid cooled
Communications	Fu 5 and Fu 2, intercom	Engine displacement	11.9 liters
Weapon, main	7.5 cm Kw.K 40 L/43 (later L/48)	Engine horsepower	265 @ 2600 rpm

Patton Museum, Fort Knox, KY

This is a closeup of the relatively hard to find Winterketten. These were used during the winter of 42/43 were actually normal track links cast with an extended blade and using a regular length track pin. These are often confused with Ostketten, which were used during the following winter. Ostketten had an entirely different design, very much resembling Panther track.

Panzerkampfwagen IV Ausf. H

Because of the increased effectiveness of Allied cannons, heavier armor became a requirement for Germany's tanks. The three assembly firms, Krupp-Grusonwerk, Vomag and Nibelungenwerke, converted to Ausf. H production in May/June 1943.

Except for a few of the initial tanks, these were up armored to have solid 80mm-thick plate to the front of the hull and superstructure. The final drive ratio made higher (reducing top speed, but providing greater torque), reflecting the steadily increasing weight of the Panzerkampfwagen IV, which had by then soared from the Ausf. A's 18 metric tons to 25 metric tons for the Ausf. H.

During the June 1943 production it was decided to eliminate the visors on the hull sides, as they were now blocked by the schürzen. Zimmerit began to be applied at the factories in September 1943, and steel, rather than rubber-tired return rollers, began to be used the following month. Also in October, the idler wheel reverted to a casting instead of the welded assembly introduced with the Ausf. F.

Krupp-Grusonwerk stopped producing Panzerkampfwagen IV in December 1943. At that time they had produced 379 Ausf. H. It had been decided that Krupp-Grusonwerk resources would be better used in producing the Sturmgeschütz IV. Nibelungenwerke and Vomag, however, continued to produce the Ausf. H, building more than 1,200 and nearly 700, respectively, through February 1944. Sixty of Nibelungenwerke's Ausf. H chassis were used in the production of the Sturmpanzer IV, and an additional 30 were used for Sturmgeschütz IV.

There was very little external difference between the late Panzerkampfwagen IV Ausf. G and the early production Ausf. H. Both were built without Zimmerit antimagnetic mine coatings, and with schürzen for protection against antitank rounds. This vehicle has been prepared for rail transport and its hull schürzen was loaded face down in front of the tank.

The late Ausf. H was difficult to distinguish from its successor, the Ausf. J. Both had schürzen and, until discontinued on the Ausf. J in September 1944, they both had Zimmerit. Midway through the Ausf. H production run the bullet splash rail around the driver's and radio operator's hatches was simplified, becoming three-sided.

Like the Ausf. G, the Ausf. H had five-sided bullet splash guards around the driver's and radio operator's hatches. Along the right side of the tank can be seen the Filzbalgfilter, introduced on the G in May 1943 and discontinued from the H in February 1944.

Panzerkampfwagen IV, Ausf. H

Length	7.02 m	Weapon, coaxial	7.92mm MG 34
Width	2.88 m	Weapon, ball mounted	7.92mm MG 34
Height	2.68 m	Ammo stowage, main	87 rnds
Weight	25 tons		
Fuel capacity	470 liters	Ammo stowage, secondary	3,150 rnds
Maximum Speed	38 km/h (23.56 mph)		
Range, on road	210 km (130.2 miles)	Engine make	Maybach
Range, cross country	130 km (80.6 miles)	Engine model	HL 120 TRM
		Engine configuration	V-12, liquid cooled
Crew	5		
Communications	Fu 5 and Fu 2, intercom	Engine displacement	11.9 liters
Weapon, main	7.5 cm Kw.K 40 L/48	Engine horsepower	265 @ 2600 rpm

Walter J. Spielberger

A typical mid-production Ausf. H on maneuvers. Notice the spare track links stowed on the rear hull plate. An interesting detail is that each schürzen panel is labeled as to its position, L1, L2, etc.

Patton Museum, Fort Knox, KY

Doors were provided in the turret schürzen allowing the turret hatches to continue to be open even with the schürzen in place. However, the presence of the schürzen resulted in the visors ultimately being eliminated from both the hull and the turret.

Patton Museum, Fort Knox, KY

In this closeup we see the ridged pattern of the Zimmerit antimagnetic mine paste. The corrugations formed into it increased its effective thickness. The further the magnet from the steel hull, the less likely it was to adhere. In the foreground is the empty rack for an axe. Details of the Kugelblende 50 machine gun ball mount are also visible, as is the method of mounting spare track on top of the glacis. This vehicle's chassis number was stenciled on the hull.

These Second Panzer Division Ausf. H tanks have both their hull and turret schürzen installed. While the turret schürzen was firmly attached, the hull schürzen hung rather loosely from a rail. The allowed it to be quickly removed for running gear maintenance.
Patton Museum, Fort Knox, KY

The Filzbalgfilter can clearly be seen on this mid-production Panzerkampfwagen IV Ausf. H. Both the main and auxiliary engine's mufflers show clearly, as does the rubber-tired return rollers and fabricated idler. In October 1943 a cast idler began to be used, as did all-steel return rollers.
Walter J. Spielberger

Panzerkampfwagen IV Ausf. J

The final version of the long-serving Panzerkampfwagen IV was the Ausführung J. The Ausf. J would also turn out to be the most abundant version.

The Ausf. J lacked the power-operated turret traverse that earlier models had—instead a two-speed, gear-driven, manually operated traversing mechanism was installed. The space in the hull previously occupied by the auxiliary generator was used to house an additional fuel tank, although installation of these was sporadic until a satisfactory tank could be produced.

With so many tanks of this Ausführung tank produced, and the German tendency to introduce running changes, it is not surprising that there are many variations of the Ausf. J. Pistol ports and visors were dropped from the turret side hatches beginning in May 1944, as the schürzen prevented their use. However, once again, the German tank manufacturer's tendency toward last in-first out inventory control of components meant that tanks with these features continued to show up on the production line sporadically throughout the war.

In August, Flammentöter mufflers were introduced, and the next month Zimmerit was eliminated. Also in

From any angle other than the rear, the Panzerkampfwagen IV Ausf. J is almost indistinguishable from its predecessor, the Ausf. H. In such cases the chassis serial number is invaluable in making identification. This tank has its chassis number, 89589, conveniently stenciled on the front of the superstructure.

Bundesarchiv photo.

September, the solid steel schürzen along the hull side was replaced with schürzen made of wire mesh, which was both lighter and used less raw material. In October, the hull side plates were made longer and were drilled on the ends to act as towing eyes, eliminating the separately installed brackets previously used.

Vomag produced the Panzerkampfwagen IV Ausf. J from February through May 1944. At that time it was decided their production should be concentrated on the Jagdpanzer IV, and about 180 Ausf. J had been built when the line was converted.

Nibelungenwerke, on the other hand, built the Panzerkampfwagen IV Ausf. J until the very end of the war, making the Panzerkampfwagen IV unique in being the only German tank in production throughout the entire war. Almost 3,000 Ausf. J had been built by Nibelungenwerke by the time of surrender, in addition to nearly 200 chassis-only for use in Sturmpanzer IV production.

The hanging method of mounting hull schürzen left the lower portion of it unsupported. Gravity caused the bottoms to swing in. The leading edge of the schürzen were tapered closer to the fenders in an attempt to avoid snagging the skirts on obstacles.

Patton Museum, Fort Knox, KY

The method of mounting the hull schürzen by hanging however made it relatively easy, and common, for panels to be pulled off by trees, structures or debris, especially in rough terrain or close quarters. The Panzerkampfwagen IV in the foreground has lost some of its schürzen panels, while the tank in the background retains its.

Military History Institute, Carlisle Barracks, PA.

Panzerkampfwagen IV, Ausf. J

Length	7.02 m	Weapon, coaxial	7.92mm MG 34
Width	2.88 m	Weapon, ball mounted	7.92mm MG 34
Height	2.68 m	Ammo stowage, main	87 rnds
Weight	25 tons		
Fuel capacity	680 liters	Ammo stowage, secondary	3,150 rnds
Maximum speed	38 km/h (23.56 mph)		
Range, on road	320 km (198.4 miles)	Engine make	Maybach
		Engine model	HL 120 TRM
Range, cross country	210 km (130.2 miles)	Engine configuration	V-12, liquid cooled
Crew	5	Engine displacement	11.9 liters
Communications	Fu 5 and Fu 2, intercom		
Weapon, main	7.5 cm Kw.K 40 L/48	Engine horsepower	265 @2600 rpm

Later in the war, mesh skirts, known as Thoma schürzen, began to be mounted on the hull. Plate schürzen continued to be used on the turret, however. The Thoma schürzen was supported on a structure made of tubing, rather than the rectangular structure used previously.

Ultimately, dual flammentöeter mufflers began to be installed in lieu of the previous canister muffler. The tank in the foreground has this new installation, while the tank in the background has the traditional exhaust system installed. From this angle positive identification of the Ausf. J can be made due to the lack of a muffler for an auxiliary power plant. This small engine was eliminated from the design commencing with the Ausf. J production.

Command tanks, or Panzerbefelswagen, differed from standard tanks primarily in that they carried a much more extensive suite of communications equipment. Of course, this meant additional antenna as well. Some combat tanks, such as the one shown here, were converted from conventional combat tanks in the field. In the left foreground of this photo can be seen the unusual star antenna, or Sternantenne D.

Military History Institute, Carlisle Barracks, PA.

Panzerbefelswagen

Like many of Germany's armored vehicle families, a certain number of the Panzerkampfwagen IV were outfitted as command vehicles, or Panzerbefelswagen IV. The conversion of Panzer IV into Panzerbefelswagen began in March 1944. The work involved reducing stowage to 72 rounds of 7.5 cm ammunition, and mounting additional radio equipment instead. A GG400 auxiliary generator was installed, along with a 30-watt transmitter and receiver set (Fu 8), as well as a 10-watt set (Fu 10). The Fu 8 utilized a Sternantenne D (star aerial), which rather resembled a broken umbrella, while the Fu 10 was connected to a 2-meter rod antenna mounted on the turret roof. Some vehicles were equipped for ground-to-air communication via Fu 7 transmitter/receiver, with 1.4-meter antenna mounted on the left rear hull.

During August and September 1944, 17 Panzerbefelswagen were built using new Panzerkampfwagen IV Ausf. J. The 88 vehicles produced from March through July were converted from rebuilt Panzerkampfwagen IV.

The 2-meter rod antenna used by the Fu 5 ultra short wave set can be seen on the turret roof of this Panzerbefelswagen. This was one of the 17 vehicles built new as Panzerbefelswagen based on Panzerkampfwagen IV Ausf. J. It is now with the Tank Museum in Brussels.

National Archives and Records Administration

The armored guard for the antenna base can be seen between the right flammentoeter muffler and the fender on this Panzerbefelswagen. The additional antenna readily identified these as command vehicles to enemy gunners.

National Archives and Records Administration

Patton Museum, Fort Knox, KY

When German troops encountered the Soviet KV and T-34 series tanks in 1941 the existing German tanks were instantly rendered obsolete. The Panther, with its powerful gun and heavy, sloped armor was seen as the counter to the Soviet armored force. This is an example of the second production series, the Ausf. A.

Panther

As the German Army's push reached deeper into the Soviet Union it began to encounter formidable foes. The tanks they encountered, the KV series and T-34/76 vehicles, were both better armed and better protected than any of the tanks the German Army had in the field at that time.

Although Germany had been experimenting with designs for a new, heavier medium tank for a while, it wasn't until the Soviet tanks were encountered that this process gained a sense of urgency. Hitler himself ordered Wa Pruef to start work on a better tank on November 25, 1941.

Wa Pruef contracted Daimler-Benz and M.A.N. (Maschinenfabrik Augsburg-Nürnberg) for firm design proposals in December 1941. The specifications called for a weight of 30 tons and armament consisting of the 75mm KwK L/70. The turret design work was contracted to Rheinmetall-Borsig. The experimental series was known as the VK3002.

Daimler-Benz completed its design in March of 1942, basing much of it on its earlier rejected VK3001, which had been a copy of the T-34. Two versions of the VK3002 were offered by Daimler-Benz, one with conventional spring suspension and another with torsion bar suspension.

Machinefabrik Augsburg-Nurnberg (M.A.N.) completed its design in May 1942. It featured a centrally located turret, sloping armor, and many of the other characteristics that are today associated with the Panther.

Prototypes of each version were built and tested, then reviewed by Hitler. He selected the M.A.N. design for production, with deliveries targeted to begin in December 1942. The initial production version of the Panther was the Ausf. D. Ulitimately the MAN-design Panther was produced by Daimler-Benz as well as MAN. MNH and Henschel also joined in this production in an all-out effort to equip the German army with the new medium tank.

The second version, the Ausf. A, entered production at MNH in August, 1943, followed by Daimler-Benz, Demag and M.A.N. in September. Demag effectively replaced Henschel in the manufacturing pool. The true difference between the Ausf. A and the earlier Ausf. D was in the mechanics of the turret. Shortly after production of the Ausf. A began, the hull construction was changed so that the "letterbox" machine gun opening was replaced with a ball mount. This has led many to believe the hull

Patton Museum, Fort Knox, KY

The first production model of the Panther, the Ausf. D, did not have a ball mount for the hull machine gun. Instead, a "letter box" type flap was installed. This characteristic was also carried over early into the second series, or Ausf. A, production. Beginning in April 1943 side skirts were mounted on the Panther. The objective of this spaced armor was to detonate Soviet anti-tank rounds before they contacted the hull itself.

National Archives and Records Administration photo.

Twin headlights were installed on the earliest of the Panther Ausf. D, but by July 1943 the right headlight had been eliminated. Also, prior to June 1943 smoke grenade launchers were mounted on either side of the turret near the front.

Walter J. Spielberger

This MAN-built Ausf. A displays the feature many believe to be the distinguishing characteristic of the improved Panther: the radio operator's ball-mounted machine gun. In fact, however, the true differences were hidden features of the turret construction, and until December 1943, A models continued to use the same machine gun flap as the earlier Ausf. D.

Two large stowage bins were mounted on the rear of the Panther Ausf. D hull outboard of the exhaust stacks. The crew of this tank has mounted spare road wheels, a valuable spare near the front, on either side of the engine compartment.

Patton Museum, Fort Knox, KY

A tube for carrying gun cleaning rods was mounted on the left side of the Panther's hull, along with spare track sections, a C-hook and a wire rope for towing. The crewman standing in front of the tank serves as a good scale of the size of the imposing vehicle.

Walter J. Spielberger

National Archives and Records Administration photo.

The heater on the Panther Ausf. A worked off the left side of the engine cooling system. Due to this design, this meant that the left exhaust manifold was no longer cooled. Therefore, a new manifold cooling system was engineered, that incorporated an air duct on either side of the left exhaust stack. Cooling air only passed through the flanking pipes.

Patton Museum, Fort Knox, KY

Unlike the broader Tigers, the Panther could fit within normal railroad clearances, thus it could be transported by rail directly into action without delay. Here a Panther in winter camouflage is being guided from a railcar.

Walter J. Spielberger

The evenly tapered side armor immediately identifies this Panther as an Ausf. G, the final production model which was introduced in March 1944. This particular tank is equipped with 800 mm diameter steel rimmed road wheels rather than the 860 mm diameter rubber tired road wheels used on most earlier models.

was changed between the ausführung, but this is not the case.

The final version of the Panther, the Ausf. G, did have a much different type of hull construction. Production of this version began in March 1944 at M.A.N., followed by Daimler-Benz and MNH in May in July, respectively. Demag did not build the Ausf. G as a combat tank, instead building Bergepanther recovery vehicles. More Panther Ausf G were produced than previous models, with production continuing for the duration of the war and totaling more than 2,900 units.

The Ausf. G's most visible difference from previous models was the tapered one-piece upper hull side plate. The top hull hatches were also redesigned, and the driver's visor in the glacis plate was eliminated. Periscopes replaced the visor. Ultimately, a new mantlet design was introduced as well that had a distinctive, squared-off chin to eliminate the shot trap presented by the earlier design.

The main weapon chosen for the Panther was a good one, and the armor was high quality and s positioned for good ballistic characteristics. However, the drive train was not reliable.

An interesting side note: After the British captured the MNH Panther production line in Hannover, they had a few more examples produced by the German workers. These factory-fresh tanks were then used for evaluation purposes.

Panther Ausf. D

Length	8.86 m	Secondary	7.92mm MG 34
Width	3.27 m	In hull	7.92mm MG 34
Height	2.99 m		
Weight	44.8 tons	Ammo stowage, main	79 rnds
Fuel capacity	730 liters		
Maximum speed	55 km/hr (34.1 mph)	Ammo stowage, secondary	5,100 rnds
Range, on road	200 km (124 miles)	Engine make	Maybach
Range, cross country	100 km (62 miles)	Engine model	HL 230 P30
Crew	5	Engine configuration	V-12, liquid cooled
Communications	Fu 5 and Fu 2, intercom	Engine displacement	23 liters
Weapon, main	7.5 cm Kw.K. 42 L/70	Engine horsepower	700 @ 3000 rpm

Panther Ausf. G

Length	8.86 m	In hull	7.92mm MG 34
Width	3.42 m		
Height	2.98 m	Ammo stowage, main	79 rnds
Weight	45.5 tons	Ammo stowage, secondary	5,100 rnds
Fuel capacity	730 liters		
Maximum speed	55 km/hr (34.1 mph)	Engine make	Maybach
Range, on road	200 km (124 miles)	Engine model	HL 230 P30
Range, cross country	100 km (62 miles)	Engine configuration	V-12, liquid cooled
Crew	5	Engine displacement	23 liters
Communications	Fu 5 and Fu 2, intercom	Engine horsepower	700 @ 3000 rpm
Weapon, main	7.5 cm Kw.K. 42 L/70		

Panther Ausf. A

Length	8.86 m	In hull	7.92mm MG 34
Width	3.42 m		
Height	3.10 m	Ammo stowage, main	79 rnds
Weight	45.5 tons	Ammo stowage, secondary	5,100 rnds
Fuel capacity	730 liters		
Maximum speed	55 km/hr (34.1 mph)	Engine make	Maybach
Range, on road	200 km (124 miles)	Engine model	HL 230 P30
Range, cross country	100 km (62 miles)	Engine configuration	V-12, liquid cooled
Crew	5	Engine displacement	23 liters
Communications	Fu 5 and Fu 2, intercom	Engine horsepower	700 @ 3000 rpm
Weapon, main	7.5 cm Kw.K. 42 L/70		

Patton Museum, Fort Knox, KY

One of the distinguishing features of the Ausf. G was its lack of a driver's vision port. The uninterrupted glacis of this captured 11th Panzer Division Ausf. G is evident here.

Military History Institute, Carlisle Barracks, PA

Initially the Ausf. G continued to use the rounded mantlet as seen here, a design that had been carried over from its predecessors. A cast commander's cupola was used on the Ausf. G, as it had been on the late Ausf. A. This captured example was part of the Pz.Lehr division.

Military History Institute, Carlisle Barracks, PA

Armin Sohns

The armored hull sides of the G also sloped at a lesser angle than they did on their predecessors. Notice the 20-ton jack mounted vertically. During production of the Ausf. A the switch was made from a 15-ton capacity horizontally stowed jack to the one shown here.

During September 1944 a new gun mantlet was introduced. This new mantlet had a cast "chin," or ledge added to the bottom to prevent incoming rounds from being deflected off the earlier rounded mantlet and through the hull roof. However, the German tank industry did not use first in-first out inventory management, which resulted in Panthers being produced with mixed features, including the round mantlet, up to the war's end.

The Panther Ausf. G did not have pistol ports in its turret sides. Rather, like the late production Ausf. D, it was designed to incorporate the Nahverteidigungswaffe (close defense weapon). This 2nd Panzer Division tank was destroyed by aircraft during the Battle of the Bulge.

As was the case with many models of German tanks, a certain number of Panthers were equipped as command vehicles. These tanks carried less ammunition in order to accommodate additional communications equipment. The additional antenna, visible here, were a tell-tale sign of these tanks.

This photo of a knocked out Panther Ausf. G shows many of the classic features of the model. The visor-free glacis can be seen, as can the chin-type mantlet, cast cupola and tapered hull side. The Panther's frontal armor was fairly heavy, but the side armor was 2" thick or less.

Porsche Tiger

Dr. Ferdinand Porsche's firm began design work on a new German tank, known as the Leopard, in 1939. Because Dr Porsche was firmly convinced that conventional mechanical powertrain design would not be able to withstand the high loads imposed by a heavy tank, a new system was employed. The Porsche Typ 100, also known as Leopard or VK 3001 (P), would use a gas-electric drivetrain. Two large, air-cooled V-10 gasoline engines powered generators, which in turn powered electric motors that acted as final drives. This was not all that radical of an idea, as the same propulsion method was, and is still, commonly used for railroad locomotives. One wooden mockup and three trial vehicles were ordered, but only the mockup and one unarmed trial vehicle were completed.

In May 1941, Hitler ordered that the new heavy tank was to have its frontal armor increased to a thickness of 100mm. He also ordered that the 8.8 cm armament

The gas-electric driven Porsche Tiger was considerably longer than the more successful, conventionally driven Henschel Tiger. The turrets however were essentially the same, with the Henschel's turret being derived from the one designed for the Porsche.

proposed for the VK 3001 (P) be retained, although he desired increased penetration. The redesigned tank was designated VK 4501 (P) by the Army, and Typ 101 by

On the front of the superstructure were a ball mount for a MG 34, driver's vision port, and driver's periscope. The track skids, needed to prevent the track from fouling on weld seams, can also be seen in this view.

This is one of two Tiger P sent to Doellersheim for testing in August of 1942. The test vehicles did not have the full suite of on-vehicle material that would have been stowed on combat vehicles.

With the turret mounted well forward as it was, and the long barrel of the 8.8 cm L/56 cannon, considerable room was needed to turn the vehicle around when the gun was trained forward. Thus photos with the gun in that position are rarely seen.

Shown here are three of the 10 Porsche Tigers completed. The tanks in the background have just extricated the tank in the foreground from a bog. The great weight of the Tigers meant that often times the only thing powerful enough to pull it was another Tiger.

Porsche. In June 1942, it was designated Panzerkampfwagen VI Tiger. The twin V-10 air-cooled engines were increased in displacement from 10 to 15 liters.

Much of the Typ 101 was merely reworked or modified Typ 100 components, including the unusual longitudinal torsion bar suspension, and the basic turret design. This basic turret design, by Krupp, was also used on the Henschel-designed Tiger.

By August 1941, this project had fallen under the realm of the "Tigerprogramm," and an all-out effort to complete the prototypes was under way. One hundred vehicles were on the initial order. After some delays due to defects with the newly designed engines, produced by Simmering, a trial vehicle was delivered to Rastenburg for a head-to-head competition with the Henschel vehicle. Hitler viewed the vehicle, and the delivery took place as part of his birthday celebration on April 20, 1942.

In testing, the engines continued to be problematic, with excessive oil consumption and short service lifes. Breakdowns were frequent, and the vehicle often became mired.

The vehicles were assembled by Nibelungenwerke, although due to ongoing changes and problems production was not consistent. The hull armor, turret and weapon were manufactured by Krupp, and shipped by rail to Nibelungenwerke. Many of the hulls traveled back and forth between the two facilities as the design was refined and Krupp made the needed modifications. Changes were not confined only to the hull, however. The first eight turrets had slightly lower sides and a roof with a raised center section (to permit full depression of the main gun), but the balance of the turrets had taller sides and a flat roof.

Ultimately, only 10 of the 100 Porsche Tigers were completed. Most were used for training and testing purposes. These vehicles represented a sizeable investment, not only in money, but in resources as well. Therefore, the remaining components were reused. The 90 unused turrets and guns were adapted for use on Henschel Tigers. Three of the hulls and chassis were repowered with liquid-cooled Maybach HL120 engines replacing the troublesome Simmering-built Porsche air-cooled engines. These chassis were further modified to become Berge-Panzer VI recovery vehicles. Another 91 were similarly repowered, then used as the basis for the construction of the Panzerjaeger "Tiger P." The very last Tiger P was completed as a command tank, or Panzerbefelswagen. After being used for testing from November 1942 through September 1943, in early 1944 it was returned to Nibelungenwerke. While there it received many of the modifications associated with the Panzerjaeger "Tiger P," including the repowering with Maybach engines, increased frontal armor and the application of Zimmerit.

After the modifications were complete, this Tiger was assigned to schwere Heeres Panzer-Jaeger-Abteilung 653 and deployed to the Eastern front in April 1944. It was reported lost in action in July of the same year. This is the only example of the Porsche Tiger known to have seen combat.

Panzerkampfwagen VI P Tiger

Length	9.54 m	Weapon, coaxial	7.92mm MG 34
Width	3.4 m	Weapon, ball mounted	7.92mm MG 34
Height	2.9 m	Ammo stowage, main	80 rnds
Weight	60 tons		
Fuel capacity	520 liters	Ammo stowage, secondary	4,350 rnds
Maximum speed	35 km/hr (21.7 mph)		
Range, on road	105 km (65.1 miles)	Engine make originally,	2 x Porsche
Range, cross country	48 km (29.76 miles)	Engine model	Typ 101
Crew	5	Engine configuration	V-10, air cooled
Communications	Fu 5, Fu 2, and intercom	Engine displacement	15 liters each
Weapon, main	8.8 cm Kw.K. 36 L/56	Engine horsepower	310 hp each

Large grilles covering cooling air ducts covered much of the sloping hull rear. As built the vehicles were powered by twin V-10 air-cooled engines turning generators. The generators supplied current to one large motor for each track.

Patton Museum, Fort Knox, KY

Bundesarchiv photo.

The initial production Tiger I tanks are easily identified by the curved notches in the front towing ring brackets. These notches were intended to provide clearance for the moveable Vorpanzer armor. The hull components had already been fabricated by the time the Vorpanzer idea was abandoned.

The Tiger I (Tiger Ausf. E)

Initial development of the Tiger I was begun in 1937. Designs for heavy tanks were submitted by Damlier-Benz, Henschel and M-A-N. Porsche became involved in late 1939. Ultimately, the Henschel and M-A-N designs evolved into the Panther, while the Porsche and Henschel designs became the famed Tiger tank.

As originally conceived, the Henschel was to have used a taper-bore 0725 main gun, but this was dropped because of the limited amount of tungsten available to German industry due to the war effort. Instead, the Henschel Tiger was armed with the Krupp-built turret with 8.8 cm gun originally developed for the Porsche-designed vehicle. At this stage the vehicle became known as the VK4501 (H).

The Porsche and Henschel designs were to be tried against each other, but from the outset the Porsche design was favored by many in high places, including

Patton Museum, Fort Knox, KY

These are Tigers of the 8th company of Panzer Regiment 7 lost during Operation "Ochsenkopf," sometime after February 26th, 1943. These tanks were disabled by mines and artillery and were later blown up by their crews. These Tigers had previously been the Second Company of the Schwere Heeres Panzer Abteilung (Army Heavy Tank Battalion) 501 and were renumbered prior to the battle.

A Tiger of the 503 Schwere Heeres Panzer Abteilung after Kursk in the Summer of 1943. This tank appears to be early spring 1943 production with drum cupola. The front track hangers are unit made, while the stowage box was factory made.

Here is a mid-production tank with dome-shaped cupola and rubber-rimmed road wheels of the Third Company of the 502nd Army Heavy Tank Battalion (Schwere Heeres Panzer Abteilung).

Hitler himself. However, almost from the beginning of the trials the Porsche prototype was unable to perform adequately. In October 1942, Speer set up an independent Tiger Commission to evaluate the competing designs. The results came firmly down in favor of the Henschel design.

The first four production Tigers were delivered August 18, 1942. Their first combat action was near Leningrad on the September 16 by four Tigers of the 502nd Tank Battalion. All four vehicles returned undamaged. However, on their second engagement, all four were put out of action

The Tiger was not terribly reliable, and oftentimes broke down. Repair and maintenance needs often overwhelmed the support personnel, requiring the crew perform many of these chores themselves.

With its normal tracks in place, the Tiger exceeded the recommended clearance standards for railcars. Therefore, the tanks were supplied with a second, narrower, set of tracks known as transport tracks. The side fenders and outer roadwheels were removed, the front fenders folded, and the transport tracks installed in lieu of the regular track. This reduced the width of the tank to an acceptable dimension. This tank, of the Panzergrenadier Division Grossdeutschland, was in such a configuration when photographed at Trakehnen, East Prussia.

A Tiger of the Third Company of the 502ND Army Heavy Tank Battalion (Schwere Heeres Panzer Abteilung) in service on the Russian front in summer 1943. The factory applied RAL 7028 dark yellow has had red and green camouflage oversprayed on it in the field. Third Company applied their tactical markings on the lower part of the turret in black during this time.

A Tiger of the Second Company s.SS-Pz.Abt. 101 with steel wheels, binocular sight, loader's hatch with offset handle and short hinges tows tank 231 of the same unit near Villers-Bocage by a second Tiger. Such towing put a severe strain on the towing vehicle's already overburdened driveline. Notice that the lead tank has the later type steel rimmed road wheels.

Tank 311, a Tiger of the Third Company s.SS-Pz.Abt. 101 sits patiently as battle plans are made. The Zimmerit anti-magnetic mine paste is particularly apparent on the side of the turret in this photo.

This Tiger was built in May, 1943 and has characteristics typical of production at that time. Note the placement of the track changing cable stowage as well as the track tool box above the left rear fender. An S-mine launcher can be seen mounted on the rear corner of the hull.

and the guns of three of the vehicles were damaged. One tank was burned out.

On February 27, 1944, Hitler banned the designation "Mark VI tank," instead ordering that the designation "Tiger Tank Ausf. E" be used. The last tank of this type was completed in August 1944.

During the development process the weight of the vehicle continually increased, which brought about the need to mount an additional roadwheel outboard of the originally designed roadwheel stations. Incidental to this

was the increase in track width from 520mm to 725mm. This resulted in the vehicle exceeding the railroad loading limitations. This problem was addressed by providing a second set of tracks, 520mm wide, known as transportation tracks. The outer roadwheels and combat tracks were removed and the transportation tracks installed for rail movement. Once offloaded, the process was reversed, which could be accomplished by an experienced crew in about a half-hour per side.

These tanks had torsion bar suspension, and beginning in January 1944, after about the first 800 tanks had been

This Tiger I of the First Company schwere Heeres Panzer Abteilung 501 was photographed while advancing through Tunisia. Notice the apparently unpainted electrical leads for the headlights and the camouflage covering of the gun barrel and hull sides.

This rear view of Tiger I, tactical number 142, First Company schwere Heeres Panzer Abteilung 501 shows clearly the Feifel air filters mounted on the rear of the hull as well as the 501st's unit-modified sheet metal exhaust stack heat shields.

The Tiger also served in the harsh winter weather of the Russian front. The large escape hatch is visible on the side of the turret. This was introduced during the December 1942 production. Note the impressive size of the 8.8 cm rounds compared to the men handling them.

On this captured tank we can see much of the mid-production stowage. Alongside the hull is a cable used when replacing the track, and just visible on top of the hull is a heavier wire rope that was used for towing.

produced, they were equipped with what is commonly known as steel road wheels. These road wheels were based on a Russian design found on captured tanks. Previously, the road wheels were constructed with a heavy rubber tire applied to a metal wheel, much like a forklift tire. The new design used a steel tire essentially isolated from the steel wheel by O-ring-type rubber cushions. When the new style road wheels were introduced, the number of road wheels per axle was reduced again from three to two.

The first 250 of these vehicles were powered by the Maybach HL210P30 with a 21-liter, 650-horsepower rating. Beyond the first 250 vehicles, the 23-liter Maybach HL230P45 engine was used, which had an additional 50 horsepower.

After 391 vehicles were built, the turret was redesigned to include a new commander's cupola, based on that used on the Panther, as well as numerous other improvements. Other changes implemented at this time include the gun barrel clamp and escape hatch. In June 1943, an improved cupola mounting for the MG34 antiaircraft weapon was introduced.

Two months later the number of headlights on the Tiger was reduced to one. Of the 1,346 Tiger I tanks produced, the final 54 were unique. Most of these vehicles were actually more accurately described as extensively rebuilt. The hulls of these vehicles were salvaged from damaged vehicles that were unrepairable, although this project required the new build of 22 turrets. Tiger I

Near the front corner of the turret is the smoke grenade launcher. The ball mount for the hull machine gun is also plainly visible.

For rail travel, the outer road wheels and fenders were removed and a narrower set of tracks installed as shown here. This reduced the width of the vehicle enough that it could travel on railroad lines.

The rubber-rimmed road wheels were characteristic of most Tigers. This tank has its normal track installed, along with a full complement of road wheels and its fenders.

production, which had begun in August 1942, ceased in August 1944.

The Tiger was well armed and well protected, but its great weight (56 tons) pushed the limits of its suspension and powertrain. Most likely more Tigers were destroyed by German forces after running out of fuel or spares than were knocked out in action by Allied tanks. However, this fact should not be construed to mean the Tiger was invulnerable. Allied forces learned that their tanks could deal with the Tiger, but to do so required skill and cunning, rather than a simple duel.

Military History Institute, Carlisle Barracks, PA.

The outer edges of the front and rear fenders were hinged so that they could fold to reduce the width when the side skirts were removed. The initial production Tigers did not have the large stowage bin seen here on the rear of the turret. Units fabricated their own or retrofitted bins off of other tanks until they became factory installed.

Panzerkampfwagen VI Ausf. E (Tiger)

Length	8.45 m	Weapon, coaxial	7.92mm MG 34
Width	3.70 m	Weapon, ball mounted	7.92mm MG 34
Height	2.93 m	Ammo stowage, main	93 rnds
Weight	57 tons		
Fuel capacity	540 liters	Ammo stowage, secondary	4,800 rnds
Maximum speed	38 km/hr (23.56 mph)		
Range, on road	140 km (86.8 miles)	Engine make	Maybach
Range, cross country	195 km (120.0 miles)	Engine model	HL210P45
Crew	5	Engine configuration	V-12, liquid cooled
Communications	FuG 5	Engine displacement	21.0 liters
Weapon, main	8.8 cm Kw.K. 36 L/56	Engine horsepower	700 @ 3000 rpm

Military History Institute, Carlisle Barracks, PA

The complex Fiefel air cleaner system is clearly shown here, as well as the engine starting crank stowed on the lower hull rear. Crews hoped to avoid using this.

Walter J. Spielberger

This factory photo shows the elaborate ductwork required by the Fiefel system. The entire system was somewhat delicate.

The three prototype Tiger II, or Tiger Ausf. B, differed from the production vehicles in detail, although the basic form was the same. The prototypes did not have Zimmerit coating, and were painted dark yellow, except for the gun tubes, which were left red oxide primer.

Tiger Ausf. B, or Tiger II

The German Tiger II was arguably the best-armed and protected tank fielded during WWII. Fortunately for the Allies, the Tiger II's effectiveness was hampered by low production numbers, an inadequate power train and poor tactical decisions.

The Henschel-designed tank initially included a Krupp-designed turret, with the three prototypes and the first 47 production vehicles featuring turrets originally designed for the ill-fated Porsche Type 180. Armament was, per Hitler's mandate, based on the 88mm Flak 41, now taking the form of the 8.8 cm L/71 KwK 43.

Although originally intended to be based on the Tiger I, the Tiger II drew much of its design, and even components, from the stillborn M.A.N. Panther II project. In the end, the transmission was essentially the only component taken over from the Tiger I, and even it was modified slightly. Production of the powerful new tank began in January 1944 and continued through March of 1945, although ultimately only 474 vehicles were built.

Although the production totals were low, there were some variations in the run. As previously mentioned, the first 50 tanks were built with Krupp turrets designed for the Porsche heavy tank project (thus these have been dubbed "Porsche" turrets). The balance of the run had

Patton Museum, Fort Knox, KY

This Tiger II of the 503rd Army Heavy Tank Battalion was photographed near Canteloup castle, in the Argences vicinity southeast of Caen, in early July 1944.

turrets designed by Krupp especially for the Henschel Tiger B.

The earliest vehicles had a telescoping snorkle for fording, but this feature was eliminated after only a few tanks were produced. In April 1944, the front and rear hull extensions were modified near the tow shackles to permit the use of "C" hooks. At about the same time a four-segment turret ring guard was added and the glacis notched near the radio operator's periscope. The addition of the turret ring guard required the modification of the screens on the rear deck of the tank. Concurrently, the binocular T.Z.F. 9b/1 gunners sight was replaced with the monocular T.Z.F. 9d sight. To accommodate this change, the left hole in the turret face was plugged.

Most of the tanks built after this time also used a two-piece stepped gun barrel, rather than the single-piece tapered tube used previously.

The original track design, which had small bar links, and hence was very flexible, was replaced in May 1944. The new track used a solid bar connecting link, and was not a flexible. It increased rolling resistance, but decreased the likelihood of a track walking off the sprocket. The drive sprocket used with the new track had only nine

The training of the 503rd Army Heavy Tank Battalion near Canteloup castle was well documented, yielding many clear photos early Tiger II with narrow mantlet and segmented turret ring guards.

Patton Museum, Fort Knox, KY

The heavy armor of the Tiger II was resistant to most contemporary tanks and tank destroyers. However, it was vulnerable to shaped charges such as bazookas and magnetic mines. Thus, we can see here the Zimmerit anti-magnetic paste which was applied to counter this threat.

Patton Museum, Fort Knox, KY

Dust flies as an 8.8 cm round hurries on its way during a firing exercise. The Tiger II's weapon was formidable, and not many opponent's tanks could resist it, even at long ranges.

Patton Museum, Fort Knox, KY

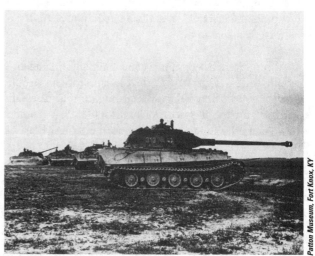

Most of the 503rd Army Heavy Tank Battalion's tanks, shown here almost new, were lost during fighting in northern France just a short time after these photos were taken.

Patton Museum, Fort Knox, KY

The tank in the foreground has a single-piece "monobloc" gun barrel, while the tank in the distance has the later, more common, two-piece stepped gun barrel.

The huge size of the Tiger II is apparent in this photo of a German soldier applying camouflage paint in the field. At the time this tank was built, they were factory painted with the base coat of yellow, and the green and brown were field applied.

The mud guards, or fenders, hung along either side of the tank. Made of armor plate, each segment had two slotted holes near the end. These slots engaged bolts that were screwed into the side of the tank superstructure. Removal, necessary for certain rail transport, required only loosening the bolts and lifting the heavy panels off.

Tank, stowage and all were painted during these camouflaging operations. Note as well the steel rimmed road wheels, characteristic of all Tiger II.

teeth, rather than the 18 used with the earlier track. At about the same time a vane sight was added to the turret roof for the commander's use.

The following month was a month of major changes in Tiger II production. Three sockets were added to the turret roof for mounting a 2-ton-capacity jib boom crane. At about the same time, a shorter muzzle brake began to be used as well. But the major change in June was the introduction of a new turret. Known now as the "production," or "series," turret, it had little in common with its predecessor. Whereas the Porsche turret had a rounded face and a bulge in its left side to accommodate the cupola, the series turret had a flat face and its side armor was not as steeply sloped. This negated the need for the bulged side.

Beginning in August 1944, the commander's cupola was bolted, rather than welded on. These are easily distinguished by the lack of a weld seam, which is prominent on the earlier models. Also in August the Tiger IIs began to be factory camouflaged in a three-color scheme.

This paint scheme was short lived, however, as in September the Tigers began to be left in their red oxide primer with patches of dark yellow, red brown and olive green. Also, beginning in September, the Zimmerit anti-magnet mine coating was discontinued.

During the next month the 20-ton jack previously furnished on the tanks was eliminated, as were its mounting brackets. Except for changes in the latch design on the hull

Patton Museum, Fort Knox, KY

The Zimmerit antimagnetic mine coating is apparent on this tank. Zimmerit application was discontinued due to concerns that it was flammable. Later it was determined that these concerns were unwarranted, but application was not reinstated.

Patton Museum, Fort Knox, KY

The turret face and mantlet of the series turret differed substantially from those of the Porsche turret. As this photo clearly shows, the series turret had a flat face and a circular mantlet. The hole in the mantlet beside the gun tube was the mounting of the coaxial machine gun.

Patton Museum, Fort Knox, KY

The hubs of the even numbered road wheel stations on each side of the Tiger II were extended, whereas the odd numbered hubs mounted nearer the face of the roadwheels.

Patton Museum, Fort Knox, KY

The hole in the turret face adjacent to the mantlet was for the monocular T.Z.F. 9d sight for the main gun. Tigers had various heavy wire rope assemblies stored on their hulls. The two heaviest of these, including the one in this photo, are for towing the tank. The lighter cable was used when changing the tracks. One end was attached to the track, the other wound around the empty drive sprocket, the sprocket acting as a windlass. The three-piece main gun-cleaning rod is also visible in this photo.

personnel hatches, and the intermittent addition of a rain shield over the gunner's sight aperture, things remained the same until January 1945.

Beginning in January, the armor components were delivered to Henschel's assembly plant prepainted RAL 6003 olive green After assembly, RAL 8017 red brown and RAL 7028 were sprayed on in a hard-edge camouflage scheme.

The final major change came in March 1945, when the track was changed again. In contrast to the previously used double-link track, this track was of a single-link design. This change required that the drive sprocket once again have 18 teeth. U.S. troops captured Henschel's Kassel plant, home of the Tigers, in March of 1945, so not many tanks with this track were produced.

Panzerkampfwagen VI Ausf. B (Tiger II)			
Length	10.30 m	Weapon, ball mounted	7.92mm MG 34
Width	3.76 m	Ammo stowage, main	72 rnds
Height	3.08 m		
Weight	68 tons	Ammo stowage, secondary	5,850 rnds
Fuel capacity	860 liters		
Maximum speed	35 km/hr (21.7 mph)	Engine make	Maybach
Range, on road	170 km (105.4 miles)	Engine model	HL 230 P30
		Engine configuration	V-12, liquid cooled
Crew	5		
Communications	FuG 5	Engine displacement	23 liters
Weapon, main	8.8 cm Kw.K. 43 L/71	Engine horsepower	700 @ 3000 rpm
Weapon, coaxial	7.92mm MG 34		

A Second Company of the 503rd Army Heavy Tank Battalion (Schwere Heeres Panzer Abteilung) Tiger II breaches a road block in Budapest, Hungary. The first digit of the tank number, 2, indicates second company. The second digit, 0, indicates it is the company commander or deputy commander (other tanks have 1, 2, or 3 to designate platoon), the third digit indicates vehicle number, again with the commanders and deputy commanders using 0, 1 or 2 while line tanks used 1, 2, or 3.

Third tank, third platoon, Second Company, 503rd Army Heavy Tank Battalion patrolling the streets of Budapest in October 1944. Its antiaircraft machine gun mount is visible behind the commander's head.

The first of these Maus behemoths was delivered with a turret-shaped ballast weight, rather than a functional turret for automotive trials.

Maus

The Maus has reached almost mythical stature in postwar literature. This enormous vehicle was designed by Ferdinand Porsche at the behest of Adolph Hitler himself. Two trial chassis were completed, but only one turret was finished.

Work on Germany's super-heavy tanks began in 1941, but the VK10001 project under Porsche was not initiated until May of 1942. Originally conceived as a 100-ton tank, the Maus ultimately grew to more than 180 tons. Various combinations of armament were proposed, but the sole turret produced was fitted with a 12.8 cm Kw.K. 44 L/55 gun mounted coaxial with a 7.5 cm Kw.K. 44 L/36.5 gun and 7.92mm MG34,

Delivery of the first tank was projected for May of 1943. The trial vehicle was to be followed by production models at a rate of five per month. As with many official German tank designations, the vehicle was renamed many times. Porsche Typ 205 ("Mammoth") and VK10001 were used through April of 1942, when it was renamed Maeuschen (Mousy) in December of 1942. It finally became Maus (Mouse) in February of 1943.

Krupp fabricated the armor plate, and Alkett did the assembly work, completing the first chassis seven months behind schedule, on Christmas Eve, 1943. Two months prior to this the original order for 150 vehicles had been cancelled, and a month prior development work was ordered ceased.

The size of the Maus is apparent when compared to the various test personnel standing on the tank. Despite the broad tracks, the tank had limited off-road mobility.

The first vehicle was powered by a derivative of the Daimler-Benz DB 603 aircraft engine known as the MB 509. Two of these engines were installed, each driving a generator, which in turn supplied power to the vehicle's traction motors. This setup was customary for Porsche-designed heavy tanks. Despite the enormous power plant, the vehicle could only attain a top speed of 13 km/hr (8.06 mph) during trials—far below the designed maximum of 20 km/hr (12.4 mph).

Prototype number one was given automotive trials sans turret, and when the first turret was completed it was installed and trials resumed. The second prototype was completed and shipped bereft of both turret and engines. Diesel engines were installed in it as soon as they were ready, with diesel power being a nod towards Germany's increasing gasoline shortages. Its turret had not been completed or installed by the time the second prototype was captured intact by Soviet troops.

The first prototype was destroyed by its crew after their attempt to flee the Russian advance failed. Under the direction of the Red Army, the turret from the destroyed vehicle was salvaged and installed on the second vehicle, which was then shipped to Russia for evaluation.

Panzerkampfwagen VIII Maus

Length	10.09 m	Weapon, secondary coaxial	7.92mm MG 34
Width	3.67 m		
Height	3.63 m	Ammo stowage, main	55+ rounds
Weight	188 tons		
Fuel capacity	2,650+ liters	Ammo stowage, secondary	200 rnds 7.5 cm
Maximum speed	13 km/hr (8.06 mph)		
Range, on road	160 km (99.2 miles)	Engine make	Daimler-Benz
		Engine model	MB 509 gas or MB 517 diesel
Range, cross country	62 km (38.44 miles)		
Crew	6	Engine configuration	V12, liquid cooled
Weapon, main	12.8 cm Kw.K. 44 L/55	Engine displacement	44.5 liters
		Engine horsepower	1,080 gas/1,200 diesel
Weapon, coaxial	7.5 cm Kw.K. 44 L/36.5		

The turret of the Maus had three weapons mounted in it. The three included a 12.8 cm cannon, 7.5 cm coaxial cannon, and a 7.92 mm machine gun.

Patton Museum, Fort Knox, KY

Once the turret was completed, it was installed on the first Maus prototype, and additional tests performed. The second prototype was not fitted with a functional turret during the war.

Patton Museum, Fort Knox, KY

The men sitting on the gun barrels and turret give scale to both the enormous weaponry and vehicle.

Patton Museum, Fort Knox, KY

As fighting neared the Kummersdorf proving ground, the first Maus prototype was destroyed as it fled. The Soviets later installed the salvaged turret of the first prototype on the second chassis of the second prototype, which had been captured intact.

Patton Museum, Fort Knox, KY

Intended as a more reasonably-sized and conventional competitor for the Maus, the E-100 was nevertheless to have been a massive tank.

E-100

As the prime contractor for the turret for the Maus, Krupp was well aware of Hitler's desire for a super heavy tank. Eager for the revenue, and ever mindful of the rivalry between Krupp and Porsche designers, Krupp offered an alternative to the Maus.

Utilizing the Maus turret, thereby reducing expense and development time, in December 1942 Krupp proposed

the so-called Tiger-Maus. This included a chassis utilizing many of the proven Tiger drivetrain components, with the 55-ton Maus turret mounted on top.

Among the advantages touted were lower raw material consumption (due to the estimated 100-ton weight reduction compared to the Maus). It was also easier to transport due to the use of transport tracks to move the tank on conventional rail cars. The Maus required special cars and extraordinary clearances for this task.

An indication of the amazing size of this vehicle can be seen by comparing the width of the rolled up track to the size of the Jeep parked next to them.

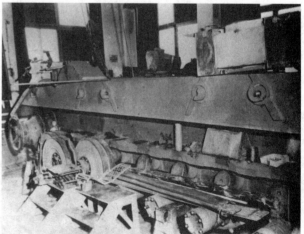

The E-100 was supposed to have the same turret as the Maus, but this never happened. In fact, the chassis was incomplete at the time of its capture.

Despite these benefits, Hitler rejected the proposal, continuing to favor Porsche's Maus instead. However, the Tiger-Maus's design was revived scarcely 6 months later as the basis for the E-100—the largest in a proposed series of standardized tanks.

Strangely, development of this massive vehicle was assigned to Adler, whose previous armored vehicle work was limited to armored cars. A hull was fabricated in May 1944, and Henschel began assembly of the trial vehicle at its facility near Paderborn. It was found there semi-complete in March 1945. Spirited off to England, it languished until the 1950s before it was unceremoniously scrapped.

E-100			
Length	10.27 m	Weapon, coaxial	7.5 cm Kw.K. 44 L/36.5
Width	4.48 m	Weapon, secondary coaxial	7.92mm MG 34
Height	3.29		
Weight	140 tons		
Maximum speed	40 km/hr (24.8 mph)	Ammo stowage, main	32 rounds
Range, on road	120 km (74.4 miles)	Ammo stowage, secondary	200 rnds 7.5 cm
Crew	5		
Communications	Fu 5	Engine make	Maybach
		Engine model	HL234
Weapon, main	12.8 cm Kw.K. 44 L/55	Engine configuration	V-12 liquid cooled
		Engine displacement	23.4 liters

The layout of the E-100 was the same as a conventional tank. In fact, the driveline of the prototype was taken over from the Tiger, although an improved but basic driveline was intended for the production models.

The chassis, with its tracks and suspension installed, languished under a shed a Bovington for years before being scrapped in the 1950s.

Patton Museum, Fort Knox, KY

Sturmgeschütz Ausf. A

The Sturmgeschütz was conceived to provide advancing infantry close armored artillery support. Its armament was intended to knock out fortified machine gun nests, and also to deal with any tanks that were encountered. The goal was for these vehicles to be deployed either independently or in small platoon-sized groups. Ultimately, the Sturmgeschütz was to find its greatest fame as an antitank weapon.

A trial group of five Sturmgeschütz were built on Daimler-Benz-built Panzerkampfwagen III Ausf. B chassis. These trial vehicles, known as the 0-series, had all been delivered by 1939. They were fully operational, including armament, but their superstructures were made of mild steel, rather than armor, precluding their combat use. These vehicles were used instead in testing and training.

The Sturmgeschütz trial series, or 0-series, vehicles can be distinguished by the round access hatches in the front of the transmission. These vehicles were built on chassis originally intended for Panzerkampfwagen III Ausf. B.

Walter J. Spielberger

Although the five 0-series vehicles were fully operational, and mounted live weapons, their superstructures were constructed of mild steel, rather than armor plate, so they were relegated to testing and training roles.

Patton Museum, Fort Knox, KY

The next series vehicles, the Sturmgeschütz Ausf. A, had armored superstructures and were extensively used in combat in France. The Sturmgeschütz Ausf. A had slightly narrower tracks than later vehicles.
Michael Harpe

A contract was awarded to Daimler-Benz for a production series of 30 combat-capable Sturmgeschütz, which were to be delivered in full by April 1, 1940. Various production delays, primarily involving the Maybach SRG 32 8 45 transmission, resulted in the deliveries not being completed until the end of April.

A supplemental group of Sturmgeschütz were produced from June through September 1940 utilizing Sturmgeschütz Ausf. B superstructures mounted on Panzerkampfwagen III Ausf. G chassis. Because these vehicles were equipped with the 10-speed Maybach SRG 32 8 45 transmission they, too, were designated Sturmgeschütz Ausf. A.

The Sturmgeschütz Ausf. A was used in France, where its success proved the merit of the concept.

Sturmgeschütz Ausf. A

Length	5.38 m	Communications	receiver only
Width	2.92 m		
Height	1.95 m	Weapon, main	7.5 cm StuK L/24
Weight	20.7 tons		
Fuel capacity	310 liters	Ammo stowage, main	44 rnds
Maximum speed	40 km/hr (24.8 mph)	Engine make	Maybach
		Engine model	HL 120 TRM
Range, on road	160 km (99.2 miles)	Engine configuration	V-12, liquid cooled
Range, cross country	100 km (62 miles)	Engine displacement	11.9 liters
Crew	4	Engine horsepower	265 @ 2600 rpm

Patton Museum, Fort Knox, KY

The entire crew, save the driver, of this Sturmgeschütz Ausf. A rides atop the superstructure as it rolls through town. All armored fighting vehicles were cramped inside, and crewmen welcomed the chance to be outside..

Walter J. Spielberger

The low profile of the Sturmgeschütz made them difficult for opposing forces to hit. These vehicles were equipped with radio receivers, but not transmitters or intercoms.

The unequal return roller spacing distinguished the Sturmgeschütz B from the earlier Ausf. A, which had a similar superstructure. The skull markings of the Sturmgeschütz-Abteilung 192 (192nd Stug battalion) are visible on the front of the superstructure.

Sturmgeschütz B

Unlike the Sturmgeschütz A, of which only 30 were produced, the Sturmgeschütz B went into mass production. Alkett received an order for 250 of the vehicles, which were produced from July 1940 through March 1941.

This new version of the Sturmgeschütz used a SSG 77 transmission and new steering gear. Its tracks were wider, and the suspension components changed accordingly. The return rollers, which had been evenly spaced on previous models, were now unevenly spaced, with a considerable gap between the first and second return roller. The armament of the Sturmgeschütz continued to be the 7.5 cm L/24.

These vehicles saw service in the Balkans, and in the advance on Russia.

Sturmgeschütz Ausf. B

Length	5.40 m	Communications	HF receiver only
Width	2.95 m		
Height	1.96 m	Weapon, main	7.5 cm StuK L/24
Weight	19.6 tons		
Fuel capacity	310 liters	Ammo stowage, main	44 rnds
Maximum speed	40 km/hr (24.8 mph)	Engine make	Maybach
Range, on road	160 km (99.2 miles)	Engine model	HL 120 TRM
		Engine configuration	V-12, liquid cooled
Range, cross country	100 km (62 miles)	Engine displacement	11.9 liters
Crew	4	Engine horsepower	265 @ 2600 rpm

The gun sight ribbed aperture of the Ausf. B, like that of the Ausf. A, was located in the left front of the superstructure, as seen here. This was later identified as a weakness in the vehicle's armor protection, and subsequent models were redesigned to eliminate this identifying feature.

Patton Museum, Fort Knox, KY

This Sturmgeschütz B was photographed during the summer 1941 advance into Russia. The Sturmgeschütz was designed as an infantry support vehicle, and it is not surprising that infantry soldiers, such as this eight-man heavy machine gun platoon, often hitched rides on the superstructure.

Bundesarchiv photo

This Sturmgeschütz B is being resupplied with ammunition. Internal stowage was provided for 44 rounds of 7.5 cm ammo, which could be quickly depleted supporting rapidly advancing units.

The Ausf. B was the first Sturmgeschütz to see widespread use. As the war progressed the "Stus" was increasingly used as an antitank weapon, and many of the Ausf. G models were supplied to Panzer units.

Sturmgeschütz Ausf. C and Ausf. D

The merit of the Sturmgeschütz concept was proven by the early success of Germany's offensive operations against Russia. However, one weakness in the design of the Ausf. B was the sight aperture in the left front of the superstructure. As a result of this, a periscopic sighting system was developed that allowed the superstructure to be reconfigured and eliminate this weakness.

The new vehicle, the Sturmgeschütz Ausfrung C, entered production at Alkett in April 1941. With only 50 vehicles on this contract, production was completed the next month. Automotively, the vehicle was little changed from the Ausf. B version, with only oil bath air cleaners and new design road wheels being introduced.

The production lines at Alkett were not idle for long, though. In May, production of the Ausfrung D began. Visually indistinguishable from the Ausf. C, the D had its frontal armor hardened to a greater extent, a reflection of the increased power of enemy tank and antitank gun.

The new shape of the superstructure front of the Sturmgeschütz C is visible on this vehicle captured by the British in North Africa.

Walter J. Spielberger

The new Sturmgeschütz Ausf. C superstructure eliminated the shot trap, which had been presented by the sight aperture on the earlier models, and replaced it with slabs of armor. The cavities presented by the new armor shape were often filled with concrete by troops looking for more protection. It's doubtful the concrete did much good, but it did overload the suspension.

Military History Institute, Carlisle Barracks, PA

The Ausf. D was indistinguishable from the Ausf. C. However, the chassis number of this captured example was determined to be 90683, making it a Sturmgeschütz D. The rack on the back is a field modification to haul fuel and water cans.

Patton Museum, Fort Knox, KY

A total of 150 of the Sturmgeschütz D were produced by Alkett between May and September 1941. The armament of the D, like the B and C, was the 7.5 cm L/24 gun.

Sturmgeschütz Ausf. C & D

Length	5.40 m	Communications	VHF receiver
Width	2.95 m	Weapon, main	7.5 cm StuK L/24
Height	1.95 m	Ammo stowage, main	44 rnds
Weight	22 tons		
Fuel capacity	310 liters	Engine make	Maybach
Maximum speed	40 km/hr (24.8 mph)	Engine model	HL 120 TRM
Range, on road	160 km (99.2 miles)	Engine configuration	V-12, liquid cooled
Range, cross country	100 km (62 miles)	Engine displacement	11.9 liters
Crew	4	Engine horsepower	265 @ 2600 rpm

The gunner and commander's hatches of this captured Sturmgeschütz are open, as are the engine compartment hatches. The torsion bar suspension of the vehicle is also evident.

The unusual shape of the gunner's hatch was necessary to accommodate the scissors periscope. The many openings in the top of the superstructure made the Sturmgeschütz far from waterproof.

This Sturmgeschütz D was not quite a year old when it was captured by the British near Bir Hacheim, North Africa, in May 1942. Extra track links were often stowed on these vehicles not only as spare parts, but also as extra armor protection.

A canvas cover was clamped to the mantlet and superstructure front to protect the gun's trunnions from dirt and moisture.

Because combat vehicles are expected to push their way through heavy brush, heavy guards must be used to protect lights and other gear attached to the vehicle. Notice the loose track pins in the spare track, no doubt left loose to expedite repair.

The commander and loader hang on as they ride a Sturmgeschütz C or D down an incline. One of the glacis hatches is open.

In addition to extra track links, extra roadwheels were carried on the rear of the Sturmgeschütz C or D. Roadwheels were susceptible to damage from mines and road debris.

Sturmgeschütz Ausf. E

Encouraged by the success of the earlier vehicles, the Waffenamt ordered 500 of an improved model, the Ausf. E. These vehicles were automotively the same as the earlier Ausf. C and Ausf. D, but their superstructure was redesigned slightly to include an armored pannier on the right side to house additional radio equipment. The pannier on the left hand side was also lengthened. Alkett produced these vehicles from September 1941 through February 1942. At that time production was switched to the long-barreled StuK 40-armed Ausf. F.

The square boxes on either side of the superstructure identify the Sturmgeschütz Ausf. E. Previous models had sloping side boxes, but an increase in the amount of radio equipment carried required more space inside, resulting in this change to the design.

Sturmgeschütz Ausf. E

Length	5.40 m	Communications	10WS h/VHF receiver, intercom
Width	2.95 m		
Height	1.95 m	Weapon, main	7.5 cm StuK L/24
Weight	22 tons		
Fuel capacity	310 liters	Ammo stowage, main	44 rnds
Maximum speed	40 km/hr (24.8 mph)	Engine make	Maybach
Range, on road	160 km (99.2 miles)	Engine model	HL 120 TRM
Range, cross country	100 km (62 miles)	Engine configuration	V-12, liquid cooled
Crew	4	Engine displacement	11.9 liters
		Engine horsepower	265 @ 2600 rpm

This Sturmgeschütz Ausf. E has slipped off of a snowy road in Russia and is about to get a helping hand from a Panzer. The harshness of Russian weather on both men and equipment exceeded the expectations of many in Germany's military.

This Sturmgeschütz Ausf. E has been outfitted as a platoon leader's vehicle, as evidenced by the two mounted antennas.

Sturmgeschütz Ausf. F

The German Army began to depend increasingly on the Sturmgeschütz as an antitank weapon. As the war advanced into Russia, the better-protected Soviet T34 and KVI tanks were introduced, making it important for the Germans to find a way to mount a high-velocity cannon on the low-profile Sturmgeschütz.

A trial vehicle was created using a Sturmgeschütz E as the basis. The new weapon was a combination of a Krupp-designed short chamber and a Rheinmetall Pak 40 L/46 barrel. The new gun was designated 7.5 cm Stuk 40 L/43. However, after installation in only 120 vehicles, this weapon was discontinued in favor of the longer-tubed 7.5 cm StuK 40 L/48. The later weapon was used on the balance of the Ausf. F production.

Production of the Ausf. F by Alkett began in early 1942, but was superceded in September of the same year by the introduction of the Sturmgeschütz Ausf. F/8.

Walter J. Spielberger

The very first Sturmgeschütz Ausf. F was built by modifying the front of the superstructure of an Ausf. E to accept the longer and more powerful 7.5 cm StuK L/43 gun.

Bundesarchiv photo

Only 366 Sturmgeschütz Ausf. F were built before production was converted to the Ausf. F/8. The side plates of true Ausf. F, such as this one belonging to the Grossdeutschland Division, end at the front plate, the hull sides extended to form towing eyes on the later F/8.

The longer-barreled 7.5 cm cannon made the Sturmgeschütz Ausf. F and later models much more effective tank killers than they were with the shorter cannon. Tank busting became increasingly important as the war dragged on.

Patton Museum, Fort Knox, KY

Sturmgeschütz Ausf. F

Length	6.31 m (6.77 with L/48)	Weapon, main	7.5 cm StuK 40 L/43 early, L/48 late
Width	2.95 m	Weapon, secondary	7.92mm MG 34
Height	2.15 m	Ammo stowage, main	44 rnds
Weight	23.2 tons	Ammo stowage, secondary	600 rnds
Fuel capacity	310 liters	Engine make	Maybach
Maximum speed	40 km/hr (24.8 mph)	Engine model	HL 120 TRM
Range, on road	140 km (86.8 miles)	Engine configuration	V-12, liquid cooled
Range, cross country	85 km (52.7 miles)	Engine displacement	11.9 liters
Crew	4	Engine horsepower	265 @ 2600 rpm
Communications	Fu. 15 or Fu. 16, intercom		

Unusually, the headlights of this Ausf. F did not have their protective covers hiding them. The first 120 Sturmgeschütz Ausf. F were armed with the 7.5 cm StuK L/43, like this one. Later vehicles had the slightly longer 7.5 cm StuK L/48.

Walter J. Spielberger

Infantry on foot could pass harmlessly over antitank mines that heavy tracked vehicles would detonate. In its intended infantry support role the Sturmgeschütz was susceptible to such mines. This Ausf. F has had a field-fabricated fuel can rack installed, as well as additional post-factory spare track links and brackets.

Bundesarchiv photo.

The armored box on each side of the superstructure, a feature of the Ausf. E, F, and F/8 versions, housed radio equipment. An extra track bracket has been welded to this box in the field on this Ausf. F.

Walter J. Spielberger

This captured Sturmgeschütz F/8 was photographed while undergoing evaluation at Aberdeen Proving Ground. It is an early model, based on the armor plate welded to the front of the hull.

Sturmgeschütz F/8

The change of Sturmgeschütz designation from F to F/8 denoted the upgrading of the chassis to the standards of the Panzerkampfwagen III 8./Z.W. This included extending the armored hull sides to include towing brackets, adding 50mm thick rear armor, shortening the front track guards, and enlarging the rear engine louvers for improved cooling. Production of the new model began in September 1942.

During the course of production, additional changes were incorporated. These involved bolting the 30mm additional front armor on rather than welding it, and using redesigned hatches on the glacis. Some of the 250 Sturmgeschütz Ausf. F/8 built were equipped with an experimental hinged machine gun shield mounted in front of the loader's hatch. Sturmgeschütz Ausf. F/8 production was completed in December 1942.

The machine gun shield fitted to some of the Ausf. F/8 has been folded down flush with the superstructure top.

Beginning in May 1943, schürzen side skirts were retrofitted to the Ausf. F/8 Sturmgeschütz. These were intended to protect the relatively vulnerable hull from antitank rounds.

Sturmgeschütz Ausf. F/8

Length	6.77 m	Weapon, main	7.5 cm StuK 40 L/48
Width	2.95 m	Weapon, secondary	7.92mm MG 34
Height	2.15 m	Ammo stowage, main	44 rnds
Weight	23.2 tons		
Fuel capacity	310 liters	Ammo stowage, secondary	600 rnds
Maximum speed	40 km/hr (24.8 mph)		
Range, on road	140 km (86.8 miles)	Engine make	Maybach
		Engine model	HL 120 TRM
Range, cross country	85 km (52.7 miles)	Engine configuration	V-12, liquid cooled
Crew	4		
Communications	Fu. 15 or Fu. 16, intercom	Engine displacement	11.9 liters
		Engine horsepower	265 @ 2600 rpm

This is the same vehicle shown in the previous views, sans schürzen. The machine gun shield is in the raised position, but the machine gun itself is absent.

The cramped conditions inside the Sturmgeschütz often led to a great deal of external stowage. This Sturmgeschütz F/8 has been fitted with a stowage bin on the engine deck to protect some of the crew's gear.

GI's prowl for souvenirs on a captured Sturmgeschütz F/8. Two of the smoke dischargers mounted on the right side of been knocked off in service. The branches were placed on the vehicle to aid concealment.

Sturmgeschütz Ausf. G

The final, and most abundant, production vehicle of the Sturmgeschütz was the Ausf. G. Alkett began producing this new version in December 1942. Muhlenbau-Industrie AG (Miag) joined in Sturmgeschütz G production in February 1943. Maschinenfabrik Augsburg-Nürnberg (M.A.N.) also became involved, as the chassis they were building for use in Panzerkampfwagen III Ausf. M production were diverted for use producing Sturmgeschütz Ausf. G. In the latter case, M.A.N. produced only the chassis, with the other firms doing the final assembly.

With the exception of the few units mentioned above that used Panzerkampfwagen III Ausf. M chassis, the Ausf. G utilized the same chassis as the earlier Sturmgeschütz III Ausf. F/8. However, the superstructure incorporated many refinements. The most apparent of these were the commander's cupola and the sloping superstructure sides—a feature reminiscent of those of the earliest Sturmgeschütz. Other changes implemented in the new production were raising the middle of the roof , which included the exhaust fan, and replacing the reverse sloped rear fighting compartment wall with a vertical one.

With production of the Ausf. G continuing for the duration of the war, of course a number of running changes were made. Among these were the introducton of the cast

Topfblende mantlet, replacing the driver's side vision slit with a pistol port, deleting the driver's periscopes, adding a coaxial machine gun, and altering the slope of the leading edge of the panniers. Numerous other small refinements to both the secondary armament, superstructure and chassis were made as the total production soared beyond 7,800 units.

Sturmgeschütz Ausf. G

Length	6.77 m	Weapon, main	7.5 cm StuK 40 L/48
Width	2.95 m	Weapon, secondary	7.92mm MG 34
Height	2.16 m		
Weight	23.9 tons	Ammo stowage, main	54 rnds
Fuel capacity	310 liters		
Maximum speed	40 km/hr (24.8 mph)	Ammo stowage, secondary	600 rnds
Range, on road	155 km (96.1 miles)		
Range, cross country	95 km (58.9 miles)	Engine make	Maybach
		Engine model	HL 120 TRM
Crew	4	Engine configuration	V-12, liquid cooled
Communications	Fu. 15 or Fu. 16, intercom	Engine displacement	11.9 liters
		Engine horsepower	265 @ 2600 rpm

The Sturmgeschütz Ausf. G commander's position was fitted with a cupola that included seven periscopes.

This Sturmgeschütz Ausf. G knocked out by the U.S. 28th Infantry Division has many of the features typical of a mid-production vehicle. Notice the shot deflector mounted just ahead of the cupola, and the mixed use of all-steel and rubber-tired return rollers.

This is a close-up view of the deflector mounted ahead of the commander's cupola. This was first introduced in October 1943, and by February 1944 it was standard on all new Sturmgeschütz. Those vehicles already fielded were ordered to retrofit a similar item using steel rods and concrete. Without this deflector it was possible for Allied troops to target the cupola and knock it off the vehicle.

This captured Sturmgeschütz Ausf. G being evaluated at Aberdeen Proving Ground was produced between February and May 1943, as indicated by the smoke dischargers on either side of the hull near the front. The installation of these devices was discontinued after reports that enemy small arms fire could cause them to be discharged at inopportune times.

This view of a captured vehicle shows an unusual field modification: the attachment of spare track sections to the hull sides near the suspension. The spare road wheel stowage on the rear deck was standard.

This Sturmgeschütz was produced prior to the February 1943 change from the laminated hull front to the single-piece hull front. The bolts holding the 30mm supplemental armor plate are evident in this photo of an advancing vehicle.

This Sturmgeschütz Ausf. G has many of the late features, including the faintly visible coaxial machine gun port introduced in June 1944, Rundumfeuer remotely operated machinegun on the roof, and external travel lock for the main gun introduced in July 1944. This phot was taken at Heiderscheid (Luxemburg) during the Battle of the Bulge.

Sturmhaubitze

The Sturmhaubitze self-propelled howitzer looked very much like a Sturmgeschütz self-propelled gun, and for good reason. Alkett built the first Sturmhaubitze in March 1942 by installing a light field howitzer in a converted Sturmgeschütz E. Hitler himself was impressed by the new self-propelled artillery piece, which certainly helped shephard it into series production.

There is some indication that the first dozen or so of the new vehicles were built by converting used Sturmgeschütz chassis. However, the bulk of the almost 1,300 Sturmhaubitze were built new by Alkett using a chassis and superstructure very similar to that used by the Sturmgeschütz G.

The 10.5 cm howitzer of the Sturmhaubitze was shorter than the 7.5 cm gun of the Sturmgeschütz, as well as appearing thicker and more heavily tapered. Prior to September 1944, new Sturmhaubitze were delivered with a muzzle brake installed. From September until the Soviet

capture of the Alkett plant in April 1945 the muzzle brake was omitted. The remainder of the changes in the vehicle throughout production paralleled the changes made in its contemporary, the Sturmgeschütz G.

Patton Museum, Fort Knox, KY

The production version of the Sturmhaubitze utilized many of the components of the Sturmgeschütz Ausf. G, which Alkett was producing concurrently. Running changes made in the production of the Sturmgeschütz were also made to the Sturmhaubitze, including the addition of smoke grenade launchers, as seen on this vehicle the were subsequent deleted.

Walter J. Spielberger

The first Sturmhaubitze was built by Alkett by modifying a Sturmgeschütz Ausf. E. The le. F. H. 18 mounted in the low profile, armored and mobile chassis was successful, and the design impressed Hitler, who immediately ordered it into production.

When parked adjacent to each other, the difference in the barrel lengths of the Sturmhaubitze (foreground and the Sturmgeschütz background become very apparent).

The track stowed on the hull front of this Sturmhaubitze is clearly there to serve as additional armor, as it is far too wide to actually be used on the vehicle. The crew has also poured concrete onto the front of the superstructure roof in an effort to gain additional protection.

This Sturmhaubitze was captured and returned to Aberdeen Proving Ground for evaluation. Evidently it was not captured without a fight, as there is considerable damage in the area of the loader's hatch. Also, close examination reveals that the entire upper plate of the superstructure has been unbolted and is merely sitting on the vehicle.

The low profile of the Sturmhaubitze, and indeed the Sturmgeschütz that it was based on, is illustrated by the 6-foot APG measuring stick at the muzzle.

A late Sturmhaubitze rolls through the countryside with both human and avian passengers. Note the waffle-pattern Zimmerit and the shop-made travel lock.

Sturmhaubitze Ausf. G

Length	6.14 m	Weapon, secondary	7.92mm MG 34
Width	2.95 m	Ammo stowage, main	36 rnds
Height	2.16 m	Ammo stowage, secondary	600 rnds
Weight	23.9 tons		
Fuel capacity	310 liters		
Maximum speed	40 km/hr (24.8 mph)	Engine make	Maybach
Range, on road	155 km (91.6 miles)	Engine model	HL 120 TRM
Range, cross country	95 km (58.9 miles)	Engine configuration	V-12, liquid cooled
Crew	4	Engine displacement	11.9 liters
Communications	Fu. 15 or Fu. 16, intercom	Engine horsepower	265 @ 2600 rpm
Weapon, main	10.5 cm StuH 42		

Sturmgeschütz IV

The concept of a Sturmgeschütz based on the Panzerkampfwagen IV chassis was first broached early in 1943. However, the design submitted by Krupp at that time was based on a proposed future 9./B. W., rather than the 8./B.W. then in production. The proposed Sturmgeschütz IV design was rejected, largely because they was no savings in weight compared to the Sturmgeschütz III. However, it was later revealed that this was largely due to the proposed use of the 9./B.W. chassis.

When Alkett's plant was heavily damaged by Allied bombing later that year, the concept of mounting a Sturmgeschütz superstructure on the Panzerkampfwagen IV chassis resurfaced. This time, it was proposed to mount the Sturmgeschütz fighting compartment on the Panzerkampfwagen IV chassis then in production.

It was found that these two major components could be fitted together with a relatively minimal amount of conversion work. A driver's compartment was fabricated and added to the front left side of the superstructure, and a plate was made to fill the gap between the transmission cover and the leading edge of the Sturmgeschütz superstructure.

Krupp Grusonwerk completed the first 30 Sturmgeschütz IV in December 1944, and by the time the war ended more than 1,100 had been built. As the production of the Panzerkampfwagen IV Ausf. H, upon which the Sturmgeschütz IV was initially based, was phased out in favor of the Panzerkampfwagen IV Ausf. J,

A column of Sturmgeschütz IV slows to a halt. The protruding driver's position and eight road wheels per side distinguish these Panzerkampfwagen IV-based Stugs from the standard Panzerkampfwagen III-based Sturmgeschütz.

these chassis began to be used for the Sturmgeschütz IV as well. Among the running changes was the reduction of return rollers from four per side to three per side, forming the tow brackets integral with the hull sides, converting to flame-arresting mufflers, and adding brackets for use with tow bars to the rear of the hull. Changes were made in the Sturmgeschütz IV superstructure just as they were to the Sturmgeschütz III Ausf. G that was being produced concurrently.

The bulk of the Sturmgeschütz IV production was used to equip single Sturmgeschütz companies attached to infantry divisions. They served on both fronts.

This view of a group of captured vehicles collected by British forces provides a side-by-side comparison of the Sturmgeschütz IV foreground with the Sturmgeschütz III Ausf. G next to it. The longer distance between the mantlet and hull front on the Sturmgeschütz IV is immediately evident.

This Sturmgeschütz IV has been captured by U.S. troops who are looking it over for gear they can use. The GI at the right front of the vehicle is peering in the open brake cover.

Patton Museum, Fort Knox, KY

Although it was proven to be ineffective, and often detrimental, troops continued to add concrete to their vehicles in an effort to increase protection. That appears to be the case on this vehicle with the area just ahead of the driver's station.

Patton Museum, Fort Knox, KY

The asymmetrical layout of the superstructure front, due to the extended driver's compartment, is apparent here. A travel lock had to be designed for the Sturmgeschütz IV that would hold the main gun in an elevated position. At 0-degree elevation, as seen here, the gun tube completely obscured the driver's vision to the right of the vehicle.

Armin Sohns collection

As with most of Germany's armored vehicles, the Sturmgeschütz IV had schürzen mounted to protect the running gear and hull sides from antitank rounds. Many of the Sturmgeschütz IV were produced with separately installed front towing brackets, as was this one. Later production vehicles had these brackets integrated into the hull sides.

National Archives and Records Administration

A GI looks in the open transmission cover of a knocked-out Sturmgeschütz IV. The armor bolted to the right front of the superstructure was factory installed. Although one of them appears to have been knocked of during the destruction of the vehicle, from their spacing it seems that this Stug had three steel return rollers on each side.

Sturmgeschütz IV

Length	6.70 m	Weapon, secondary	7.92mm MG 34
Width	2.95 m	Ammo stowage, main	61 rnds
Height	2.20 m		
Weight	25.9 tons	Ammo stowage, secondary	600 rnds
Fuel capacity	450 liters		
Maximum speed	38 km/hr (23.56 mph)	Engine make	Maybach
Range, on road	220 km (136.4 miles)	Engine model	HL 120 TRM
Range, cross country	130 km (80.6 miles)	Engine configuration	V-12, liquid cooled
Crew	4	Engine displacement	11.9 liters
Communications	Fu. 15 or Fu. 16, intercom	Engine horsepower	265 @ 2600 rpm
Weapon, main	7.5 cm StuK 40 L/48		

Sturminfanteriegeschuetz 33

The Sturminfanteriegeschuetz 33 was developed to provide a well-protected, self-propelled artillery piece whose primary purpose was to destroy non-fortified structures, depriving the enemy of cover.

The main armament of the Sturminfanteriegeschuetz 33 was a 150mm heavy infantry support gun. Previous attempts to mount this weapon on a tracklaying chassis, specifically on the Panzerkampfwagen I and Panzerkampfwagen II chassis, were not successful. So when the Führerkonferenz of September 1942 closed on the 22nd, a directive was given to mount the weapon in the turret of a Panzerkampfwagen III or Panzerkampfwagen IV. If that failed, the weapon would be mounted in a Sturmgeschütz. The directive further called for a minimum of six, and preferably 12, of the new vehicles to be constructed.

Protection for the crew was considered of highest priority, and an incredible delivery schedule of 14 days was requested. Amazingly, the first six of the sIG tanks were completed by October 7, with a second group of six completed by October 10. A second group of 12 was completed by the end of the month. The first 12 vehicles were deployed in the assault on Stalingrad, where six each were assigned to Sturmgeschütz-Abteilung 177 and Sturmgeschütz-Abteilung 244. The vehicles were in the

area of Stalingrad by November 8, 1942. None of them survived the combat there.

The second group of 12 vehicles were also sent to Stalingrad. They had been assigned to the Sturm-IG Batterie of the XVII Lehr Battalion of the XVII Armee Korps. It was hoped that these vehicles would

Military History Institute, Carlisle Barracks, PA

This Sturminfanteriegeschutz 33 has had a spare road wheel pair mounted on the face of its superstructure. The boxy fighting compartment of the Sturminfanteriegeschutz was similar to that of the Sturmpanzer, which was built for the same purpose.

Armin Sohns collection

The Sturminfanteriegeschutz 33 was based on the Sturmgeschütz III chassis, but with a new superstructure. The frontal armor was 80mm thick, while the sides were 50mm thick. The rear had only 15mm protection, and the roof 10mm.

Stu.-I.G. 33

Length	5.40 m	Weapon, main	15 cm sIG33/1
Width	2.90 m	Weapon, secondary	7.92 mm MG 34
Height	2.30 m		
Weight	21 tons	Ammo stowage, main	30 rnds
Fuel capacity	310 liters		
Maximum speed	20 km/hr (12.4 mph)	Ammo stowage, secondary	600 rnds
Range, on road	110 km (68.2 miles)	Engine make	Maybach
Range, cross country	85 km (52.7 miles)	Engine model	HL 120 TRM
Crew	5	Engine configuration	V-12, liquid cooled
Communica-tions	Fu. Spr. d, intercom	Engine displacement	11.9 liters
		Engine horsepower	265 @ 2600 rpm

aid in breaking through the Soviet encirclement of Stalingrad. On April 11 1943, this unit, which had seven Sturminfanteriegeschutz 33 remaining, was assigned to the 201st Panzer-Regiment of the 23rd Panzer Division as "Stu.I.G. Battr./Pz.Regt.201." The last of the Sturminfanteriegeschutz was lost in October 1943.

Military History Institute, Carlisle Barracks, PA

The Sturminfanteriegeschutz had a five-man crew. This vehicle's entire crew, sans driver, is riding outside the superstructure to escape the heat, cramped conditions and noise.

Military History Institute, Carlisle Barracks, PA

A Sturminfanteriegeschutz 33 leads a halftrack towing a field piece. In addition to its heavy armor protection for the gun crew, the Sturminfanteriegeschutz could be brought into action sooner and withdrawn quickly.

Patton Museum, Fort Knox, KY

With so few Sturminfanteriegeschutz 33 produced, and their service life so brief, photos of the of this model are difficult to find, especially right side views. Barely visible here is the ball-mounted machine gun installed in the right side of the frontal armor.

Patton Museum, Fort Knox, KY

Though all the Sturminfanteriegeschutz 33 were lost, the concept of a demolition-oriented armored vehicle was not. The later Sturmpanzer and Sturmmörserwagen were built for the same purpose

Sturmpanzer

In the fall of 1942, Hitler became very interested in producing an armored vehicle mounting a short-range weapon capable of firing a shell with great high-explosive capacity. Alkett designed such a vehicle, which had a special short-barreled 15 cm StuH 43 L/12 howitzer ball-mounted in a well-armored box-like superstructure, which in turn was mounted on a Panzerkampfwagen IV chassis.

This design was approved and production began in early 1943 using rebuilt Panzerkampfwagen IV chassis as a basis. Unlike most of Germany's armored vehicles, the Sturmpanzer (often referred to as Brummbär" in postwar literature, but not by the wartime German military) were assembled not in a factory, but in the Army's own workshops in Vienna. In June 1944, this work was transferred to workshops in Duisberg.

As with many of Germany's armored vehicles, there were some changes made during the production of the vehicle. A pistol port was added to each rear side of the superstructure. The roof design was changed, the two-piece gunner's hatch was eliminated and a new ventilator was added near the front. Additionally, the armored sleeve of the gun tube was lengthened.

The oversize superstructure and ammunition load overloaded the vehicle, leading to mechanical problems. In December 1943, a redesigned, lighter howitzer, designated the StuH 43/1 L/12, began to be installed. At about the same time the superstructure was modified. The installation of the driver's Fahrersehklappe 80 direct vision port, adapted from the Tiger I, was discontinued.

The early production Sturmpanzer used a Fahrersehklappe 80 direct vision port for the driver. It had the extremely short-barreled 15 cm s.I.G. and field-modified Schürzen.

Because of the critical shortage of Panzerkampfwagen IV tanks, upon whose chassis the Sturmpanzer was built, rebuilt chassis were initially used for these vehicles. However, the supply of rebuilt chassis was inadequate, and new chassis were used as well. This Sturmpanzer was built on a Panzerkampfwagen IV Ausf. H chassis.

After the initial production run with direct vision ports, periscopic vision ports were introduced for the driver. This example, photographed in 1946 at Aberdeen Proving Ground, had this type installation. This vehicle remains on display today.

Even shorn of its stubby main weapon, like this example being evaluated by the British, the Sturmpanzer presented a distinctive profile. Later production vehicles utilized steel-tired road wheels on the forward stations to combat wear due to the vehicle's overloading.

In its place a box containing periscopic vision blocks was installed.

As a result of successful infantry attacks against the Sturmpanzers, a later improvement involved the mounting of an MG 34 in a Kugelblende 80 ball mount on the face of the superstructure.

The Sturmpanzers first saw combat at Kursk, and were used throughout the rest of the war.

Sturmpanzer			
Length	5.80 m (later 5.93 m)	Weapon, main	15 cm StuH43
Width	2.86 m	Weapon, secondary	7.92mm MG 34
Height	2.45 m (later 2.52)	Ammo stowage, main	32 rnds
Weight	24 tons (later 28.2)	Ammo stowage, secondary	600 rnds
Fuel capacity	470 liters		
Maximum speed	40 km/hr (24.8 mph)	Engine make	Maybach
Range, on road	200 km (124 miles)	Engine model	HL 120 TRM
Range, cross country	130 km (80.6 miles)	Engine configuration	V-12, liquid cooled
Crew	5	Engine displacement	11.9 liters
Communications	Fu. 5 and Fu.2, intercom	Engine horsepower	265 @ 2600 rpm

Patton Museum, Fort Knox, KY

Because the bulk of the early Sturmpanzer were built on rebuilt Panzerkampfwagen IV chassis, there was some variation in detail from vehicle to vehicle. The right engine compartment door is open here, exposing the fans.

Patton Museum, Fort Knox, KY

Two large hatches were in the back plate of the superstructure one of which is missing in this photo. The chassis number, 80976, can be seen stenciled just beneath the spare road wheels on the left rear of the vehicle.

Walter J. Spielberger

Until the final production version, which had an MG34 in a ball mount, the Zimmerit coating was the Sturmpanzer's first line of defense against infantry with magnetic mines.

Patton Museum, Fort Knox, KY

The final version of the Sturmpanzer was equipped with a machine gun in a ball mount at the front of the superstructure. Many of the last batch of 166 vehicles were built on new chassis, rather than the rebuilt chassis used previously.

Stefan De Meyer collection

GI's advance past an abandoned Sturmpanzer with a dust cover on the ball mount.

Sturmmörserwagen

Because of the problems they had encountered during the siege-like battle for Stalingrad, the Germans decided to develop a heavily armed and armored vehicle capable of leveling large structures with a single round. Even though work began on this project in mid-1943, the first production vehicle was not completed until August 1944. Such a vehicle was originally envisioned to be built on new Tiger I chassis, but the critical need for Tigers led to the decision to put the Sturmmörserwagen on rebuilt chassis. Delays such as this resulted in only 18 of the massive machines getting built. Alkett in Berlin built all of these vehicles

The main armament of the Sturmmörserwagen was a Raketenwerfer 61. This stubby weapon fired a 38 cm rocket. Additionally, two 7.92mm machine guns were carried—an MG 34 and an MG42.

National Archives and Records Administration

The massive size of the Sturmmörserwagen made it unmistakable. Despite Hitler's visions of companies of 14 of these vehicles being assigned to each of several divisions, and expending a combined 300 rounds per month of ammunition, only 18 vehicles total were ultimately assembled. The MG 34 has already been removed from its ball mount on this captured example. The front of the hull has been reinforced with an additional 50mm-thick armor plate.

National Archives and Records Administration

This Sturmmörser, belonging to Sturmmörser Kompanie 1000, was captured and evacuated by U.S. troops in February 1944. The massive Tiger-based vehicle dwarfs the diminutive Sherman-based recovery vehicle with Commonwealth crew passing by.

Sturmmörser

Length	6.28 m	Weapon, secondary	7.92mm MG 34, or 7.93mm MG 42
Width	3.57 m		
Height	2.85 m		
Weight	65 tons	Ammo stowage, main	14 rnds
Fuel capacity	540 liters		
Maximum speed	37.5 km/hr (23.25 mph)	Ammo stowage, secondary	2,550 rnds
Range, on road	120 km (74.4 miles)		
Range, cross country	85 km (52.7 miles)	Engine make	Maybach
		Engine model	HL 230 P45
Crew	5	Engine configuration	V-12, liquid cooled
Communications	Fu. 5, intercom	Engine displacement	23 liters
Weapon, main	38 cm StuM	Engine horsepower	650 @ 2500 rpm

After its retrieval by the Americans, the Sturmmörser was sent to England for study at the school of tank technology. From there it crossed the Atlantic for further study at Aberdeen Proving Ground. The crane just behind the superstructure was used to hoist the huge shells and place them inside the vehicle.

Rebuilt Tiger I chassis were used as a basis for these vehicles. While the chassis were updated with steel-rimmed road wheels, etc., some variances were present among the Sturmmörser. Thus, this Sturmmörser has Zimmerit on its lower hull, while the other vehicle shown does not.

This upper view of the Sturmmörser allows shows the loading hatch, which is partially open here. Also visible are the the lugs for mounting a counterweight near the muzzle.

The bolts that secure the superstructure were massive, as are the welds joining the interlocking upper armor sections. A right side track has been installed on the Sturmmörser for the evaluation—it was missing when the vehicle was captured.

Patton Museum, Fort Knox, KY

The holes surrounding the gun tube are for expelling gases generated by the launching of the rocket. The unusual rocket and launcher were based on an antisubmarine weapon developed by the Kriegsmarine. The weapon is shown here at zero elevation.

Patton Museum, Fort Knox, KY

This rear view clearly of the Sturmmörser shows the mounting for the ammunition davit, as well as three holes shot in the left rear of the vehicle prior to its capture. The chassis number of this vehicle, 250327, reveals that the chassis was originally produced in June 1943 as a tank.

Patton Museum, Fort Knox, KY

This weapon has been raised to its maximum elevation. On the right of this photo is the periscopic visor of the driver, and above it the port for the PaK ZF3 gun sight. On the left is the ball-mounted machine gun.

Jagdpanzer 38

The Jagdpanzer 38 was born out of compromise. The German Army was increasingly reliant on the Sturmgeschütz assault guns as antitank weapons. When the Allies bombed the Alkett plant in Berlin, the source of the Stug, in November 1943, work began in earnest to find an alternate production facility. Among the facilities reviewed for this work by the Oberkommando des Herres (the OKH was the German Army high command) was the Boemisch-Märische Maschinenfabrik (BMM) plant in Prague. The BMM plant was not suitable for the production of Sturmgeschützs, but was well suited for the production of a new type vehicle—a light tank hunter.

Eleven days after the December 6, 1943, report to Hitler that the BMM plant was unsuitable for Sturmgeschütz production, design drawings for the new vehicle were completed. The new vehicle was initially named "Sturmgeschütz neur Art mit 7.5 cm PaK 39 L/40 auf Fahrgestell Pz.Kpfw. 38(t)." The vehicle was based on the proven automotive components of the Pz.Kpfw 38(t) alter Art and the Pz.Kpfw 38(t) neur Art and armed with the same main gun as was mounted in the Jagdpanzer IV.

A wooden mockup was constructed and shown to the Heeres Waffenamt on January 26, 1944.

The mockup was well received and the vehicle was placed into immediate production with relatively few changes. The first three vehicles were delivered on schedule by BMM in March 1944 and accepted the following month by the Herres Waffenamt. These three were followed by an additional 20 vehicles the next month

Patton Museum, Fort Knox, KY

From this angle, the thin side and rear armor of the Jagdpanzer 38 would be easily penetrated by tank and antitank guns.

Patton Museum, Fort Knox, KY

This photo shows two factory-fresh Jagdpanzer 38, one wearing camouflage paint, at the Škoda factory, Pilsen. The front armor of the Jagdpanzer 38 was substantial.

as production ramped up to fill the large orders placed for the new tank destroyer. In addition to BMM, orders were placed with Škoda, which began deliveries in July 1944.

In November 1944, the vehicle was officially redesignated Jagdpanzer 38 (SdKfz 138/2). The name Hetzer was intended for the never-produced Jagdpanzer E-10 project, but troops mistakenly applied it to the Jagdpanzer 38. Because this mistake has been repeated so widely, and for so long, the Jagdpanzer 38 will no doubt forever be known as the Hetzer while the real Hetzer, the E-10, is essentially forgotten.

Production of the Jagdpanzer 38 was often delayed due to Allied bombing, either of the main assembly plants, or of suppliers' plants. The PaK 39 was often in short supply, and further delays were introduced by relocating part of the Jagdpanzer production to satellite plants.

The Jagdpanzer 38 was intended to be used to equip each infantry division with its own tank destroyer unit. Through January 1945, 14 Jagdpanzer 38 were issued to each of the affected Panzer Jäger companies. After that time, due to Germany's worsening war situation, only 10 of the tank hunters were issued to each company.

The Jagdpanzer 38 had an excellent ballistic shape, but its greatest defense was its diminutive size.

Later production vehicles used a lighter gun mantlet and mount, like the one seen on this tank destroyer.

The Jagdpanzer 38's armor had the shape of a truncated pyramid, with every side sloped. This design helped it survive in the field.

CKD archive via Kliment collection

CKD archive via Kliment collection

While the early Jagdpanzer 38s were camouflaged by troops in the field, later production vehicles were factory painted in the "ambush" paint scheme shown here. The antennas stowed on the left rear of the vehicle identify this as a command vehicle.

Patton Museum, Fort Knox, KY

Most Jagdpanzer 38 vehicles were equipped with a large horizontal muffler. The machine gun mount is pivoted 90 degrees to the right.

As was customary with fighting vehicles of all nations, as experienced was gained in both combat and production of the Jagdpanzer 38, numerous minor changes were introduced. The basic form of the vehicle, though, remained the same throughout production.

CKD archive via Kliment collection

Jagdpanzer 38 tank destroyers produced after October 1944 utilized the Flamm-Vernichter muffler shown here. The reinforced idler wheel was another refinement introduced during the production run.

Specifications Jagdpanzer 38

Length	6.27 m	Weapon,	secondary 7.92mm MG 34
Width	2.63 m		
Height	2.10 m	Ammo stowage, main	41
Weight	16 metrics		
Fuel capacity	320 liters	Ammo stowage, secondary	600
Maximum speed	40 km/hr (24.8 mph)		
Range, on road	180 km (111.6 miles)	Engine make	Praga
Range, cross country	130 km (80.6 miles)	Engine configuration	six-cyl., liquid cooled
Crew	4	Engine displacement	7.75 liters
Communications	Fu.Spr.f	Engine horsepower	150 @ 2600 rpm
Weapon, main	7.5 cm Pak 39 L/48		

National Archives and Records Administration

The remote-controlled machinegun and binocular range finder are clearly shown in this photograph.

Patton Museum, Fort Knox, KY

Various configurations of road wheels and idlers were used throughout production. The towing brackets formed by extending the hull sides were characteristic of the bulk of the production.

CKD archive via Kliment collection

The Jagdpanzer 38 starr was an attempt to speed production and reduce cost by eliminating the recoil-absorbing system from the gun mount. The full recoil force was instead transferred to the vehicle. As a result, the cast gun mount was quite different, as seen here.

CKD archive via Kliment collection

Critical shortages of gasoline led to efforts to dieselize the Jagdpanzer. The rear view of the Jagdpanzer 38 starr shows the very different rear hull arrangement required by the air-cooled diesel. Such an installation would have required considerable changes in parts fabrication, with resultant delays in production. Accordingly, the diesel program was abandoned.

Jagdpanzer IV (Sd. Kfz. 162)

As the German Army began to face increased armor threats, especially from heavily armed and armored Soviet tanks, the need for purpose-built tank destroyers became increasingly evident. Low-profile, turretless assault guns had been pressed into this roll, and performed admirably, but by and large they were controlled by the infantry, and the armored force wanted its own dedicated tank hunters.

The Jagdpanzer IV was such a vehicle. It was based on the proven Panzerkampfwagen IV chassis and incorporated

The sloped armor of the Jagdpanzer offered greater protection that the slab-sided armor of the Sturmgeschütz.

Features that were carried over from the prototype vehicle into initial production were the mounting of spare track on the hull front and a machinegun port on either side of the front of the hull.

The Jagdpanzer IV's spare track links were relocated to the rear of the vehicle, which in turn forced the relocation of the spare road wheels.

The mockup of the Jagdpanzer IV included rounded shoulders where the side and front armor met. Due to the difficulty manufacturing vehicles in this form, this design feature was not carried over into production.

a low silhouette like the Sturmgeschütz assault guns. Whereas much of the armor on the Sturmgeschütz was vertical, the armor of the Jagdpanzer IV was well sloped, offering additional protection from the tanks it was intended to hunt.

Preliminary work on the Jagdpanzer IV began by Vomag in late 1942. A wooden mockup of the new vehicle, which was to mount a 7.5 cm PaK 39 (L/48) gun, was shown to Hitler in May 1943. Production of the new vehicle, titled the "Sturmgeschütz neue Art," began in January 1944. Production continued through November of the same year, at which time it was replaced with the similar, but better-armed, Panzer IV lang (V).

During the production run several changes were made. Significant among them were the omission of the left machinegun port and elimination of the muzzle brake in favor of a larger recoil cylinder beginning in May, and the deletion of Zimmerit anti-magnetic coating and one return roller in September. Also in September, Flammentoeter spark-arresting mufflers were introduced to the series.

Patton Museum, Fort Knox, KY

The low profile of the Jagdpanzer, coupled with its heavy frontal armor, made it difficult to defeat from this angle.

Ordnance Museum, Aberdeen Proving Ground, MD

The left machine gun port was deleted during the March 1943 production.

Patton Museum, Fort Knox, KY

It has been reported that the muzzle brake was deleted from the PaK 39 L/48 in May of 1943, but photographic evidence suggests that this change was not implemented on a specific date. Rather, it seems to have been phased in gradually based on supplies of weapons and recoil cylinders on hand.

The Jagdpanzer IV was originally coated with Zimmerit anti-magnetic mine paste.

Late-production Jagdpanzer IV vehicles, produced after September 1943, lacked the antimagnetic coating, like this vehicle captured by the Third Armored Division.

Panzer IV/70 (V) (Sd. Kfz. 162/1)

For some time the Heeres Waffenamt wanted to mount the powerful 7.5 cm L/70 in a vehicle to be employed as a tank killer. In early 1944, a Panzerjaeger IV was at last trial fitted with the long gun. A successful demonstration of the new vehicle for Hitler resulted in an order for the new vehicle to be placed into production by Vomag. In July, Hitler ordered the new tank hunter be designated "Panzer IV lang (V)." Ultimately, the Heeres Waffenamt designated the vehicle Panzer IV/70 (V) to minimize confusion with the turreted Panzerkampfwagen IV (lang).

Initial Panzer IV/70 (V) were built alongside the Jagdpanzer IV at Vomag. However, as supplies of the 7.5 cm PjK 42/L70 increased, production of the Jagdpanzer IV was phased out. During November 1944, only the Panzer IV/70 (V) was being produced.

Production continued at the Vomag plant through April 1945, although Allied bombing steadily reduced the monthly output from its peak of 185 units in January 1945.

Though various documents list differing final production numbers, just under 950 of the Panzer IV/70 (V) were built. These vehicles were issued primarily to tank killer detachments of Panzer divisions, as well as a few Independent Panzer Brigades.

Jagdpanzer IV

Length	6.85 m	Weapon, secondary	7.92mm MG 42
Width	3.17 m	Ammo stowage, main	79 rnds
Height	1.86 m		
Weight	24 tons	Ammo stowage, secondary	1,200 rnds
Fuel capacity	470 liters		
Maximum speed	40 km/hr (24.8 mph)	Engine make	Maybach
Range, on road	210 km (130.2 miles)	Engine model	HL 120 TRM
Range, cross country	130 km (80.6 miles)	Engine configuration	V-12, liquid cooled
Crew 4		Engine displacement	11.9 liters
Communications	Fu 5, Intercom	Engine horsepower	265 @ 2600 rpm
Weapon, main	7.5 cm Pak 39 L/48		

When production began, the Panzer IV/70 (V) had four return rollers on each side, and conventional roadwheels were used throughout.

Schuerzen was installed on the Panzer IV/70 (V) to protect the suspension components, while the rest of the tank destroyer's flank relied upon the sloping armor of the fighting compartment to protect the crew from small arms fire and fragments.

Walter J. Spielberger

Later production Panzer IV/70(v) had only three return rollers on each side. Steel-tired, rubber-cushioned roadwheels began to be installed on the two forward stations on each side. This was to combat excessive wear to conventional roadwheels caused by the nose-heavy stance of the vehicle.

Walter J. Spielberger

This captured example, sent to England for evaluation, lost one of its Flammentoeter flame-arresting mufflers, as well as the rear-stowed spare track, somewhere along the way.

Spare roadwheels were stowed on the engine deck, as seen here. The bar, which has broken free on the left end, is also apparent.

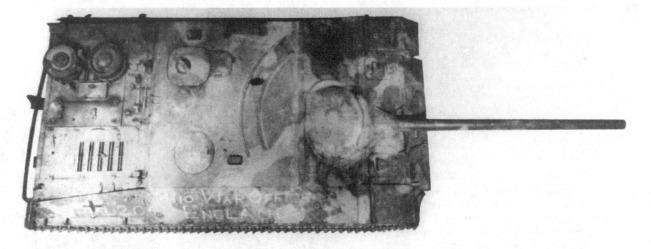

The top of the Panzer IV/70 (V) fighting compartment was uncluttered, with only the hatches and the opening for the periscopic gun sight visible in this photo.

Panzer IV/70 (A)

Much like Vomag had set out to mount a 7.5 cm L/70 cannon in the Jagdpanzer IV, and ultimately produced the Panzer IV/70 (V), the engineers at Alkett were charged with a similar mission in June 1944.

Well prior to this date, considerable research had been done regarding mounting the Kw. K. 42 L/70 tank gun in the Panzer IV turret. It had been determined that such an installation was unfeasible. Therefore, the decision was reached to mount superstructure of the Vomag-produced Jagdpanzer IV on the Alkett-produced Panzer IV chassis.

The chassis for the Panzer IV, however, was designed such that the fuel tanks were located under the turret. Had the Vomag superstructure been mounted conventionally, it would have been impossible to elevate the gun. Therefore, the superstructure was mounted on risers, raising it 38 cm.

Production of the new vehicle was undertaken by Nibelungenwerk in Austria in August 1944. When production ceased in March 1945, 278 had been completed.

Panzer IV/70 (A)

Length	8.87 m	Weapon, secondary	7.92mm MG 42
Width	2.90 m	Ammo stowage, main	90 rnds
Height	2.20 m	Ammo stowage, secondary	1,200 rnds
Weight	27 tons		
Fuel capacity	470 liters		
Maximum speed	38 km/hr (23.56 mph)	Engine make	Maybach
Range, on road	200 km (124 miles)	Engine model	HL 120 TRM
Range, cross country	130 km (80.6 miles)	Engine configuration	V-12, liquid cooled
Crew 4		Engine displacement	11.9 liters
Communications	Fu 5 and Fu 2, Intercom	Engine horsepower	265 @ 2600 rpm
Weapon, main	7.5 cm Pjk 42 L/70		

The additional riser required to mount the Vomag-based superstructure on the Alkett chassis is visible here. The Panzer IV driver's vision port was retained.

Patton Museum, Fort Knox, KY

This pair of Panzer IV/70 (A) was knocked out near Bastogne during the Ardennes offensive.

Stefan De Meyer collection

Although the design of the superstructure was based on that of the Jagdpanzer IV, the superstructures themselves were especially built for the new application. This is evident by the continuous side armor on this knocked-out Panzer IV/70 (A) on display at the Kubinka museum in Moscow.

Patton Museum, Fort Knox, KY

Jagdpanther Sd. Kfz. 173

Among the most lethal of Germany's AFVs was the Panzerjaeger Panther, or Jagdpanther. As early as 1942 Krupp had begun work on the design of this vehicle, with production scheduled to begin in July of the following year. The primary feature of the new vehicle was to be its lethal 8.8 cm Pak L/71 gun. The famed "88" had already garnered quite a reputation as a tank killing weapon.

The overwhelming work load of Krupp was cause of concern, so the Waffenamt transferred the Jagdpanther project to Daimler-Benz in October 1942. D-B intended for the vehicle to be based on the chassis of the forthcoming Panther II.

Of course, the decision not to produce the Panther II led to further delays in the Jagdpanther program, as the vehicle was redesigned again to adapt it to the Panther chassis. However, Daimler-Benz was able to retain some of the features originally intended for the Panther II.

Due once again to pressing work in the Damlier-Benz Berlin plant, the Jagdpanther project was transferred yet again. As mid-1943 approached, the project was handed off to Miag in Braunschweig. Miag finalized the design

The early production Jagdpanthers had double persicopes for the driver. Also visible is the overall Zimmerit antimagnetic coating and the tools stowed along the right-hand side of the vehicle.

Military History Institute, Carlisle Barracks, PA

During the second month of Jagdpanther production the outer driver's periscope was deleted. Much of the external stowage has been removed from this captured example.

Patton Museum, Fort Knox, KY

The thin section of the casting of the outer gun shield is visible on this early Jagdpanther, as is the rain deflector over the dual driver periscopes. The gun tubes on the early vehicles were one piece, with a smooth, tapered outer surface.

Walter J. Spielberger

Although well protected from frontal attack, like most German tank destroyers, the Jagdpanther had vulnerable flanks, as evidenced by the four holes fired into the sides of this captured example.

Close inspection of this photograph of the same tank suggests that the hatches were blown off by an internal explosion.

Note the size of the three 88mm rounds laying beside the track in this rear view of the same vehicle.

This overhead view of the same vehicle shows many of the rooftop details. Many of the hatches are absent.

and completed to prototype vehicles in October and November of 1943.

Mass production began and Jagdpanther deliveries began in January 1944. However, all was not yet well for the Jagdpanther production line. Allied bombers began to target Miag's Braunschweig plant, delaying production. In response to this, additional Jagdpanther assembly lines were established at Maschinenfabrik Niedersachsen-Hannover (MNH) in Hannover as well as Maschinenbau und Bahnbedarf AG Nordhausen (MBA) at Potsdam-Drewitz. It was hoped that deliveries from the two additional firms would begin in November. Despite operating three production facilities, the persistent delays at the design stage, and the Allied bombing efforts, combined to limit production to just over 400 units.

The Jagdpanther was well armed and armored, and had reasonable automotive performance, making it a menacing presence on the battlefield. It was used by both tank destroyer and tank units.

Jagdpanther

Length	9.88 m	Weapon, secondary	7.92mm MG 42
Width	3.45 m	Ammo stowage, main	60 rnds
Height	2.72 m		
Weight	46 tons	Ammo stowage, secondary	1,200 rnds
Fuel capacity	700 liters		
Maximum speed	46 km/hr (28.52 mph)	Engine make	Maybach
Range, on road	160 km (99.2 miles)	Engine model	HL 230 P30
Range, cross country	80 km (49.6 miles)	Engine configuration	V-12, liquid cooled
Crew 5		Engine displacement	23.1 liters
Communications	Fu 5 and Fu 2, Intercom	Engine horsepower	600 @ 2500 rpm
Weapon, main	8.8 cm Pjk 43/3 L/71		

The stepped barrel of this Jagdpanther's 88 is indicative of a later-production vehicle with a sectional 8.8 cm Pak43/3 cannon. This gun was introduced in May 1944. The 7.92mm MG 34 mounted to the right of the main gun protected the vehicle against infantry assault.

The torsion bar suspension of the Jagdpanther offered excellent performance off road. Unfortunately the drivetrain was not up to the standards of the suspension system.

Late production Jagdpanthers (post October 1944) utilized a heavier outer gun shield casting, like the one on this captured example photographed at Aberdeen Proving Ground in December 1946.

The sloping plates of the Jagdpanther's armor, the heavy plate used for the superstructure front, and its low profile made it nearly immune to front assault by contemporary Allied tanks.

The knocked-out Jagdpanther commanded by noted armor historian and contributor to this work, Walter J. Spielberger. A GI is shown examining the fractured hull side armor.

Ferdinand/Elefant Sd. Kfz. 184

Considerable raw materials, engineering and man-hours had been devoted to the aborted Porsche designed gas/electric-powered Tiger (P) project. These were all resources the Germany could ill afford to merely discard. In September 1942, the military brain trust decided to modify a significant portion of the Tiger (P) chassis into self-propelled gun armed with an 8.8 cm Pak L/71 cannon. This weapon was installed in a boxy superstructure featuring frontal armor a whopping 200mm thick.

Alkett completed the design work in November 1942. Two of the 100 hulls, which had been completed by Krupp and shipped to Nibelungenwerk prior to the suspension of the Tiger (P) program, were shipped to Alkett. Alkett used these to produce two trial vehicles, and it was originally envisioned that Alkett would produce all the superstructures, while Nibelungenwerk would complete the chassis. However, in February 1943, it was decided that Nibelungenwerk would assemble the vehicles in their entirety, save for the two prototypes.

Production of the 89 Ferdinands, so named in honor of Dr. Ferdinand Porsche, took only two months. Nibelungenwerk began production in April 1943, and the job was complete in May.

When initially produced, the Ferdinand had no close-in defensive weaponry. This proved problematic on the Russian front. The smooth sides indicate that these vehicles were produced prior to Zimmerit being mandated on combat vehicles.

During the post-Kursk rebuild, the Ferdinand was equipped with a hull-mounted 7.92mm MG 34 machine gun. A cupola with vision ports was also added for the commander. The cupola is faintly visible in this photo, taken in 1946 at Aberdeen Proving Ground, of a captured example.

The massive new tank killers were dispatched to the Russian front the next month, in the charge of PanzerjägerAbteilungen 656. The first combat operation of the new vehicles was at Kursk, as part of operation Zitadelle. By December, their number had been reduced to 48—all of which were returned to Nibelungenwerk for rebuilding.

Based on the lessons learned in combat, the rebuild included a ball-mounted machinegun, to be fired by the radio operator, added at the hull front. The commander's hatch was replaced with a cupola at the same time, and Zimmerit was added to such a height as to protect the vehicle from magnet mines placed by a man on foot. The vehicles retained their unusual twin gasoline engines, which each powered a generator. Those generators in turn supplied current to electric motors that drove the vehicle.

The rebuild program was completed in March 1944 and the vehicles were redeployed to Italy, assigned to schwere PanzerjägerAbteilungen 653. Coincidental, but unrelated to the rebuild program, the name of the vehicle was changed from Ferdinand to Elefant at Hitler's suggestion. The change became official in February 1944.

Ordnance Museum, Aberdeen Proving Ground

During the same rebuilding program that added the commander's cupola, Zimmerit was applied to the lower portion of the hull.

Ferdinand/Elefant

Length	8.14 m	Weapon, main	8.8 cm Pak 43/2 L/71
Width	3.38 m	Weapon, secondary	7.92mm MG 42
Height	2.97 m	Ammo stowage, main	50 rnds
Weight	65 tons		
Fuel capacity	950 liters	Ammo stowage, secondary	600 rnds
Maximum speed	30 km/hr (18.6 mph)		
Range, on road	150 km (93 miles)	Engine make	2 x Maybach
Range, cross country	90 km (55.8 miles)	Engine model	HL 120 TRM
		Engine configuration	V-12, liquid cooled
Crew 6			
		Engine displacement	11.9 liters each
Communications	Fu 5 and Fu 2, Intercom		
		Engine horsepower	265 @ 2600 rpm

Patton Museum, Fort Knox, KY

A shell ejection port was centered on the large access hatch in the superstructure rear. The Ferdinand, renamed the Elefant in early 1944, was largely blind and defenseless from the rear and sides.

National Archives and Records Administration.

The shell ejection door and rear pistol port are open on the rear of this example, photographed after action. The large access door was retained by eight bolts. It was likely dislodged here by an internal explosion.

Jagdtiger Sd. Kfz. 186

Germany's continuous quest for heavier-armed and armored vehicles touched tank destroyers as well. In early 1943, a vehicle armed with a 12.8 cm gun was proposed. It was believed such a vehicle would be useful for infantry support against well-armored targets, as well as targets beyond the effective range of lesser cannons.

Around the main armament developed for the Maus superheavy tank, albeit installed in a different mounting,

This is one of the 11 Jagdtigers completed with the Porsche-type suspension, as evidenced by the eight road wheels.

These Jagdtigers with Henschel suspension have met a more civil fate—they were surrendered by their crews at Iserlohn in April 1945.

This Jagdtiger has met its demise, perhaps a result of destruction by its crew.

This eight-wheel suspension system of the Jagdtiger was eventually abandoned in favor of the simpler Henschel-designed suspension.

This is one of a pair of Jagdtigers captured by the U.S. Third Armored Division.

wheels on each side, before the Henschel suspension was adopted as standard. The Henschel suspension featured nine road wheels each side, each slightly larger than those used on the Porsche suspension-equipped vehicles.

Only 85 of the huge vehicles were completed before the war ended. All were assigned to only two units: the Panzerjagerabteilung 653, and the schwere Panzerabteilung 512. Their tremendous weight was detrimental to these machines' performance, both on and off road. These factors, and their limited numbers, greatly reduced their effectiveness.

Henschel began designing the new Panzerjaeger. The Tiger II was used as the automotive basis for the new vehicle, although the hull had to be lengthened some 40 cm in its new role. At the insistence of Ferdinand Porsche, Hitler agreed to utilize a new type torsion bar suspension on some of the vehicles.

Nibelungenwerk finished the first two Jagdtigers, one with the Porsche-designed suspension, the other with the Henschel-designed suspension in February 1944. A further 10 units were assembled with the Porsche-designed suspension, distinguished by having eight road

Jagdtiger

Length	10.5 m	Weapon, secondary	1 x 7.92mm MG 42 and 1 x 7.92mm MG 34
Width	3.77 m		
Height	2.95 m		
Weight	75.2 tons	Ammo stowage, main	40 rnds
Fuel capacity	860 liters		
Maximum speed	34.6 km/hr (21.45 mph)	Ammo stowage, secondary	3,300 rnds
Range, on road	100 km (62 miles)	Engine make	Maybach
Range, cross country	70 km (43.4 miles)	Engine model	HL 230 P30
Crew	6	Engine configuration	V-12, liquid cooled
Communications	Fu 5 and Fu 2, Intercom	Engine displacement	23.1 liters
Weapon, main	12.8 cm Pjk 80 L/55	Engine horsepower	600 @ 2500 rpm

The same vehicle was photographed in December 1946 at Aberdeen Proving Ground, where it had been taken for evaluation.

Ordnance Museum, Aberdeen Proving Ground

Bergepanzer 38

As initially produced, the Bergepanzer 38 had no winch and was simply an open-top prime mover provided with rudimentary towing and repair equipment. A jib crane could be installed on the right side of the vehicle.

Vehicles produced post-February 1945 were equipped with a ground anchor mounted on the rear and a winch mounted internally in the vehicle. Using both these items in concert, the Bergepanzer 38 could retrieve even larger vehicles that were stuck or disabled.

The first of the 181 Bergepanzer 38 (Sd. Kfz. 136) were built in May 1944 by Boehmisch-Mahrische Maschinenfabrik in Prague, where production continued until April 1945. Like the Jagdpanzer 38, a variety of idler and road wheels were used throughout production of the

Bergepanzer 38. One Bergepanzer 38 was supplied to each Jagdpanzer unit equipped with the Jagdpanzer 38.

Bergepanzer 38			
Length	4.87 m w/o ground anchor	Crew	2
		Weapon, main	7.92mm MG
Width	2.63 m	Ammo stowage, main	600 rnds
Height	1.97 m		
Weight	13 tons	Engine make	Praga
Fuel capacity	320 liters	Engine model	AC
Maximum speed	40 km/hr (24.8 mph)	Engine configuration	six-cyl., liquid cooled
Range, on road	180 km (111.6 miles)	Engine displacement	7.75 liters
Range, cross country	130 km (80.6 miles)	Engine horsepower	150 hp @ 2600 rpm

Patton Museum, Fort Knox, KY

When initially produced, the Bergepanzer 38 didn't have a recovery winch or ground anchor, limiting it largely to towing. This captured example was photographed at Aberdeen Proving Ground after the war.

CKD archive via Kliment collection

Beginning in February 1945, the Bergepanzer 38 began to leave the factory with a large ground anchor attached to the rear hull. This was used in conjunction with the newly installed drag winch to retrieve mired or disabled vehicles that the Bergepanzer might not otherwise be able to recover.

CKD archive via Kliment collection

This Bergepanzer 38 was not equipped with a winch. Crews improvised by breaking a track and using that side's drive sprocket as a capstan winch, with the wire rope wrapping around its hub.

All Bergepanzer 38s carried a variety of tools and recovery gear, including towbars and jib booms. Their body was a cut-down version of the Jagdpanzer 38.

CKD archive via Kliment collection

Gravity was used to lower the Bergepanzer 38 ground anchor. Its blade was set at an angle and pointed so that it would dig into the ground during winching operations.

CKD archive via Kliment collection

A winch was used to pick up the blade after recovery operations were complete. The wire rope is visible here along with a sheave.

CKD archive via Kliment collection

This late Bergepanzer 38 was photographed positioned for recovery outside the CKD factory. These vehicles were intended for issue to units using Panzerkampfwagen 38(t)-based families of vehicles. This kept the weights manageable for the Bergepanzer as well as providing a commonality of parts and training.

CKD archive via Kliment collection

Bergepanzer III Sd. Kfz. 144

In the early stages of the war, the German Army relied upon its 18-ton halftrack prime mover as its chief recovery vehicle. Shortages of these halftracks, and the increasing weight of German tanks, resulted in the adaptation of tank chassis to recovery roles. To ease maintenance and facilitate parts availability, typically each unit's recovery vehicle would share a common chassis with that unit's tanks.

One of the earliest of these recovery vehicles was the Bergepanzerwagen III. Construction of these vehicles, utilizing rebuilt Panzer III chassis as a basis, was begun in March 1944. The construction of these vehicles amounted to installing a heavy wooden box in the area formerly occupied by the tank's turret. Although the Bergepanzer III was equipped with tow bars and couplings, a jib boom and a variety of recovery gear, it had neither a winch, nor a ground spade. When necessary, winching was done by breaking a track and using the drive sprocket as a windlass.

Between March and November 1944, 167 of these vehicles were constructed. A further nine were assembled in the first quarter of 1945. These were issued to a variety of units that employed Panzer III and Sturmgeschütz vehicles.

Bergepanzer III (Sd.Kfz. 144)

Length	5.52 m	Weapon, main	7.92mm MG 34
Width	2.97 m	Ammo stowage, main	600 rnds
Height	2.40 m		
Weight	20 tons	Engine make	Maybach
Fuel capacity	320 liters (19.84 mph)	Engine model	HL 120 TRM
Maximum speed	42 km/hr (26.04 miles)	Engine configuration	V-12, liquid cooled
Range, on road	155 km (96.1 miles)	Engine displacement	11.9 liters
Range, cross country	95 km	Engine horsepower	265 @ 2600 rpm
Crew	2		

Patton Museum, Fort Knox, KY

One-hundred seventy-six older Panzer III returned for rebuild were reconstructed as recovery vehicles, known as the Bergepanzer III.

Patton Museum, Fort Knox, KY

The box-like superstructure of the Bergepanzer III was constructed of wood with angle-iron reinforcement.

Bergepanzer IV Sd. Kfz. 164

Like the Bergepanzer III, this vehicle was based on rebuilt combat tanks. Installing a heavy wooden decking over the turret ring of a Panzer IV began the transformation to a Bergepanzer IV. Inside, more heavy wooden decking was installed to protect the fuel tanks from the heavy recovery gear that was stowed internally. Sockets to receive a 2-ton crane were welded to the roof of the vehicle superstructure.

Without a purpose-built winch at their disposal, the crews of the Bergepanzer IV had to rely upon using a drive sprocket as a windlass. The track was broken, and

Bergepanzer IV (Sd.Kfz. 164)

Length	5.92 m	Weapon, main	7.92mm MG 34
Width	2.88 m	Ammo stowage, main	600 rnds
Height	2.10 m		
Weight	20 tons	Engine make	Maybach
Fuel capacity	470 liters	Engine model	HL 120 TRM
Maximum speed	42 km/hr (26.04 mph)	Engine configuration	V-12, liquid cooled
Range, on road	210 km (130.2 miles)	Engine displacement	11.9 liters
Range, cross country	130 km (80.6 miles)	Engine horsepower	265 @ 2600 rpm
Crew	2		

a wire rope was attached between the sprocket and the vehicle to be winched. By placing the Bergepanzer in gear, the sprocket was turned, and the wire rope wound around it. Though labor-intensive, this was an effect recovery means. However, its utility was hampered by the lack of a ground spade, requiring the Bergepanzer to be anchored to another heavy vehicle or large tree.

Only 21 Panzer IV were converted to Bergepanzer, all between October 1944 and March 1945.

Bergepanther Sd. Kfz. 179

The Bergepanther, unlike the Bergepanzer III and Bergepanzer IV, was purpose-built as a recovery vehicle. The Bergepanther was also built on freshly assembled chassis, rather than on rebuilt chassis. M.A.N., the primary contractor on the Panther project, also did the design work on the Bergepanther, and built the first 12, converting the chassis of in-process Panther D models to the new configuration.

Further, from July through December 1943 Henschel produced 70 Bergepanthers with the characteristics of the Panther A. Daimler-Benz built an additional 40 Bergepanther Ausfrung A in the early months of 1944 before production of these vehicles was transferred to Demag. In March 1944, Demag delivered its first Bergepanther A. Production of this model concluded in October 1944, when the Bergepanther A was superceded by the Bergepanther G. Demag's production of both types totaled 168 units.

Although plans for the Bergepanther included a large 40-ton-capacity recovery winch from the outset, equipment shortages forced many of the vehicles to be completed without this key component. During the course of the long production run, many running changes were made. Naturally, most of the changes to regular Panther production were applied to the Bergepanther as well. Additionally, the mounting location of the jib boom was moved from the superstructure sides to the rear deck with the introduction of the Bergepanther G.

Bergepanzerwagen Panther

Length	8.86 m w/ ground anchor	Weapon, main	2 cm Kw.K 38 (on some models)
Width	3.42 m	Weapon, secondary	7.92mm MG 34
Height	2.70 m		
Weight	43 tons	Ammo stowage, main	600 rnds
Fuel capacity	1,075 liters	Engine make	Maybach
Maximum Speed	46 km/hr (28.52 mph)	Engine model	HL 230 P30
Range, on road	320 km (198.4 miles)	Engine configuration	V-12, liquid cooled
Range, cross country	160 km (99.2 miles)	Engine displacement	23.1 liters
Crew	3	Engine horsepower	600 @ 2500 rpm
Communications	Fu 5		

After 12 turretless Panther Ausf. D were delivered for use as recovery vehicles, a more refined approach was taken. Henschel produced 70 vehicles, such as this one, based on the Ausf. A chassis, which were well equipped for towing and recovery work.

In order to anchor the vehicle while using the recovery winch, a spade was attached to the rear. Initially, the spade was of a simple design, as shown here, but later a more effective and more elaborate spade was used. The jib boom is also shown erected here.

Walter J. Spielberger

Walter J. Spielberger

A mount was installed on the glacis of some of the Bergepanther for installation of a 2 cm Kw.K. for self-defense. The folding sides of the superstructure were made of wood.

This Bergepanther Ausf. A is using the early spade. The wire rope extending from the winch has been rigged as a two-part line using a sheave to return it to an anchor point on the engine access cover. This effectively doubled the pulling effort of the 40-ton-capacity recovery winch.

The recovery winch was used to lift the heavy ground anchor. The jib boom could be erected on either side of the Bergepanther's hull.

Patton Museum, Fort Knox, KY

Later Bergepanther Ausf. A had the more elaborate spade shown here, which was more effective at anchoring the vehicle. Note the extensive reinforcement on the underside of the ground anchor.

Patton Museum, Fort Knox, KY

A heavy wooden timber was carried as part of the recovery gear and stowed along the left side of the hull when not in use. A mount for a MG34 antiaircraft machine gun has been installed on the 2 cm Kw.K.'s bracket on this Bergepanther.

Patton Museum, Fort Knox, KY

In addition to use in repair work (the Bergepanther was assigned a mechanic as part of its crew), the jib boom was also useful when handling the recovery gear. Sheaves, clevis, and wire ropes for heavy recovery all weigh more than one might expect.

Patton Museum, Fort Knox, KY

The harder the pull on the drag winch, the more firmly the ground anchor is seated. No doubt a major factor in its redesign, which added the upper "lip," was the desire to keep from simply burying the spade and plowing with it rather than anchoring.

Stefan De Meyer collection

The final version of the Bergepanther was built on the Panther Ausf. G chassis, and naturally had the tapered armored side that characterized that ausfrüng. This vehicle was assigned to s.Pz.Jg.Abt. (heavy tank destroyer battalion) 512, which surrendered to U.S. forces at Iserlohn in March 1945.

Stefan De Meyer collection

The Bergepanther Ausf. G was not equipped with the mount for the 2 cm Kw.K. that had been installed on some of the Ausf. A. One example so equipped survives today in a museum, but this feature was added post-war.

Bergepanzer Elefant

The 90 huge self-propelled guns, known as Ferdinand, which were built on chassis of the ill-fated Tiger (P), exceeded the towing capacity of the standard German 18-ton halftrack recovery vehicle. To address this problem, three of the Tiger (P) chassis were converted to recovery vehicles.

The superstructure installed was considerably smaller than that of the self-propelled gun, and the armor was not as thick. The gas-electric power plant, powered by twin Maybach HL 120 engines, was carried over in the recovery variant. A jib boom was provided, as was a 7.92mm MG 34 for self-defense. Nibelungenwerk completed the three recovery vehicles in August 1943, and they were supplied to schwere Heeres Panzer-Jaeger-Abteilung 653. One was eventually shipped to Italy and the other two to the Russian Front.

At more than 60 tons, these were the largest recovery vehicles fielded by the German Army during WWII.

Bergepanzer Ferdinand/Elefant

Length	6.97 m	Communications	Fu 5
Width	3.38 m		
Height	2.97 m	Weapon, main	7.92mm MG 34
Weight	60 tons		
Fuel capacity	950 liters	Ammo stowage, main	600 rnds
Maximum speed	30 km/hr (18.6 mph)	Engine make	2 x Maybach
		Engine model	HL 120 TRM
Range, on road	150 km (93 miles)	Engine configuration	V-12, liquid cooled
Range, cross country	90 km (55.8 miles)	Engine displacement	11.9 liters
Crew	3	Engine horsepower	265 @ 2600 rpm

The three Bergepanzer Ferdinand were Germany's largest recovery vehicles and were based on the VK4501 (P) Porsche Tiger. The ball-mounted machine gun has been relocated to the upper superstructure.

The outline of the machine gun's former location in the hull is faintly visible to the right of the driver's visor in this photo. The large shackles added to the front of the vehicle aided its new role of recovery vehicle.

The suspension of the VK 4501 (P) was retained, as were the vehicles' gas-electric drive, although the engines were moved to a central location in the hull.

Panzerkampwagen 38 füer 2 cm Flak 38 Sd. Kfz. 140

As the Allies wrestled control of the sky from the Luftwaffe, the need for organic antiaircraft defense within armored units became critical. A variety of self-propelled antiaircraft artillery were conceived utilizing chassis already in production.

Such was the case with the Panzerkampwagen 38. Boemisch-Märische Maschinenfabrik, which had previously begun production of Geschuetzwagen 38 Ausfürung K "Grille," was tasked with the creation of a flakpanzer based on the same chassis. The new vehicle was to be armed with the 2 cm Flak 38 antiaircraft cannon.

While this chassis shared many components with the panzer 38 (t), its engine was mounted midships, like that of the Geschuetzwagen. The superstructure, although resembling that of the Grille, was different and included hinged upper armor sections. These sides could be folded down when it was necessary to bring the 2 cm cannon into action. With the sides hinged down, the cannon mount could be rotated through 360 degrees, and the barrel depressed enough to engage ground targets.

Between November 1943 and February 14, B.M.M. completed 141 of these vehicles. The bulk of the new vehicles were assigned in batteries of 12 to flak units attached to panzer units. The new vehicles were used in Italy as well as on the Western front.

Although closed here, the upper portions of the Panzerkampfwagen 38 antiaircraft gun's enclosure were hinged, and were designed to be lowered when using the gun.

The Panzerkampfwagen 38 fuer 2 cm Flak 38 was built on a mid-engine chassis based on the 38 (t).

Flakpanzerkampfwagen 38 fuer 2 cm Flak 38

Length	4.61 m	Communications	Fu 5
Width	2.135 m	Weapon, main	1 x 2.0 cm Flak 38
Height	2.252 m	Ammo stowage, main	1,040 rnds
Weight	9.8 tons		
Fuel capacity	218 liters	Engine make	Praga
Maximum speed	42 km/hr (26.04 mph)	Engine model	AC
Range, on road	185 km (114.7 miles)	Engine configuration	six-cylinder, liquid cooled
Range, cross country	140 km (86.8 miles)	Engine displacement	7.75 liters
Crew	4	Engine horsepower	150 @2600 rpm

With the sides swung down and the crew in place, this well-camouflaged Flakpanzer is ready for action.

The exhaust system of this captured example has been damaged, and the tailpipe (in the foreground) is no longer connected to the rear-mounted muffler.

With the armored sides folded down, the 2 cm Flak 38 and its mount can be clearly seen. This weapon could be used against lightly armored vehicles and infantry, as well as against aircraft.

Flakpanzer III

By late 1944, the Sturmartillerie was growing anxious for its own indigenous antiaircraft protection. It was important that this vehicle be based on the Panzerkampfwagen III chassis, as this would provide not only parts commonality the most abundant Sturmgeschütz, but similiar maneuverability as well.

Toward this end, a representative was sent to Ostbau Sagen, where Panzer IV-based Ostwind and Wirbelwind were being assembled in the army's own shops. Finding the management at Sagen less than helpful, the Sturmartillerie set out to create their own Panzer-III based flak vehicle. While authorization was given to create 90 of these vehicles, it appears materials were only released to build 18 of them. It is unknown if even this handful were actually built, as no photos or records of them have surfaced in the intervening 60 years.

2 cm Flakvierling auf Fahrgestell Panzerkampfwagen IV

In February 1943, Krupp began work on a Flakpanzer based on the tried chassis of the Panzer IV medium tank. Krupp mounted a quadruple 2 cm antiaircraft mount on top of a Panzer IV chassis. The vehicle's superstructure consisted of an open top box with hinged double wall sides of 12mm armor.

Although the trial vehicle was completed on schedule and satisfied the requirements of General Guderian, the decision was made to pursue development of a vehicle armed with the 3.7 cm Flak 43 instead. As a result, the series production of the 2 cm Flakvierling auf Fahrgestell Panzerkampfwagen IV ordered by General Guderian was cancelled. The single trial 2 cm Flakvierling auf Fahrgestell Panzerkampfwagen IV was rearmed with a 3.7 cm Flak 43.

Walter J. Spielberger

This vehicle was a result of the first attempt to create an antiaircraft tank on the chassis of a Panzerkampfwagen IV, however, only this single example was produced.

It was possible to rotate the mount and engage high-flying targets without lowering the armored sides.
Walter J. Spielberger

With the double-walled armored superstructure front lowered the business end of the quadruple 2 cm antiaircraft mount is visible.

With all four sides lowered, the quad mount could be brought to bear on low-flying aircraft or ground targets.

Flakpanzerkampfwagen IV "Möbelwagen"

After the decision was made to abandon the quad 20mm mount Flakpanzerkampfwagen in favor of a single 3.7cm mount in December 1943, Krupp set out to design such a vehicle.

After first considering a newly designed chassis utilizing some Panzer IV components, Krupp saw the requirement changed to include instead a standard Panzer IV chassis. The basic configuration of the 2cm Flakvierling auf Fahrgestell Panzerkampfwagen IV was employed with fold-down sides. However, these sides were somewhat shorter than those previously used. While lessening protection for the crew, this allowed the 37mm mount to be used without lowering the sides. The mount chosen was the standard 3.7cm Flak 43, with a shortened right side gun shield and other minor modifications.

Per its February contract, Deutsche Eisenwerke AG-Werk Stahlindustrie began production of 100 of the new vehicles on chassis provided by Krupp, with the initial delivery coming in March 1944.

The new vehicle was dubbed Möbelwagen by using troops because its slab sides resembled those of a moving van. Like the 2cm Flakvierling auf Fahrgestell Panzerkampfwagen IV, the first 45 vehicles had double wall sides—first of 12mm, and later of 10mm, plate. After these were completed, the balance of the 240 Möbelwagens constructed had superstructure sides made of single-thickness 25mm plates.

Once the later Wirbelwind was introduced, the Möbelwagen and Wirbelwind were issued one for one to flak units attached to armored units.

Flakpanzerkampfwagen IV Möbelwagen

Length	5.92 m	Weapon, main	1 x 3.7 cm Flak 43/1
Width	2.95 m	Weapon, ball mounted	—
Height	3.0 m		
Weight	25 tons	Ammo stowage, main	400 rnds
Fuel capacity	470 liters		
Maximum speed	38 km/hr (23.56 mph)	Engine make	Maybach
		Engine model	HL 120 TRM
Range, on road	200 km (124 miles)	Engine configuration	V-12, liquid cooled
Range, cross country	130 km (80.6 miles)	Engine displacement	11.9 liters
Crew	5	Engine horsepower	272 @ 2800 rpm
Communications	Fu 5 and Fu 2		

The Möbelwagen sides could be opened partially, allowing the gun to engage high-flying targets while still protecting crew from shell fragments and small arms fire.

Walter J. Spielberger

The boxy appearance of the Möbelwagen with the sides folded to the transport position led to its name, which means "moving van."

Patton Museum, Fort Knox, KY

The basis of the Möbelwagen was the standard Panzerkampfwagen IV chassis. This vehicle was on display at Aberdeen Proving Ground.

Ordnance Museum, Aberdeen Proving Ground

A hinged, asymmetrical gunshield was attached to the 3.7 cm Möbelwagen weapon.

Walter J. Spielberger

With the sides fully lowered, the gun could be trained on low-flying aircraft or ground targets, however, the gun crew was totally exposed.

Imperial War Museum

Flakpanzerkampfwagen IV Wirbelwind Sd. Kfz 161/4

The 3.7 cm-armed Möbelwagen did not mark the last of the idea of arming a flakpanzer with quadruple 2 cm mount. The idea resurfaced in 1944 with the installation of a 2 cm Flakvierling in an open-topped nine-sided turret.

Named the "Wirbelwind," or whirlwind, the new vehicle offered a distinct advantage over the Möbelwagen in that its weapons were immediately employable. The three-man crew could immediately bring the guns into play in any direction with the Wirbelwind's turret,

whereas, in most instances, the Möbelwagen's crew had to lower the sidewalls before their single 3.7 cm gun could be brought to bare.

A further advantage was the protected position of the crew. The Möbelwagen crew was totally exposed to ground and strafing fire when in firing position, while the Wirbelwind's crew was protected from small arms fire

A three-man crew manned the Wirbelwind turret. The gunner, who was also the vehicle commander, sat behind the weapons, while two loaders, one on each side, fed the gun's voracious appetite for ammunition. The driver and radio operators stations were in the hull, as they were in the Panzer IV.

Walter J. Spielberger

The Wirbelwind was armed with 2 cm Flak 38 on a quad mount. The Panzerkampfwagen's ball-mounted MG 34 was retained at the radio operator's station, even though the quad 2 cm guns could be devastating against infantry.

Walter J. Spielberger

One of the most effective self-propelled antiaircraft weapons developed by Germany during the war was the Wirbelwind. Rather than being manufactured by industrial firms, these vehicles were constructed in an Army depot.

Walter J. Spielberger

as well as shell fragments from all sides except directly above.

Unlike most German AFVs, which were produced by commercial concerns, the Wirbelwind was produced by the German army itself. The turret housing was constructed by Deutsche Rohrenwerk, and assembled with the 2 cm Flak 38-Vierling onto rebuilt Panzer IV chassis at the panzer repair facility in Sagan, Schlesien. Between July 1944 and March 1945, 122 Wirbelwind were produced. As rebuilt chassis were used, the details varied from vehicle to vehicle.

As mentioned previously, once the Wirbelwind was introduced, it and the Möbelwagen were issued one for one to flak units attached to armored units.

Flakpanzerkampfwagen IV Wirbelwind

Length	5.92 m	Weapon, main	4 x 2.0 cm Flak 38
Width	2.90 m	Weapon, ball mounted	7.92mm MG 34
Height	2.76 m		
Weight	22 tons	Ammo stowage, main	3,200 rnds
Fuel capacity	470 liters		
Maximum speed	38 km/hr (23.56 mph)	Ammo stowage, secondary	1,350 rnds
Range, on road	200 km (124 miles)	Engine make	Maybach
Range, cross country	130 km (80.6 miles)	Engine model	HL 120 TRM
Crew	5	Engine configuration	V-12, liquid cooled
Communications	Fu 5 and Fu 2	Engine displacement	11.9 liters
		Engine horsepower	272 @ 2800 rpm

Because an assortment of rebuilt chassis were supplied for the Wirbelwind program, there was quite a variety of detail differences. This Wirbelwind, displayed at one time at Aberdeen Proving Ground, lacked the bolted-on front superstructure armor seen on the "new" vehicle photographed at the conversion center. Two of the guns have been removed.

Ordnance Museum, Aberdeen Proving Ground

Rebuilt used Panzerkampfwagen IV chassis were used as the basis for the Wirbelwind. The nine-sided turret shell was manufactured by Deutsche Rohrenwerk. This vehicle was constructed on a Panzerkampfwagen IV Ausf. G chassis with Zimmerit coating.

Walter J. Spielberger

The victors are looking over the tools of the vanquished in this image. These GI's examine a pair of Wirbelwind lost during the Battle of the Bulge. Though well armed against infantry, the thin armor of these antiaircraft tanks made them vulnerable to moderately sized weapons, while their open top exposed the crew to air bursts and grenades.

Patton Museum, Fort Knox, KY

Flakpanzerkampfwagen IV "Ostwind"

In mid-1944, efforts were made to mount the German Army's preferred antiaircraft weapon, the 3.7 cm Flak 43, in a closed-sided rotating turret similar to that used by the Wirbelwind. The troops at Ostbau Sagan assembled a trial vehicle using a rebuilt conventional Panzer IV chassis. This trial vehicle had a mild steel six-sided turret, rather than armored, like the Wirbelwind turret.

After trials, some changes were recommended prior to placing the vehicle in series production. Foremost among these was the replacement of the Panzer IV turret ring with the larger turret ring from a Tiger I. This required the turret ring to extend further forward than the standard ring, which in turn required the relocation of the hatches on the superstructure top.

Due to the extensive revisions, it was necessary for new chassis to be constructed for this new vehicle, known as the "Ostwind," or east wind. The chassis were ordered from Krupp-Grusonwerk, and were mechanically comparable to the Panzer IV J. The turret shells were made by Deutsche Roehrenwerke. Of the 80 Ostwind ordered in September 1944 and scheduled to be assembled by

Deutsche Eisenwerke, only six were known to have been completed.

Flakpanzerkampfwagen IV Ostwind

Length	5.92 m	Communications	Fu 5 and Fu 2
Width	2.95 m	Weapon, main	1 x 3.7 cm Flak 43/1
Height	2.96 m		
Weight	25 tons	Weapon, ball mounted	7.92mm MG 34
Fuel capacity	470 liters		
Maximum speed	38 km/hr (23.56 mph)	Engine make	Maybach
		Engine model	HL 120 TRM
Range, on road	200 km (124 miles)	Engine configuration	V-12, liquid cooled
Range, cross country	130 km (80.6 miles)	Engine displacement	11.9 liters
Crew	5	Engine horsepower	272 @ 2800 rpm

The pilot model of the Ostwind, shown here (no photos of production versions have surfaced), was built using a remanufactured Panzerkampfwagen IV Ausf. G chassis. Production vehicles used new chassis incorporating a Tiger I turret ring and with a relocated radio operator's hatch.

The turret of the production vehicle would have overhung most of the forward part of the superstructure due to its larger turret ring. This was needed to provide room to properly serve the 3.7 cm Flak.

While the Wirbelwind (background) was the most effective self-propelled antiaircraft system fielded in quantity by Germany, a weapon with a heavier punch was desired. The Ostwind, armed with 3.7 cm Flak 43/1, was to have been the answer to this problem.

Military History Institute, Carlisle Barracks, PA

Walter J. Spielberger

Walter J. Spielberger

Contracts for the production of Ostwind turrets were awarded in September of 1944. Allied bombing caused repeated delays, however, and only a handful of vehicles were actually completed.

Walter J. Spielberger

Like the Wirbelwind, the Ostwind had a five-man crew. Unlike the Wirbelwind, two different men served as gunner and commander. The offset position of the radio operator's hatch identifies this as the pilot vehicle.

Walter J. Spielberger

"Kugelblitz"

In January 1944, with the Allies having achieved air supremacy, the need for a flakpanzer with a high rate of accurate fire, and protection for its crew, was becoming urgent. It was suggested that a 3 cm flak gun with turret, originally developed for use on U-boats, be trial fitted to a Panzer IV as a solution to this problem.

The transplantation of the U-boat turret was not successful, but the idea remained and a new turret was designed by Daimler-Benz. The new installation, resembling an oversized aircraft ball turret, mounted twin 3 cm M103 belt-fed aircraft cannon. This new turret was to be mounted on a redesigned Panzer IV chassis. The redesign involved the installation of a Tiger I turret ring and relocating the driver's and radio operator's hatches to accommodate the larger ring.

In July 1944, Daimler-Benz was ordered to produce two trial vehicles in September, with series production

to begin by Stahlindustrie in January. However, the aggressive air and ground campaign being waged by the Allies prevented this plan from being implemented, and ultimately only three Kubelblitz were completed.

Flakpanzerkampfwagen IV Kugelblitz

Length	5.92 m	Weapon, main	2 x 3 cm M.K.103
Width	2.95 m		
Height	2.40 m	Weapon, ball mounted	7.92mm MG 34
Weight	23 tons		
Fuel capacity	470 liters	Ammunition, main	1,200 rnds
Maximum speed	38 km/hr (23.56 mph)	Ammunition, secondary	1,200 rnds
Range, on road	200 km (124 miles)	Engine make	Maybach
		Engine model	HL 120 TRM
Range, cross country	130 km (80.6 miles)	Engine configuration	V-12, liquid cooled
Crew	5	Engine displacement	11.9 liters
Communica-tions	Fu 5 and Fu 2	Engine horsepower	272 @2800 rpm

Patton Museum, Fort Knox, KY

Although records indicate three Kugelblitz were completed, no photographic evidence of their use has yet surfaced. It is unclear whether this image is a heavily retouched photo of one of these vehicles, or an artist's rendering.

The Kugelblitz had the only totally enclosed turret mounted on a Flakpanzer during the war. Its design was a bit cramped, despite the large Tiger turret ring.

Patton Museum, Fort Knox, KY

A light touch would have been required on the trigger to be effective on the Kugelblitz, despite the 1,200 rounds of 3 cm ammunition on board. This was due to the cannon's 15 rounds-per-second appetite.

8.8 cm Flak auf Sonderfahrgestell (Pz.Sfl.IVc)

The chassis of this vehicle was developed to provide a mounting for 8.8 cm Flak guns for use as an assault gun. Later, this was revised to be a Panzerjäger, but by the end of 1941 even this idea had been abandoned. In June of 1942, this chassis design was again revived, this time for use as a Flakpanzer. With this intention, two experimental models were ordered from Krupp, with delivery anticipated in mid-1943.

By this time it had been decided to arm the vehicle with an 8.8 cm Flak 41. Like many of Germany's wartime production goals, this order was not met. By November 1943, neither vehicle had been completed, and the Luftwaffe, which was responsible for these vehicles procurement, cancelled the second unit. In January of 1944, citing a variety of reasons, Reichminister Speer ordered an end to development work on the 8.8 cm Flak auf Sonderfahrgestell (Pz.Sfl.IVc).

The sole example was finally tested in March 1944 in Denmark. The weapon that had been installed was worn and obsolete, and was replaced with an 8.8 cm Flak 37. After conversion, it was shipped to Heeres Flakartillerie-Abteilung (Sf) 304, which was assigned to the 26th Panzer Division for troop trials in Italy.

8.8 cm Flak auf Sonderfahrgestell (Pz.Sfl.IVc)			
Length	7.00 m	Communications	Fu.Spr.Ger.
Width	3.00 m		
Height	2.80 m	Weapon, main	8.8 cm Flak 41
Weight	26 tons		
Fuel capacity	600 liters	Ammo stowage, main	48
Maximum speed	60 km/hr (37.2 mph)	Engine make	Maybach
Range, on road	300 km (186 miles)	Engine model	HL90P
Range, cross country	200 km (124 miles)	Engine configuration	V-12, liquid cooled
Crew	9	Engine displacement	9.0 liters
		Engine horsepower	360 @ 3600 rpm

Looking somewhat like an enlarged Mobelwagen, the 8.8 cm Flak auf Sonderfahrgestell (Pz.Sfl.IVc) poses for a photo at the Krupp plant. Originally intended as a bunker buster, the chassis evolved into a Flakpanzer.

Patton Museum, Fort Knox, KY

Even with the sides down, the Flak 41 looks huge. Problems with battery fire control was a primary reason for this project's abandonment.

Patton Museum, Fort Knox, KY

The sides of the vehicle were hinged, allowing them to fold down to form platforms for the gun crew and provide room for the weapon to traverse. The armor protection was adequate only against small arms and splinters. The Flak 37 has been fitted on this vehicle..

Patton Museum, Fort Knox, KY

Self-propelled fully tracked howitzers and mortars

15cm sIG auf Pz. Kpfw. I Ausf. B

Due to the need to provide fire support to armored infantry units, in February 1940 Alkett converted 38 obsolete Panzer IB tanks into self-propelled artillery. The turrets and superstructure were removed from the tanks, and a tall gun shield was mounted on the chassis, increasing the overall height of the vehicle to more than 10 feet. The gun shield protected the gun crew from frontal fire, and had a bit of shielding on the sides. The top and rear were open.

Behind the gun shield was a 15cm sIG heavy infantry howitzer complete with its normal field carriage. A crew of five served the vehicle and piece. Only three ready rounds were carried on the vehicle, but an Sd.Kfz. 10 served as an ammunition carrier for the vehicle, as well as transport for three of the crew.

The chassis of the 15cm sIG auf Pz. Kpfw. I Ausf. B was overloaded by the addition of the field piece and its armored shield which, coupled with its raised center of gravity, limited its mobility. These vehicles saw active service in Heavy Infantry (SP) companies from mid-1940 through mid-1943 in campaigns from Belgium to Russia.

15 cm schwere Infanteriegeschütz (mot S) Pz Kpfw I Ausf B

Length	4.42 m	Weapon, main	15 cm s.I.G. 33 L/11
Width	2.17 m	Ammo stowage, main	3 rnds
Height	2.70		
Weight	7 tons	Engine make	Maybach
Fuel capacity	146 liters	Engine model	NL 38 Tr
Maximum speed	40 km/hr (24.8 mph)	Engine configuration	six-cylinder
Range, on road	170 km (105.4 miles)	Engine displacement	3.8 liters
Range, cross country	115 km (71.3 miles)	Engine horsepower	100 @ 3000 rpm
Crew	4		

Patton Museum, Fort Knox, KY

The 15 cm schwere Infanteriegeschuetz (mot S) Pz Kpfw I Ausf B was an excellent example of how the German Army reused obsolete chassis. A standard 15 cm schwere Infanteriegeschuetz-towed field piece was simply placed atop an otherwise obsolete Panzerkampfwagen I Ausf. B chassis and a gun shield installed in front of it.

Walter J. Spielberger

The large cannon could be fired with devastating effect at soft targets, and was well suited for supporting infantry in assaults. This vehicle was photographed on a snowy Russian road.

Walter J. Spielberger

Though ungainly looking, the Infanteriegeschuetz's simple design allowed for rapid replacement of damaged or worn chassis with a minimum of tools.

Military History Institute

Just visible on the left rear fender of this Infanteriegeschuetz are two of the woven containers that each contained one round for the field piece.

15 cm sIG33 auf Fgst Pz Kpfw II (Sf)

The mounting of the 15 cm sIG33 heavy infantry howitzer on the Panzerkampfwagen I chassis was considered a qualified success. Its shortcomings were its tall profile and its reliance on the obsolescent Panzerkampfwagen I chassis.

In 1940, attempts were made to mount the heavy field piece on the more modern Panzerkampfwagen II chassis. Testing revealed that the standard tank chassis was not large enough to mount the heavy gun and service the piece. Therefore, a trial series of vehicles were ordered built on modified chassis. The modifications included widening the hull and lengthening it enough so that an additional roadwheel was required. Additional space was gained by mounting the engine transversely. Rather than mounting

15 cm sIG33 on a Panzerkampfwagen II as originally intended, a new chassis utilizing some Panzerkampfwagen II components had been created.

The 12 trial vehicles were issued as two companies of self-propelled heavy howitzers, the 707th and 708th. In 1942, both companies were dispatched to North Africa, where the chassis proved woefully inadequate for the rigors of the desert. Grossly underpowered and difficult to maneuver, their engines responded by overheating, leading to the 90th light division, to which they were assigned, to report the vehicles as unusable.

After El Alamein, the British captured half of the total production in local repair shops.

15 cm schwere Infanteriegeschütz 33B Sfl.

Length	5.48 m		Weapon, main	15 cm s.I.G. 33B
Width	2.60 m		Ammo stowage, main	10 rnds
Height	1.98			
Weight	16 tons		Engine make	Büssing
Maximum speed	45 km/hr (27.9 mph)		Engine model	Typ GS
Range, on road	100 km (62 mph)		Engine configuration	eight-cyl., liquid cooled
Crew	4		Engine displacement	7.91 liters
Communications	Fu.Spr. Geraet a		Engine horsepower	155 @ 3000 rpm

Patton Museum, Fort Knox, KY

North Africa was the site of the only deployment of the 15cm sIG33 mounted on a Panzerkampfwagen II-based chassis. The heavy howitzer itself was a potent weapon, but the chassis was an inadequate carriage for it.

One of Alkett's design goals for the 15cm sIG33 auf Fgst Pz Kpfw II (Sf) was to create a vehicle with a lower silhouette than the 15cm sIG33 on Panzerkampfwagen I chassis had presented. In this it succeeded, as the new vehicle was about the same height as a standard Panzerkampfwagen II.

Patton Museum, Fort Knox, KY

Howitzers are indirect-fire weapons, lobbing shells at targets, rather than firing along line of sight. This makes them effective at hitting targets behind structures and berms, as well as being able to strike the relatively vulnerable upper surfaces of tanks. The weapon here is at its maximum elevation.

Leichte Feldhaubitze 18/2 auf Fgst Pz Kpfw II (Sf) (Sd Kfz 124) "Wespe"

While many innovative tanks were designed and produced by Germany during the course of WWII, self-propelled artillery design tended to be placed on the back burner. Existent tank chassis were often converted to serve as a basis for the mobile artillery. Some conversions meant little more than the removing the turret and placing a field piece on top of the hull. The "Wespe" (Wasp) was a little more advanced than that. While based on the Panzerkampfwagen II components, the engine was moved forward and the drivetrain shortened to make room for a large open-topped fighting compartment at the rear. Not

On production Wespe such as this one the front of the driver's compartment was squared and its front plage hinged to open for greater visibility. This vehicle lacks the stowage boxes often seen on th front of the superstructure, but its crew has stored fuel containers and spark track on the side and front of the hull.

The entire crew of this Wespe has clambered into the fighting compartment for this photo on the Eastern front. The Panzerkampfwagen heritage of the vehicle is evident in the suspension and front hull. The stowage boxes mounted on the outer front of the fighting compartment were a popular unit-made conversion, given the cramped conditions in the vehicle.

Dust and dirt fly and the crew of the howitzer hang on tightly as a Wespe ascends a rise in the terrain at speed. The torsion bar suspension gave a relatively smooth ride over such terrain. Note the MG 34 on the superstructure front. This was the field gun's only defense against aircraft or infantry attack.

This is the preproduction prototype of the Sd. Kfz. 124. The rounded front, protruding driver's compartment and wide flat muzzle brake were distinguishing features of this vehicle. The basic form of the vehicle, however, was to remain unchanged through its entire production run of 676 vehicles.

This captured Wespe, under evaluation by the British, has lost its muffler, although one of the muffler mounting straps is still present. "Wespe" was one of a number of vehicle names which was officially discouraged beginning in early 1944.

having to mount the field piece above the engine allowed the vehicle to have a much lower profile than would otherwise have been possible.

Famo began production of these vehicles in February 1943 and the vehicles remained in production through June 1944. Though intended as an interim vehicle, the Wespe served throughout the war.

Leichte Feldhaubitze 18/2 auf Fgst Pz Kpfw II (Sf) (Sd Kfz 124) "Wespe"

Length	4.81 m	Communications	Fu.Spr. Geraet f
Width	2.28 m	Weapon, main	10.5 cm le.F.H. 18/2
Height	2.30 m		
Weight	11 tons	Ammo stowage, main	32 rnds
Fuel capacity	200 liters		
Maximum speed	40 km/hr (24.8 mph)	Engine make	Maybach
		Engine model	HL62TR
Range, on road	140 km (86.8 miles)	Engine configuration	six-cyl., liquid cooled
Range, cross country	95 km (58.9 miles)	Engine displacement	6.23 liters
Crew	5	Engine horsepower	140 @ 2600 rpm

Military History Institute, Carlisle Barracks, PA.

The upper portion of the rear armor plating was hinged. This allowed it to be folded out, allowing easier ammunition resupply as well as greater freedom of movement by the gun crew. The brackets just below the hinge line originally held aiming stakes.

Military History Institute, Carlisle Barracks, PA

The bulk of the small, cramped fighting compartment was filled with the 10.5 cm Leichte Feldhaubitze 18/2 (light field howitzer). Four men also rode and worked in this area, which left room for only 32 rounds of 10.5 cm ammunition. This was a two-part ammunition with the propellant and the projectile separate.

This crew posed with their nearly new self-propelled howitzer. Notice the headlight with blackout cover on the front fender and the spare track section stowed on the front of the hull. This gave the vehicle needed spare parts and additional protection from incoming rounds striking the hull front.

Patton Museum, Fort Knox, KY

The Wespe was reliable, though cramped, and, despite being based on an obsolescent tank chassis, served on every front throughout the war.

Bundesarchiv photo.

Geschützwagen 38 füer s.I.G. 33/1 (Sf)(Sd.Kfz. 138/1) "Grille"

As Germany's military moved towards mechanization, it was natural for it to want to increase the mobility of field artillery as well. The 15 cm sIG (schwere Infanteriegeschütz) 33 had been developed in the early 1930s. Termed a heavy infantry howitzer, the tube was originally mounted on carriages suitable for towing either by vehicle, or by horse. The limitations of towed artillery are many, chief of which is the emplacement time. After attempts at mounting this formidable field piece alternately on Panzerkampfwagen I or Panzerkampfwagen II chassis (discussed elsewhere in this book), the proven Panzerkampfwagen 38 (t) chassis was tried as a motor carriage.

Work on a gun mount for the new vehicle was begun by Skoda in mid-1941, but a year later responsibility for the project had been shifted to Rheinmetall-Borsig. Rheinmetall-Borsig was the firm that had originally developed the towed version of this howitzer. An all-new mount was designed, although the recoil mechanism and tube of the towed field piece were retained.

Alkett was tasked with adapting the Czech light tank chassis for its new use. Ultimately, the 38 (t) chassis was equipped with an all-new superstructure from the fender line up. The new superstructure was made of thin armor plate and open topped, so it provided only basic protection for the crew and ammunition from small arms

The prototype of the Grille, shown here, differed only in details from the production vehicles. The stowage was slightly different, as were the fender supports. In this view the howitzer has been raised to its maximum 72-degree elevation.

Charles Kliment collection.

This BMM factory photograph of a Geschützwagen 38 füer s.I.G. 33/1 (Sf)(Sd.Kfz. 138/1), or Grille, provides an excellent view of the howitzer's travel lock. Two visors, one on the front and one of the right corner of the superstructure, were provided for the driver.

Stefan De Meyer collection

This Ausf. H Grille had its radio rack mounted centered on the left wall of the fighting compartment. A box for stowing the periscopic sight was mounted at the top of the short angular armor plate near the front of the superstructure.

CKD archive via Kliment collection

This view from the left of the Grille looking into the fighting compartment shows four canvas ammunition containers hanging from the right superstructure wall. Boxes for charges are just forward of bags.

CKD archive via Kliment collection

CKD archive via Kliment collection

The interior of the fighting compartment of the Grille had little space to spare. Shown here is an Ausf. H. Five men worked in this small area. The 15 cm field piece was termed a schwere Infanteriegeschütz (s.I.G.), or heavy infantry howitzer.

Netik

This is another configuration of the Grille interior layout. Note the relocated radio rack and charge boxes compared to the other photos.

CKD archive via Kliment collection

The tapered walls of the superstructure minimized the vehicle's silhouette. Being lightly armored and often remaining stationary for extended periods, concealment was a major concern for artillery. The low profile helped.

Geschützwagen 38 füer s.I.G. 33/1 (Sf)(Sd.Kfz. 138/1) "Grille"

Length	5.6 m	Communication	Fu.Spr.16
Width	2.15 m		
Height	2.40 m	Weapon, main	15 cm s.I.G. 33/1
Weight	11.5 tons		
Fuel capacity	218 liters	Ammo stowage, main	15 rnds
Maximum speed	42 km/hr (26.04 mph)	Engine make	Praga
Range, on road	185 km (114.7 miles)	Engine model	TNHPS/II
Range, cross country	140 km (86.8 miles)	Engine configuration	six-cyl., liquid cooled
Crew	5	Engine displacement	7.75 liters
		Engine horsepower	150 @ 2600 rpm

and splinters. However, this was deemed sufficient given that this vehicle was intended for infantry support, rather than breakthrough roles.

A trial vehicle was delivered in April 1942, and was well received. This led to BMM being awarded a contract for production of the new self-propelled howitzers, termed Geschützwagen 38 füer s.I.G. 33/1 (Sf)(Sd.Kfz. 138/1). However, the vehicle was commonly known as "Grille," or cricket. Between February and June of 1943 BMM delivered 200 of these vehicles. The first 90 were built on Ausf. H chassis, with the remainder built on Ausf. K chassis. A final batch of 10 were built in October of that year.

The Grille was provided to Panzer-Grenadier-Regiments in companies of six vehicles. The Grille provided excellent service and was used throughout the remainder of the war.

Stefan De Meyer collection

Footman loops near the top of the armored sides were used to secure a canvas cover. This was only installed in non-combat situations and is rarely seen in photographs. Similar loops lower on the side were used to secure camouflage.

Patton Museum, Fort Knox, KY

The Panzerkampfwagen 38 (t), upon which the Grille was based, had a ball-mounted machine gun on the left front of the hull. However, no such weapon was provided on the Grille as it was not intended to operate at the front. Hence, no visors are present on this side of the vehicle.

Stefan De Meyer collection

Large numbers of Grille were first used on the Eastern front. As was the custom of armies operating in snowy climates, this Grille has been camouflaged by white washing. Operation through mud and thaw has removed much of the whitewash from the road wheels.

Geschützwagen 38 M füer s.I.G. 33/2 (Sf)(Sd. Kfz. 138/1) "Grille"

While the Geschützwagen 38 füer s.I.G. 33/1 (Sf)(Sd.Kfz. 138/1) "Grille" was considered a success by the Waffenamt, there was still room for improvement. The fighting compartment was cramped, the vehicle was poorly balanced and it was felt that its barn-like sides presented too large of a target.

Therefore, efforts were made to mount the 10.5 cm howitzer in the mid-engined 38(t)-based chassis developed for the Panzerjaeger 38 Ausf. M. The larger bore of the schwere infanteriegeschütz required that the superstructure sides and front be modified for the chassis 's new role.

Designated the Geschützwagen 38 Ausf. K, production began by BMM in December 1943 and continued through August 1944. During this time period 152 of the contracted 200 vehicles were produced. The increased need for tank hunters caused the production emphasis to be shifted to the Jagdpanzer 38 at that time. A further 17 Geschützwagen 38 Ausf. K were produced in February and March of 1945. In the field these vehicles were used interchangeably with the earlier Geschützwagen 38 füer s.I.G. 33/1 (Sf)(Sd.Kfz. 138/1) "Grille."

The improved Grille, with its engine relocated centrally, was a better-balanced vehicle than its predecessor. This arrangement was based on that used by the Panzerjaeger 38.

CKD archive via Kliment collection

Geschützwagen 38 M füer s.I.G. 33/2 (Sf)(Sd. Kfz. 138/1) "Grille"

Length	4.835 m	Communica- tion	Fu.Spr.16
Width	2.150 m	Weapon, main	15 cm s.I.G. 33/1
Height	2.400 m		
Weight	11.5 tons	Ammo stowage, main	15 rnds
Fuel capacity	218 liters		
Maximum speed	42 km/hr (26.04 mph)	Engine make	Praga
		Engine model	AC
Range, on road	185 km (114.7 miles)	Engine configuration	six-cylinder, liquid cooled
Range, cross country	140 km (86.8 miles)	Engine displacement	7.75 liters
Crew	5	Engine horsepower	150 @ 2600 rpm

Although not readily apparent, the new style superstructure did offer the crew a little more room in the fighting compartment, but it was still far from spacious. The circular racks visible primarily on the right of this photo held the projectiles. The adjacent square boxes held the propellant charges.

CKD archive via Kliment collection

The driver's compartment projected from the sloping front plate of the Grille and incorporated visors permitting visibility forward and to the right. Spare track links were stowed on the hull front and on left side of the glacis to serve both as replacement parts and as supplemental armor.

Viewed from the behind with the rear apron closed, the muffler is visible. The Ausf. K utilized a Praga AC engine, while the earlier model was powered with a TNHPS/II from the same manufacturer.

A factory-fresh Grille Ausf. K with its gun at maximum elevation. Notice how the top bows have been disengaged and swung toward the rear to make way for the gun crew.

Prepared for a road march or rail transport, this Grille has its canvas cover in place over the fighting compartment and its cannon secured in its travel lock. Despite the success of this design, production was curtailed in order to produce more tank killers, required by Germany's increasingly defensive position.

Ordnance Museum, Aberdeen Proving Ground, MD

The shield beneath the howitzer was hinged and spring-loaded on the Ausf. K, unlike the sliding shield used previously. This Grille was photographed not long after the war at Aberdeen Proving Ground in Maryland.

Patton Museum, Fort Knox, KY

This captured Grille, being evaluated by the British, has lost much of its exhaust system. However, it retains the wires strung about its superstructure to aid in the attachment of foliage for camouflage purposes.

Patton Museum, Fort Knox, KY

Most Grilles, rather than being captured, met a violent end. The thin armor, coupled with large amounts of propellant powder and projectile explosives, often meant that enemy hits were fatal.

15 cm s.I.G. 33/2 (Sf) on Bergepanzerwagen 38

This little vehicle is shrouded in a cloak of mystery. For the past 40 years various sources have stated that up to 24 of these vehicles were built either from converted Bergepanzerwagen 38 or as new construction based on that chassis. However, no reliable documentation has surfaced to support these claims. Indeed, there is no mention of

series production of these vehicles in either the BMM or Škoda records. These vehicles were reportedly produced as a stopgap measure to provide troops with a self-propelled

Photographed outside the Boemisch-Märische Maschinenfabrik (BMM) plant is a 15 cm s.I.G. 33/2 (Sf) on Bergepanzerwagen 38.

As the howitzer was elevated, a spring-loaded shield rose to close the opening in the frontal armor.

The open-topped superstructure of the Bergepanzer was extended upward, forming a superstructure around the s.I.G. 33/2., the same weapon mounted on the Marder Ausf. K.

15 cm s.I.G. 33/2 (Sf) on Bergepanzerwagen 38

Length	4.87 m	**Ammo stowage, main**	15 rnds
Width	2.63 m		
Height	2.40 m	**Ammo stowage, secondary**	600 rnds
Weight	16.5 tons		
Maximum speed	38 km/hr (23.56 mph)	**Engine make**	Praga
		Engine model	AE
Range, on road	130 km (80.6 miles)	**Engine configuration**	six-cyl., liquid cooled
Crew	4	**Engine displacement**	7.75 liters
Weapon, main	15 cm s.I.G. 33/2 L/11	**Engine horsepower**	150 @ 2600 rpm
Weapon, secondary	7.92mm MG34		

howitzer after Grille production had ceased. Like the late Grille, this vehicle was armed with the 15 cm s.I.G. 33/2 cannon. Only this handful of photographs, apparently of a prototype, proves the vehicle existed at all.

Patton Museum, Fort Knox, KY

Faintly visible in this photograph are the shell racks and charge boxes. The 15 cm howitzer was a powerful weapon and a valuable asset to infantry movements.

CKD archives via Kliment collection

The muffler for the rear-mounted engine is visible here, as are the usual tow cable and spare track stowage. There are no known survivors of this vehicle type.

With its forward-mounted gun, this vehicle was in many ways a return to the Geschützwagen 38 füer s.I.G. 33/1 (Sf)(Sd. Kfz. 138/1) "Grille" design. It is unknown if more than this one vehicle was built on the Bergepanzer chassis.

Patton Museum, Fort Knox, KY

L.g.s.F.H.13 (Sfl.) auf Lorraine-Schlepper

When France fell, Germany captured a large number of relatively new French Lorraine carriers. Rather than scrap these fine vehicles, the Germans used them as chassis for self-propelled artillery. Alkett began converting 30 of these vehicles in June of 1942, and due to their urgent need by Rommel, completed all 30 that same month. The weapon mounted was the formidable 15 cm heavy field howitzer 13.

Immediately dispatched to North Africa, seven of the vehicles were lost in transit. The remaining 23 vehicles performed admirably, but all were lost in combat by the end of the year. The powerful cannon mounted on the reliable and mobile Lorraine chassis proved an excellent combination.

Meantime, an additional 64 vehicles were converted at Army depots in Paris in July and August of 1942. These were issued on the basis of six per battery to Gepanzerte Artillerie-Regiments 1 (Sfl) and 2 (Sfl). Gepanzerte Artillerie-Regiments 2 (Sfl) was later reorganized as Artillerie-Regiment 931 and still later as Panzer-Artillerie-Regiment 155 for the 21st Panzer Division. All were involved in the fighting at Normandy, and by the end of 1944 only one L.g.s.F.H.13 (Sfl.) auf Lorraine-Schlepper was left.

L.g.s.F.H.13 (Sfl.) auf Lorraine-Schlepper

Length	5.31 m	Communications	FuG Spr f
Width	1.83 m	Weapon, main	15 cm sFH13/1
Height	2.23 m		
Weight	8.49 tons	Ammo stowage, main	8 rnds
Fuel capacity	111 liters		
Maximum Speed	34 km/hr (21.08 mph)	Engine make	DelaHaye
		Engine model	103TT
Range, on road	135 km (83.7 miles)	Engine configuration	six-cylinder
Range, cross country	88 km (54.56 mph)	Engine displacement	3.55 l
Crew	4	Engine horsepower	70 @ 2800 rpm

This vehicle was captured intact by the British in North Africa. Built by the Germans on captured French Lorraine personnel/ammunition carrier chassis, the L.g.s.F.H.13Sfl. auf Lorraine-Schlepper was one of the more effective pieces of self-propelled artillery in this theater.

Patton Museum, Fort Knox, KY

The vehicles supplied to the Afrika Korps were converted by Alkett. German Army depot forces converted other units, which were retained on the western front.

The narrow width of the vehicle, less than 6 feet, is apparent in this view, as is the large bore of the howitzer. Note the open visor.

A ground anchor was installed on the rear of the vehicle. This spade was lowered when firing so that it could transfer recoil forces to the ground and lessen the punishment on the vehicle's suspension and brakes.

Radio racks, antenna mounts and ammunition stowage are all visible in this overhead view taken during evaluation of a captured L.g.s.F.H.13Sfl. auf Lorraine-Schlepper.

Two styles of howitzer travel lock were used. The style used here used a T-cross-sectioned lug that engaged the rest. The other style, visible in the photos taken in North Africa, used a simple rest.

Later ground anchors were longer than the early models, perhaps a result of lessons learned in the field. The spade was raised using a winch, to which it was connected via the chain visible here.

The early, short ground spade had to be operated from outside the vehicle, which was a definite hindrance to quick escape from attack. The heavy construction of the anchor was indicative of the recoil forces of the howitzer.

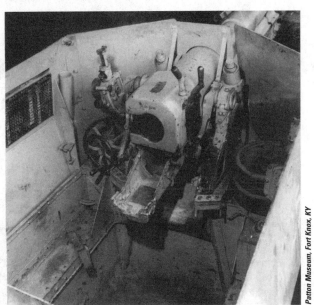

Aiming of the weapon was done manually. With only eight rounds stowed on board, both accurate fire and support vehicles were a necessity.

15cm s Pz H 18/1 auf Fgst Pz III/IV (Sf) (Sd Kfz 165) "Hummel"

The Sd. Kfz. 165 was originally conceived as a stop-gap self-propelled mount for the 15 cm field howitzer. Using an amalgamation of previously tried components, the design firm of Rheinmetall-Borsig/Alkett created a vehicle with the proven transmission, steering units and final drive from the Panzerkampfwagen III. The suspension and engine used in the Panzerkampfwagen IV were adopted. The hull and superstructure were newly designed especially for this vehicle.

With the gearboxes in the front and howitzer mounted in the rear, the engine had to be placed in the center of the vehicle. The tall, open-topped fighting compartment offered only modest armored protection, resisting only shell fragments and bullets up to 7.92mm.

The first vehicles of an eventual 881-unit production run were completed in February, 1943. Despite being intended as an interim vehicle, the "Hummel," or Bumble Bee, remained in production throughout the war. Unarmed versions were built to serve as ammunition carriers to support the armed vehicles.

The Hummels were deployed in batteries of six, with their first combat coming July 5, 1943, while taking part in Operation Zitadelle.

15cm s Pz H 18/1 auf Fgst Pz III/IV (Sf) (Sd Kfz 165) "Hummel"

Length	7.17 m	Weapon, secondary	MG34
Width	2.97 m		
Height	2.81 m	Ammo stowage, main	18
Weight	23 tons		
Fuel capacity	600 liters	Ammo stowage, secondary	600
Maximum speed	25 km/hr (15.5 mph)		
Range, on road	215 km (133.3 miles)	Engine make	Maybach
		Engine model	HL 120 TRM
Range, cross country	135 km (83.7 miles)	Engine configuration	V-12, liquid cooled
Crew	6	Engine displacement	11.9 liters
Communications	Fu.Spr.Ger. f	Engine horsepower	265 @ 2600 rpm
Weapon, main	15 cm s.F.H. 18/1		

The side-mounted cooling air grilles for the centrally located engine are evident on this Hummel trial vehicle. The high profile of the vehicle is also apparent. The muzzle brake was not a feature included on series vehicles.

Ordnance Museum, Aberdeen Proving Ground

Half of a battery of six Hummel vehicles prepare to fire. Armor piercing, high-explosive, demolition and smoke ammunition rounds were available for the 15 cm howitzer. Its maximum range was 14,630 yards. Like all howitzers, it was designed for indirect fire—lobbing the shell at the target—thus the high elevation of the gun.

The open-topped body of the Hummel meant that the crews were exposed to the weather. The crews of these vehicles are bundled up to face a cruel winter. The lightweight framework attached to the front of the vehicle was used by the driver to crudely aim the piece.

This crewman is freeing the travel lock on the howitzer in preparation of elevating the weapon. The mounting base for the radio antenna is visible on the side of the vehicle just behind the headlight.

Patton Museum, Fort Knox, KY

Late model Hummels, such as this one, did not have mufflers. The four-man gun crew, plus commander, worked in rather cramped surroundings. The alternately colored poles affixed to the rear of Hummels were painted red and white and were ranging devices used in the howitzer's indirect fire mission.

Patton Museum, Fort Knox, KY

With the main gun elevated, the weapon is ready to fire. The back doors are open to provide easy access for the crew. The muffler visible on the rear of the vehicle is indicative of an early vehicle.

Patton Museum, Fort Knox, KY

With very little armor, and little secondary armament, concealment was the Hummel's best defense.

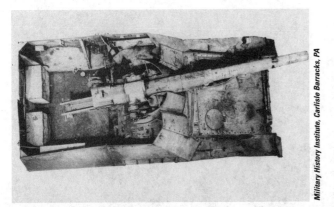

The general layout of the open-topped fighting compartment can be seen here. The main weapon could be traversed 15 degrees left or right of center. The open design presented a tempting target for grenade and moltov cocktail-armed enemy soldiers, as well as exposing the crew to shell fragments.

This Hummel has been fitted with an elaborate mesh covering to keep out grenades, but it does little to protect the crew from the surrounding cold of the Russian winter.

The crew of this Ninth SS Division has slung a camouflage net across the howitzer barrel and stowed poles to support it on the travel lock. However, the dark yellow and green paint scheme stands out against the stark white snow-covered Russian countryside.

Early in 1944, the front of the Hummel was redesigned so that the front plate of the driver's compartment extended across the full width of the superstructure, as seen on these two late production vehicles. This enlarged the radio operator's compartment. The lead vehicle here also has a tarp covering part of the fighting compartment.

The very final version of the Hummel had shrouding placed over the grilles. The all-steel return rollers were instituted in response to the critical rubber shortage in Germany.

10.5 cm le.F.H.16 Geschützpanzer

When the British forces were withdrawn from France they left behind a number of serviceable vehicles. Among these were a number of Light Tanks Mark VI. Six of these were taken over by Artillerie-Regiment 227, which had a 10.5 cm light field howitzer mounted on each of them in an open-topped armored superstructure. The six vehicles entered service in October 1941.

The light field howitzer 16 was a proven weapon, with adequate range and good bursting qualities. A ground spade was installed at the rear to stabilize the vehicle when firing the howitzer above charge three. No secondary weapon was installed. Instead, close-in defense was provided by machinepistols fired by the gun crew.

10.5 cm le.F.H.16 Geschützpanzer

Length	4.00 m	Crew	4
Width	2.20 m	Communications	Fu.Spr.Ger
Height	2.00 m		
Weight	6.5 tons	Weapon, main	10.5 cm le.F.H.16
Fuel capacity	159 liters		
		Engine make	Meadows
Maximum speed	50 km/hr (31 mph)	Engine configuration	six-cyl., liquid cooled
Range, on road	280 km (173.6 miles)	Engine displacement	4.43 liter
Range, cross country	180 km (111.6 miles)	Engine horsepower	68 @ 3000 rpm

Patton Museum, Fort Knox, KY

The light field howitzer 16 was nearly obsolete when it was adapted as self-propelled artillery by installing it on a motor carriage. The chassis began life as a British Mark VI light tank, which had left behind in France.

Patton Museum, Fort Knox, KY

Though compact, the vehicle had adequate space for a three-man gun crew plus driver. With a top speed of 50 km/hr31 mph, the Geschützpanzer was faster than many of its contemporaries.

The driver is faintly visible in his compartment in this view, while the commander, loader and gunner ride in the open-topped superstructure. They are protected by 22mm frontal armor and 15mm-thick side armor.

Military History Institute, Carlisle Barracks, PA

10.5 cm le.F.H. 16 auf gep.Sfl. FCM

Immediately prior to the war, the French had begun purchasing a new series of light tanks. The FCM-36 was a design competitive to the R-35, and featured welded hull construction. However, the diesel-powered FCM-36 was considerably more expensive than the R-35, so only 100 were procured.

After the fall of France, the German military found itself in possession of these vehicles. In the fall of 1942, eight of these were modified as self-propelled artillery by mounting the proven 10.5 cm le.F.H. 16 field howitzer. To accomplish this conversion, the turret of the tank was removed and a boxy armored superstructure added to house the field piece.

These eight vehicles were assigned to the 1st and 2nd Batteries of gepanzerte Artillerie-Abteilung (Sfl) z.B.V. By 1944, all eight had been lost.

10.5 cm le.F.H. 16 auf gep.Sfl. FCM			
Length	4.60 m	Weapon, main	10.5 cm le.F.H. 16
Width	2.14 m		
Height	2.15 m	Weapon, secondary	7.92mm MG
Weight	12.2 tons		
Fuel capacity	260 liters	Ammo stowage, main	50 rnds
Maximum speed	28 km/hr (17.36 mph)	Ammo stowage, secondary	2,000 rnds
Range, on road	200 km (124 miles)	Engine make	Ricardo-Berliet
Crew	4	Engine configuration f	our-cylinder, diesel
Communications	Fu.Spr.Ger.	Engine horsepower	91 @ 1550 rpm

Walter J. Spielberger

Extensive modifications were required to mount the dated le.F.H. 16 on the FCM chassis, which may have contributed to the decision to only construct eight of the unwieldy-looking vehicles.

Much of the interior was devoted to ammunition stowage. The rounds were stowed tip-down in special racks. Note the striped aiming poles, needed for indirect fire, stowed on the fender.

Walter J. Spielberger

The compact size of the self-propelled howitzer is apparent when compared to the soldier posing in front of this one. While a compact size was beneficial for maneuverability and concealment, it did create hardships for the gun crew.

Patton Museum, Fort Knox, KY

Geschützwagen IVb für 10.5 cm le.F.H.18/1(Sf) (Sd Kfz 165/1)

In September of 1939, Wa Pruef 6 received a design proposal from Krupp for a purpose-built self-propelled howitzer. Unlike earlier motorized artillery, this was not an adapted or converted vehicle. It was expressly designed for this role.

A 10.5 cm le.F.H. 18/1 was mounted in an open-topped turret. The light field howitzer could be rotated in this turret through a 70-degree arc. The sides of the turret were tapered downward toward the rear, allowing excellent side visibility. The new vehicle, initially known as Pz.Sfl. IVb, was later designated Geschützwagen IVb für 10.5 cm le.F.H.18/1(Sf) (Sd Kfz 165/1).

Two vehicles were ordered for testing and were delivered in January 1942. Even before that, during Fall 1941, a series of 10 of the new vehicles were ordered for troop trials. Krupp-Grusonwerk produced these vehicles from August through December 1942. These test vehicles were assigned to Artillerie-Regiment 16 of the 16th Panzer Division and deployed to the Russian front.

Enthusiasm for the new design was such that even before the first vehicle was delivered, Krupp was in possession of a contract for 200 production vehicles. However, none of these were produced because it was discovered that an adequate carriage could be made from obsolete Panzerkampfwagen II chassis, allowing the valuable manufacturing capacity to be put to better use.

Geschützwagen IVb für 10.5 cm le.F.H.18/1(Sf) (Sd Kfz 165/1)

Length	5.90 m	Communications	Fu.Spr.Ger.f
Width	2.87 m	Weapon, main	10.5 cm le.F.H. 18/1
Height	2.25 m		
Weight	18 tons	Ammo stowage, main	60 rnds
Fuel capacity	410 liters	Engine make	Maybach
Maximum speed	35 km/h (21.7 mph)	Engine model	HL 66
Range, on road	240 km (148.8 miles)	Engine configuration	six-cyl., liquid cooled
Range, cross country	130 km (80.6 miles)	Engine displacement	6.6 liters
Crew	4	Engine horsepower	188 @ 3200 rpm

The Sd.Kfz. 165/1 utilized a suspension consisting of six dual roadwheels mounted in tandem pairs on leaf springs. This suspension, with 520mm-diameter wheels, had also been proposed for the Panzerkampfwagen IV.

Patton Museum, Fort Knox, KY

The turret was wider than the superstructure of the Sd Kfz 165/1, and the resultant overhang is visible in this photo taken at the Krupp-Grusonwerk facility..

A small muffler for the Maybach HL 66 engine was mounted at the rear of the hull. Spare track links were stowed on the back wall of the turret.

The tapered turret sides minimized weight and provided excellent vision for the howitzer's crew. The short hull required carefully planned stowage for the myriad of on-vehicle material on the Geschützwagen IVb.
Patton Museum, Fort Knox, KY

Patton Museum, Fort Knox, KY

The optical rangefinding and sighting equipment can be seen here, as can some of the ammunition stowage. The turret could only be traversed 35 degrees either side of center.

10.5 cm le.F.H. 18/3 (Sf.) auf Geschützwagen B2

When Germany conquered France, many of the French Army's serviceable vehicles were assimilated into the Wermacht. Some were used as they were, others were the basis for various conversions.

One such conversion was proposed for the Renault Char B and entailed mounting a flamethrower in place of the normal turret. As flamethrower tanks have limited range, and are thus somewhat vulnerable, it was desirable to provide an escort with cannon-armed vehicles. It was natural that they, too, would use the Char B chassis to provide a commonalty of replacement parts and skills.

While the idea of having flamethrower-equipped Char B tanks was abandoned after their unsuccessful use in Russia in mid-1941. Production of the howitzer-armed vehicles continued to be scheduled for early 1942.

Five of these vehicles, armed with 10.5 cm le.F.H. 18/3 howitzers in fixed superstructures, were produced in January 1942. Five more were delivered the following month, and the final six in March 1942.

These vehicle were shipped to the 26th Panzer Division, where they were assigned to the I.Abteilung/ Artillerie Regiment 93. In mid-1943 these vehicles were replaced with the new Wespe. It is not known if the 10.5 cm le.F.H. 18/3 (Sf.) auf Geschützwagen B2 saw combat use, or what their final fate was.

10.5 cm le.F.H. 18/3 (Sf.) auf Geschützwagen B2

Length	7.62 m	Communications	Fu.5
Width	2.40 m		
Height	3.00	Weapon, main	10.5 cm le.F.H. 18/3
Weight	32.5 tons		
Fuel capacity	400 liters	Weapon, secondary	7.92mm MG 34
Maximum speed	25 km/hr (15.5 mph)	Engine make	Renault
		Engine model	307
Range, on road	140 km (86.8 miles)	Engine configuration	six-cylinder, liquid cooled
Range, cross country	100 km (62 miles)	Engine displacement	16.5 liters
Crew	5	Engine horsepower	300 hp @ 1900 rpm

Sixteen captured French Renault Char B tanks were refitted with fixed superstructures and mounted with 10.5 cm howitzers in early 1942. The resultant vehicle was the 10.5 cm le.F.H. 18/3 (Sf.) auf Geschützwagen B2.

Patton Museum, Fort Knox, KY

Geschützwagen Lorraine-Schlepper füer le.F.H. 18/4

In addition to being used as carriages for the 15 cm howitzer, some of the captured Lorraine-Schlepper carriers were used to mount the 10.5 cm le.F.H. 18/4. An armored superstructure similar to that used with the larger cannon was mounted on the chassis. The fairly modern light field howitzer was installed inside. Ammunition stowage was also provided in the open-topped superstructure, as was seating for four of the crew. The driver, naturally, was in the chassis.

The side armor of converted Geschützwagen Lorraine-Schlepper füer le.F.H. 18/4 was tapered toward the rear of the vehicle. These vehicles were employed in an effort to throw back the Allied invasion at Normandy.

Geschützwagen Lorraine-Schlepper füer le.F.H. 18/4

Length	4.40 m	Communications	FuG Spr Ger.
Width	1.85 m	Weapon, main	10.5 cm le.F.H. 18/4
Height	2.20 m		
Weight	7.7 tons	Ammo stowage, main	20 rnds
Fuel capacity	111 liters		
Maximum speed	34 km/hr (21.08 mph)	Engine make	DelaHaye
		Engine model	103TT
Range, on road	120 km (74.4 miles)	Engine configuration	six-cylinder
Range, cross country	75 km (46.5 miles)	Engine displacement	3.56 l
Crew	4	Engine horsepower	70 @ 2800 rpm

The first 12 of these conversions were completed in September, 1942. These were supplied to Battery 6 of the gerpanzerte self-propelled Artillery Regiments 1 and 2.

In December 1942, an improved superstructure was designed, and two more vehicles converted with this revision. No further conversions are known to have been made until mid-1943, when 12 more were produced.

In addition to the previously named units, Geschützwagen Lorraine-Schlepper füer le.F.H. 18/4 were supplied to 15 Batterie/Artillerie-Regiment 227 and Artillerie-Regiment 155 of the 21st Panzer Division.

The final conversions on this vehicle included armor that was the same height front to rear. A ground anchor at the rear of the chassis was employed to relieve stresses on the suspension when firing.

Walter J. Spielberger

10.5 cm le.F.H. 18/6 (Sf.) auf Geschützwagen III/IV "Heuschrecke IVb"

The German high command was desperate for a versatile self-propelled howitzer with a cannon that could be dismounted and used as towed artillery as well. Considerable effort over a number of years by a variety of firms went into this objective, but none of the efforts were considered true successes.

Krupp's attempt to solve this problem involved mounting a 10.5 cm light field howitzer on an extensively modified Hummel chassis. The engine and cooling system were moved to the rear of the vehicle, in positions much as they were on the Panzerkampfwagen III and IV. A new glacis and superstructure was fabricated by Stahlindustrie and installed by Krupp. A hydraulic system for dismounting the turret was installed as well. The cannon itself was based on that used in the Sturmhaubitze 42.

The design was initially well received, although the immobility of the turret and high purchase price were noted as disadvantages. A trial vehicle was subsequently produced and tested in October 1943. The military requested that a provision be made for manually removing the turret in the event of hydraulic failure, and for a wheeled carriage for the dismounted turret. The changes were made and the modified test vehicle was demonstrated in May 1944. At that time it was determined the turret was unwieldy when removed from the chassis, and the project was abandoned.

Patton Museum, Fort Knox, KY

This is what the unusual design was all about: The turret of the Heuschrecke IVb could be dismounted, and fired from the ground or towed using the carriage stowed on the motor carriage.

Patton Museum, Fort Knox, KY

Although the Heuschrecke IVb was a purpose-built vehicle, it utilized many components from other designs. The chassis was taken over from the Hummel, albeit extensively modified. Much of the weapon had been previously used in the Sturmhaubitze 42.

Military History Institute, Carlisle Barracks, PA

The sole Heuschrecke IVb was of sufficient interest to U.S. engineers that after its capture it was shipped to Aberdeen Proving Ground, where this photo was taken shortly after its arrival. It remains at Aberdeen today.

Patton Museum, Fort Knox, KY

A parallelogram lifting device was used to remove the turret. In this, the final form of the prototype, the dismounting could be accomplished manually.

10.5 cm le.F.H. 18/6 (Sf.) auf Geschützwagen III/IV "Heuschrecke IVb"

Length	6.57 m	Communications	Fu.Spr.Ger.	
Width	2.90 m	Weapon, main	10.5 cm le.F.H. 18/6	
Height	2.65 m			
Weight	24 tons	Ammo stowage, main	87 rnds	
Fuel capacity	360 liters	Engine make	Maybach	
Maximum Speed	38 km/hr (23.56 mph)	Engine model	HL120TRM	
Range, on road	225 km (139.5 miles)	Engine configuration	V-12, liquid cooled	
Range, cross country	120 km (74.4 miles)	Engine displacement	11.9 liters	
Crew	5	Engine horsepower	285 @ 2600 rpm	

The initial design did not include a means for moving the dismounted turret, so no wheels were carried. The turret of the Heuschrecke IVb could be rotated through 360 degrees. Notice the unique engine deck.

Another major difference between the original and modified form of the prototype Heuschrecke IVb was the original design's reliance on an on-board hydraulic system for removing the turret.

The wheels for the carriage were stowed on the rear of the final design. The rear of the turret was hinged, providing maximum crew protection while traveling, yet allowing easy ammunition resupply and room to man the weapon.

Geschützpanzer 39H(f) le.F.H. 16 & 18 Hotchkiss

Germany used captured equipment more than any other country involved in WWII. Czech arms makers built equipment for the Wermacht's use, and captured Russian artillery was issued en masse to German units, sometimes without modification. Captured French tanks were also used as platforms for various self propelled artillery, such as the one shown here.

The Hotchkiss 39 was a French medium tank constructed with bolted-together cast hull sections. In 1943, the Germans removed the turret with 37mm gun from a dozen of these prizes and fabricated an armored open-topped superstructure on top of the hull. Inside of this they installed their own 10.5 cm howitzers—either the le.F.H. 16 or 18. These vehicles, known as Geschützpanzer 39H(f), were assigned to Sturmgeschütz-Abteilung 200 in September. The following February another dozen similar conversions were also provided to the unit. Like so many of the German conversions of French vehicles, these remained in France and were used in the futile attempt to throw back the Allied landings in June of 1944. It was in this arena that all these conversions had been lost by August 1944.

Walter J. Spielberger

As with most self-propelled artillery, the Geschützpanzer were lightly armored, and loaded with ammunition. These two factors, combined with their low production quantity, means they are rare today.

Geschützpanzer 39H(f) le.F.H. 16 & 18 Hotchkiss

Width	1.85 m	**Weapon, main**	10.5 cm le.F.H. 16 or 18
Weight	12.5 tons		
Fuel capacity	207 liters	**Ammo stowage, main**	36 rnds
Maximum speed	35 km/hr (21.7 mph)	**Engine make**	Hotchkiss
Range, on road	180 km (111.6 miles)	**Engine configuration**	6-cyl., liquid cooled
Range, cross country	95 km (58.9 miles)	**Engine displacement**	5.97 liter
Crew	4	**Engine horsepower**	120 @ 2800 rpm
Communications	Fu.Spr.Ger.		

Military Miniatures in Review

After their conversion, these Geschützpanzer were hardly recognizable as being based on the Hotchkiss R-39, especially when the suspension was obscured.

le.F.H. 18/40/2 (Sf.) auf Geschützwagen III/IV

In addition to Krupp's design, a proposal from Alkett was considered as well for a dismountable howitzer using the Hummel chassis. Wa Pruef 4 was presented with the Alkett proposal in September 1943, and a contract for the production of a trial vehicle was awarded.

The significant difference of this design was that it involved the mounting of a conventional le.F.H. 18/40/2 on a rotating platform recessed in the hull. The howitzer's wheels and trails were carried on the rear of the vehicle. With this arrangement it was possible to raise the weapon, reinstall the trails and wheels, and roll it down ramps to the ground for conventional use. Unfortunately, these components were heavy, and handling them was slow and difficult work. These points were reinforced during the vehicle's March 1944 tests. Despite the problems, this design was ordered into production utilizing the Panzerkampfwagen IV chassis, with initial deliveries scheduled for October 1944. As was the case with many of Germany's AFVs, there were numerous delays in

beginning production, and in December 1944 the order was cancelled before any production vehicles had been built.

le.F.H. 18/40/2 (Sf.) auf Geschützwagen III/IV

Length	7.195 m	Weapon, main	10.5 cm le.F.H. 18/40/2
Width	3.000 m		
Height	2.875 m	Ammo stowage, main	85 rnds
Weight	25 tons		
Fuel capacity	500 liters	Engine make	Maybach
Maximum speed	42 km/hr (26.04 mph)	Engine model	HL120TRM
Range, on road	190 km (117.8 miles)	Engine configuration	V-12, liquid cooled
Range, cross country	150 km (93 miles)	Engine displacement	11.9 liters
Crew	5	Engine horsepower	285 @ 2600 rpm
Communications	Fu.Spr.Ger.f		

Patton Museum, Fort Knox, KY

Alkett's Geschützwagen with 18/40/2 was somewhat taller than Krupp's competing design. Its height is emphasized in the view by virtue of its being transported on a low loader trailer. The disadvantage of the larger silhouette was partially offset by the greater range of the howitzer Alkett selected.

Patton Museum, Fort Knox, KY

The trails and wheels of the howitzer's conventional carriage were stowed on the rear of the Geschützwagen, but they were rather heavy and awkward to handle.

Patton Museum, Fort Knox, KY

Close examination of the chassis reveals its Hummel heritage. The empty spindle above the second road wheel was for the mounting of spare road wheels. The vehicle's rear deck was kept clear to speed dismounting of the howitzer.

Gerät 040 and Gerät 041, "Karl"

Among the heaviest self-propelled weapons ever built were Germany's super-heavy mortars, often referred to as "Karl." They were originally conceived in the mid-1930s, and by the late 1930s Rheinmetall had designed a 60 cm mortar capable of heaving a 2,000 kg shell 4,000 meters. It was carried on a unique, tracklaying chassis. The vehicle design was such that prior to firing, the chassis was lowered to the ground, removing the firing stresses from the suspension components. The breech-loading mortar tube was mounted in a carriage that traveled with recoil, further reducing the abuse transmitted to automotive components. The muzzle faced toward the rear of the

The soldier beside this Karl aids in judging the size of the massive vehicle. The suspension system and track varied from vehicle to vehicle, as did the engine setup.

Patton Museum, Fort Knox, KY

The manpower needed to operate one of these weapons was enormous. A team of 21 men were directly involved.

Patton Museum, Fort Knox, KY

This is Karl number I or II, as evidenced by the suspension. The tube could be elevated a maximum of 70 degrees, and provision was made for 4-degree traverse.

Patton Museum, Fort Knox, KY

vehicle, allowing a quick getaway after firing, although with a top speed of 10 km/h or less, quick was a relative term.

By July 1940, plans for the massive weapon had become a reality, and the first unit was shown to representatives from Wa Pruef 4. These huge mortars were enormous consumers of resources, not only in production but also logistically, and only seven were built, with the last one completed in 1942. With such a low production number, and being such a huge machine, there was a certain amount of variation between the units.

A 2-ton shell leaves the tube. The pistons of the counter-recoil cylinders can be seen in this view. The crew did not stay on the vehicle during firing, which was done electrically, due to the concussion of the muzzle blast.

Originally referred to simply as Project 4, it was known as Geraet 040 by late 1940, then Geraet-Karl in February 1941. During that month, Hitler ordered the range increased by decreasing the bore. Three of the mortars, I, IV and V, were retubed to a 54 cm bore, which also involved some changes to the carriage, including lengthening it slightly. The smaller-bore version was referred to as Geraet 041. In late July 1942, the names were reversed, becoming Karl-Geraet—the name they are most widely known by today.

These vehicles were used primarily on the Eastern front, although one did fire at the bridge at Remagen in 1945 in an attempt to deny the Allied forces a crossing.

Gerät 040 and Gerät 041, "Karl"

Length	11.15 m	Crew	21 (18 with 041)
Width	3.16 m	Weapon, main	60 cm (54 cm with 041)
Height	4.78 m		
Weight	123 tons (126.4 with 041)		
		Engine make	Daimler-Benz
Fuel capacity	1,200 liters	Engine model	MB503A (gasoline) MB 507C (diesel)
Maximum speed	10 km/hr (6.2 mph)		
Range, on road	42 km gasoline (26.04 miles), 60 km diesel (26.04 miles)	Engine configuration	V-12 liquid cooled
		Engine displacement	1200 liters
		Engine horsepower	580 @ 1850 rpm

Even though the Karl was self-propelled, its speed, weight and inefficiency meant that rail transport was utilized to bring the mortar as near as possible to the action. Special equipment was designed to handle such moves.

The tube of the 54 cm mortar was just over 7 meters long, whereas the 60 cm tube was just over 5 meters in length.

Special ammunition transporters and loaders, based on Panzerkampfwagen IV chassis, were assigned to each of the massive mortars. This is another view of "Thor," one of the 54 cm mortars.

Aufklärungspanzerwagen 38 (2 cm)(Sd.Kfz. 140/1)

Despite its inclusion in this chapter, this vehicle isn't truly a Panzerjäger. It is included here because it was open-topped and was armed with a tank gun (not an antiaircraft gun or howitzer). The Aufklärungspanzerwagen 38 was built as a reconnaissance vehicle.

In essence, these vehicles were created by mounting the 2 cm cannon-armed turret, similar to the one used on the Sd.Kfz. 234/1, on the proven chassis of the Panzerkampfwagen 38(t) tank. An improved engine with a slightly higher horsepower rating was installed, raising the top speed to 45 km/hr.

ČKD initiated construction of the 70 vehicles of this series with delivery scheduled to begin in October 1943. Production ended in March 1944. The next month 25 of the vehicles were supplied to Panzer-Grenadier-Division "Grossdeutschland." A second group of 25 were supplied in September 1944 to the Third Panzer Division, thus the vehicles were used on both the Eastern and Western fronts.

Aufklärungspanzerwagen 38 (2 cm)(Sd.Kfz. 140/1)			
Length	4.51 m	Weapon, main	2 cm KwK 38 L/55
Width	2.14 m		
Height	2.17 m	Weapon, coaxial	7.92mm MG42
Weight	9.75 tons	Engine make	Praga
Maximum speed	45 km/hr (27.9 mph)	Engine configuration	six-cylinder, liquid cooled
Range, on road	210 km (130.2 miles)	Engine displacement	xxxx
Crew	4	Engine horsepower	180 @ 2800 rpm
Communications	Fu.Spr.Ger.f (9 equipped with Fu 12)		

Patton Museum, Fort Knox, KY

The turret of the vehicle was taken from the 234/1 eight-wheeled armored car. Similar turrets were also mounted on halftracks.

The Aufklärungspanzerwagen 38 was built to perform relatively high-speed armored reconnaissance. The reliable Czech 38(t) chassis was its basis.

Production of the vehicles occurred during the winter of 1943-1944. CKD was the manufacturer of the entire 70-vehicle series.

CKD archive via Kliment collection

Hinged mesh screens were provided to keep debris and, more importantly, grenades from entering the vehicle.

The vehicle's primary armament was a 2 cm Kw.K. 38. A coaxially mounted MG34 was also provided. These were intended for self-defense and overcoming very light resistance.

The vehicles were powered with a 180-hp engine, rather than the 150-hp engine originally used in the Panzerkampfwagen 38(t). This gave them a top speed of 45 km/hr.

Though not really Panzerjäger, or tank destroyers, Aufklärungspanzerwagen 38 were armed with a tank gun, albeit small, and were open-topped, so they are included here.

4.7cm PaK(t) (Sfl) auf Pz Kpfw I Ausf B

To the German wartime military, there was little distinction between Panzerjäger and Jagdpanzer: both were built and employed to destroy enemy tanks. However, in the postwar years it has evolved that Jagdpanzer refers to a closed-topped tank destroyer, while Panzerjäger has come to mean open-topped tank hunters.

Prior to WWII, and throughout much of the war, German (and U.S.) military strategy called for tanks to be used to break through enemy lines and attack strong points. Tanks were not intended to do battle with other tanks. That was the job of the tank destroyer, on Panzerjäger.

One of the earliest Panzerjägers was the result of the marriage of the excellent Czech-made Škoda 4.7 cm kanon P.U.V vz. 36, known to the Germans as the 4.7 cm PaK36(t), with the Panzerkampfwagen I Ausf. B chassis. The cannons used were not war prizes confiscated by Germany upon its annexation of Czechoslovakia; rather, they were new production contracted for by the Waffenamt.

Alkett was contracted to produce a trial vehicle of this type, which was demonstrated to Hitler in February 1940. The resultant vehicle was officially known as the 4.7cm PaK(t) (Sf) auf Panzerkampfwagen I Ausf B, but is more commonly known today as the Panzerjäger I. Alkett began delivering the converted vehicles in series in March of 1940, when 30 were accepted. These were followed by 60 more in April and a further 30 in May. Alkett delivered two final vehicles in September 1940 and July 1941.

A second series of vehicles was contracted for in September 1940. Only 10 of these were to be completed by Alkett; the remaining 60 vehicles on this order were to be assembled by Klockner-Humboldt-Deutz. Ten vehicles were delivered in November 1940, 30 in December and the final 30 the following January. The shape of the gunshield of the second series Panzerjäger had seven sides, rather than the five found on the first series.

Though the Panzerjäger I was initially effective, by late 1943 the improving armor of opposing tanks rendered it obsolete and it was removed from service.

4.7cm PaK(t) (Sfl) auf Pz Kpfw I Ausf B			
Length	4.42 m	Communications	Fu.Spr.Ger. "a"
Width	2.06 m		
Height	2.14	Weapon, main	4.7 cm PaK(t)
Weight	6.4 tons		
Fuel capacity	146 liters	Ammo stowage, main	74 rnds
Maximum Speed	40 km/hr (24.8 mph)	Engine make	Maybach
Range, on road	170 km (105.4 miles)	Engine model	NL 38 Tr
Range, cross country	115 km (71.3 miles)	Engine configuration	six-cylinder, liquid cooled
Crew	3	Engine displacement	3.8 liters
		Engine horsepower	100 @ 3000 rpm

The Panzerjäger I was created by mounting the Škoda 4.7 cm antitank gun on the chassis of the Panzerkampfwagen I Ausf. B tank. The result was an effective tank destroyer. The vehicle shown here was assigned to the 670 Panzerjäger Abteilung.

Bundesarchiv photo

This early Panzerjäger I hitches a ride on a Sd.Anh. 115 trailer behind a 12-ton halftrack. Combat vehicles are often hauled to minimize wear on drive train components.

Somewhere in Russia a Panzerjäger I completes a fording operation. The log it is climbing over was deliberately placed there to increase traction on the muddy riverbank.

A vehicle formerly assigned to the 605 Panzerjäger Abteilung, captured intact at El Almein and returned to England for examination. Early vehicles such as this one had five-sided gun shields.

Patton Museum, Fort Knox, KY

There was very little space behind the gun shield of the Panzerjäger I. The early vehicles, with the five-sided gun shields such as this one, were all assembled by Alkett.

Patton Museum, Fort Knox, KY

Though a good weapon for its time, the Czech 4.7 cm cannon was soon faced with heavier armor than it could penetrate upon entering Russia.

Patton Museum, Fort Knox, KY

This vehicle has its tarpaulin covering its gun mount, but lacks its tracks. This vehicle is a later-production machine with the seven-sided gun shield, which offered slightly better protection.

Although Alkett built 10 of the final 70 vehicles, the balance of the order was filled by Klockner-Humboldt-Deutz. One machine from the first order was not delivered until July 1941, the rest of both orders had been finished by January 1941.

Patton Museum, Fort Knox, KY

Patton Museum, Fort Knox, KY

The Panzerjäger of the platoon leader of the first platoon of the first company of Panzerjäger Abteilung 605 is shown here. Note the extra water can racks, and the antenna mount fastened to the gun shield.

Panzerselbstfahrlafette 1 für 7.62 cm PaK36(r) auf fahrgestell Panzerkampfwagen II Ausf. D (Sd. Kfz. 132)

Although Krupp's proposed Panzerkampfwagen II, known as the LaS 138, was not accepted for production, that decision did not sound the death knell for the Krupp chassis design. In addition to being used as the basis for the Panzerkampfwagen II Ausf. D and E, as well as the Panzer II flamethrower variant, it also served as the basis for a self-propelled antitank gun.

In December 1941, the Waffenamt contracted with Alkett to create a Panzerjäger utilizing the LaS 138 chassis components and Russian 7.62 cm anti-tank guns. In Soviet service these were known as the 76.2mm F-22 Model 1936 divisional field gun, but they were captured in such large quantities that the Germans rechambered the weapons to accept 7.5 cm PaK 40 ammunition and redesignated them the 7.62 cm PaK 36(r) L/51 anti-tank gun. By mid-May 1942, the first order for 150 units was finished, and a further 60 superstructures had been ordered for use converting Flammpanzer II into Panzerjäger. Wegmann joined Alkett in producing these vehicles.

During the course of the conversion, the superstructure front and sides were raised in order to create a protected fighting compartment for the gun crew. The gun was mounted inside this area on its cutdown field carriage. Stowage was provided for 30 rounds of main gun ammunition, and provision was made to carry a 7.92mm MG 34 as a close defense weapon. The main gun could be traversed 50 degrees either side of center.

Designated Panzerselbstfahrlafette 1 für 7.62 cm PaK36(r) auf fahrgestell Panzerkampfwagen II Ausf. D, the vehicles were also known as LaS 762. Those vehicles

constructed on Panzer II Ausf. D and E chassis were known as the Ausf. D1, while those converted from Flammpanzer II were referred to as Ausf. D2.

The earliest conversions can be distinguished by having a wire mesh-enclosed area at the rear of the hull. Later versions lacked this, although two different style gun shields were used on the later vehicles. Not all of the guns were fitted with a muzzle brake. The vehicles began to be used on the Eastern Front in April 1942, primarily by tank destroyer detachments of Panzer and Panzer-Grenadier divisions, including SS units. By 1944, these vehicles were relegated to secondary areas after better thank destroyers began being fielded by the German military.

Panzerselbstfahrlafette 1 für 7.62 cm PaK36(r) auf fahrgestell Panzerkampfwagen II Ausf. D (Sd.Kfz. 132)			
Length	5.65 m	Weapon, main	7.62 cm Pak 36(r) L/51
Width	2.30 m	Weapon, secondary	7.92mm MG34
Height	2.65 m		
Weight	11.5 tons	Ammo stowage, main	30 rnds
Fuel capacity	200 liters		
Maximum speed	55 km/hr (34.1 mph)	Ammo stowage, secondary	900 rnds
Range, on road	220 km (136.4 miles)		
Range, cross country	140 km (86.8 miles)	Engine make	Maybach
		Engine model	HL 62 TRM
Crew	4	Engine configuration	six-cylinder, liquid cooled
Communications	FuG Spr d	Engine displacement	6.2 liters
		Engine horsepower	140 hp

This illustration from the operator's manual shows the original form of the Panzer II-based tank destroyer. Later models varied in rear superstructure configuration as well as the shape of the gun shield.

Visible here is the expanded metal grating on the rear of the superstructure. This mesh was characteristic only of the earliest vehicles.

Patton Museum, Fort Knox, KY

These vehicles mounted captured Soviet PaK36(r) antitank guns on Krupp-designed chassis originally used for the Panzerkampfwagen II Ausf. D and E.

Later production versions deleted the metal grating on the rear in favor of armor plate extending the full height. Alkett and Wegmann performed the conversions that produced these vehicles.

The Soviet guns were rechambered so that they could fire standard German PaK 40 ammunition. The three-man gun crew was protected from small arms fire by the sides of the superstructure, as well as by the gun shield.

The vehicle's small size permitted only 30 rounds of 7.5 cm ammunition to be carried. The crew was provided with a 7.92 mm MG 34 with which to defend the vehicle from infantry attack.

The main gun could be traversed 50 degrees either side of center. Elevation was from –5 to +16 degrees. Both elevation and traverse were driven manually with hand cranks.

7.5 cm PaK40/2 auf fahrgestell Panzerkampfwagen II (Sf)(Sd.Kfz. 131)

Faced with the growing obsolescence of Panzerkampfwagen II and the overwhelming need for a self-propelled antitank gun with reasonable firepower, the leadership of Germany's military opted to mount the 7.5 cm PaK 40/2 L/46 antitank gun on the Panzer II chassis.

Of course, the new gun was far too big for the Panzerkampfwagen's turret, so a new, fixed, open-topped fighting compartment was designed to permit the antitank gun's installation. The resultant vehicle was designated 7.5cm PaK40/2 auf Fahrgestell PzKpfw II (Sf), but is popularly known as the Marder II.

The standard Ausf F hull and superstructure were utilized in large part, with driver retaining his former position, and a two-man gun crew riding in the new fighting compartment. This vehicle protected the crew better than the Panzerjäger I, as there was at least some armor along the sides of the fighting compartment, even if it was open at the top and rear.

The mounting of the PaK 40 permitted 32 degrees traverse to the left and 25 degrees to the right of the centerline. The crew as defense against infantry attack carried a 7.92mm MG 34 inside the fighting compartment.

Daimler-Benz, FAMO, and M.A.N. and Daimler-Benz produced 576 Marder II vehicles from June 1942 through June 1943. At that time all new Panzerkampfwagen II chassis were diverted to Wespe production. An additional 75 Marder II were built from older Panzerkampfwagen II returned for overhaul between July 1943 and March 1944.

The Marder IIs were used by Panzerjäger Abteilungen on all fronts from until the end of the war.

7.5 cm PaK40/2 auf fahrgestell Panzerkampfwagen II (Sf)(Sd.Kfz. 131)

Length	3.63 m	Weapon, secondary	7.92mm MG34
Width	2.28 m	Ammo stowage, main	37 rnds
Height	2.20 m		
Weight	10.8 tons	Ammo stowage, secondary	600 rnds
Fuel capacity	200 liters		
Maximum speed	40 km/h (24.8 mph)	Engine make	Maybach
Range, on road	190 km (117.8 miles)	Engine model	HL62TRM
Range, cross country	125 km (77.5 miles)	Engine configuration	straight six-cylinder
Crew	3	Engine displacement	6.2 liter
Communications	FuG.Spr.d	Engine horsepower	140 @ 2600 rpm
Weapon, main	7.5 cm Pak 40/2 L/46		

Patton Museum, Fort Knox, KY

The mounting of the main gun permitted 32 degrees traverse to the left and 25 degrees to the right of its centerline. The driver's visor is visible through the gun's travel lock in this view.

Patton Museum, Fort Knox, KY

Popularly known as the Marder II, but officially designated 7.5cm PaK40/2 auf Fahrgestell PzKpfw II (Sf), this vehicle had better crew protection that the older Panzerjäger I.

Patton Museum, Fort Knox, KY

This crew has chalked up a number of victories judging from the rings on the barrel of the gun. The PaK 40/2 L46 gave the Marder II sufficient firepower to take on most WWII-era tanks.

Patton Museum, Fort Knox, KY

The delicate nature of the aiming apparatus, combined with the length and weight of the PaK 40, meant that the travel lock had to be used at all times, except when actually firing.

Patton Museum, Fort Knox, KY

Though obsolete as a tank, mechanically the Panzerkampfwagen II chassis was a successful design, making it a natural choice for conversion to an open-topped Panzerjäger.

Panzerjäger 38 (t) für 7.62cm PaK36(r) (Sd. Kfz. 139) "Marder III"

In late June 1941 the German Army first encountered the Soviet KV-series tanks. Instantly the German antitank guns were rendered obsolete. The 3.7 cm and 5.0 cm rounds they fired simply bounced off of the new Russian vehicles.

Scrambling to meet this new threat, the German military was compelled to use captured Russian 7.62 cm field gun 36. This was due to the manufacturing lead time required to produce a comparable German weapon. This was ironic in that the Russian field gun was itself developed from a 1930s German Rheinmetall-Borsig design. Enough of these guns were captured that they were given the classification 7.62 cm PaK 36(r) in the German military. However, there were not adequate stocks of captured ammunition. Therefore, a program began to

rechamber the weapons to fire the German PaK 40 7.5 cm round. These rechambered guns were classified as 7.62 cm PaK36.

The chassis of the vehicle came from the Panzerkampfwagen 38(t) Ausf. G which, though automotively reliable, was no longer adequately armed or armored for use as a front-line tank. For use as a gun motor carriage, naturally the turret and turret ring were removed, as was the cover for the fighting compartment and existent ammo stowage. A flat engine deck replaced the sloping one found on the tank.

A T-shaped gun mount was bolted across the hull, and the PaK36 with a gun shield was installed. The fighting compartment was open-topped and the crew was exposed to the weather. A canvas cover was provided that could protect the gun's mechanism, but it wasn't suitable for use as crew protection.

The first production vehicle, dubbed the Marder III, was completed by the ČKD plant in April 1942. From April 1942 through July 1942, the gun motor carriage and the 38(t) tank were concurrently produced. In July, the basis of the vehicle was changed to the Panzerkampfwagen 38(t) Ausf. H, which had a more-powerful engine. The last of the 344 Panzerjäger 38 (t) für 7.62cm PaK36(r) (Sd. Kfz. 139) "Marder III" were delivered in October 1942.

The Sd.Kfz. 139 was initially supplied to both Army and SS armored self-propelled antitank battalions. After improved Panzerjäger became available for these units, the remaining Sd.Kfz. 139 were transferred to infantry antitank battalions.

CKD archive via Kliment Collection

Photographed at the CKD factory, this Marder III shows its high profile. This height would be on of the vehicle's few shortcomings.

CKD archive via Kliment Collection.

The length and weight of the 7.62 cm PaK36(r) required a travel lock be used to protect the gunlaying apparatus. Shown here is the earliest type, which was a simple pole-like brace.

Patton Museum, Fort Knox, KY

The supporting bow for the canvas cover can be seen on this 2nd Panzerjäger Battalion, 7th Panzer Division Marder III somewhere in France.

Panzerjäger 38 (t) fur 7.62cm PaK36(r) (Sd. Kfz. 139) 'Marder III'

Length	5.85 m	Weapon, secondary	7.92mm MG 37(t)
Width	2.16 m	Ammo stowage, main	30 rnds
Weight	10.67 tons	Ammo stowage, secondary	1,200 rnds
Maximum speed	42-47 km/hr (26-28 mph)	Engine make	Praga
Range, on road	185 km (114.7 miles)	Engine model	TNHP or AC
Range, cross country	140 km (86.8 miles)	Engine configuration	six-cylinder, liquid cooled
Crew	4	Engine displacement	7.75 liters
Communications	Fu 5 SE 10 U	Engine horsepower	125 or 150
Weapon, main	7.62 cm PaK36		

Kliment Collection

A canvas cover for the fighting compartment was provided, but it was primarily to protect the weapon during transport. The cover restricted visibility and movement too much to be of use as weather protection for the crew during combat. .

CKD archive via Kliment Collection.

The small, open-topped fighting compartment offered little protection for the gun crew. Even side armor was lacking, with the only protection being the gun shield.

Later vehicles had reinforced gun travel locks. The first reinforced version was a triangular arrangement of steel tubing. Later, sheet steel filled in the triangle, strengthening it and resulting in the version shown here.

This is a Marder III captured by the British somewhere in Tunisia. Note the seat hurled over the side. Though the Russian gun gave the Marder a heavy punch, its lack of armor meant mobility was its best defense.

Military History Institute, Carlisle Barracks, PA

The Panzerkampfwagen 38 (t) chassis, in either the Ausf. G or Ausf. H version, was the basis for the 388 Sd.Kfz. 139 assembled by CKD.

Little room was wasted behind the gun shield. With the limited amount of ammunition stowage, crews often stored additional rounds in any available space.

Panzerjäger 38(t) für 7.5cm PaK40/3 Ausf. H (Sd. Kfz. 138) 'Marder III'

The Panzerjäger 38(t) für 7.62cm PaK36(r) was successful, but with the German-built PaK40 now becoming available in quantity, the decision was made to incorporate that weapon in future Panzerjäger 38(t) production. This vehicle, the Panzerjäger 38(t) für 7.5cm PaK40/3 Ausf. H, however, was more than simply a rearming of its predecessor. The PaK40 was mounted differently, and considerably more forward on the chassis than was the Russian gun. This change meant that the driver and radio operator no longer had their own hatches in the hull top; rather, they entered and exited the vehicle through the fighting compartment.

Also, the chassis itself was different that those used on the early Soviet-armed vehicles. The new vehicle was built on the Panzerkampfwagen 38(t) Ausf. H chassis, which featured a more-powerful engine. It should be noted that no actual Panzerkampfwagen 38(t) Ausf. H were ever actually built, and all the chassis were used for self-propelled guns.

The gun was mounted to the chassis by means of a T-shaped supporting structure that spanned the hull. Crew protection was improved in the new design. In addition to the gun shield, which traversed with the gun, there was additional frontal armor as well as sloping, tapered side armor plates. This armor was sufficient to stop small arms fire. A final improvement had to do with the travel lock. Unlike the earlier vehicle, which required a crewman to expose himself to release the guns travel lock, the driver could release the lock from inside his compartment.

From November 1942 through April 1943, ČKD built 242 of these vehicles. Additional vehicles were converted from existing Panzerkampfwagen 38(t) combat tanks. These vehicles were issued to Panzerjäger units from their initial deliveries and served through the end of the war.

Panzerjäger 38(t) für 7.5cm PaK40/3 Ausf. H (Sd. Kfz. 138) 'Marder III'

Length	5.77 m	Weapon, main	7.5 cm PaK40/3
Width	2.16 m	Weapon, secondary	7.92mm MG 37(t)
Height	2.51 m		
Weight	10.8 tons	Ammo stowage, main	38 rnds
Fuel capacity	220 liters		
Maximum speed	47 km/hr (29.14 mph)	Ammo stowage, secondary	600 rnds
Range, on road	185 km (114.7 miles)	Engine make	Praga
Range, cross country	140 km (86.8 miles)	Engine model	AC
Crew	4	Engine configuration	six-cylinder, liquid cooled
Communications	Fu 5 SE 10 U	Engine displacement	7.75 liters
		Engine horsepower	150

The gun of the Panzerjäger 38(t), a German-made PaK 40, was mounted well forward of the position that had been taken by the Soviet PaK36(r) on its predecessor. The GI standing next to this captured vehicle gives the viewer an idea of the compact size of the tank destroyer.

Patton Museum, Fort Knox, KY

The rear of the fighting compartment was completely open. A decking was provided to allow the crew room to serve the weapon. The driver and radio operator had to enter their positions from this area.

CKD archive via Kliment collection

An armored roof provided minimal protection from overhead shell bursts and strafing aircraft. However, this, and the minimal amount of side armor provided, were a considerable improvement over the crew protection on previous 38(t)-based tank destroyers.

Ordnance Museum, Aberdeen Proving Ground, MD

National Archives and Records Administration

The open fighting compartment of the Panzerjäger 38(t) led to casualties. The best defense for a Panzerjäger crew was to strike first and move after each shot, as the vehicle's armor was only protection against rifles and light machineguns.

Patton Museum, Fort Knox, KY

Panzerjäger crews often tried to conceal their vehicles in brush. The hope was that they would remain undetected until they fired their first shot. The strong muzzle blast of the PaK 40 meant that as soon as a shot was fired, the vehicle's position was revealed.

Bundesarchiv photo

The wounded crew of a Marder III Ausf. H ride their vehicle home. The mechanical reliability of the Panzerkampfwagen 38(t) was superb, and in most conditions its performance was more than adequate.

Patton Museum, Fort Knox, KY

When a Panzerjäger got in a dual with a tank the results were often devastating to the Panzerjäger. Their armor simply could not withstand armor piercing rounds of any size, as witnessed by the massive destruction of this vehicle.

Panzerjäger 38(t) für 7.5cm PaK40/3 Ausf. M (Sd. Kfz. 138) Marder III

This final improvement of the Marder was introduced in the opening months of 1943. Although the vehicles were built by ČKD, Alkett influenced the design of the fighting compartment. The Panzerkampfwagen 38(t) chassis design was revised, with the fighting compartment moved to the rear, and the engine compartment moved to the middle of the tank. Among the advantages to rearranging the vehicle was the elimination of the long gun overhang evident on previous models, and the direct coupling of the engine to the transmission.

The running gear and suspension were only slightly modified, with the new vehicle having only one return roller on each side, rather than the two previously used.

In the redesigned vehicle, the radio operator's station was moved from beside the driver to inside the fighting compartment. The driver's station was a compartment that protruded slightly from the superstructure. For most

of 1943, this compartment was a combination of cast and bolted construction, while later vehicles had a more angular welded compartment. The early Ausf. M also had their exhaust pipes routed internally along the right side of the vehicle. The balance of the vehicles had the exhaust pipe routed externally.

Protection for the crew was improved with the Ausf. M, which had armor on all four sides of the fighting compartment. However, main gun ammunition stowage was reduced to 27 rounds. The radio operator was repositioned, which meant the elimination of the hull-mounted Czech machine gun found on the Ausf. H. It had been deemed of little use, anyway.

Though the prototype was complete by February 1943, delivery of series production Marder III Ausf. M did not begin by ČKD until May 1943. Through October of the same year, 374 vehicles were built on the Panzerkampfwagen 38(t) Ausf. K chassis. From October onwards, the Panzer 38(t) Ausf. M chassis was used, with 568 vehicles ultimately being built on this improved chassis.

Panzerjäger detachments on all fronts used these vehicles for the duration of the war.

CKD archive via Kliment collection

The earliest version of the Panzerjäger 38(t) für 7.5cm PaK40/3 Ausf. M, or Marder III M, had fenders extending behind the track.

CKD archive via Kliment collection

The fighting compartment of the Ausf. M was located at the rear of the vehicle, greatly reducing the gun's overhang. This was an aid to driver training and vehicle maneuverability in cities and forests.

CKD archive via Kliment collection

For most of 1943 the driver's compartment was made of bolted-together steel castings. This chassis number of this particular vehicle, 2193, has been stenciled on its superstructure.

Panzerjäger 38(t) für 7.5cm PaK40/3 Ausf. M (Sd. Kfz. 138) "Marder III"

Length	5.02 m	Weapon, secondary	7.92mm MG 34
Width	2.15 m	Ammo stowage, main	27 rnds
Height	2.35 m	Ammo stowage, secondary	1,500 rnds
Weight	10.15 tons		
Maximum speed	47 km/hr (29.14 mph)	Engine make	Praga
		Engine model	AC
Range, on road	240 km (148.8 miles)	Engine configuration	six-cylinder, liquid cooled
Crew	4		
Communications	Fu 5 SE 10 U	Engine displacement	7.75 liters
Weapon, main	7.5 cm PaK40/3	Engine horsepower	150

CKD archive via Kliment collection

The rear fenders were eliminated from production fairly early. This vehicle has the early Panzerkampfwagen 38(t) drive sprocket, distinguishable by the eight holes in its outer ring.

CKD archive via Kliment collection

The muffler was mounted across the rear of all Ausf. M, just below the hinged armor. The exhaust pipe on much of the production was routed internally, as seen here, exiting at the rear.

CKD archive via Kliment collection

A rear view of the fighting compartment with the rear armor folded down. This aided re-supply and gave the crew more room. This gun's rear travel lock is in the engaged position.

CKD archive via Kliment collection

In addition to the internal travel lock, visible inside the fighting compartment, a second travel lock was attached to the superstructure. To ensure accurate fire, these supported the gun during maneuvers, relieving the strain on the gun-laying apparatus.

Although the redesigned Marder offered better protection for its crew from small arms fire, the Marder's best defense still was camouflage and mobility.

The 7.5 cm PaK 40 remained an effective antitank gun throughout the war. When the vehicles were captured, Allied troops often used them against the former owners.

Bundesarchiv photo

Later production Marder III had their exhaust routed out the air duct and along the outside of the vehicle to the rear-mounted muffler. Note the intricate camouflage paint scheme.

Photographed at Aberdeen Proving Ground in December 1946, this Marder has the welded fabricated driver's compartment. Note the single return roller, characteristic of the Marder III M.

National Archives and Records Administration

10.5cm K. Panzer Selbstfahrlafette IVa

Development work on the 10.5cm K. Selbstfahrlafette IVa began by Krupp as early as 1938. At that time the work was concentrated toward creating a vehicle capable of knocking out the strongest fortifications on the Maginot line. Like many of Germany's arms projects, as the design wound its way through the procurement process many changes were made, which brought many delays.

In the case of the 10.5cm K. Panzer Selbstfahrlafette IVa, by the time the manufacture of a trial vehicle was eminent, the original need had passed. However, it was decided to press on with the project, because by this time well-protected Soviet tanks had been encountered. It was felt that the Selbstfahrlafette Iva, with its 10.5 K18 L/52 cannon, would make an excellent tank destroyer.

The basic chassis was that of the Panzerkampfwagen IV, but the smaller six-cylinder 180-hp Maybach HL 66 Pla engine was used instead of the 265 hp HL 120 V-12 found in the Panzer IV. This engine was coupled to a SSG 46 transmission, which limited the vehicle's speed to 27 km/hr. The 10.5 cm gun used two-part ammunition, and two different types of projectiles were provided, allowing it to be used as either field artillery or an antitank gun.

Krupp completed two trial vehicles in January 1941, several months behind schedule. Had troop trials been successful, production of 100 series vehicles was to have begun in the Spring of 1942. In July 1941, the two trial vehicles were assigned to Tank Destroyer Battalion 521 for use on the Russian front.

The two-part ammunition was blamed for the total destruction of one of the vehicles as it moved into Russia. A fire broke out in the propellant storage area as the vehicles were on a road march. The crew abandoned the

By the time an operational vehicle was ready for field trials, a bunker-buster was no longer needed, but a powerful tank destroyer was.

Krupp began creating what would become the 10.5cm K. Panzer Selbstfahrlafette IVa, more popularly known as the Dicker Max, in 1938. It was to be used to break through Maginot line.

Selbstfahrlafette prior to the explosion. It is believed that heat from the engine caused the powder to ignite.

The other vehicle fought until late 1941, when it was returned to Krupp for rebuild. It was redeployed to the east after a rebuild in mid-1942. It was lost later that year.

Though the Selbstfahrlafette's gun was lethal, the chassis was underpowered, and the armor inadequate. The need to aim the entire vehicle took a heavy toll on the drive train as well.

10.5cm K. Panzer Selbstfahrlafette IVa

Length	7.47 m	Communications	speaking tube
Width	2.86 m	Weapon, main	10.5 cm Kanone L/52
Height	2.53 m		
Weight	22 tons	Ammo stowage, main	26 rnds
Fuel capacity	xxxxx		
Maximum speed	27 km/hr (16.74 mph)	Engine make	Maybach
		Engine model	HL 66 Pla
Range, on road	170 km (105.4 miles)	Engine configuration	six-cylinder, liquid cooled
Range, cross country	120 km (74.4 miles)	Engine displacement	6.6 liters
Crew	5	Engine horsepower	180 @ 3200 rpm

Walter J. Spielberger

The 10.5 K18 L/52 cannon fired two-part ammunition, so two loaders joined the commander and gunner in the open-topped fighting compartment.

In the foreground is the scissors periscope of one of the loaders. Note the back rests for the seats, shown in the folded down position.

Walter J. Spielberger

Only two of these vehicles were built, and they differed in detail. The vehicle shown here had a dummy mirror image of the driver's compartment mounted on the right side of the vehicle.

Nashorn

The Nashorn, or rhinoceros, was developed as a temporary measure to meet a specific objective. When the German Army had faced the British Matilda, and later the Russian T-34 and KV-1 tanks, it found the opposing vehicles to be relatively immune to their antitank weapons. Almost in desperation, the high-velocity 8.8 cm Flak guns were used in an antitank role. The guns were devastatingly effective, and the legend of the 88 was born. But the flak guns were towed, and it was desirable to have a self-propelled carriage for 88, which would then provide a potent and mobile antitank force.

The decision was made to mount a version of the potent 88 on a chassis being developed for the 10.5 howitzer. This chassis was a hybrid of Panzer III and Panzer IV components and was intended as a stopgap prior to the production of a specialized chassis. The specialized chassis never materialized, and the howitzer version, known as the Hummel, as well as the 88 version, the Nashorn, soldiered on until the war ended.

The chassis, while physically large enough to accommodate the 88, was less than ideal as a tank destroyer due to its thin armor. The Nashorn's best defense was the long range of the 88, which allowed it to knock out opposing tanks while still outside of the range of the tank's guns.

Production of the Nashorn was not given the same priority as the Hummel, and its design was not updated as frequently. Production of the new vehicle began in May-June 1943, and the total production was 494 units at war's end. Prior to January 27, 1944, the vehicle was known as the "Hornisse" (Hornet), but on that date Hitler ordered it renamed Nashorn.

The long tube of the 8.8 cm Pak 43/41 L/71 made a travel lock essential, or else the gunlaying and sighting mechanism would drift out of calibration during movement. When in place, the webbed reinforcement is visible beneath the gun barrel.

The Nashorn, originally known as the Hornisse, did not have as many variations as its sister vehicle, the Hummel. Basically, only two types were built: the early model, and the later, or standard model. The early models used the same type of travel lock as the Hummel, which when released, criss-crossed on the glacis, as seen here. Spare road wheels were mounted on the front corners of the fighting compartment as well.

Nashorn

Length	8.44 m	Ammo stowage, secondary	600
Width	2.95 m	Engine make	Maybach
Height	2.94 m	Engine model	HL 120 TRM
Weight	24 tons	Engine configuration	V-12, liquid cooled
Fuel capacity	600 liters	Engine displacement	11.9 liters
Range, on road	235 km (145.7 miles)	Engine horsepower	265 @ 2600 rpm
Range, cross country	135 km (83.7 miles)		
Crew	5		
Weapon, main	8.8 cm PaK43/1 L/71		
Weapon, secondary	MG34		
Ammo stowage, main	40		

Patton Museum, Fort Knox, KY

Some interim vehicles were built with the early travel lock, but with the spare roadwheels relocated to the rear. The disadvantage of the early, or Hummel travel lock, was that releasing it required a crewman to stand on the glacis and loosen a bolt. While this was acceptable for long-range artillery like the Hummel, for a tank destroyer likely to be called into action at a moments notice this was less than ideal.

A canvas cover was provided for the fighting compartment, but it was primarily only used in rear areas or when in transit. It functioned chiefly to protect the weapon and ammunition.

Patton Museum, Fort Knox, KY

Later Nashorn had the spare road wheel racks located on the rear of the vehicle, and the barrel-style muffler of the early vehicles was eliminated.

The standard Nashorn used this type of travel lock. The release cable dangling from it ran into the fighting compartment, allowing the crew to unlock the weapon without leaving the fighting compartment. The full-width driver's compartment developed for the Hummel was never used on the Nashorn.

Military Miniatures in Review

Patton Museum, Fort Knox, KY

Springs at the base of the travel lock forced it to lay back against the glacis when released, rather than falling forward. Standard Nashorns had only one Bosch headlight mounted on the fender, whereas early vehicles had two.

Patton Museum, Fort Knox, KY

This Nashorn, with the name "Puma" painted on the side, was operating in Russia with s. H. Pz. Jg. Abt. (heavy army antitank battalion) 519 in early 1944. The two rear doors allowed relatively easy re-supply of ammunition.

Patton Museum, Fort Knox, KY

Snow flies as "Puma" makes a right turn. The scissors-type periscopic sight can be seen above the armor. Also notice the aiming pole standing in the rear doorway.

Patton Museum, Fort Knox, KY

Patton Museum, Fort Knox, KY

The Nashorn was designed as a direct fire weapon intended to fire its projectile along the line of sight. The cannon's long range and the vehicle's mobility were its defense, as its thin armor and open top offered the crew little protection. Proper camouflage was critical, especially as Germany lost control of the skies.

A circular hatch in the top of the driver's compartment was his means of access. In the front of his compartment a hinged armored vision port could be opened providing maximum visibility when not in combat. When the port was closed the driver relied on a vision block, visible here on the open port.

Patton Museum, Fort Knox, KY

The famed 88 unleashed. The Pak 43/41 L/71 had a maximum range of 17,500 meters, and destroyed opposing tanks as far as 3,500 meters away.

Patton Museum, Fort Knox, KY

In rare circumstances the Pak 43/41 L/71 could be used as an indirect fire weapon, as appears to have been the case with this Nashorn prior to its capture by New Zealand troops. The high-explosive round had excellent fragmentation characteristics, making it lethal against soft-skinned vehicles and troop concentrations.

12.8 cm Selbstfahrlafette L/61

While the leadership of the German Army had been interested in powerful "bunker busters" like the Dicker Max early in war, they seemed blissfully unaware of the heavily armored (and armed) Soviet T-34 and KV-I tanks until they were encountered on the battlefield.

Suddenly, there was a rush to develop a weapon system that would be able to eliminate these Russian tanks before they could decimate the German's underarmed and underarmored Panzer III and IV units.

One of the most powerful weapons in the German arsenal at that time was the 12.8 cm Flak gun. This was adapted by Rheinmetall into a field weapon, the 12.8 cm K L/61. A suitable chassis had to be found to mount the massive cannon, and toward this end the Germans turned to the chassis which had been developed by Henschel for the VK3001 tank. This tank project had been supplanted by the Tiger project, leaving these chassis excess. Two of the VK3001 chassis were lengthened, and an open-topped fighting compartment mounted on the rear. In the front of the fighting compartment the huge cannon was installed.

Only two trial vehicles were built, one which had been completed during 1941, the other in the spring of 1942. Both were subsequently deployed to Russia, one with

the 521st schwere Panzerjäger Abteilung and the other with the 2nd Panzer Division. The 2nd Panzer Division's vehicle was destroyed in combat, but the other one fought until it was captured intact near Stalingrad in January 1943. By that time it had claimed 22 kills.

The slow speed and lack of turret, as well as their being mechanical "orphans," were major hindrances to their utility, as was there low rate of fire due to their two-part ammunition. However, the long range and high muzzle

To build the Sturer Emil, or stubborn Emil, the VK3001 was extended to the rear, and an additional roadwheel assembly was added to each side. The open-topped fighting compartment was then added to the top rear.

Looking somewhat like an oversized Dicker Max, the Sturer Emil was based instead on larger VK3001 tank chassis. Built by Henschel, the Sturer Emil, more properly known as the 12.8 cm Selbstfahrlafette L/61, also had a much more powerful gun.

velocity of their massive cannon offset these disadvantages to a certain extent. These vehicles were able to claim T-34 kills at ranges to 4,500 yards, something no other vehicle could do.

12.8 cm Selbstfahrlafette L/61

Length	9.7 m	Ammo stowage, main	15-18 rnds
Width	3.16 m	Ammo stowage, secondary	600 rnds
Height	2.7 m		
Weight	35 tons	Engine make	Maybach
Fuel capacity	450 liters	Engine model	HL 116
Maximum speed	20-25 km/hr	Engine configuration	six-cylinder, liquid cooled
Crew	5		
Communications	FuG5	Engine displacement	11.6 liters
Weapon, main	12.8 cm PaK 40 L/61	Engine horsepower	300
Weapon, secondary	7.92mm MG34		

Even with a 300-horsepower engine, the massive Sturer Emil was underpowered, especially considering the entire vehicle had to be maneuvered to roughly aim the weapon.

Patton Museum, Fort Knox, KY

The leading and trailing torsion bars of the VK3001 suspension had to be strengthened in order to support the overhanging weight of the long cannon.

Patton Museum, Fort Knox, KY

The second prototype lacked the dummy "driver's" compartment on the right side. Both vehicles were dispatched to the Russian front, where one was destroyed and the other captured.

Patton Museum, Fort Knox, KY

Part of the five-man crew of the first prototype pose with their vehicle at their home base of Wünstorf.
H. Fleischer via Thomas Anderson

Patton Museum, Fort Knox, KY

Projectiles were stowed vertically in racks, while the cased powder charges were stored horizontally in the lockers to the left of the photo.

Patton Museum, Fort Knox, KY

Ammunition storage on the left side of the superstructure was almost a duplicate of that found on the right side. The two-part ammunition caused a relatively low rate of fire.

Patton Museum, Fort Knox, KY

A door was installed in the rear of the fighting compartment, the latches for which are visible here. In spite of the size of the vehicle, crew conditions were crowded.

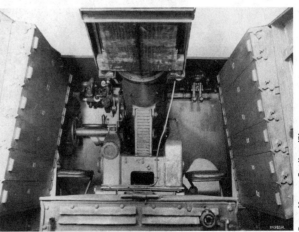

Patton Museum, Fort Knox, KY

Though the vehicle was underpowered, it certainly was not under-armed. The Sturer Emil was credited with destroying well-protected Soviet tanks at ranges to 4,500 meters.

4.7 cm PaK(t) (Sfl) auf Panzerkampfwagen 35R 731(f)

With the fall of France, Germany had captured hundreds of Renault R35 tanks. Because Germany's tanks were superior, many of these war prizes were used as chassis for other vehicles. Previously, the mounting of the Czech 4.7 cm antitank gun on the Panzerkampfwagen I had been successful, so a similar installation was tried on the R35 chassis. Improvements were made in armor protection, primarily by creating a four-sided fighting compartment, rather than merely relying on the gun shield, as had been the case with the Panzerjäger I.

Briefly used on the Russian front, for which the French chassis was ill-suited, the vehicles were returned to the West to serve out the rest of their careers. They were armed with the Czech 4.7 cm antitank gun.

Patton Museum, Fort Knox, KY

Alkett was contracted to do the design and assembly work, and it produced a mild-steel prototype in February 1941, and in turn was awarded a contract for 200 series vehicles. These vehicles were completed between May and October 1941. Twenty-six of these were command vehicles armed only with a ball-mounted MG34, rather than the 4.7 cm antitank gun.

The new vehicles were dispatched to Russia, where the French-designed chassis quickly failed en masse due to the severity of the Russian winter. Other vehicles dispatched to the West, in climates that the R35 had been designed for, were substantially more reliable, and were used for many years.

4.7 cm PaK(t) (Sfl) auf Panzerkampfwagen 35R 731(f)

Length	4.30 m	Communications	Fu.Spr. Ger."a"
Width	1.87 m	Weapon, main	4.7 cm PaK(t)
Height	2.11 m		
Weight	10.5 tons	Engine make	Renault
Fuel capacity	168 liters	Engine configuration	four-cylinder, liquid cooled
Maximum speed	20 km/hr (12.4 mph)		
Range, on road	130 km (80.6 miles)	Engine displacement	5.8 liters
Range, cross country	80 km (49.6 miles)	Engine horsepower	85 @ 2200 rpm
Crew	3		

Germany captured many relatively new armored vehicles when France fell. Many of these they adapted to new uses in the Wehrmacht. Among these were Renault R35 tanks. Some of these were converted to Panzerjäger, as seen here.

Patton Museum, Fort Knox, KY

Panzerselbstfahrlafette 1a 5 cm PaK38 auf Gepanzerter Munitionsschlepper

In July of 1940, Rheinmetall was tasked with developing a light tank destroyer suitable for use by airborne troops, as well as dismounted infantry. Using the recently developed Borgward VK3.02 artillery tractor as a basis, a vehicle armed with the 5 cm PaK38 L/60 was developed.

The fighting compartment, such as it was, was the area behind the antitank gun's spaced armor gunshield. This offered protection only from 7.92mm armor piercing ammunition.

Despite initial plans to have produced 200 of these by April 1945, only two were completed. These were sent forth for troop trials in July 1942. By that time the 5 cm PaK38 was no longer a viable antitank gun and the project was abandoned.

The gunshield was essentially all the armor protection offered the gun crew. The driver was protected by the vehicle's hull. The welded-up vision port of the artillery tractor is visible here.

Panzerselbstfahrlafette 1a 5 cm PaK38 auf Gepanzerter Munitionsschlepper

Width	1.83 m		Engine make	Borgward
Weight	4.5 tons		Engine model	6M RTBV
Maximum speed	30 km/hr (18.6 mph)		Engine configuration	six-cylinder
Crew	3		Engine displacement	2.3 liters
Weapon, main	5 cm PaK 38 L/60		Engine horsepower	50 hp @ 3300 rpm

Work began in 1940 to develop this light tank destroyer, the Panzerselbstfahrlafette 1a, utilizing the chassis of the experimental Borgward artillery tractor.

The gun crew's position on this vehicle was very cramped. Only two of these were produced for trial purposes before production plans for the vehicle were scrapped.

Patton Museum, Fort Knox, KY

The vehicle was armed with the 5 cm PaK 38 L/60, and, among other uses, was intended for use by German airborne troops.

Panzerselbstfahrlafette 1c 5 cm PaK 38 auf Panzerkampfwagen II Sonderfahrgestell 901

In July 1940, Rheinmetall was contracted to design a light tank destroyer based upon the M.A.N. VK9.01 Panzerkampfwagen II chassis.

The armament selected for this program was the 5 cm Kanone l/60, which was based on the PaK38.

Four men crewed the small, high-speed (60 km/hr) vehicle, and two fully equipped trial vehicles were built. These two vehicles were dispatched to the East for troop trials with the unit ultimately known as the 559th Tank Destroyer Battalion.

As a result of these trials, plans for the production of more than 2,000 series vehicles were abandoned.

Looking rather like a miniaturized Marder, this 1940 Rheinmetall design Panzerselbstfahrlafette 1c never went into production. Two trial vehicles, built in late 1941, were the sole examples.

7.5 cm PaK40/1 auf Geschützenwagen Lorraine Schlepper (f) (Sd.Kfz. 135)

Very similar to the howitzer-armed Geschützwagen Lorraine-Schlepper für le.F.H. 18/4 except for the weapon, the 7.5 cm PaK40/1 auf Geschützenwagen Lorraine Schlepper (f) (Sd.Kfz. 135) was another example of Germany's adaptive reuses of captured vehicles.

The French Lorraine artillery tractor had an open-topped armored superstructure installed instead of the original cargo compartment. Its relatively thin armor was proof only against small arms and splinters, and was intended to protect the gun crew from infantry, not against tanks. Inside that superstructure was installed the excellent German PaK 40/1 L/46 7.5 cm antitank gun. The gun shield of the PaK was placed outside the front of the superstructure. This arrangement permitted the weapon to be traversed 32 degrees either side of center.

Army workshops in Paris and Krefeld produced 170 of these conversions in 1942. The resultant vehicles were used throughout the remainder of the war. Though first issued to Panzerjäger units of Infantry Divisions on the Eastern front, the vehicles were soon recalled to the Western front. Once there, they were used in the defense of Normandy with some degree of success.

7.5 cm PaK40/1 auf Geschützenwagen Lorraine Schlepper (f) (Sd.Kfz. 135)

Width	1.85 m	Weapon, secondary	7.92mm MG34
Weight	8 tons	Ammunition stowage, main	40 rnds
Fuel capacity	111 liters		
Maximum speed	34 km/hr (21.08 mph)	Engine make	DelaHaye
		Engine model	103TT
Range, on road	120 km (74.4 miles)	Engine configuration	six-cylinder
Range, cross country	75 km (46.5 miles)	Engine displacement	3.56 l
Crew	4		
Communica-tions	FuG 5.	Engine horsepower	70 @ 2800 rpm
Weapon, main	7.5 cm PaK 40/1		

Patton Museum, Fort Knox, KY

This Panzerjäger was built on the French Lorraine carrier chassis. The box-like superstructure was added at German Army workshops in Paris.

Patton Museum, Fort Knox, KY

The vehicles were fitted with the 7.5 cm PaK 40/1. The gunshield was external to the superstructure, allowing room for 32-degree traverse either side of center.

Ordnance Museum, Aberdeen Proving Ground, MD

This captured vehicle was displayed indoors at Aberdeen Proving Ground following its evaluation by U.S. engineers. It was moved outdoors many years ago.

Bundesarchiv photo

The open nature of the Panzerjäger made for harsh conditions for their crews during the bitter cold of the Russian winters. Note the snow shovel strapped to the side of the fighting compartment and the whitewashed winter camouflage scheme.

Geschützpanzer 39 H(f) 7.5 cm PaK40(Sf) Hotchkiss

Similar in design to the 7.5 cm PaK40/1 auf Geschützenwagen Lorraine Schlepper (f), these vehicles were built based on the captured French Hotchkiss H-35 light tank chassis. However, the conversion work was much more complicated, resulting in essentially only the floor pan and drive line of the French tank being reused.

About 24 of these tank destroyers were built, each armed with the 7.5 cm PaK 40 L/46 anti-tank gun. Designated 7.5cm PaK40(Sf) auf Geschutzwagen 39H(f), this vehicle, like others, is popularly known as the Marder I.

Its open-topped fighting compartment housed the weapon and four-man crew. The main weapon had a traverse of 30 degrees left and right, and its gunshield was external to the fighting compartment. A 7.92mm MG 34 was carried inside the fighting compartment. The conversion work was done at Army workshops in Paris under the command of Capt. Alfred Becker during 1942. The resulting vehicles were used in France.

Geschützpanzer 39 H(f) 7.5 cm PaK40(Sf) Hotchkiss

Width	1.85 m	Communications	Fu.Spr.Ger.
Weight	12.5 tons		
Fuel capacity	207 liters	Weapon, main	7.5 cm PaK40 L/46
Maximum speed	35 km/hr	Engine make	Hotchkiss
Range, on road	180 km	Engine configuration	six-cylinder, liquid cooled
Range, cross country	95 km	Engine displacement	5.97 liter
Crew	4	Engine horsepower	120 @ 2800 rpm

Patton Museum, Fort Knox, KY

This Hotchkiss conversion was more complicated than the similar Lorraine Schlepper-based conversion, with most of the H-35 being cut away. Only 24 of these were produced by the Paris workshops.

7.5 cm PaK40/1 auf Geschützenwagen FCM(f)

Just before the outbreak of World War II, France had developed the FCM-36 light tank. Designed to compete with the R-35, the FCM-36 featured welded hull construction. Unfortunately, the diesel-powered FCM-36 was considerably more expensive than the R-35, so only 100 were procured.

Germany captured about 50 of these vehicles when France was conquered. During 1943, 10 of these were used as the basis for conversion to Panzerjäger.

To accomplish this conversion, the turret of the tank was removed and a boxy armored superstructure added to house a 7.5 cm PaK 40 L/46 anti-tank gun. The newly created Panzerjägers were designated 7.5cm PaK40(Sf) auf Geschutzwagen FCM(f) and, like so many other vehicles, are loosely referred to as Marder I. Like most of the other Marder I variants, these conversions were done at Army workshops in Paris. The four-man crew, as well as the antitank gun, was housed in an open-topped fighting compartment with armor protection ranging from 10 to 40mm. This was sufficient against small arms.

The vehicles were deployed in France with "Schnelle Brigade West," which became part of the 21st Panzer Division in 1943.

7.5 cm PaK40/1 auf Geschützenwagen FCM(f)

Length	4.77 m	Weapon, main	10.5 cm le.F.H. 16
Width	2.14 m	Weapon, secondary	7.92mm MG
Height	2.23 m		
Weight	12.8 tons	Ammo stowage, main	50 rnds
Fuel capacity	260 liters		
Maximum speed	28 km/hr (17.36 mph)	Ammo stowage, secondary	2,000 rnds
Range, on road	200 km (124 miles)	Engine make	Ricardo-Berliet
Crew	4	Engine configuration	four-cylinder, diesel
Communications	Fu.Spr.Ger.	Engine horsepower	91 @ 1550 rpm

Patton Museum, Fort Knox, KY

Only 10 Panzerjäger were built by reusing captured FCM-36 chassis. The vehicle was named the 7.5 cm PaK40/1 auf Geschützenwagen FCM(f). It was armed with a 7.5 cm PaK 40 L/46 gun and used exclusively in France.

Pz Kpfw II (Flamm) Ausf. A and B (Sd Kfz 122) Flamingo

Development of this flamethrowing tank, based on the Panzerkampfwagen II, began in early 1939. Prior to this, a few Panzer I's had been retrofitted with flamethrowers by troops in the field. Those field-modified tanks were only marginally successful, as the useable range of the flamethrowers, which were originally man-packs, was so short it made the tank vulnerable.

The Panzerflammwagen (Sd.Kfz. 122), later known as the Panzerkampfwagen II (Flamm), addressed this problem in a variety of ways. A specially designed flame nozzle, known as a Spritzköpf, was mounted on each front fender. These spray heads were independently traversable through 180 degrees. These nozzles were engineered to maximize the range of the flame oil. The fluid was propelled by compressed nitrogen that was stored in four cylinders inside the tank. Ignition of the oil was provided by an acetylene-fueled torch.

An MG 34 was mounted via a ball mount in the turret, allowing the vehicle a moderate amount of conventional offensive capability.

Production of the Ausf. A began in April 1939. Wegmenn built 46 vehicles on Panzerkampfwagen II Ausf. D chassis manufactured by M.A.N. by the end of August. Additional flamethrowers were built by Wegmann on conventional gun tanks returned for conversion.

Orders for 150 Ausf. B vehicles were placed even before the first series was completed. Production of this series, utilizing newly assembled M.A.N. chassis, began in August of 1941, but prior to that date the order had been reduced to 90 vehicles. After that decision was subsequently reversed, new orders came down for the remaining chassis be used to construct tank-killers. Sixty-two Ausf. B flamethrowers had been constructed by that time. These were subsequently converted to tank killers with no flamethrower structure.

Though they saw limited action, these vehicles, like most flame weapons, were very effective.

Specifications Pz Kpfw II (Flamm) Sd.Kfz. 122

Length	4.90 m	Weapon, coaxial	7.92mm MG 34
Width	2.40		
Height	1.85	Flame oil stowage	160 liters
Weight	12.0 tons	Ammo stowage, secondary	2,250 rnds
Fuel capacity	200 liters		
Maximum speed	55 km/hr (34.1 mph)	Engine make	Maybach
Range, on road	200 km (124 miles)	Engine model	HL62TR
Crew	3	Engine configuration	straight six-cylinder
Communica-tions	FuG 5	Engine displacement	6.2 liter
Weapon, main	2 x Flam-menwerfer	Engine horsepower	140 @ 2600 rpm

The Panzerkampfwagen II (Flamm) had only a ball-mounted machine gun in its turret. However, a special nozzle for spraying flame oil was mounted on the leading edge of each fender. These nozzles were aimed independently from inside the tank.

Bundesarchiv photo

Panzer B2 (F)

Consistent with the German military practice of reusing or adapting captured vehicles, the decision was made to build a flame-projecting tank utilizing the French Char B as a basis. The French hull-mounted 7.5 cm gun was removed, and the same type Flammenwerfer-Spritzköpf that had previously been used on the Panzerkampfwagen II (F) was installed in its place. Twenty-four tanks were converted in this manner. These were issued to Panzerabteilung (F) 102, which employed them in operation Barbarossa.

Development of Char B-based flamethrowers continued with a second series. These vehicles differed from the initial production in that a pump was used to induce the flow of the flame oil, rather than the compressed nitrogen used previously. The flame oil was stored on the rear of the tank in a fuel compartment made of armor plate. At least 60 of these improved flamethrowers were built beginning in December 1941, and the vehicles served on both fronts for the duration of the war.

The main armament of the Char B was normally a 7.5 cm gun mounted in the hull. This gun was removed as part of the flammpanzer conversion process, and the space it occupied was taken up by the flame projector.

The German military liked the idea of a flamethrowing tank, and the Panzer II-based flamethrower was reasonably successful. A second series of Flammpanzers was based on captured French Char B tanks. This one was knocked out in Holland in 1944.

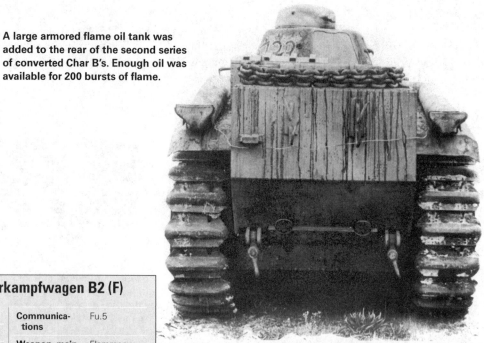

A large armored flame oil tank was added to the rear of the second series of converted Char B's. Enough oil was available for 200 bursts of flame.

Specifications Panzerkampfwagen B2 (F)

Length	6.86 m	Communications	Fu.5
Width	2.52 m	Weapon, main	Flammenwerfer-Spritz-köpf
Height	2.88 m		
Weight	32 t		
Fuel capacity	400 liters	Weapon, secondary	4.7 cm cannon
Maximum speed	28 km/hr	Engine make	Renault
Range, on road	140 km	Engine model	307
Range, cross country	100 km	Engine configuration	six-cyl, liquid cooled
Crew	4	Engine displacement	16.5 liters
		Engine horsepower	300 @ 1900 rpm

The mount for the flamethrower, which replaced the 7.5 cm gun, was designed by Wegmann, while Köebe designed the flamethrower itself.

Unlike earlier systems that used pressurized gasses (usually nitrogen) as a propellant, the second series of Char B conversions used a pump to force the flame oil through the nozzle.

Mechanically, the Panzer B2 (F) remained essentially as they were under French ownership. These vehicles served on both the Eastern and Western fronts.

Panzerkampfwagen III (F1)

Pleased with the success of the Koebe pump-driven flame system mounted in the second series of Panzerkampfwagen B2 (F), the Waffenamt had the same system installed in the turrets of Panzerkampfwagen III. The Panzer III Ausf. M was used as the base vehicle for these conversions. The hull-mounted MG 34 was retained, and a second was mounted coaxially with the flame projector in the turret. A small Auto-Union engine powered the pump, which was fed from two containers holding a combined 1,020 liters of flame oil. Ignition for the flame oil was electrical, as opposed to the acetylene used with the Panzerkampfwagen II-based Flammpanzers.

Wegmann in Kassel completed 100 of these vehicles, all on chassis produced by Miag. These vehicles were used in platoon-sized units in both Italy and along the Eastern front.

Patton Museum, Fort Knox, KY

Flame is an extremely demoralizing weapon, and naturally is very effective against infantry. However, it has an extremely short range, and the smoke generated makes it fairly easily for opposing artillery to target return fire.

Panzerkampfwagen III (FL)

Length	6.41 m		Weapon, coaxial	7.92mm MG 34
Width	2.97 m		Weapon, ball mounted	7.92mm MG 34
Height	2.50 m		Flame oil stowage	1,020 liters
Weight	23.8 tons		Ammo stowage, secondary	3,450 rnds
Fuel capacity	320 liters			
Maximum speed	40 km/hr (24.8 mph)		Engine make	Maybach
Range, on road	155 km (96.1 miles)		Engine model	HL 120 TRM
Range, cross country	95 km (58.9 miles)		Engine configuration	V-12, liquid cooled
Crew	5		Engine displacement	11.9 liters
Communications	Fu. G. 5		Engine horsepower	265 @ 2600 rpm
Weapon, main	14 mm Flammwerfer			

Patton Museum, Fort Knox, KY

Crews of the Flammpanzers, such as this Panzerkampfwagen III (Fl), had to undergo specialized training, not only in the equipment, but tactics as well. This crew was photographed during a training exercise.

The Panzerkampfwagen III (Fl) used a variation of the pump-supplied flame projection system that had been developed for the late Panzer B2 (F). Raw oil could be projected 50 meters, while burning oil could reach a little further, on out to 60 meters.
Patton Museum, Fort Knox, KY

Patton Museum, Fort Knox, KY

The flame oil itself was a powerful irritant. Dousing infantry even without ignition would induce surrender. Of course, leaks and spills inside the tank were hazardous to the tank crew. The oil had a good saturation effect, and once sprayed and ignited, most frame structures were completely destroyed.

Sturmgeschütz-I (FLAMM)

In December of 1943, Hitler approved the conversion of 10 Sturmgeschütz into flamethrowers. Initially it was thought new chassis would be used for these vehicles, but in the end it was decided to utilize 10 older vehicles that had been returned for depot overhaul. Nine of these converted vehicles were available in May 1943, with the 10th one being completed the following month.

Very little information about these 10 vehicles has surfaced. One was involved in an accident and had to be rebuilt in July. At least two of these vehicles were again converted, this time reverting to their original assault gun configuration in 1944.

Sturmgeschütz III (F1)

Length	5.52 m	Weapon, main	14 mm Flammnwerfer
Width	2.95 m		
Height	2.16 m	Weapon, secondary	7.92mm MG 34
Weight	23 tons		
Fuel capacity	310 liters	Ammo stowage, secondary	600 rnds
Maximum speed	40 km/hr (24.8 mph)		
Range, on road	140 km (96.8 miles)	Engine make	Maybach
		Engine model	HL 120 TRM
Range, cross country	85 km (52.7 miles)	Engine configuration	V-12, liquid cooled
Crew	4	Engine displacement	11.9 liters
Communications	Fu. 15 or Fu. 16, intercom	Engine horsepower	265 @ 2600 rpm

National Archives and Records Administration photo.

A limited number of Sturmgeschütz were converted to flamethrowers per Hitler's request. The superstructure was modified, and an unusual-looking mounting assembly installed in its place. Some of these vehicles were later converted back into standard Sturmgeschütz.

Flammpanzer 38

Once again, Hitler's special interest in flamethrowers came into play during November 1944. At that time he demanded that a large number of flame tanks be made available in a short period of time. In response to this, 20 Jagdpanzer 38 were drawn from the ČKD factory on December 8, 1944, for conversion to flamethrowers.

The Koebe pump-operated projection system was chosen for the Flammpanzer 38. Cartridge-type igniters were used with this installation, having been perfected in May of 1944. Seven hundred gallons of flame oil were carried, which meant that the Flammpanzer could fire 60 or so short bursts without refilling. A sleeve was installed around the flame projector tube to camouflage the vehicle as a normal tank destroyer. Unfortunately, this tube was flimsy, and when damaged fouled the flame projector, preventing its operation.

Mechanically, the Flammpanzer 38 was identical to the familiar Jagdpanzer 38, but the lighter load on the front suspension due to the flame gun improved steering.

The Flammpanzer 38 saw their first combat during Operation Nordwind during the winter of 1944-45. The vulnerability of flame tanks to conventional tank and antitank weapons resulted in high losses, but the vehicles continued to be employed well into 1945.

Flammpanzer 38

Length	4.87 m without projector	**Weapon, main**	14mm Flammenwerfer 41
Width	2.63 m	**Weapon, secondary**	7.92mm MG 34
Height	2.10 m		
Weight	16 metrics	**Flame oil stowage**	700 liters
Fuel capacity	320 liters	**Ammo stowage, secondary**	600
Maximum speed	40 km/hr (24.8 mph)		
Range, on road	180 km (111.6 miles)	**Engine make**	Praga
Range, cross country	130 km (80.6 miles)	**Engine model**	AC
Crew	4	**Engine configuration**	six-cyl., liquid cooled
Communications	Fu.Spr.f	**Engine displacement**	7.75 liters
		Engine horsepower	150 @ 2600 rpm

One of Germany's more successful attempts at a flamethrowing tank was based on the Jagdpanzer 38. Its most notable weakness was the easily damaged dummy gun that hid the flame mechanism. Damage to the sheet metal housing could render the flamethrower inoperable.

Patton Museum, Fort Knox, KY

The same characteristics that served it well as a tank destroyer, low profile, narrow track, and well-sloped armor, benefited the Flammpanzer 38. However, it also had the same weakness: thin side and rear armor.

The Flammpanzer 38 retained the remote-controlled machinegun of the Jagdpanzer 38. Though the machinegun was removed from this captured example, the mount can be seen atop the hull.

An array of German military vehicles described in this book are visible in this period photo. Visible are a Panzerkampfwagen III tank, a Kübelwagen, Sd.Kfz. 250 and Sd. Kfz. 251 halftracks, and a Medium Uniform Car, as well as other vehicles. Note the variety of paint schemes.

Germany mastered the combined use of infantry and tanks, as seen by these soldiers keeping close company with a Panzer III. One arm, without the other, is almost always doomed to failure.

The 5.0 cm Kw.K. 38 L/42, as seen on this Panzer III, was largely obsolete by 1942. Soviet and British tanks were arriving on the battlefield with heavier armor than this weapon could defeat from a safe distance.

Maintenance of combat equipment is always intensive, and this was especially the case in the rigors of operations in Russia and North Africa. Here, the Maybach power plant has been removed from a Panzer IV. Note the cooling fans on the underside of the open engine compartment hatch.

According to prewar planning, the Panzer IV, shown here, was to be the heavy tank in Germany's armored formations. Its purpose was to destroy enemy fortifications and antitank weapons at long ranges, allowing the Panzer II and III tanks to roam the battlefield freely, supporting an infantry advance. As the war progressed, the Panzer II became quickly obsolete, and the distinctions between the purpose of Panzer III and IV blurred.

Patton Museum, Ft. Knox, KY

The forward-swinging, one-piece turret doors used on the early Panzer IV are evident on the Ausf. E in the foreground. There are 30mm-thick supplemental armor plates on the side of the superstructure.

Patton Museum, Ft. Knox, KY

The Panzer II introduced widespread use of torsion bar suspension on tanks. The Panzer III, Panther, Tiger, and even modern day U.S. tanks such as the M60 and M1 Abrams all utilize torsion bar suspension.

National Archives and Records Administration

The Tiger is widely perceived to have ruled the battlefield, and indeed was a formidable opponent, but the vehicles were not invincible. This knocked-out Tiger has been pushed off the roadway and rolled partially on its side, permitting the victorious Allied troops to advance.

Patton Museum, Ft. Knox, KY

A Panther hull, nearing completion, is lowered onto its tracks. The Panther was quite likely Germany's best tank, but was beset by mechanical problems early on. Those teething problems, coupled with the Allied war effort crippling component suppliers, and the usual internal struggle within the Reich weapons program prevented the design from being fully exploited.

A Demag Sd.Kfz. 10 halftrack, owned and restored by Bob Graebe, pauses near a Swiss G13, converted to resemble a Jagdpanzer 38 (alias Hetzer), during an exhibition at the Patton Museum, Ft. Knox, Kentucky.

The 1-ton Sd. Kfz. 10 halftrack was widely used as a light prime mover and infantry transport. Like much of Germany's war material, few survive today.

American halftracks had rubber-band tracks and a driven front axle, while German halftracks such as this one had steel link tracks and a non-driven front axle. The German vehicles were designed so that the tracks assisted in making sharp turns.

The G13, like the Jagdpanzer 38 it was based on, was mechanically reliable and had well-shaped, although thin, armor. Its best defense was its low profile and small frontal area. This example is owned by the Patton Museum, Ft. Knox, Kentucky.

One of the most immediately recognized German vehicles to emerge from WWII was the Type 82 VW Kubelwagen. Built by Volkswagen, this vehicle was the German Army's equivalent to the Jeep. Its lighter weight and air-cooled engine made it in some ways superior to the American vehicle.

The mainstay of Germany's wheeled transport was the Opel Blitz. Produced by GM's German subsidiary, the Blitz was originally a commercial truck offered in 1-, 1 1/2- and 3-ton capacities. The 1 1/2- and 3-ton versions saw widespread military use, and four-wheel-drive versions of the 3-tonner were even built.

Denise Moss

This 3-ton Blitz is owned and restored by Bob Graebe. It was configured as a general service cargo and troop transport vehicle. Blitzes were also equipped with van, workshop, tanker, and communications bodies, among others.

Denise Moss

Another Volkwagen-built military vehicle was this, the Schwimmwagen (Type 166). A scouting and reconnaissance vehicle with limited load carrying capacity, its distinction was its amphibious abilities.
Ideal for calm, inland waters, the Schwimmwagen was decidedly out of its element in rough water.
Denise Moss

This restored Panzer IV, part of the Ordnance Museum collection on display at Aberdeen Proving Ground, wears the markings of Rommel's famed Afrika Korps.

The supplemental armor protecting the sides and face of the superstructure, a stop-gap measure at best in the face of the British Matilda and the Soviet T34, can be seen in this view.

The Sd. Kfz. 2 Kettenkraftrad is often thought of as a tracked motorcycle. Even though its maker, NSU, was a motorcycle builder, the Kettenkraftrad was really a small halftrack prime mover. Its unique appearance made it a tempting toy when captured by curious Allied soldiers.

This Sd. Kfz. 10 halftrack coupled to a Nebelwerfer 41 six-tube rocket launcher was on display at the annual military vehicle show at Beltring, England. Although the Sd. Kfz 10 was a prime mover, its small size limited it to light loads.

Simon Thomson

The Sd. Kfz. 250 was a small halftrack designed to transport half of a heavy machinegun section with some degree of armor protection. Engineered by Demag, it was based on the Sd.Kfz. 10 soft-skin halftrack.

Simon Thomson

Abwurfvorrichtungen on Panzerkampfwagen I

For years the Abwurfvorrichtungen on Panzerkampfwagen I has been misidentified as a Ladungsleger, which had been intended to perform a similar function. That function was to place (or, more accurately, drop) explosive charges on bunkers and obstacles.

One hundred Pz.Kpfw.I were equipped with Abwurfvorrichtungen (the charge dropping device), following orders issued in late December 1939. The completed vehicles were assigned to Panzer-Pionier-Kompanien (armored engineer companies) for use in the French Campaign during May and June 1940.

A cable was used to release the 50-kilogram charge suspended from the Abwurfvorrichtungen mounted on the rear of the Panzerkampfwagen I. This arrangement allowed demolition charges to be placed on obstacles without exposing the troops to small arms fire.

The Panzer I remained able to fight as a normal combat tank, but the Abwurfvorrichtungen mounted on the rear interfered with rearward firing of the gun. It was intended that these vehicles be issued two each to the five destruction platoons within the Panzer-Pionier-Kompanie.

B I Minenräum-Wagen (Sd.Kfz. 300)

This small vehicle was developed by Borgward for clearing mine fields. Capable of being driven either directly or via remote control, the concrete-bodied vehicle was designed to tow a set of mine clearing rollers. The crew consisted of only the driver, when the vehicle was not being radio controlled.

Development work began in late 1939, and by May 1940 the full order of 50 vehicles had been completed, although at this point they had not had their radio gear installed. When completed, the vehicles were assigned to the Minen-Räum-Kompanie of Panzer-Abteilung 67.

The cast concrete body of the B I conserved the use of strategically important armor plate while protecting the mechanical components from the effects of detonated mines. The roller assembly shown behind the vehicle was designed to be towed through mine fields to set off charges. Evidently, it was hoped that somehow the Minenräum-Wagen itself would not trigger any antitank mines with its tracks.

B II Minenräum-Wagen (Sd.Kfz. 300)

The second series of Borgward Minenräum-Wagen entered production in July 1940. These vehicles were longer and heavier than the previous series, and featured an armor plate on the front of the concrete hull. The earlier model's four-cylinder engine was replaced with a six-cylinder.

Like its predecessor, it could tow mine rollers or carry a charge that could be detonated by remote control. The concussion of an exploding 300-kilogram charge would detonate mines in a 20-meter radius around the vehicle.

The two-speed transmission allowed a top speed of 5 km/hr, making it necessary to haul the vehicles to front-line areas. The first use of these vehicles came with the onset of operation Barbarossa in June 1941. Almost immediately they were found to be ineffectual, as their charges were too easily set off.

The B II Minenräum-Wagen from Borgward was slightly longer and heavier than the earlier model, but both had hulls made of concrete. The new version was powered by a six-cylinder engine, rather than the four-cylinder used previously.

"Goliath" leichte Ladungsträger (Sd.Kfz. 302 & 303)

Certainly one of the most interesting German engineer vehicles, at least in the eyes of the average GI or Tommy facing off against them was the diminutive Goliath. Consistent with the tongue-in-cheek naming of certain German vehicles (the 200-ton super-heavy tank was name "mouse"), Goliath was about 5 feet long and weighed about 400 kilograms.

These vehicles, developed by Borgward, were actually tethered remote-controlled demolition charges. Development took place from 1940 through 1942, when series production began.

Two versions of these vehicles were built. The first one to enter production was the electrical-powered Sd.Kfz. 302. These were manufactured from April 1942 through January 1944, with production totaling 2,635 units.

The positioning of the return rollers on these units readily identify them as the electrically operated version.

U.S. forces encountered the Goliath self-propelled mine first at Anzio, then again at Normandy, where this photo was taken. In most cases, the vehicles were not successful, as they were too vulnerable to small arms fire. Wherever they were found, when disarmed they were of great curiosity to GI's.

Capable of speeds up to 10 km/hr, these vehicles carried a 60-kilogram demolition charge. The vehicle was fitted with 6mm frontal armor for protection from small arms fire. However, there was no armor on the sides, leaving these areas vulnerable. Small arms could be used to set off the charge, or, more commonly, disable the unit's drive mechanism.

A slightly larger version entered production in April 1943. Rather than dual electric motors, these units were driven by a two-stroke Zundapp gasoline engine. Two variants of the gasoline-powered Goliath were produced—one carrying a 75-kg charge, the other a whopping 100 kilograms of explosives. The armor on the gasoline-driven units was upgraded to 10mm, but the sides were still vulnerable. The last of the 4,929 of these machines was built in January 1945. As with the electrically driven unit, a drum in the rear of the vehicle dispensed the tether cable as the vehicle moved forward.

These vehicles were employed by German armored engineer units on all fronts, but never achieved the success hoped for by their users.

A gasoline-powered Goliath is being removed from its transport wagon prior to use in Warsaw in August 1944. Electromagnetic clutches were used to steer the vehicle. The vulnerability of the wire tether and the unarmored side were the Goliath's two major weaknesses.

The return idler of the gasoline-powered Goliath was much closer to the ground. The gas version carried a larger charge than the electric unit, but more importantly, it had a much greater range.

Goliath Sd.Kfz. 302

Length	1.50 m	Range, on road	1.5 km (.93 miles)
Width	.85 m	Range, cross country	.8 km (.49 miles)
Height	.56 m	Explosive charge	60 kg
Weight	370 kg	Power plant	2 x 2.5 kw motor
Fuel capacity	2 batteries		
Maximum Speed	10 km/hr (6.2 mph)		

Goliath Sd.Kfz. 303a

Length	1.62 m	Explosive charge	75 kg
Width	.84 m	Engine make	Zundapp
Height	.60 m	Engine model	xxxx
Weight	365 kg	Engine configuration	two-cylinder, two-stroke, air-cooled
Fuel capacity	6 liter	Engine displacement	703 cc
Maximum speed	11 km/hr (6.82 mph)	Engine horsepower	12.5 @ 4500 rpm
Range, on road	1.2 km (.74 miles)		
Range, cross country	.6-8 km (.37-.45 miles)		

National Archives and Records Administration

This was the fate of many of the Goliath: captured, and stacked like so much cordwood in a dump. Most of the vehicles visible in this photo are the gasoline-powered version. Even with their destruction eminent, they were fascinating to GIs.

Sprengladungsträger (Sd Kfz 301) Ausf. A and B

Interest in remote-controlled charge layers remained high within the German Army High Command. With the earlier attempts not very successful, in October 1941 work began on a new series of these vehicles. As it had with several earlier designs, the Waffenamt turned to Borgward, Bremen as the prime contractor.

The result was the B IV, which Borgward based loosely on its VK 302 experimental munitions carrier. The basic premise of its design was that it could be driven normally to a point near the action. At that time, the driver would exit the vehicle, and the vehicle continue via radio control. A 500-kilogram charge was secured to the front of the vehicle. This charge was designed to slide off, and the vehicle could then back away prior to detonation. This was an improvement over earlier designs that took their transport vehicle's destruction as a matter of course. However, the B IV was also equipped with a belly-mounted pressure switch. This switch could be connected to the demolition charge and the vehicle steered across a minefield. When the B IV sat off a mine, that blast would close the pressure switch, detonating the demolition charge. The concussion of that much larger blast would then off any other mines in a 20-meter radius.

Production of the first series, the Ausf. A, totaled only 120 units. The remainder of the almost 800 B IV were Ausf. B. These vehicles included side and rear armor, in addition to frontal armor, folding armored flaps to protect the driver, as well as an escape hatch. Some of these vehicles were equipped with dry pin tracks. Production of the Ausf. B ended in December 1943.

The Sprengladungsträger were issued to radio-controlled tank companies, which used Panzerkampfwagen III or Sturmgeschütz as control vehicles.

B IV Sprengladungsträger Ausf. A

Length	3.650 m	Communications	EP, UKE6
Width	1.800 m	Explosive charge	500 kg
Height	1.185 m		
Weight	3.6 tons	Engine make	Borgward
Fuel capacity	123 liters	Engine model	6M 2.3 RTBV
Maximum speed	38 km/hr (23.56 mph)	Engine configuration	six-cylinder, liquid cooled
Range, on road	200 km (124 miles)	Engine displacement	2.247 liters
Range, cross country	125 km (77.5 miles)	Engine horsepower	49 @ 3300 rpm
Crew	1		

Patton Museum, Fort Knox, KY

The earliest series of B IV, the Ausf. A, had only a windshield to protect the driver. These vehicles also rode on rubber-cushioned tracks.

One of the first deployments of the new series of demolition charge carriers came in 1942 in Crimea. The B IV was a considerable improvement over earlier designs.

The Ausf. B had numerous improvements over the Ausf. A, not the least of which was the installation of folding armored shields for the driver. They are shown here in the raised position.

Patton Museum, Fort Knox, KY

The Ausf. B also had 5mm armor added to its sides and rear, while the Ausf. A only had armor protection on the front.

Patton Museum, Fort Knox, KY

The explosive charge was carried on the sloping glacis at the front of the vehicle, which slid to the ground when released. Because the charge was equipped with a delayed-action fuse, the vehicle could be backed a safe distance away prior to detonation.

Patton Museum, Fort Knox, KY

The small size of the Sprengladungsträger is apparent here. Weighing between 3.5 and 4 tons, the vehicle had a six-cylinder engine that propelled it up to 38 km/hr (23.56 mph)

Schwere Ladungsträger (Sd Kfz 301) Ausf. C

Reports from the field indicated that there was room for improvement in the B IV, particularly in the areas of protection and maneuverability. Accordingly, the vehicle was redesigned, and the Ausf. C introduced. The driver's compartment was relocated to the left side of the vehicle, and the escape hatch introduced on the Ausf. B was deleted. Armor protection was increased to 20mm, and a six-cylinder engine installed. The latter modification resulted in a major redesign of the rear of the vehicle.

Production of this version of the Ladungsträger began by in December 1943 and continued until Speer's October 1944 order curtailed production. At that time, Borgward had completed 322 out of the 400 vehicles ordered.

These vehicles were utilized and deployed in the same manner as their predecessors.

Patton Museum, Fort Knox, KY

The Schwere LadungsträgerSd Kfz 301 Ausf. C utilized dry-pin steel track. Its driver's compartment was located to the left of the vehicle centerline. Earlier Ausf. had the driver's compartment to the right.

B IV c schwere Ladungsträger

Length	4.10 m	Communications	EP, UKE6
Width	1.83 m	Explosive charge	500 kg
Height	1.25 m		
Weight	4.8 tons	Engine make	Borgward
Fuel capacity	135 liters	Engine model	6B 3.8 TV
Maximum speed	40 km/hr (24.8 mph)	Engine configuration	six-cylinder, liquid cooled
Range, on road	250 km (155 miles)	Engine displacement	3.745 liters
Range, cross country	125 km (77.5 miles)	Engine horsepower	78 @ 3000 rpm
Crew	1		

Patton Museum, Fort Knox, KY

The driver's protective armored flaps had small vision slits in them. Visible on the left rear of the body is the muffler for the six-cylinder engine.

Installation of the larger, more powerful engine on the Schwere LadungsträgerSd Kfz 301 Ausf. C necessitated the enlargement of the engine compartment. This resulted in the rear deck being raised considerably from its former height.

The rear of the vehicle was rather plain. An access hole for installation of a manual engine starter crank was low on the rear panel. Two masts supported lights that were used as an aid in steering the vehicle via radio control.

This well-traveled vehicle crossed the Atlantic twice. Careful examination of the stenciling on the engine deck reveals this captured vehicle was shipped from Aberdeen Proving Ground, Maryland, to England for further evaluation. The charge box has been opened and is empty, and its upper plate is missing..

The charge box is absent from this vehicle. The ability of the B IV series to drop their charges, withdraw, and be rearmed was a considerable improvement over the disposable nature of their predecessors.

Mittler Ladungsträger "Springer" (Sd Kfz 304)

The Mittler Ladungsträger, popularly known as the "Springer," marked the reversion to the "disposable" charge-laying vehicle, rather than reusable vehicles such as the B IV. In the interest of speeding the design and manufacturing efficiency, the contractor for the Springer, NSU, utilized many components from its successful Kettenkraftrad semi-tracked motorcycle.

The vehicle was designed to be controlled either by a driver on board, or through radio signals. Its payload was a 350-kilogram demolition charge, which was carried internally. When Speer halted the manufacturing of the Borgward B IV in October 1944, the debut of the Springer moved up accordingly, though it was not originally scheduled to enter production until May 1945.

Only 50 of these vehicles were built, the last being completed in February 1945. It is not known if any were used operationally.

Patton Museum, Fort Knox, KY

Folding armored panels could be raised to protect the driver when the vehicle was locally controlled. When the Springer was operated by radio control these panels were folded down, lowering the vehicle's silhouette.

Springer mittler Ladungsträger

Length	3.15 m	Crew	1
Width	1.43 m	Communications	KE6, UKE6
Height	1.45 m		
Weight	2.4 tons	Explosive charge	330 kg
Fuel capacity	65 liters	Engine make	Opel
Maximum speed	42 km/hr (26.04 mph)	Engine configuration	four-cylinder, liquid cooled
Range, on road	200 km (124 miles)	Engine displacement	1.5 liters
Range, cross country	80 km (49.6 miles)	Engine horsepower	38

Patton Museum, Fort Knox, KY

The Mittler Ladungsträger, or "Springer," shared many of its suspension components with the Kettenkraftrad, which was also produced by NSU.

National Archives and Records Administration

A 350-kilogram charge was carried in the forward compartment of the vehicle. Unlike the Borgward B IV, the self-destructive Springer could not drop its charge.

National Archives and Records Administration

This view from the rear of a captured vehicle reveals the motorcycle-style handlebars used to control the vehicle from onboard. An Opel four-cylinder engine powered the machine.

Patton Museum, Fort Knox, KY

One of the first 12 experimental Springers undergoes testing. These vehicles lacked the track covers incorporated in the production vehicles.

Minenräumgerät mit Pz.Kpfw.Antrieb

Little is known about this vehicle. The sole example was captured by U.S. forces. Based on the Panzerkampfwagen III, the suspension was extended considerably in order to distance the hull from the blast of exploding mines. The design included a forward-projecting boom carrying mine rollers, but this arrangement proved unwieldy and difficult to control.

This captured Minenräumgerät mit Pz.Kpfw.Antrieb was transported to Aberdeen Proving Ground, Maryland, where these photos were taken, for evaluation.

It was hoped that the unusual reinforced extended suspension would protect both the vehicle and its crew from the mines it was designed to detonate.

Schweres Minenräumfahrzeug "Räumer-S"

This odd-looking vehicle was designed by Krupp with the purpose of exploding mines with its reinforced wheels. The articulated machine had an engine and driver's position in each end. Total seating was eight men, with four in each end. The articulated steering was hydraulically actuated. Even though work on this project began in 1942, at the end of the war only a sole example existed, which the U.S. captured.

The only Räumer S was captured by U.S. forces at the Krupp facility in Hillersleben near the end of the war. The GI posing beside it illustrates the huge size of the veicle. Less apparent is its incredible weight—110 tons!

Brückenleger II

Rivers and chasms have delayed advancing armies for time immemorial. It was natural then that Germany developed a means of overcoming these type obstacles as part of their doctrine of rapidly advancing mechanized warfare. As early as 1939 the Waffenamt was developing armored vehicle-launched bridges.

For bridges with an 8-ton capacity, the Panzerkampfwagen II chassis was selected for the basis. M.A.N. completed at least three Brückenleger on Panzer II chassis in 1939. Total production is unknown.

The Brückenleger II were used during the German advance into Poland. The 8-ton capacity of the bridge limited the system's utility.

Brückenleger IV

A heavier bridge, with an 18-ton capacity, was designed for installation on Panzer IV chassis. In mid-1939 Krupp completed 6 Panzerkampfwagen IV Ausf. C chassis for use as a basis of such vehicles. Both Krupp and Magirus were tasked with assembling armored bridgelaying equipment on what would become a total of 20 chassis. In addition to the Ausf. C chassis mentioned above, Ausf. D chassis were also produced for this purpose in early 1940. By the end of April, 20 Brückenleger IV had been produced.

The weight-reducing holes in the beams of the Brückenleger IV c were circular, rather than oval. During a demonstration, this vehicle has deployed its bridge panel on the ground to show how the bridge equipment can be used to scale obstacles.

These vehicles were issued in platoons of four to the Engineer Companies of five Panzer divisions for use in France and Belgium. Their usage in these areas proved to be less than successful, and resulted in the scrapping of plans to produce 40 more. However, an experimental series of four Brückenleger IV c was built in January 1941. These were used with some success on the Eastern front by the 3rd Panzer Division. Of note is that the bridging equipment of the IV c was transported by truck, and transferred to the armored chassis just prior to emplacement.

A Brückenleger IV b demonstrates how assault bridging can be used to breach dragon's teeth tank barriers. The Brückenleger IV b can be distinguished from the IV c by the oval holes in the bridge beams, as well as the radically different launching mechanism.

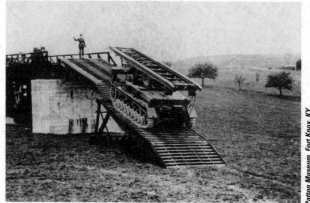

A second bridge layer has moved in and placed its bridge panel to span between the first panel and the elevated objective. The chassis, sans panel, ascends the obstacle by way of the bridge panels.

Again, two bridge panels are being used, this time in a more conventional means. Although 20 Brückenleger IV b were constructed, only four of these Brückenleger IV c were built, and they were used on the Eastern front.

Brückenleger IV s (Sturmstegpanzer)

Another variation of bridging equipment mounted on the Panzerkampfwagen IV chassis was the Sturmstegpanzer. Looking very much like what they were (aerial firefighting ladders adapted to tank hulls), these ladders could be extended across rivers and gaps. Two ladders could be extended parallel to each other and bridging timbers laid between them. Only four of these vehicles were built in early 1941. The chassis used were those of Panzerkampfwagen IV Ausf. C. The Third Panzer Division took these vehicles with it to Russia in 1941, and successfully used them in July of that year. However, chassis failure caused half the vehicles to be lost.

The Brückenleger IV s, also known as the Sturmstegpanzer, utilized large telescoping ladders to span distances. This one appears to have fallen victim to antitank mines.

Landwasserschlepper

Work developing these unusual vehicles began in May 1935. The combined efforts of Alkett, Huettenwerke, Rheinmetall-Borsig, Sachsenberg, and Maybach produced a vehicle to fulfill the Army's broad requirement.

The objective was to produce a single vehicle that could be a tractor, tugboat and a ferry. As the Landwasserschlepper was intended for use by engineers in a support role, it was neither armed nor armored. Delivery of trial vehicles began in late 1940 and continued into 1941. Less than 30 of these vehicles were built, with most used for testing and training, although at least one was sent to North Africa.

The earliest Landwasserschleppers had the large windows in the pilothouse, like those on this example. However, these proved vulnerable to breakage by waves, and were soon reduced in size. Likewise, the fenders over the front of the tracks were eliminated on later models.

A Maybach HL120TRM engine drove the vehicle both on the ground and in the water, with water propulsion coming from 800mm propellers. Its 600-liter fuel tank allowed it to operate for about 6 hours without refueling.

The large side window was eventually replaced with a large porthole, and the number of rear portholes reduced from three to two on later vehicles.

Landwasserschlepper

Length	9.0 m	Crew	3	
Width	3.0	Engine make	Maybach	
Height	3.15 m	Engine model	HL 120 TRM	
Weight	15 tons	Engine configuration	V-12, liquid cooled	
Fuel capacity	600 liters	Engine displacement	11.9 liters	
Maximum speed, land	40 km/hr (24.8 mph)	Engine horsepower	265 @ 2600 rpm	
Maximum speed, water	12.5 km/hr (6.25 mph)			

In this photo taken by the British during evaluation, the Landwasserschlepper looks very much like a boat sitting on Panzer tracks.

Steps were cut into the sides of the hull on the later vehicles to make boarding easier for the crew. Note the large centrally located exhaust stack for the Maybach HL120 TRM tank engine that powered the vehicle.

The two 800mm propellers that drove the vehicle through water can be seen here. The vehicle consumed 100 liters of gasoline per hour when operating in the water.

A captured Landwasserschlepper languishes at Aberdeen Proving Ground after the war. These vehicles were not armored. They were constructed of sheet metal and designed as they were to keep water out. They also kept rainwater in, making periodic maintenance a necessity.

Panzerfähre

Rather than the Jack-of-all-trades intent of the Landwasserschlepper, the Panzerfähre was developed especially to transport tanks and other combat vehicles across water while under fire.

The Panzerfähre shown here is undergoing trials. It is doubtful either of the vehicles saw combat use. The vehicles shared many components with the Panzerkampfwagen IV.

Patton Museum, Fort Knox, KY

The bold concept was that two of these vehicles, with decking between them, would work as a normal ferry, shuttling across rivers and lakes.

Work on these odd armored vehicles began in April 1941, with metalwork starting in July. Magirus did the final assembly, although a host of other firms were also involved in the production of the two experimental vehicles. The vehicles shared a powertrain with the Panzer IV, and had armor protection against small-arms fire.

Panzerfähre

Length	8.25 m	Engine model	HL 120 TRM
Width	2.8 m	Engine configuration	V-12, liquid cooled
Height	2.5 m	Engine displacement	11.9 liters
Weight	17 tons		
Engine make	Maybach	Engine horsepower	265 @ 2600 rpm

Patton Museum, Fort Knox, KY

The Panzerfähre, unlike the Landwasserschlepper, was armored and protected its crew against small arms fire. Only two of these vehicles are known to have been built. This one was photographed at the Magirus plant.

Fully tracked armored support vehicles

Munitionsschlepper auf Pz Kpfw I (SdKfz 111)

As the Panzer I tanks became obsolete they were converted for a number of other uses. Beginning in September 1939, one of these uses was the conversion into an ammunition carrier. This was done mainly by removing the turret and covering the turret ring with an armored hatch. The new vehicle was designated Munitionsschlepper auf Pz Kpfw I. In early 1943, it was mandated that all of the remaining Panzer I tanks were to be converted in this manner. In some instances, the entire superstructure was removed, but in most cases just the turret was removed. These turrets were then reused in fixed fortifications.

Patton Museum, Fort Knox, KY

The conversion of obsolete Panzerkampfwagen I tanks for use as tractors and ammunition carriers was straightforward. In most cases, including the one shown here, the conversion amounted to merely removing the turret and installing plating over the resulting opening.

Artillerie Schlepper 35(t)

A few of the Panzerkampfwagen 35 (t) taken over by the German army were converted into open-topped artillery tractors. Some were used to provide armored ammunition and crew transport for field artillery, while others had a small mortar installed, creating a motorized mortar carrier. Only a handful of these conversions were performed.

Patton Museum, Fort Knox, KY

The Artillerie Schlepper 35(t) was one of many adaptive reuses the German Army had for captured or obsolete tanks and equipment.

Patton Museum, Fort Knox, KY

A canvas cover, supported at the rear by a bow, covers the opening resulting from the removal of the Panzerkampfwagen 35(t)'s turret.

Heavy draft gear was installed on the rear of the former tank chassis, in order to allow the secure attachment of field artillery.

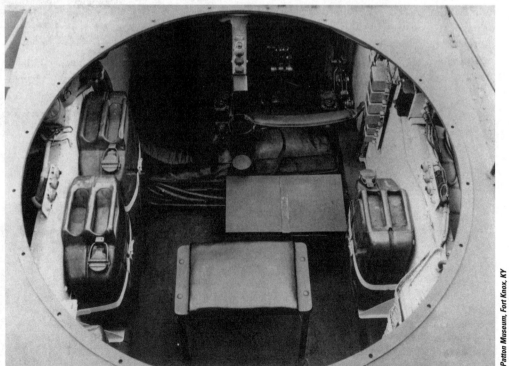

The interior of the Artillerie Schlepper 35(t) had little room to spare. The open bolt holes previously secured the turret ring.

Patton Museum, Fort Knox, KY

Munitionspanzer 38(t) (Sf) Ausf. M (Sd.Kfz. 138/1M)

One of the major shortcomings of the Grille was its limited ammunition stowage. In an effort to combat that, 103 ammunition carriers were built using the same chassis and hull. These vehicles had racks allowing them to transport 40 15 cm howitzer rounds. This commonality was advantageous for parts supply and training. The ammunition carriers had additional ammunition stowage racks that could be removed, plating over the weapon aperture, and a howitzer installed. This allowed the field conversion of the vehicle into an armed Grille, providing the units with a ready source of spare chassis for repair.

The first 10 of these vehicles were built in November 1943 using the rear-engined Ausf. H chassis. The remaining 93 were built in the first half of 1944 on Ausf. M chassis.

Munitionspanzer 38(t) (Sf) Ausf. M (Sd.Kfz. 138/1M)			
Length	4.835 m	Weapon, main	7.92mm MG34
Width	2.150 m	Ammo stowage, cargo	40 15 cm rnds
Height	2.400 m		
Weight	11.5 tons	Engine make	Praga
Fuel capacity	218 liters	Engine model	AC
Maximum speed	42 km/hr (26.04 mph)	Engine configuration	six-cylinder, liquid cooled
Range, on road	185 km (114.7 miles)	Engine displacement	7.75 liters
Range, cross country	140 km (86.8 miles)	Engine horsepower	150 @ 2600 rpm
Crew	5		
Communication	Fu.Spr.16		

CKD archive via Kliment collection

The munitionspanzer 38(t) was built to provide a carrier to resupply Grille batteries with ammunition. Each battery of six howitzers was supposed to have two carriers.

Munitionspanzer auf Fahrgestell Panzerkampfwagen III

As the German Army advanced into Russia, the Wehrmacht leadership made a number of discoveries. One of these was that the Panzerkampfwagen III was woefully inadequate to deal with the better Soviet tanks. The other was that the weather made Russian road conditions horrendous. These two revelations came together, and in an effort to make the best of bad situations, beginning in May 1943 obsolete Panzerkampfwagen III had their turrets removed and were converted into ammunition carriers. Of greater advantage than their armor protection was their tracks, which provided better mobility in mud and snow than either transport trucks or even halftracks.

Patton Museum, Fort Knox, KY

A Munitionspanzer III resupplies a Tiger I along the Eastern front. The Munitionspanzer's armor protected the crew and cargo from small arms fire, but the vehicle's biggest asset was its mobility in these conditions.

Munitionsfahrzeug III/IV

The ammunition stowage on board the Hummel was only 30 rounds—woefully inadequate for sustained bombardment. An ammunition carrier was developed that utilized not only the same chassis, but the same superstructure. The mobility of these vehicles was the same as that of the Hummel, as were repair procedures and parts. Called the Munitionsfahrzeug III/IV (ammunition carrier), this vehicle could be converted to a standard Hummel by removing the extra armor plate closing the front of the fighting compartment and installing the howitzer and mount from a donor Hummel. This allowed the quick "repair" of a Hummel that had sustained severe chassis or drivetrain damage. A total of 157 of these vehicles were built, and they were intended to be assigned two Munitionsfahrzeug per battery of six Hummel.

Munitionsfahrzeug III/IV

Length	6.20 m	Communications	Fu.Spr.Ger. f
Width	2.97 m		
Height	2.81 m	Ammo stowage, cargo	48
Weight	23 tons		
Fuel capacity	600 liters	Engine make	Maybach
Maximum speed	42 km/hr (26 mph)	Engine model	HL 120 TRM
Range, on road	215 km (133.3 miles)	Engine configuration	V-12, liquid cooled
Range, cross country	135 km (83.7 miles)	Engine displacement	11.9 liters
Crew	6	Engine horsepower	265 @ 2600 rpm

Patton Museum, Fort Knox, KY

As was the case on the early Hummel, the early Munitionsfahrzeug III/IV had a narrow driver's compartment extending from the sloping hull front. The armor plate that closed the gap in the superstructure, caused by the removal of the howitzer and its mount, is visible here.

The Munitionsfahrzeug III/IV was identical to the Hummel, which allowed the quick conversion of the vehicle into self-propelled artillery if circumstances demanded it.

Late-production Munitionsfahrzeug III/IV had the full-width driver's and radio operator's compartment. This example was captured by U.S. troops.

Munitionsschlepper für Karlgerät

The immense size of the ammunition for the giant "Karl" mortars—each shell weighed about 2 tons—required specialized equipment for both transport and handling. For this purpose an unknown number of Panzerkampfwagen IV chassis, both new construction and rebuilt, were modified as ammunition carriers for the huge mortars. Only four rounds could be carried by each Panzer IV, on special racks on the rear of the superstructure. Naturally there was no turret.

A derrick built by Demag and driven by the Panzer IV's turret drive was used to load and unload the shells. It was located in the approximate position of the radio operator's compartment on a normal tank. Ausf. D, E and F chassis are known to have been used as the basis for these unusual vehicles. Of course, these vehicles were assigned only to units with the Karl mortars.

Walter J. Spielberger

Photographed just outside of the Krupp-Gruson plant where it was assembled, this Munitionsschlepper für Karlgerät's crane is near its maximum effective reach.

Although the derrick could reach either side of the Munitionsschlepper, normally it was positioned with its right side toward the mortar.

Walter J. Spielberger

Walter J. Spielberger

The compartment on the rear of the superstructure could store up to four of the huge shells for the Karl mortars. The hook is positioned here over the cargo area.

Walter J. Spielberger

The cable-operated derrick was folded down for transport, as shown here. Panzerkampfwagen III D, E and F chassis were used as the basis for these vehicles.

National Archives and Records Administration.

This Munitionsschlepper for Karl was displayed after WWII at Aberdeen Proving Ground. Notice how the front of the superstructure of these vehicles was very different than the front of the Panzerkampfwagen IV.

Wheeled and semi-tracked armored vehicles

Maschinengewehrkraftwagen (Kfz 13)/ Funkkraftwagen (Kfz 14)

Among the earliest armored cars built during Germany's rearmament immediately prior to WWII were these two vehicles. Based on strengthened Daimler-Benz and Adler automobile chassis, they were far from ideal armored vehicles.

The two vehicles, Maschinengewehrkraftwagen (Kfz 13) and Funkkraftwagen (Kfz 14), were quite similar to each other, regardless of which chassis was used. Daimler-Benz did the conversion work on both their own as well as the Adler chassis, and mounted the armored bodies on the vehicles. The thin armor cold resist only 7.92mm fire, and even at that only the front was proof against armor piercing rounds.

As its name implies, the Maschinengewehrkraftwage n Kfz 13 was armed with a machinegun—a 7.92mm MG 13. This weapon was pedestal mounted and could rotate 360 degrees. One thousand rounds of ammunition were carried for the weapon.

The Funkkraftwagen (Kfz 14) lacked the machinegun armament of its cousin. Instead, the interior space was occupied by a 5-watt transmitter and receiver capable of both voice and key operation.

Thirty radio vehicle and 116 machinegun carriers were completed between 1933 and 1935. It is unlikely that any of these vehicles saw front-line service during the war.

Kfz. 13 and Kfz. 14-Daimler-Benz construction

Length:	4.20 m	Tire size	6.00-20
Width	1.70 m	Weapon, main	7.92mm MG13 in Kfz. 13 only
Height	1.46 m		
Weight	2.1 tons	Ammo stowage, main	1,000 rnds
Fuel capacity	45 liters		
Maximum speed	70 km/hr (43.4 mph)	Engine make	Daimler-Benz
		Engine configuration	6 cyl., liquid cooled
Range, on road	250 km (155 miles)		
Range, cross country	150 km (93 miles)	Engine displacement	2.6 liter
Crew	2	Engine horsepower	50 hp
Communica- tions	Fu9 SE 5 in Kfz. 14 only		

Here are two of the Kfz. 13 armored reconnaissance cars, with a similar Kfz. 14 radio car barely in the photo to their right. The Kfz. 14 Funkkraftwagen, or radio car, had a small radio set instead of the pedestal-mounted machinegun of the Kfz. 13.

Patton Museum, Fort Knox, KY

The Maschinengewehrkraftwagen, also known as the Kfz. 13, was a 4x4 light reconnaissance car armed with an MG 13. Its armor was proof only against 7.92mm ammunition.

Patton Museum, Fort Knox, KY

The passenger car heritage of these vehicles was evident by their styling. These vehicles carried only two-man crews.

Patton Museum, Fort Knox, KY

The Kdz. 14 was readily identified by its frame-type radio antenna. A large radio set was carried in lieu of a machine gun. While both Adler and Daimler-Benz built these vehicles, the example shown is a Daimler-Benz product.

Patton Museum, Fort Knox, KY

Sd. Kfz. 221

Unlike its predecessor, the Sd. Kfz. 221 was built on a chassis especially engineered for armored cars. Hence its Sd. Kfz. designation, rather than Kfz. designation. The vehicle had four-wheel drive and four-wheel steer and a relatively powerful engine, which combined to give the vehicle acceptable off- and on-road operation.

What appears to be a turret on the roof of the vehicle was actually a manually rotated open-topped gun shield. Folding screens were provided in an effort to prevent grenades from being tossed in. Initially, an MG13 was installed on the vehicle, but later MG34 machineguns were retrofitted in their place. Ultimately some vehicles had the 2.8 cm s.Pz.B.41 mounted on them.

During the 1935 through 1940 production run the vehicles were not equipped with radios, although beginning in 1941 radios were installed in some of the vehicles.

Sd.Kfz. 221

Specifications	Sd.Kfz. 221	Communications	none from factory
Length	4.80 m	Tires	210-18
Width	1.95 m	Weapon, main	7.92mm MG 34
Height	1.70 m		
Weight	4.0 tons	Ammo stowage, main	1,000 rnds
Fuel capacity	110 liters		
Maximum speed	80 km/hr (49.6 mph)	Engine make	Horch
		Engine model	801
Range, on road	320 km (198.4 miles)	Engine configuration	V-8, liquid cooled
Range, cross country	200 km (124 miles)	Engine displacement	3.5 liters
Crew	2	Engine horsepower	75 @ 3600 rpm

Patton Museum, Fort Knox, KY

This is one of two pre-production prototypes of the Sd. Kfz. 221 built by Eisenwerk Weserhütte AG. The slightly raised area forward of the gun mount and just above the driver distinguished the prototype vehicles. The single vision flap for the driver set the 221 apart from the later 222 and 223.

The square rear grille of the Sd. Kfz. 221 was also found on a few of the earliest Sd. Kfz. 223, so is not a sure-fire identifier. The triangular plates mounted on the wheels are hub protectors.

Maschinenfabrik Niedersachsen in Hannover and Schichau built production versions of the 221. Both used the four-wheel-drive and four-wheel-steer chassis, built by Horch in Zwickau, known as the Einheitsfahrgestell (uniform chassis 1 (801) for heavy motor vehicles). The evenly sloped rear armor also separated the 221 from the later 222 and 223, which had stepped rear armor.

The Sd. Kfz. 221 had a two-man crew. Here, one of the crew watches a building burn, probably in Russia. With only a 75-hp liquid-cooled engine, the Sd. Kfz. 221 had a hard time in such conditions.

Beginning early in 1942, the armament of the Sd. Kfz. 221 was upgraded from the previously carried 7.92mm machinegun (either MG13 or later the MG 34) with a 2.8 cm s.Pz.B.41 antitank gun.

The new weapon profoundly increased the firepower of the vehicle, but it was far too lightly armored to linger if the first round did not knock out the opposing vehicle. The Sd. Kfz. 221's armor could only withstand 7.92mm rifle and machinegun rounds.

The Sd. Kfz. 221 closely resembled the Sd. Kfz. 223 from the front. However, the leading edge of the 221 fenders turned down much more sharply than did those of the 223. The Sd. Kfz. 221 also had only a single forward visor for the driver.

Kliener Panzerfunkwagen (Sd.Kfz. 260 and 261)

Like the Sd.Kfz. 221, 222, and 223, these vehicles were built on the Einheits-fahrgestell I f.s.Pkw, or standardized chassis for heavy armored cars. Like the other vehicles in this series, they were equipped with four-wheel steering and four-wheel drive. However, unlike the other vehicles on this chassis, they were bereft of any armament.

These were strictly communications vehicles, with the Sd.Kfz. 260 equipped for ground-to-air communications, while the Sd.Kfz. 261, with its large frame antenna, was used for long-range communications on the ground.

Two different chassis were used in the production of these vehicles, with the Ausf. B having a slightly more powerful engine. Delays prevented both the trial vehicles and initial production vehicles from being completed on schedule. However, almost 500 of these vehicles were built from April 1941 through April 1943.

Sd.Kfz. 260 and Sd.Kfz. 261

Length	4.83 m	Communications, Sd.Kfz. 261	kl.Pz.Fu.Tr. d, Fu 10 SE 30, Fu.Spr. Ger. a
Width	1.99 m		
Height	1.78 m		
Weight	4.3 tons	Tires	210-18
Fuel capacity	100 liters	Weapon	none
Maximum speed	75 km/hr (46.5 mph)	Engine make	Horch
		Engine model	801
Range, on road	320 km (198.4 miles)	Engine configuration	V-8, liquid cooled
Range, cross country	200 km (124 miles)	Engine displacement	3.5 liters
Crew	4	Engine horsepower	75 @ 3600 rpm
Communications, Sd.Kfz. 260	kl.Pz.Fu.Tr. c, Fu 7 SE 20, Fu.Spr. Ger. a		

Unlike the other vehicles built on this common chassis, neither the Sd.Kfz. 260, nor 261, carried any mounted weapons. Instead, they were used purely for radio communications.

Patton Museum, Fort Knox, KY

This Sd.Kfz. 261 traveling through North Africa by rail allows us to see the arrangement of the rear of the vehicle. Its antenna is in the raised position, forming a handy seat for some of the crew.

This Sd.Kfz. 261 has its antenna folded down. Not only did this protect the antenna from damage, it also lowered the vehicle's silhouette and made its command/communications role less visible.

The preproduction prototype of the Sd.Kfz. 260 was not completed until April 1940, more than 2 years behind schedule. Note the guard surrounding the turn signal indicator on the side of the hull.

Sd.Kfz. 222

The Sd. Kfz. 222 was built on a common chassis with the Sd. Kfz. 223. This was a chassis especially engineered for armored cars. Like the Sd. Kfz. 221 and 223, this vehicle had four-wheel drive and four-wheel steer and a relatively powerful engine. It was slightly heavier than the Sd. Kfz. 221 while using the same Horch 801 V-8 engine, so off-road performance suffered slightly. The Sd. Kfz. 222 had a three man crew: driver, gunner and commander, who also loaded the machinegun.

What appears to be a turret on the roof of the vehicle is actually a manually rotated open-topped gun shield. Folding screens were provided in an effort to prevent grenades from being tossed in. Initially, an MG13 was installed on the vehicle, but in later production MG34 machineguns were installed instead.

During the 1937-42 production run the vehicles were not equipped with radios, although beginning in 1942 and continuing until production ceased in 1944 radios were installed in some of the vehicles.

Sd.Kfz. 222			
Length	4.80 m	Weapon, main	2 cm Kw.K. 30.38
Width	1.95 m	Weapon, secondary	7.92mm MG 34
Height	2.00 m		
Weight	4.8 tons	Ammo stowage, main	180 rnds
Fuel capacity	100 liters		
Maximum speed	70 km/hr (43.4 mph)	Ammor stowage, secondary	1,050 rnds
Range, on road	300 km (186 miles)	Engine make	Horch
Range, cross country	200 km (124 miles)	Engine model	801
Crew	3	Engine configuration	V-8, liquid cooled
Communications	none from factory	Engine displacement	3.5 liters
Tires	210-18	Engine horsepower	75 @ 3600 rpm

Patton Museum, Fort Knox, KY

The Sd.Kfz. 222 was much more heavily armed than the preceding German four-wheel armored cars. It had both a 2 cm Kw.K. and a 7.92mm machinegun in its open-topped turret. Hinged mesh covers were provided to keep out grenades.

The left-side muffler and exhaust pipe are visible on this captured example. A mirror image of this exhaust system was installed on the opposite side.

The engine was installed in the rear, as it was also on the Sd.Kfz. 221 and 223. The round hub protectors visible here were typical of later armored car production.

A canvas cover has been installed to keep the interior dry during overseas shipment of this vehicle. Notice the mounting location of the spare tire.

The spare has been removed from this captured Sd.Kfz. 222, revealing its mounting bracket. The measuring sticks of the evaluators show just how small these vehicles were.

The Sd.Kfz. 222 presented a small target for enemy gunners, especially from head-on.

The dual weapon mount has been elevated and the protective screens opened in this photo, providing an excellent view of both. Although better armed than its predecessors, the Sd.Kfz. 222 was nevertheless a scouting vehicle, and the weapons were for self-defense.

The Sd. Kfz. 223 was built on a chassis specially engineered for armored cars. Like the Sd. Kfz. 221 and 222, this vehicle had four-wheel drive and four-wheel steer and a relatively powerful engine, which combined to give the vehicle acceptable off- and on-road operation. It was slightly heavier than the Sd. Kfz. 221 while using the same Horch 801 V-8 engine, so off-road performance suffered slightly. The Sd. Kfz. 223 had a three-man crew: driver, radio operator and commander, who also operated the machinegun.

What appears to be a turret on the roof of the vehicle is actually a manually rotated open-topped gun shield. Folding screens were provided in an effort to prevent grenades from being tossed in. Initially, an MG13 was installed on the vehicle, but MG34 machineguns were installed instead in later vehicles.

Throughout the 1936-44 production run the vehicles were equipped with radios, At first the vehicles were equipped with 30-watt radio sets. Later-production vehicles came with 80-watt sets, which were also retrofitted to older vehicles.

Sd.Kfz. 223

Length	4.56 m	Tires	210-18
Width	1.95 m	Weapon, main	7.92mm MG 34
Height	2.00 m		
Weight	4.4 tons	Ammo stowage, main	1,050 rnds
Fuel capacity	100 liters		
Maximum speed	75 km/hr (46.5 mph)	Engine make	Horch
		Engine model	801
Range, on road	300 km (186 miles)	Engine configuration	V-8, liquid cooled
Range, cross country	200 km (124 miles)	Engine displacement	3.5 liters
Crew	3	Engine horsepower	75 @ 3600 rpm
Communications	Fu.10 SE 30		

Patton Museum, Fort Knox, KY

The Sd. Kfz. 223 was a standard radio vehicle for the German military throughout WWII. Early vehicles, such as this one, are distinguished by their equal-sized front vision ports.

Initially, these vehicles were equipped with 30-watt Fu. 10 radio sets, but later versions had the 80-watt Fu. 12 sets installed. The frame antennas folded down to afford a greater field of fire for the MG34 7.92mm self-defense machinegun.

This captured vehicle, being evaluated at Aberdeen Proving Ground, has its antenna swung up into the normal operating position. Note the "step" in the rear armor at the rear antenna mount, a feature that distinguished the Sd. Kfz. 223 from the earlier Sd. Kfz. 221.

The tapered hatch over the rear engine compartment also distinguished the 4.8-ton 223 from the 4-ton 221, which had a rectangular hatch in this position. These vehicles also had four-wheel drive and four-wheel steer.

The turret of the Sd. Kfz. 223 was small and housed only the antiaircraft machine gun, whereas the turret of the similar Sd. Kfz. 222 housed a machine gun and coaxial cannon.

National Archives and Records Administration

This knocked-out Sd. Kfz. 223 has the different-sized front vision ports characteristic of later production vehicles. Bulletproof tires were installed on these vehicles prior to 1943, although it is doubtful that they would have helped in this case.

ww2mm.com

A spare tire was carried on the right side of the vehicle. A stowage box occupied a similar position on the left side of the vehicle.

ww2mm.com

Large, irregular-shaped doors provided access to the interior of the Sd. Kfz. 223, and its sister vehicle, the Sd. Kfz. 222. The white balls on the ends of the shafts were markers to aid the driver in judging distance. This was necessary due to the poor visibility from inside the vehicle.

Sd.Kfz. 231 (6-rad)

The Sd.Kfz. 231 (6-rad), like its companion vehicle the Sd.Kfz. 232 (6-rad), was based on contemporary German 6 x 4 truck design. Most of the chassis used for the Sd.Kfz. 231 were provided by Daimler-Benz, with the bodies being fabricated by armor manufacturers. The armor was designed to protect the vehicle and occupants from 7.92mm fire from ranges exceeding 30 meters.

Although the conventional engine-in-front layout was retained, an additional driver's station was provided at the rear of the vehicle. This allowed the vehicle to reverse

directions, even without enough space for a 180-degree turn.

On top of the vehicle was a manually traversed turret fitted with a 2 cm cannon and a coaxial MG 13 machinegun.

Production of these vehicles ran from 1932 through 1937, at which time they were superceded by eight-wheeled armored cars that offered superior off-road mobility. Beginning during the 1935, production an antiaircraft machinegun began to be installed outside the turret, and a spare tire was carried. In spite of their limitations, these vehicles did see limited service in Austria, Poland and France.

Patton Museum, Fort Knox, KY

While the bulk of the Sd.Kfz. 231 (6-rad) were built on Daimler-Benz chassis, this particular example was built on chassis supplied by Magrius, as given away by the front fenders extending so far downward. Operationally there was little difference between vehicles, regardless of chassis builder.

Sd.Kfz. 231 (6-rad)

Length	5.57 m	Weapon, coaxial	7.92mm MG 13
Width	1.82 m		
Height	2.25	Ammo stowage, main	200 rnds
Weight	5.7 tons		
Fuel capacity	105 liters	Ammo stowage, secondary	1,500 rnds
Maximum speed	70 km/hr (43.4 mph)		
Range, on road	250 km (155 miles)	Engine make	Daimler-Benz
		Engine model	MO9
Tire size	6.00-20	Engine configuration	6 cyl., liquid cooled
Crew	4	Engine displacement	3.7 liters
Weapon, main	2 cm Kw.K. 30	Engine horsepower	65

Walter J. Spielberger

Büssing-NAG also provided chassis for the 6-rad vehicles. Shown here is one of the G31p chassis before installation of the armored body.

The Sd.Kfz. 231 (6-rad) lacked the large frame antenna that characterized its companion vehicle, the Sd.Kfz. 232 (6-rad). Internally, it also lacked the powerful long-range radio set that the 232 carried.

Early vehicles did not include a spare tire, but later production vehicles did, and they were retrofitted to the earlier armored cars as well. The spare tires were carried on the rear of the vehicle.

Not mired, but clearly demonstrating the need for all-wheel drive, which these vehicles lacked, this Second Panzer Division Sd.Kfz. 231 (6-rad) pauses next to a radio-equipped four-wheeled armored car somewhere in France. Its fender style identifies it as having a Büssing-NAG chassis. Smoke canisters are mounted ahead of its grille.

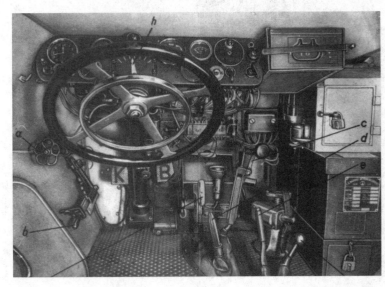

This illustration from the operator's manual shows a characteristic that the Sd.Kfz. 231 (6-rad) shared with many German armored cars, a backwards-canted steering wheel.

Scherer Panzerspähwagen (Fu) Sd.Kfz. 232 (6-rad)

The Sd.Kfz. 232 was little more than a radio-equipped version of the Sd.Kfz. 231 heavy reconnaissance car that had been introduced in the mid-1930s. Built primarily on the Magirus chassis, a few were also assembled using chassis built by Daimler-Benz and Büssing-NAG. The vehicle was originally classified as gepanzerten Kraftwagen (Fu)(Kfz.67a) before being reclassified to the more familiar Schwerer Panzerspähwagen (Fu) Sd.Kfz. 232 (6-rad) in April 1936.

Their limited cross-country mobility, due in large part to their basis on commercial 6 x 4 truck chassis, quickly rendered these vehicles obsolete, and they were withdrawn from front-line use after operations in France.

Patton Museum, Fort Knox, KY

The radio-equipped Sd.Kfz. 232 (6-rad) was easily differentiated from its radio-less counterpart, the Sd.Kfz. 231 (6-rad), by the large framework antennas.

Sd.Kfz. 232 (6-rad)

Length	5.57 m	Weapon, coaxial	7.92mm MG 13
Width	1.82 m		
Height	2.87 over antenna	Ammo stowage, main	200 rnds
Weight	6 tons	Ammo stowage, secondary	1,500 rnds
Fuel capacity	110 liters		
Maximum speed	62 km/hr (38.44 mph)	Engine make	Magirus
		Engine model	s88
Range, on road	250 km (155 miles)	Engine configuration	six-cyl., liquid cooled
Tire size	6.00-20	Engine displacement	4.6 liters
Crew	4		
Weapon, main	2 cm Kw.K. 30	Engine horsepower	70

Two Sd.Kfz. 232 (6-rad) bracket an Sd.Kfz. 231 (6-rad). The pennant on the fender displays maneuver markings. The rods with white-painted balls on the end mark the corners of the vehicle—an aid for the driver who had limited visibility from his position in the armored hull.

Patton Museum, Fort Knox, KY

An Sd.Kfz. 231 radio car speeds past another during training in 1935. The vehicle in the foreground has its turret reversed toward the rear.

Lacking all-wheel drive, these vehicles' off-road abilities were limited. Only hard-bottom crossings such as this could be attempted, as a muddy bottom would surely mire the Panzerspähwagen.

Sd.Kfz. 263 (6-rad)

In the mid-1930s, the Germans converted 12 of the then relatively new Kfz.67a (Sd.Kfz. 231 6-rad) into a radio car for use by the signal battalions of various Panzer divisions. The turret was fixed, and a flat plate formed the face of it, with a ball-mounted MG13 installed as the vehicle's only weapon.

Inside, a 100-watt radio set was installed and attached to the frame antenna. A telescoping aerial was installed as well. The new vehicles, built on Magirus-supplied chassis, were christened Kfz.67b, but that classification was superceded with Sd.Kfz. 263 (6-rad) in 1937.

Sd.Kfz. 263 (6-rad)

Length	5.57 m	**Weapon, main**	7.92mm MG 13
Width	1.82 m	**Ammo stowage, main**	1,500 rnds
Height	2.25		
Weight	5.7 tons	**Engine make**	Magirus
Fuel capacity	105 liters	**Engine model**	s88
Maximum speed	70 km/hr (43.4 mph)	**Engine configuration**	six-cyl., liquid cooled
Range, on road	250 km (155 miles)	**Engine displacement**	3.7 liters
Tire size	6.00-20	**Engine horsepower**	65
Crew	4		
Communications	FuG Spr Ger 'a'		

Walter J. Spielberger

This Sd.Kfz. of the 2nd Panzer Division was photographed as it entered Vienna in 1938. The driver, commander and radio operator are visible through the open vision ports.

Patton Museum, Fort Knox, KY

The lack of a pivot on the antenna indicates that this is a fixed-turreted Sd.Kfz. 263. From this angle the dual rear wheels used by the 6-rad can be seen.

Schwerer Panzerspähwagen Sd.Kfz. 231 (8-rad)

The off-road mobility of the German six-wheeled armored cars was limited, in part due to their modified truck chassis. To overcome these problems, the Waffenamt, through its Wa Pruef 6 automotive design office, requested Büssing NAG to design an all-new vehicle. The new vehicle, the uniform eight-wheeler, was powered by Büssing's own eight-cylinder L8V/G.S.36 engine. It entered production in late 1936.

All eight of the self-sealing tires drove and steered, and a driver's position was provided in each end of the vehicle, allowing it to be driven at top speed of 85 km/hr (52.7 mph) in either direction. A driver, a co-driver, commander and gunner made up the four-man crew.

The vehicle's armor was sufficient to protect it from 7.92mm machinegun fire at ground level. A July 1940 modification involved the addition of a spaced armor Zusatpanzer plate on the front of the vehicle. In June 1942, the thickness of the basic frontal armor was increased and the Zusatpanzer was dropped.

These vehicles were armed with a 2 cm automatic cannon and a coaxially mounted 7.92mm MG 34 machinegun. Ammunition stowage was 1,125 rounds of 7.92 and 180 rounds of 2cm, which was adequate when the cannon was fired single-shot. In May 1939, a belt-fed MG 34 with flexible mount began to be installed. At first, the 2 cm cannon was the Kw.K. 30, but in 1942 that was superceded by the Kw.K.38. The later cannon lacked the tapered profile of the former.

Beginning in 1941, the Sd. Kfz. 231 was fitted with a Funkspechgerät radio set. Prior to this no radio equipment was carried by the Sd. Kfz. 231. In 1943, this set was replaced by the more powerful Funkspechgerät f radio set.

Despite the vehicle's overtaxed drive train and the fact that its armor could be defeated by anything as small as the U.S. M2 HB .50-caliber machinegun, the Sd. Kfz. 231 (8 rad), as well as the rest of this series, continued to serve until war's end.

Schwerer Panzerspähwagen Sd.Kfz. 231

Specifications	Sd.Kfz. 231 (8-rad)	Weapon, main	2 cm Kw.K. 30/38
Length	5.85 m	Weapon, coaxial	7.92mm MG 34
Width	2.20 m		
Height	2.35 m	Ammo stowage, main	180 rnds
Weight	8.30 tons		
Fuel capacity	180 liters	Ammo stowage, secondary	2100 rnds
Maximum speed	85 km/hr (52.7 mph)	Engine make	Büssing-NAG
Range, on road	300 km (186 miles)	Engine model	L8V/GS
Range, cross country	170 km (105.4 miles)	Engine configuration	V-8, liquid cooled
Crew	4	Engine displacement	7.91 liters
Communications	none	Engine horsepower	155 hp @ 3000 rpm
Tire size	210-18		

The Sd. Kfz. 231 8-rad was the base vehicle for an entire series of eight-wheel-drive and eight-wheel-steer heavy reconnaissance cars. The Sd. Kfz. 231 8-rad was in production from 1936 through mid-1942. This vehicle is a later-production vehicle judging by the single forward vision port, pipe-type front bumper (buried beneath stowage), lack of splash guards above the visors and turn signal mounted on the fender (vertical bar above second wheel).

Bundesarchiv photo

Here is an example of a factory-fresh Sd. Kfz. 231, minus the armament. Notice the two-piece driver's hatch, twin forward visors, and turn signal semaphores mounted midships of the hull.

Walter J. Spielberger

Walter J. Spielberger

The early-production vehicles can also be identified by their flush-mounting vision ports. The mufflers, tailpipes and guards do not extend to the bottom of the fender. Later tailpipes were bent, and the muffler and guards reached nearer the bottom edge of the fender.

Fahrgestell Baumuster GS

The Sd. Kfz. 231 and its family of vehicles were built on a conventional automotive ladder-type frame. Leaf spring independent suspension was used. Notice the driver's controls at either end. The engine was installed at the rear of the vehicle.

Patton Museum, Fort Knox, KY

The Zusatpanzer plate seen extending from the front of the vehicle was intended to provide additional armor protection from heavy machineguns and light antitank rounds. The additional weight overloaded the front suspension, especially when crews packed the space between the body and the Zusatpanzer with stowage. The Viking ship painted on the hull side recognizes the service of the Hermann Göring Regiment in the Norwegian campaign.

Patton Museum, Fort Knox, KY

After the self-sealing inner tubes were discontinued in February 1943, the eight-wheeled armored cars began to carry spare tires. The antenna on the turret is for the Funkspechgerät f radio set, which was added about the same time.

Military History Institute, Carlisle Barracks, PA

The earliest vehicles did not have Zusatpanzer, or even a pipe-type front bumper. Faintly visible is the slightly tapered tube of the 2 cm Kampfwagenkanone 30. Later vehicles used the 2 cm Kw.K. 38 tank gun.

Patton Museum, Fort Knox, KY

Guards were added to protect the turn signals of this vehicle serving in North Africa. The spare tire has been removed, making its mounting bracket visible in this photo.

This overhead view of the vehicle during evaluation shows off the air intakes for the radiator, which was well protected in its almost central location. Also of interest are the mountings for the frontal armor, which had lightening holes formed in them to reduce the overhanging weight.

This captured Sd. Kfz. 231 was also photographed in North Africa, but under different circumstances! It has been recovered for evaluation. The stowage box between the front wheels is open. The "antennas" on the rear fenders are to aid the driver in judging distances from the limited-visibility vehicle.

This captured Sd. Kfz. 231 was photographed in March 1943 during its evaluation at Aberdeen Proving Ground. The rear engine access door, as well as the right side fighting compartment door, are open.

Schwerer Panzerspahwagen (Fu) (Sd Kfz 232) 8-Rad

The Sd. Kfz. 232 was intended to provide long-distance radio communications for the heavy platoon of the armored reconnaissance company of each reconnaissance battalion. For this purpose three of these vehicles were assigned to each heavy platoon.

The Sd. Kfz. 232 was developed alongside the Sd. Kfz. 231, with which it shares almost every part. They are distinguished by the powerful radio used in the 232, initially the Fu 11 SE 100, with massive frame aerial installed. With the vehicle stationary, this radio had a voice range of 70 kilometers (43.4 miles). Later, this radio was augmented with a short-range radio of the same type retrofitted to the Sd. Kfz. 231—the Funkspechgerät a. Later, the Fu 12 SE 80 radios with smaller "star" aerials were mounted instead of the Fu 11 set. In time, the Funkspechgerät f supplanted the Funkspechgerät a for short-range communications.

Production of the 232 lasted a bit longer than it did for the 231, with the last one not completed until 1943, 7 years after the first one was begun.

Bundesarchiv photo

The Sd. Kfz. 232 was distinguished from the 231 by its radio equipment. In the case of vehicles built prior to July 1942, the radio was a Fu 11 SE 100, and the antenna was the massive frame array shown here. The twin visors on the hull front also identify this as an early vehicle, later vehicles had a single larger hatch. This vehicle was photographed in the Balkans in 1941.

Sd.Kfz. 232 (8-rad)

Length	5.85 m	Weapon, coaxial	7.92mm MG 34
Width	2.20 m	Ammo stowage, main	180 rnds
Height	2.90 m		
Weight	9.10 tons	Ammo stowage, secondary	2,100 rnds
Fuel capacity	180 liters		
Maximum speed	85 km/hr (52.7 mph)	Engine make	Büssing-NAG
Range, on road	300 km (186 miles)	Engine model	L8V/GS
Range, cross country	170 km (105.4 miles)	Engine configuration	V-8, liquid cooled
Crew	4	Engine displacement	7.91 liters
Communications	Fu 11 SE 100	Engine horsepower	155 hp @ 3000 rpm
Tire size	210-18		
Weapon, main	2 cm Kw.K. 30/38		

These early Sd. Kfz. 232 are being prepared for rail shipment. Photographed from this angle, the three-point forward support for the frame antenna is clearly visible. This arrangement allowed the turret to traverse a full 360 degrees while still supporting the antenna.

Bundesarchiv photo

A brand-new Sd. Kfz. 232, at the time known as a heavy armored scout vehicle with radio Sd. Kfz. 234. The earliest vehicles, such as this, lacked both the additional frontal armor and any form of front bumper. The two-piece driver's hatch is plainly visible. The large hole in the early flush-type mantlet accepted the 2 cm cannon, while the smaller one was for the coaxial machinegun.

The engine access doors and the plate covering the emergency starter crank port are visible on the rear of the vehicle. Later mufflers and tailpipes were of a different configuration.

Surrounded by British troopers, this Sd. Kfz. 232 is already missing its armament and external stowage. Many of the doors, including one of the between-the-wheels stowage compartment doors, are open. What appears to be a handrail mounted on the side of the body is a guard to protect the turn signal arm.

This Sd. Kfz. 232's four-man crew studies a map in North Africa. A Notek night driving light has been installed on the Zusatzfrontplatte, or Zusatpanzer, which itself is a retrofitted item judging from its paint finish. The barrels of the vehicle's weapons have been covered with cloth to protect them from the grit of the desert.

The white cross centered on the rear of this Sd. Kfz. 232 is indicative of vehicles involved in the invasion of Poland. Notice the overhang of the turret when it is rotated.

Later Sd. Kfz. 232 vehicles had Fu 12 SE 80 radios and the smaller "star" aerial. The photographer did not capture the distinctive upper "star" portion of this 7th Panzer Division vehicle's antenna as it patrols the Mediterranean coast.

Schwerer Panzerspahwagen (7.5cm) (Sd Kfz 233)

The heavy armored scout vehicle armed with 7.5 cm cannon (Schwerer Panzerspahwagen (7.5cm)), known as the Sd Kfz 233 provided armored reconnaissance units with a more formidable weapon that they had previously. While the 2 cm automatic cannon of the Sd. Kfz. 231 and 232 eight wheeled armored cars was effective against lightly armored targets, the Sd. Kfz. 233's 7.5 cm StuK was much more effective against medium tanks and more substantial fortifications. These weapons were made available due to the decision to rearm the Sturmgeschütz with a higher-velocity weapon. From July 1942 through October 1943, 129 of these vehicles were built by Schichau. Most were newly constructed, but a few were built by cutting down the superstructure of rebuilt Sd. Kfz. 263 vehicles, upon which the 233 design was based.

Four men crewed these vehicles, with the commander, gunner and loader occupying the open-topped fighting compartment. Due to space and concerns about overloading the already strained chassis, only 32 rounds of ammunition were carried.

These vehicles served from Tunisia until the end of the war.

Sd.Kfz. 233

Length	5.85 m	Weapon, main	7.4 cm Kanone 37
Width	2.20 m	Weapon, secondary	7.92mm MG 34
Height	2.25 m		
Weight	8.70 tons	Ammo stowage, main	32 rnds
Fuel capacity	150 liters		
Maximum speed	85 km/hr (52.7 mph)	Ammo stowage, secondary	1,500 rnds
Range, on road	300 km (186 miles)	Engine make	Büssing-NAG
Range, cross country	170 km (105.4 miles)	Engine model	L8V/GS
Crew	3	Engine configuration	V-8, liquid cooled
Communications	Fu.Ger. a		
Tire size	210-18	Engine displacement	7.91 liters
		Engine horsepower	155 hp @ 3000 rpm

Patton Museum, Fort Knox, KY

Some of the earliest Sd. Kfz. 233 were built by cutting down the superstructure of overhauled Sd. Kfz. 263 vehicles. This accounts for the presence of Zusatzfrontplatte and turn signal guards on this vehicle. Both features were discontinued on new production prior to the July 1942 introduction of the Sd. Kfz. 233.

Bundesarchiv photo

The main armament of the Sd. Kfz. 233 was the 7.5 cm StuK L/24 cannon. A surplus of these weapons was created when the Waffenamt decided to rearm the Sturmgeschütz with the long-barreled StuK L/43 in March 1942. The Sfl.Z.F.1 periscopic dial sight is visible just to the side of the gun mount.

Preparing for action in Tunisia, these four new Sd. Kfz. 233 move up from port. Notice that each of the vehicles has four smoke canisters on each front fender. Wire mesh screens protect the headlights, as do covers.

Patton Museum, Fort Knox, KY

Military History Institute, Carlisle Barracks, PA.

Captured intact by the British, this vehicle was carefully examined. Notice the water can (so identified by the white cross painted on it) stowed on the rear of the hull. A spare tire is mounted on the rear of the vehicle, as was the case on all the eight-wheeled armored cars after the self-sealing inner tubes were discontinued.

Patton Museum, Fort Knox, KY

WH - 237 778

The cannon of the Sd. Kfz. 233 could be traversed 9 degrees left and 12 degrees to the right. Larger changes were made by repositioning the vehicle. The gun could be elevated from minus-4 to plus-20 degrees. The outboard smoke canister from each fender is missing.

This view, taken from the rear deck of an Sd. Kfz. 233 captured in Tunisia, shows the sighting mechanism clearly, as well as the breech of the StuK L/24. Only 32 rounds of ammunition were carried due to space and weight considerations.

Patton Museum, Fort Knox, KY

Patton Museum, Fort Knox, KY

This Sd. Kfz. 233 has been captured by American forces, and GI's are employing it against its former owners, as evidenced by the star painted on the front plate. The eight-wheel steering of these vehicles is apparent from the slightly different angle each wheel is in here.

Panzerfunkwagen (Sd Kfz 263) 8-Rad

The Sd. Kfz. 263 was designed to provide a mobile base station for Panzer unit communications. Intended for use in rear areas, these vehicles were equipped only with a ball-mounted 7.92mm MG 34 for self defense as their only armament. Their armor protection, like the other vehicles in this family, held up only against 7.92mm armor piercing rounds and smaller, fired from ground level.

Rather than a turret, the top of the body was extended upward as a six-sided truncated pyramid. The structure housed a powerful m.Pz.Fu.Tr.b with Fu 11 SE 100 radio set. In addition to the frame, or bow, type antenna, these vehicles were also equipped with a 9-meter telescoping antenna mounted behind the raised superstructure.

A crew of five men—a commander, and two each drivers and radio operators—were assigned to each of these vehicles.

Automotively, the Sd. Kfz. 263 was identical to the Sd. Kfz. 231 and 232 8-rad vehicles. Production of these vehicles was ordered in 1937 and continued until January 1943. At that time the production order for the remaining vehicles was changed to the 7.5 cm-armed Sd. Kfz. 233. Like all the vehicles in this series, the Sd. Kfz. 263 was built by Schichau on Büessing-NAG GS chassis.

Sd.Kfz. 263 (8-rad)

Length	5.85 m	Tire size	210-18
Width	2.20 m	Weapon, main	7.92mm MG 34
Height	2.90 m		
Weight	9.10 tons	Ammo stowage, main	1,050 rnds
Fuel capacity	180 liters	Engine make	Büssing-NAG
Maximum speed	85 km/hr (52.7 mph)		
		Engine model	L8V/GS
Range, on road	300 km (186 miles)	Engine configuration	V-8, liquid cooled
Range, cross country	170 km (105.4 miles)	Engine displacement	7.91 liters
Crew	5	Engine horsepower	155 hp @ 3000 rpm
Communications	Fu 11 SE 100		

Patton Museum, Fort Knox, KY

The pistol ports are visible on the side of the superstructure in this photo taken in North Africa of a captured Sd. Kfz. 263. Following a precedent set by Rommel, some commanders used the Sd. Kfz. 263 as a mobile command post.

A 7th Panzer Divison Sd. Kfz. 263 moves across a bridge sometime prior to 1941. The arc in the near side of the frame antenna was necessary to prevent interference with the telescopic antenna, seen here with protective cover in place.

Patton Museum, Fort Knox, KY

This brand new Sd. Kfz. 263 was posed for photos at the factory in 1939. The ball mount for the self-defense machinegun can be seen in the front of the superstructure, although the weapon itself is absent.

Walter J. Spielberger

Like the rest of
this family of
vehicles, the
Sd. Kfz. 263
had a forward-
opening storage
locker built into
each fender.
The mottled
appearance of the
paint is the result
of the two-tone
dark brown spots
on dark gray base
camouflage.

The outside of this Sd. Kfz. 263, like that of most military vehicles, was festooned with
considerable additional stowage. The extra water cans, identifiable by their what crosses, were
especially valuable for the men of the Afrika Korps. Though impressive looking, the Sd. Kfz.
263 was not a large vehicle.

PanzerMesskraftwagen mit Aggregat

The oddest-looking vehicle built on the Büssing 8-Rad GS chassis was not a combat vehicle at all. Rather, this vehicle was built to transport ballistic survey equipment on German test ranges. Completed in 1942, this vehicle was interesting enough it was shipped to Aberdeen Proving Ground for evaluation after it was captured. Unfortunately it no longer exists.

The flap that has been lowered to protect the third wheel on this side, as well as the shutters for the windows.

This unusual-looking eight-wheeled armored car is believed to have been used as a range vehicle in conjunction with the V-2 missile.

Schwerer Panzerspähwagen (2cm) (Sd. Kfz. 234/1)

While the Sd. Kfz. 231 series of eight-wheeled armored cars were largely successful, they were somewhat deficient in off-road mobility, armor protection and engine cooling. Work on the next generation of vehicles began in August 1940, with the first production vehicle being completed in 1943.

The new design, designated Sd. Kfz. 234, differed from the previous by having an armored hull, to which the other components were attached, much like a tank. The previous armored cars had utilized a truck-like chassis with an armored body attached. As with the earlier eight-wheelers, Büssing-NAG was selected as the prime contractor. The power plant selected for the new vehicle was 12-cylinder Tatra air-cooled engine.

The turret of the 234/1 was open-topped, and armed with a 2 cm Kw.K. 38 with coaxial MG 42. A crew of two sat in the hand-traversed turret; commander on the left and gunner to his right. Two hundred-fifty rounds of 2 cm ammunition was carried, as were 2,400 rounds for the machinegun. Only a few vehicles were equipped with radios.

Sd.Kfz. 234/1

Length	5.86 m	Weapon, main	2 cm Kw.K. 38
Width	2.33 m	Weapon, secondary	7.92mm MG 42
Height	2.10 m		
Weight	11.5 tons	Ammo stowage, main	250 rnds
Fuel capacity	360 liters		
Maximum speed	80 km/hr (49.6 mph)	Ammo stowage, secondary	2,400 rnds
Range, on road	1,000 km (620 miles)		
Range, cross country	600 km (372 miles)	Engine make	Tatra
		Engine model	Early 102, Later 103
Crew	4	Engine configuration	V-12, air-cooled diesel
Communications	Fu.12 SE 80 and Fu.Spr. Ger. f	Engine displacement	14.825 liters
Tire size	270-20	Engine horsepower	220 hp @ 2250 rpm

The suspension on this captured SD.KFZ. 234/1 was been so badly damaged that jacks had to be used to support the vehicle at a normal attitude for photographs. The armor of these vehicles was adequate only against small arms fire. Like all reconnaissance vehicles, its primary defense was flight.

Patton Museum, Fort Knox, KY

The early production Sd. Kfz. 234/1 had four stowage compartments in the fenders on each side. The right rear fender of this vehicle was damaged in combat, as was the suspension of the third wheel.

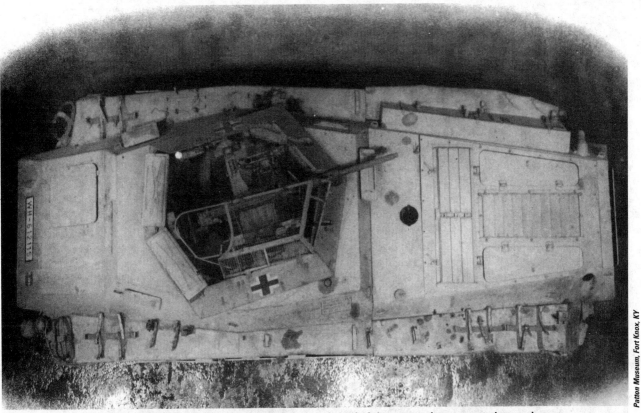

The coaxial MG34 is missing from this vehicle, as is half of the screen that prevented grenades from being tossed into the turret. The 20 cm Kw. K was lethal against low-flying aircraft, which were a menace during the later stages of the war.

Patton Museum, Fort Knox, KY

Unlike the earlier eight-wheeled armored cars, the Sd. Kfz. 234/1 and related vehicles did not have frames. Instead, the armored hull served as the basis for the vehicle, and the suspension, engine and other components were attached to it.

Stefan De Meyer

Late-production 234/1, such as this example produced in the fall of 1944, had only two stowage compartments per side. The transportation stenciling is visible on the side of the superstructure in this photo.

Sd.Kfz. 234

While the 8-rad armored cars from Büssing-NAG were a considerable improvement over the previous used 6-rad vehicles, they still fell short of the Wermacht's desire. Because of its previous experience with such matters, Büssing-NAG was awarded a contract in August of 1940 to design a new series of vehicles.

The new vehicles were to be powered by air-cooled diesel engines. This meant superior cooling in both hot and cold temperature extremes, improved fuel efficiency, and the use of a more easily produced fuel. Rather than building a vehicle on a chassis and frame like conventional automotive design, the new family of armored cars would be built more like a tank. The armored hull itself was the core structure for the vehicle, and everything else attached to it. It was, in essence, an extremely heavy-duty monobody design.

Frontal armor protection was upgraded slightly compared to the earlier eight-wheelers, with 30mm-thick armor in the front, but only 8mm-thick plate on the sides. Top speed was increased to 80 km/hr (44.8 mph) and it had a phenomenal range up to 1,000 kilometers (620 miles).

The Sd.Kfz. 234 was to be armed with a 2 cm Kw.K. 38, but this was changed to the 5 cm Kw.K. 39/1 even before the first vehicle was completed.

Production of the new vehicle, known at first as the Sd.Kfz. 234, but later as the Sd.Kfz. 234/2, ran from December 1943 through June of 1944.

Sd.Kfz. 234/2

Length	6.80 m	Weapon, main	5 cm Kw.K. 39/1 (L/60)
Width	2.33 m	Weapon, coaxial	7.92mm MG 42
Height	2.38 m		
Weight	11.7 tons	Ammo stowage, main	55 rnds
Fuel capacity	360 liters		
Maximum speed	80 km/hr (49.6 mph)	Ammo stowage, secondary	2,850 rnds
Range, on road	1,000 km (620 miles)	Engine make	Tatra
Range, cross country	600 km (372 miles)	Engine model	103
Crew	4	Engine configuration	V-12, air-cooled diesel
Communications	Fu.Spr.Ger. f	Engine displacement	14.825 liters
Tire size	270-20	Engine horsepower	220 hp @ 2250 rpm

Known to enthusiasts as the Puma, the Schwerer Panzerspähwagen (5 cm) was officially known as the Sd.Kfz. 234 until March 1944, when it was redesignated Sd.Kfz. 234/2. Notice the paint overspray on the tires.

Patton Museum, Fort Knox, KY

Stefan De Meyer

The 234 series of vehicles were considerably different than the prior eight-wheeled armored cars. The 234s were built more like tanks, with their armored hulls being the basic structure of the vehicle, rather than having a separate frame.

Patton Museum, Fort Knox, KY

Armed with a 5 cm cannon, the Sd.Kfz. 234 was fast and could deliver a reasonably heavy blow. This allowed it to roam into areas more hostile than other armored cars dared venture.

Ordnance Museum, Aberdeen Proving Ground

This vehicle was captured and returned to the United States for evaluation. Its sheet metal stowage bins show considerable signs of damage, although the armored hull itself is sound.

Patton Museum, Fort Knox, KY

National Archives and Records Administration

Although well armed and fast, the armor protection of the Sd.Kfz. 234 vehicles was proof only against 7.92mm and smaller armor piercing bullets; therefore, camouflage was essential for a long life.

A spare tire was carried on the rear of the vehicle after run-flat were previously discontinued. The star antenna was standard equipment on these vehicles.

Military History Institute, Carlisle Barracks, PA

The rear of the turret was plain, with only a pistol port interrupting its smooth surface. This vehicle was on display at Aberdeen Proving Ground after the war.

Though considered obsolete as a tank weapon, the 7.5 cm Kanone 37 continued to prove its worth when installed in the Sd.Kfz. 233. When the decision was made to upgrade Germany's fleet of eight-wheeled armored cars from Büssing-NAG GS chassis type to the larger monobody style, the 7.5 cm-armed version was updated as well. The new vehicles were to be assigned to headquarters and headquarters reconnaissance battalions of Panzer divisions.

Using essentially the same armored body as the 234/1, the 234/3 body had an open fighting compartment in lieu of a turret. At the front of this compartment, which occupied roughly the same area as the turret, the venerable 7.5 cm L/24 was mounted. The commander, as well as the loader and gunner who served the weapon, rode in this compartment as well, while the driver's position was slightly deeper in the hull. An MG42 was mounted in the upper compartment for close-in and antiaircraft defense.

The military never could seem to decide how many of these vehicles it wanted, and the production orders were constantly being changed almost from the time production

began in April 1944. Finally, in December 1944, the 234/3 was abandoned entirely, with the balance of the chassis on order being changed to the Pak40-armed 234/4.

Sd.Kfz. 234/3

Length	5.86 m	Weapon, main	7.5 cm K 51 (L/24)
Width	2.33 m	Weapon, secondary	7.92mm MG 42
Height	2.22 m		
Weight	11.5 tons	Ammo stowage, main	50 rnds
Fuel capacity	360 liters		
Maximum speed	80 km/hr (49.6 mph)	Ammo stowage, secondary	1,950 rnds
Range, on road	1,000 km (620 miles)		
		Engine make	Tatra
Range, cross country	600 km (372 miles)	Engine model	103
Crew	4	Engine configuration	V-12, air-cooled diesel
Communications	Fu.Spr.Ger. f	Engine displacement	14.825 liters
Tire size	270-20	Engine horsepower	220 hp @ 2250 rpm

Patton Museum, Fort Knox, KY

The Sd.Kfz. 234/3 was only slightly taller than the 234/1 it was based upon. While it was well armed, the 234/3's thin armor and open-topped fighting compartment made it vulnerable even to infantry units.

A drum-type muffler was mounted on each rear fender, with one muffler serving each cylinder bank of the Tatra V-12 air-cooled diesel engine.

While the hull of the 234/3 was made of armor plate, the stowage boxes mounted alongside were made only of sheet metal. The rigors of combat often caused considerable damage to these lightweight components.

The Sd.Kfz. 234/3 gun had a traverse of 20 degrees either side of center. More dramatic changes in aim were made by repositioning the entire vehicle.

In addition to better cooling in hostile weather conditions, the air-cooled power plant also eliminated the need for a vulnerable radiator.

Schwerer Panzerspahwagen (7.5 cm PaK 40)(Sd. Kfz. 234/4)

Even the large Sd.Kfz. 234-type eight-wheel armored car chassis was overburdened by the installation of the 7.5 cm PaK 40 antitank gun. Nonetheless, at Hitler's personal insistence, development and production of these vehicles proceeded beginning in November 1944.

Büssing-NAG did the design work beginning with the 234/4 as the basis. The PaK 40 L/46 was installed, with its gun shield modified to provide clearance for a limited amount of traverse, on a framework in the fighting compartment.

The new vehicle was rushed into production starting in December 1944, and almost 100 had been completed at the time of the German surrender.

Sd.Kfz. 234/3

Length	5.86 m less gun	**Communications**	Fu.Spr.Ger. f
Width	2.33 m	**Tire size**	270-20
Height	2.38 m	**Weapon, main**	7.5 cm Pak 40
Weight	11.5 tons		
Fuel capacity	360 liters	**Ammo stowage, main**	36 rnds
Maximum speed	80 km/hr (49.6 mph)	**Engine make**	Tatra
		Engine model	103
Range, on road	1,000 km (620 miles)	**Engine configuration**	V-12, air-cooled diesel
Range, cross country	600 km (372 miles)	**Engine displacement**	14.825 liters
Crew	4		
		Engine horsepower	220 hp @ 2250 rpm

Stefan De Meyer

The Sd.Kfz. 234/4 combined high speed with a powerful antitank gun. However, the size, weight and recoil of the PaK 40 taxed the limitations of the chassis.

Charles Kliment

Installation of the PaK 40 produced a very cramped fighting compartment. Obviously, the open-topped compartment was vulnerable to shell fragments as well as small arms and grenade attacks.

This view of a captured vehicle minus its wheels and a forward fender, shows the monobody construction of this series of vehicles. All the components, including the suspension, were attached directly to the armored hull.

Charles Kliment

S gl gep Personenkraftwagen (Sd Kfz 247)

The heavy cross-country armored staff car, or schwerer gelandegaengiger gepanzerter Personenkraftwagen, was intended as a command vehicle for use by armored reconnaissance staff.

The earliest version, the six-wheeled car, was based on the Krupp L2H143 chassis, also known as the Krupp limber. This chassis had been specially developed for military use. Ten of these vehicles, which were powered by Krupp's own horizontally opposed engine, were built from 1937 through January 1938.

The armor of the open-topped vehicle was sufficient to protect its driver and five passengers from 7.92mm armor piercing bullets, so long as they were fired from more than 30 yards away.

Another 58 cars were ordered in 1938, but these were radically different. The German Army's Sd.Kfz. numbers reflect the purpose of a vehicle, not its design (unlike the U.S. Army's Standard Nomenclature List, or SNL G-numbers). Therefore, these later cars, even though had only four wheels and were based on the Horch Uniform Chassis, or Einheitsfahrgestell II, retained the designation Sd.Kfz. 247.

Though equipped with four-wheel drive, the new vehicle had only two-wheel steering, unlike the other four-wheel armored vehicles being built in Germany at this time.

Several delays were encountered in beginning construction, with production finally getting under way in July 1941. Daimler-Benz completed the contract for 58 vehicles in January 1942. Like the six-wheel version, the four-wheeled Sd.Kfz. 247 accommodated the driver and five passengers. There was no provision for mounted armament or communications gear. The engine was located at the front of both the four- and six-wheeled versions.

Due to the delays in production, by the time the vehicles were produced they were no longer needed for their original purpose. The armored cars were instead assigned for headquarters use with motorcycle units.

Both the four- and six-wheel versions transported five passengers and a driver. Due to production delays and changing needs, by the time the 58 four-wheeled cars were complete in 1942 they were no longer required for their original purpose.

schwerer gelandegängiger gepanzerter PersonenkraftwagenSd.Kfz. 247 (6 rad)

Length	5.20 m	Communications	none
Width	1.96 m	Weapon, main	none
Height	1.70 m	Engine make	Krupp
Weight	5.2 tons	Engine model	M305
Fuel capacity	110 liters	Engine configuration	four-cyl. opposed pistion
Maximum speed	70 km/hr (43.4 mph)		
Range, on road	350 km (217 miles)	Engine displacement	3.5 liter
Range, cross country	220 km	Engine horsepower	65 @ 2500 rpm
Crew	1 + 5 passengers		

schwerer gelandegängiger gepanzerter Personenkraftwagen Sd.Kfz. 247 (4 rad)

Length	5.00 m	Communications	none
Width	2.00 m	Weapon, main	none
Height	1.80 m	Engine make	Horch
Weight	4.46 tons	Engine model	801
Fuel capacity	160 liters	Engine configuration	V-8, liquid cooled
Maximum speed	80 km/hr (49.6 mph)		
Range, on road	400 km (249 miles)	Engine displacement	3.8 liters
Range, cross country	270 km (167.4 miles)	Engine horsepower	81 @ 3600 rpm
Crew	1 + 5 passengers		

Later Sd.Kfz. 247 vehicles were built on Horch-designed four-wheeled chassis. Unlike Germany's other four-wheeled armored cars, these vehicles had front-mounted engines and were only two-wheel steer.

Patton Museum, Fort Knox, KY

The handsome styling and open-topped design of the six-wheeled version of the Sd.Kfz. 247 made it a popular vehicle for parade use. Perhaps this was just as well, as its off-road mobility left something to be desired.

National Archives and Records Administration

These early heavy cross-country armored staff cars were built on Krupp military truck chassis. Only 10 of these vehicles were produced. No armament or communications equipment was carried, as the vehicles were intended to serve only as armored transports.

Patton Museum, Fort Knox, KY

Polizei-Panzerkampfwagen ADGZ

Built for the Austrian Army between 1935 and 1937, the 27 vehicles produced by Austro-Daimler-Puch up to that time were of no interest to the Wehrmacht. After Germany annexed Austria, these vehicles were assigned to the state police. However, in 1942 an additional 25 units were manufactured. Some of these were used by the German Army and the SS, but only briefly.

These unusual-looking vehicles had dual wheels on their central axles, and single wheels on the leading and trailing axles. The rotating turret housed a 2 cm Kw.K. 35 (L/45) cannon. Eleven millimeter-thick armor protected the vehicle's six-man crew.

By late 1944 these vehicles had been relegated to training roles only.

Three of the early production armored cars parade through Vienna. These vehicles were being operated by the Austrian Army at this time; the 1938 celebration of Austria's unification with Germany.

Patton Museum, Fort Knox, KY

Polizei-Panzerkampfwagen ADGZ

Length	6.26 m	Ammo stowage, main	100 rnds
Width	2.16 m		
Height	2.56 m	Ammo stowage, secondary	2,500 rnds
Weight	12 tons		
Maximum speed	70 km/hr (43.4 mph)	Engine make	Austro-Daimler
Range, on road	450 km	Engine model	M612
Crew	6	Engine configuration	six-cyl., liquid cooled
Weapon, main	2 cm Kw.K. 35 L/45	Engine displacement	12 liters
Weapons, secondary	3 x 7.92mm MG 34	Engine horsepower	150 @ 1800 rpm

Here an Austro-Daimler-Puch ADGZ armored car operated by the SS is on patrol. The turret-mounted machinegun has been removed, although the hull mounted gun (directly in front of the driver) has been retained, as was the 2 cm turret-mounted cannon.

Bundesarchiv photo

S gl LKW 4.5t fur FlaK (Sf)

By mid-war Allied air superiority was becoming apparent. Both the strategic bombing of transportation and manufacturing facilities, and the tactical bombing of troops and equipment, were taking their toll on the Wehrmacht.

Germany responded with increased development of antiaircraft weapons. One of these new weapons was the 5 cm Flak 41. Fewer than 100 of these guns were actually produced. In an effort to create a mobile antiaircraft weapon, some of these new weapons were installed on the proven Mercedes-Benz L4500A 4.5-ton truck.

Armor plating was installed on the cab, and an armored splinter shield was installed in front of the radiator. The sides of the bed were hinged, allowing them to fold down and become a working platform for the gun crew, as well as providing clearance for the 360-degree rotation of the weapon mount. Outriggers were installed to stabilize the truck while the gun was in use.

With so few of these weapons being produced, this was a relatively scarce vehicle. Exact specifications are unknown.

The early versions of the Sd.Kfz. 250 had armored bodies of with a fairly complicated shape and many parts.

The Sd.Kfz. 250/1 light halftrack was built to provide an armored reconnaissance vehicle with mobility superior to that of wheeled armored cars. The small size of the vehicle is evident from the soldier examining this captured example.

Patton Museum, Fort Knox, KY

The engine compartment side flap on this example has been opened to allow better cooling of the engine. The steel tracks had rubber pads, making for a quieter, smoother ride than with all-steel track. This vehicle has a Holzgas wood-gas generator mounted on its front.

Ordnance Museum, Aberdeen Proving Ground

In October 1943 a restyled body entered production. With fewer panels and seams, this body style was easier, faster and less expensive to produce.

Leichter Gepanzerter Kraftswagen (Sd. Kfz. 250), later le SPW (Sd. Kfz. 250)

While Germany's four-, six-, and eight-wheeled armored cars offered adequate protection for their crews, at least in the early stages of the war, their shortcoming was cross-country mobility. Even the eight-wheeled armored cars had difficulty keeping ahead of tanks in mud and rough terrain.

On the other hand, halftrack vehicles were much more capable of operating with the Panzer formations, but the Sd.Kfz. 10 and Sd.Kfz. 11 1- and 3-ton halftracks lacked armor protection, an obvious shortcoming in a reconnaissance vehicle. Efforts were made to develope armored bodies to fit these basic chassis, with the goal being to attain the best of both worlds.

While prototype work on the Sd.Kfz. 250 took place in 1939, it was June 1941 before the vehicles entered production. The chassis, which was based on the Sd.Kfz. 10, was engineered by Demag, while the armored body was a Büssing-NAG design. It was designed to transport half of a machine gun section, or four men. The front wheels did the steering in most cases, but during sharp turns steering brakes on the tracks were engaged as well.

Though production got off to a slow start, it did ramp up quickly. No fewer than 12 variations of this vehicle were created for various special purposes. The vehicles were produced by Büssing-NAG, Deutsche Werke, Evans and Pistor, Ritscher, Weserhütte and Wumag.

In October 1943, a redesigned body entered production. The new design incorporated nine major armor components, whereas the earlier style had 19. The reduction in the number of parts greatly increased efficiency at the assembly plants and sped the production. From this point onward the original style vehicle was referred to as the "alte" (old) Light Shützenpanzerwagen, while the improved version was the "Neu," or new style.

The new version was produced by Deutsche Werke, Evans and Pistor, Ritscher, Weserhütte and Wumag from 1943 onward, with Wumag dropping out in July 1944. According to Germany's industrial plans, the vehicle was to be discontinued before the end of 1945. But, of course, all German military production ceased in 1945!

The base Sd.Kfz. 250 was also known as the Sd.Kfz. 250/1. Whether old or new style, there were two different loads for this vehicle. The first load was used to transport the Halbgruppe of four men. This vehicle was armed with two MG34s and provided with 2,010 rounds of 7.92 mm ammunition. The second load transported the support Halbruppe along with heavy field mountings for the MG34s.

As the MG42 became the machinegun of choice for the German Army during 1943, it replaced the MG34 on all machine gun-equipped Sd.Kfz. 250 variants.

Ultimately, more than 4,000 of the old style, and more than 2,000 new style Sd.Kfz. 250 halftracks were produced during the course of the war. These vehicles saw service on all fronts, and in a variety of roles.

As all the variants were based on either the alte or neu chasis, and the vehicles all had similar dimensions. To save space in the accompanying chart, full tabulated data is only given for the base 250/1 vehicle, with changes unique to individual models called out in the appropriate text.

Sd.Kfz. 250 alte

Length	4.56 m	Communications	Fu.Spr.Ger.f
Width	1.95 m		
Height	1.66 m	Weapon, main	2 x 7.92mm MG
Weight	5.8 tons	Ammo stowage, main	2010 rnds
Fuel capacity	140 liters		
Maximum speed	60 km/hr (37.2 mph)	Engine make	Maybach
		Engine model	HL42TRKM
Range, on road	320 km (198.4 miles)	Engine configuration	six-cylinder, liquid cooled
Range, cross country	180 km (111.6 miles)	Engine displacement	4.198 liters
Crew	2	Engine horsepower	100 @ 2800 rpm

Sd.Kfz. 250 neu

Length	4.61 m	Communications	Fu.Spr.Ger.f
Width	1.95 m		
Height	1.66 m	Weapon, main	2 x 7.92mm MG
Weight	5.38 tons	Ammo stowage, main	2,010 rnds
Fuel capacity	140 liters		
Maximum speed	60 km/hr (37.2 mph)	Engine make	Maybach
		Engine model	HL42TURKM
Range, on road	320 km (198.4 miles)	Engine configuration	six-cylinder, liquid cooled
Range, cross country	180 km (111.6 miles)	Engine displacement	4.198 liters
Crew	2	Engine horsepower	100 @ 2800 rpm

Sd. Kfz. 250/2 Telephone vehicle

Though perhaps not as celebrated as pure combat vehicles, the number of support vehicles needed to advance a modern army exceeds the number of combat vehicles many fold. An example of this was the Sd.Kfz. 250/2 leichter Fernsprechpanzerwagen, Gerät 892. The specialized variant of the Sd.Kfz. 250 was equipped with a cable drum in the rear of the vehicle and one on each front fender. This arrangement allowed it to lay three lines of telephone cable simultaneously. A crew of four served the 5.44-ton vehicle, which was armed with an MG34 for defensive use. This vehicle was the base vehicle of the light field cable troops, and was sometimes found with telephone switching equipment installed.

Telephone and signal wires were laid and hung using the Sd.Kfz. 250/2 halftrack, which retained an MG 34 for self-defense.

Patton Museum, Fort Knox, KY

A cable reel machine was mounted on each front fender, and a third in the passenger compartment of the halftrack.

Crewmen used long rods to guide the wires to the exact position they wanted. Note the antenna mount on the side of the halftrack.

The small size of the Sd.Kfz. 250 meant there was no space to spare. Crews tended to stow much of their gear outside of the vehicle.

Sd. Kfz. 250/3 light Radio vehicle

Radio communications were a key component of German military strategy at a time when many of its opponents considered radio an unusual feature in military vehicles.

One of the earliest variants of the Sd.Kfz. 250 was the Sd.Kfz. 250/3 "Leichter Funkpanzer" (Light radio panzer), of which there were four variations with regard to radio equipment. The radio equipment varied depending upon what type of unit it was assigned to and what command center it was to contact.

The 250/3 attached to mechanized forces was equipped with the Fu 12 radio set. This set was the standard radio for ground forces. This medium wave receiver operated on the 835–3,000 kilocycles per second (Kc/s) band. Its 80-watt transmitter used the 1120-3000 Kc/s band. A 2-meter rod antenna was used on the early versions, while later versions were equipped with a star antenna instead. The radio equipment was mounted on top of the fuel tank, which was reconfigured to accommodate this installation.

The antenna for the inter-vehicular Funksprechgeraet f was mounted on the right front of the fighting compartment, with the command antenna mounted on the left rear. Vehicles with this equipment were produced with both the alte and neu bodies.

This vehicle, believed to be a Sd.Kfz. 250/3 light radio vehicle, was used extensively by Rommel while he commanded the famed Afrika Korps.

Patton Museum, Fort Knox, KY

Field Marshal Rommel leans from his vehicle beside one of the supports for the large frame-type radio antenna, which was connected to an Fu 12 radio set.

Patton Museum, Fort Knox, KY

A second version of the Sd.Kfz. 250/3 was equipped with an Fu 7 radio set. The Fu 7 was comprised of an ultra-short wave receiver d1 and a 20-watt transmitter that operated on the 42100-47800 Kc/s band. This equipment had a range of 50 kilometers and was used to contact Luftwaffe support groups. A 2-meter rod aerial was required by this radio set.

For a main divisional command link Luftwaffe personnel used a third model of "Leichter Funkpanzer." Like the vehicle described previously, it also carried an Fu 7 radio set, but it also carried the Fu 8 set. The Fu 8 was a medium wave receiver. The c model used the 835-3000 Kc/s. band, while the earlier b model worked on the 580-3000 Kc/s. band. The transmitter was a 30-watt unit operating between 1,130 and 3,000 Kc/s. The early version was distinguished by the huge frame antenna used by the Fu 8, which gave the radio a range of 40 kilometers. On later models, however, this was replaced by a telescoping 8-meter mast with star antenna, which increased the radio's range to 50 kilometers. Typically, the license plates of these vehicles carried the WL prefix signifying Luftwaffe.

The fourth model of the Sd.Kfz. 250/3 was a general purpose radio vehicle. No specific radio equipment was assigned, rather it was outfitted according to the using units needs. In the case of assault gun formations, this meant the installation of Fu 15 or Fu 16 sets, while armored reconnaissance groups needed the Fu 10.

To minimize confusion, the Wehrmacht assigned the following ordnance numbers to the vehicles: Sd.Kfz. 250/3.I, Sd.Kfz. 250/3.II, Sd.Kfz. 250/3.III, and Sd.Kfz. 250/3.IV. Each of these 5.35-ton vehicles was armed with a single machine gun and crewed by four men.

The radio vehicles retained their 7.92mm machineguns for protection. The flag was placed on the hood of the vehicle to avoid attack from the Luftwaffe.

National Archives and Records Administration.

Late production Sd.Kfz. 250/3 lacked the classic frame aerial often found on German command and communications vehicles. Instead, a normal mast antenna or star antenna was used.

National Archives and Records Administration.

Sd.Kfz. 250/4

The designation Sd.Kfz.250/4 was originally assigned to a halftrack armed with twin (Zwilinglafette 36) 7.92mm MG34 machine guns. It was envisioned that this would be a Flakwagen, used to protect various units from aerial attack. However, these plans were abandoned before the vehicles entered series production.

In 1943 the Sd.Kfz.250/4 classification was reassigned to an observation and fire control vehicle for use by self-propelled artillery units (e.g. Sturmgeschütz). FuG15 and FuG16 radio sets were installed for communication with these units. Either an MG34 or MG42 was mounted on the vehicle for self-defense use by the four-man crew.

Sd. Kfz. 250/5 Artillery observation vehicle

When the Sd.Kfz. 250 series vehicles began production in June 1941, one of the initially planned variants was a leichter Beobachtungspanzerwagen, or light artillery observation vehicle. This standardized open-topped vehicle would be used to supplement and replace the closed-topped Sd.Kfz. 253, which was discontinued the same month.

Though precise production numbers of the 5.35-ton Sd.Kfz. 250/5 have not been discovered, it is believed that Evans & Pistor continued to produce these vehicles throughout the war. Naturally, these vehicles underwent the same body restyling as the rest of the series.

These vehicles were used by artillery and armored reconnaissance units, and two different radio installations could be installed. Vehicles assigned to artillery units were equipped with Fu 6 and Fu 2 radio sets, while those attached to armored recon units were equipped with a Fu 12 radio installation. Later in the war this was modified so that the artillery observation vehicles mounted the Fu 8, Fu 4 and Fu.Spr.Ger.f, while the armored recon vehicles had Fu12 sets installed in addition to the Fu.Spr.Ger.f. A four-man crew operated each vehicle. In 1944 these two sub-variants were named Sd.Kfz. 250/5I and Sd.Kfz. 250/5II.

Patton Museum, Fort Knox, KY

The Sd.Kfz. 250/5 leichter Beobachtungspanzerwagen, or light artillery observation vehicle, had the classic German frame antenna for use with the Fu 8 long-range radio set.

Bundesarchiv photo

Later in the war, the Sd.Kfz. 250/5 were also used for reconnaissance, and were designated Aufklärungspanzerwagen. In this role they had a Fu 12 radio and star antenna.

Sd. Kfz. 250/6 Ammunition supply vehicle

The Sd.Kfz. 250/6 was introduced in 1941 to provide Sturmgeschütz units with an armored ammunition carrier based on the standard Sd.Kfz. 250, rather than the special-bodied Sd.Kfz. 252.

The Sd.Kfz. 250/6 did not leave the factory as such. Rather, to speed and simplify production the machines were built as 250/1. The specialized ammunition racks were issued as kits, to be installed by the military, rather than the manufacturer.

Kits were produced in two versions. The Ausf. A configuration included racks for 70 rounds of 7.5 cm Kanone ammunition packed in pairs in cartridge boxes. The Ausf. B stowed 60 individually packed 7.5 cm StuK 40 ammunition.

The Sd.Kfz. 250/6 Ausf. B had racks installed in it to transport 7.5 cm StuK 40 ammunition individually packed in tubes.

The Sd.Kfz. 250/6 Ausf. B, shown here, as well as the Ausf. A, retained the two 7.92mm machineguns that were mounted on personnel carriers.

The Sd.Kfz. 250/6 ammunition supply vehicles were built as standard 250/1 personnel carriers. This conversions were not done by the assembly plants.

Walter J. Spielberger

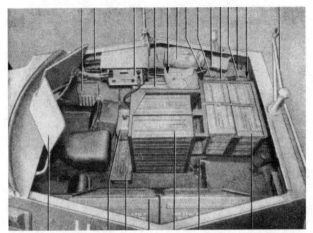

The Sd.Kfz. 250/6 Ausf. A was configured to haul 70 rounds of 7.5 cm Kanone ammunition. In both the Ausf. A and Ausf. B version, the ammo almost filled the former passenger compartment.

The Ausf. A's stowage was arranged to transport the ammo packed in pairs of rounds in crates.

Sd. Kfz. 250/7 8.0 cm mortar carrier

Because of the success of the bigger Sd Kfz 251/2 with mounted schwerer Granatwerfer 34 8.0 cm mortar, the decision was made to install the same weapon in the smaller Sd.Kfz. 250. The vehicle was known as the Sd.Kfz. 250/7. Both the old (Alte) and new (Neu) vehicles were built in this configuration.

In order to mount the heavy mortar in the vehicle, a reinforced base plate was installed. This allowed the mortar to be fired from inside the vehicle. A conventional base plate for the mortar was stowed on the right rear of the vehicle. This allowed the mortar tube to be dismounted for use as a fire base, under these circumstances the halftrack itself was then used as an ammunition carrier to keep the mortar crew supplied.

Other distinguishing features of the 250/7 were the elimination of the forward machine gun mount (to

clear the mortar round's trajectory), and the addition of ammunition stowage bins for mortar rounds—either 42 or 66, depending on vehicle configuration. The rear-mounted machine gun was retained, providing the five-man crew with a means of defending the 5.61-ton, 1.8-meter-tall vehicle.

These halftracks had five-man crews and were used in pairs. Together with another Sd.Kfz. 250 with observer team, they made up the mortar squad of the Aufklarungsschwadron heavy platoon.

When the shell was fired from inside the vehicle, the trajectory took it over the vehicle's hood. This required the elimination of the forward machine.

Much of the remaining space in the vehicle was occupied by ammunition, both for the mortar and for the rear machine

Some carriers were built without the mortar tube. These were to be used as ammunition supply vehicles for those halftracks with the tubes.

The ammunition carriers can be distinguished by having both mortar round ammo racks, and a forward machinegun mount.

Sd. Kfz. 250/8 Self-propelled 7.5 cm howitzer

As the Panzerkampfwagen IV was rearmed with long guns, large numbers of the previously used 7.5cm K 51 L/24.short gun became available. Utilizing a mounting that had been developed for the Sturmgeschütz, some of these weapons were installed in Sd.Kfz. 250 halftracks. These vehicles were then classified as Sd.Kfz. 250/8.

The installation required radical changes inside the halftrack, as well as removal of the forward machine gun mount. A number of the seats were removed, and the radio was relocated in order to accommodate the infantry support weapon, the three-man crew, and stowage for 20 rounds of ammunition. Installation of the cannon pushed

the vehicle's weight up to 6.3 tons, and its height to 2.07 meters.

Reportedly, a small number of these vehicles were produced using the alte style chassis, but no photographic evidence has surfaced to support this. However, a number of vehicles definitely were produced using the Neu chassis.

In October of 1944 these vehicles began to be produced using the 7.5 cm K51 (sf) and a simplified mounting. The Fourth Platoon of light armored reconnaissance companies was the recipient of the 250/8 and used them for the duration of the war.

Patton Museum, Fort Knox, KY

A fire support vehicle was created on the Sd.Kfz. 250 chassis by installing a surplus 7.5 cm cannon in the crew compartment. This made for a very cramped vehicle, which was designated the Sd.Kfz. 250/8.

Sd. Kfz. 250/9

In March 1942 authorization was given to develop an armed armored personnel carrier on the Sd.Kfz. 250 chassis. The pedestal mount with shield then in use on the Sd.Kfz. 222 armored car was adapted by the firm of Gustav Appel for use on the halftrack body. The armament used on the Sd.Kfz. 222 was retained—specifically the 2 cm Kw.K.38 and coaxial MG34. The vehicle created by this arrangement was designated Sd.Kfz. 250/9 and weighed 5.9 tons. It was intended to perform the same functions as the Sd.Kfz. 222 armored car, but it was felt

that the halftrack chassis would provide greater mobility off-road. Mass production was to begin in July of 1942, with assembly to be done by Appel, as well as Evans and Pistor.

When the Sd.Kfz. 250 was extensively redesigned in 1943, and the Ausf. B introduced, the Sd.Kfz. 250/9 was redesigned as well. A new turret was used that had a six-sided open top enclosure with the 2 cm cannon mounted on a suspended carriage. The coaxial gun was upgraded to the newer MG42. The new version of the vehicle was known as the Sd.Kfz. 250/9 Ausf. B and weighed 6.2 tons. The Sd.Kfz. 250/9 remained in production throughout the war, with a total of about 1,000 vehicles being produced.

A three-man crew served both versions of the vehicle. The 250/9 was used by reconnaissance units.

The new turret, with the 2 cm cannon mounted on a suspended carriage, extended slightly beyond the sides of the hull.

Military History Institute, Carlisle Barracks, PA

The early Sd.Kfz. 250/9, like this example, were armed with a 2 cm Kw.K 38 in a pedestal mount, much like the one used on Sd.Kfz. 222.

Patton Museum, Fort Knox, KY

The Sd.Kfz. 250/9 was created as a replacement for the Sd.Kfz. 222 four-wheeled armored car, due to the poor cross-country characteristics of the latter.

Patton Museum, Fort Knox, KY

National Archives and Records Administration

When the "neu" version of the Sd.Kfz. 250 base vehicle was developed with its simplified armor in 1943, the Sd.Kfz. 250/9 was updated as well.

Patton Museum, Fort Knox, KY

At the same time the Sd.Kfz. 250/9 armored body was changed, a new six-sided turret was added. Hinged screens were installed on both style turrets to prevent grenades from being tossed in.

Military History Institute, Carlisle Barracks, PA

A 7.92 mm machinegun was mounted coaxially with the cannon. On the earlier vehicles, this was an MG 34, and on the Ausf. B it was an MG 42.

Sd. Kfz. 250/10 Self-propelled 3.7 cm antitank gun

The SdKfz 250/10 leichte Schützenpanzerwagen (3.7cm PaK), Gerält 881 was created in an effort to give platoon leaders a vehicle capable of providing heavier support fire for the standard 250/1. Toward this end a 3.7 cm PaK 35/36 was mounted in place of the front machine gun. The mounting allowed a 30-degree left or right traverse. The PaK was provided with 216 rounds of ammunition, while the rear 7.92mm MG34 was supplied with 1,100 rounds.

While in the early stages of the war the 3.7 cm weapon was a reasonable antitank gun, by the time of the German push into Russia more formidable vehicles were being faced. The 3.7 cm weapon was ineffective against these new tanks, and it earned its nickname of "door knocker." However, when firing high-explosive rounds it was still an effective weapon against soft targets. Nevertheless,

production of these vehicles ceased after about 150 units. A crew of four men operated the Zugfuhrerwagen; a driver, loader, gunner and commander.

Patton Museum, Fort Knox, KY

The Sd.Kfz. 250/10 was built to be a cannon-armed platoon leaders vehicle. The intention was that this would give infantry units an indigenous anti-tank weapon.

Bundesarchiv photo

The 3.7 cm PaK lacked the power to deal with Soviet tanks. Its rounds simply bounced off, earning the weapon the name "door knocker."

Sd.Kfz. 250/11

Another attempt to provide platoon leaders with an antitank weapon resulted in the SdKfz 250/11 leichte Schützenpanzerwagen (schwere Panzerbüchse 41), Gerält 882. A 2.8cm sPzB41 taper-bore antitank gun was mounted on these vehicles. The theory behind the tapered bore, also known as a squeeze bore, was that the increasing back pressure raised the muzzle velocity of the tungsten-based round, allowing greater armor penetration. The theory itself was sound, but Germany had precious little of the required tungsten metal. It could not afford to expend its reserves on ammunition.

In addition to the Panzerbüsche, either an MG34 or MG42 machinegun was carried. The machinegun was mounted on the rear of the vehicle and intended for defensive use. One hundred sixty-eight rounds of ammunition were carried for the main gun, and 1,100 rounds of 7.92mm machine ammunition were aboard as well. Also carried along was a field carriage for the Panzerbüsche, allowing its dismounted operation. The vehicle weighed 5.53 tons and stood 2.13 meters tall. Like the Sd.Kfz. 250/10, the 250/11 was issued to platoon leaders.

A carriage for the dismounted use of the weapon was carried on the outside rear of the halftrack.

The Panzerbüchse was a potent weapon, but precious tungsten was a key component of its ammunition. This greatly limited ammunition supplies.

Patton Museum, Fort Knox, KY

Because the 3.7 cm PaK of the Sd.Kfz. 250/10 was inadequate, a different platoon leader vehicle was created. The new Sd.Kfz. 250/11 was armed with the 2.8 cm tapered bore sPzB41 Panzerbüchse.

Sd. Kfz. 250/12 Light armored survey section vehicle

This obscure variation of the Sd.Kfz. 250 was intended for use by platoon leaders and their assistants in sound ranging and flash spotting sections. Depending upon what type of unit the vehicle was assigned to, there were slight variations in the equipment carried.

The Sd.Kfz. 250/12 was discontinued prior to October 1944, and only three are confirmed to have been built prior to that.

This view from the technical manual is from the inside of the vehicle looking toward the rear.

This view looking forward shows scissors periscopes and aiming circles, as well as the mount for the forward machine gun.

Radio sets and observation equipment were mounted in the left rear interior of the halftrack.

The Sd.Kfz. 250/12 was a leichter Messtruppanzerwagen, or light artillery survey vehicle.

Walter J. Spielberger

M gep Mannschaftskraftwagen (Sd. Kfz. 251), later mittler Schützenpanzerwagen Ausf. A, B and C

Even though its Sd.Kfz. number is higher than that of the light Schützenpanzerwagen (Sd.Kfz. 251 Vs Sd.Kfz. 250), the medium halftrack actually entered production first. Based on the chassis of the Sd.Kfz. 11 3-ton halftrack, preproduction vehicles began trials at Kummersdorf in 1938. Hanomag designed the chassis, while the armored body was engineered by Büssing-NAG.

To adapt the Sd.Kfz. 11 chassis for use as a basis for the armored personnel carrier, a few changes were necessary. The steering wheel reverse-sloped at a 45-degree angle to the driver, the radiator was made larger and repositioned, a new fuel tank was installed, and the exhaust system redesigned and rerouted. The new chassis was designated Hkl 6p.

An armored superstructure was placed on this chassis. Fabricated from welded plate, the superstructure consisted of two large sections bolted together. The forward section, which ended just behind the driver, protected the driver,

The Ausf. A, shown here, as well as the Ausf. B, had tubular front bumpers and ventilation grilles on the top of the hood. The crane-like mounts for the front and rear machineguns are evident.

Patton Museum, Fort Knox, KY

The Sd.Kfz. 251 was the "classic" German halftrack—one of the most modern armored personnel carriers in the world. The Ausf. A, shown here, was the first. It was distinguished by the vision ports in the rear personnel compartment. These ports were missing on later models.

Patton Museum, Fort Knox, KY

commander and engine. The open-topped rear section was designed for the transport of 10 soldiers. An internal flange facilitated the bolting together of the two sections. Large clamshell-type doors in the rear provided access to the interior.

By spring of 1939, the vehicles began to be supplied to the troops for use in the Polish campaign. These early vehicles, designated Sd.Kfz. 251 Ausf. A, performed admirably. Two MG34 machine guns were mounted, on forward and one rear, using swing-out crane-type mounts on the personnel carriers. About 232 Sd.Kfz. 251 Ausf. A are believed to have been built.

The second series of vehicles, the Sd.Kfz. 251 Ausf. B, differed from the Ausf. A only in details. The internal stowage was rearranged slightly, with the most significant of this being the relocation of the radio from behind the

co-driver's seat to in front of his seat. The vision ports in the rear transport area of the vehicle were eliminated. The front machine gun mount became a simple pivot type, and armored gunshields were provided for the guns. The radio antenna was relocated from the right front fender to a position closer to the radio itself. Evidence suggests that approximately 250 of the Ausf. B vehicles were assembled.

The Ausf. C entered production in 1940 and more manufacturers began building these vehicles. Final assembly of the medium halftrack was done by Hanomag, MNH and Borgward, With the introduction of the Ausf. C, these firms were joined by Wesserhütte, Wugam and F. Schichau AG in building the medium halftrack.

The addition of the new firms meant that some builders now lacked experience welding armor. For this

The Ausf. B did not have the visors for troops in the back that was present on the Ausf. A. Notice the straight fender line above the tracks characteristic of only the Ausf. A and Ausf. B.

When the Ausf. C was introduced, the front bumper was discontinued. Also, the forward-most portion of the fenders over the tracks now flared upward. This vehicle has both its machineguns mounted.

While most Sd.Kfz. 251 had armored bodies of welded construction, some, like this one, were of riveted construction. Notice the bows for the passenger compartment's protective cover—an item rarely seen.

The interior of the halftrack was rather Spartan. Room in all AFVs was limited, and no space was wasted.

Riveted construction was introduced as the number of manufacturers assembling the 251 was increased. Some of the new firms lacked experience in the highly technical skill of welding armor plate.

Patton Museum, Fort Knox, KY

reason riveting was introduced as an alternate assembly method. The riveted version was less common than the version constructed with welded armor.

The most obvious change was in the front of the vehicle. The front plate of the engine compartment, which had been made of two intersecting pieces of armor, was replaced with a front plate made of a single piece of flat armor plate. Unlike earlier models, the Ausf. C had no front bumper.

The Ausf. D was considerably simpler to produce, and was made up of fewer pieces of armor. This version of the Sd.Kfz. 251 was produced in far greater numbers than any of the others.

Walter J. Spielberger

The rear of the Ausf. D had a single, reverse-slope plane. The complicated clamshell doors were replaced with simple flat doors, and external stowage bins became an integral part of the halftrack's flanks.

Armin Sohns collection

Engine cooling air was now drawn up behind the armor plate, rather than down through a grille. Large box-like structures were added to either side of the engine compartment. These were armored covers to protect the cooling air exhausts. The fenders over the tracks were changed. Previously, they were flat, but with the introduction of the Ausf. C they became slightly upswept near the front. Turn indicators were moved from the visors to the fenders.

Internally, changes included new stowage lockers behind the troop seats. The front seats were redesigned so they folded down, and were readily removable for maintenance purposes.

In early 1941, the vehicle was officially redesignated the "mittler Schützenpanzerwagen." Previously, its official name had been Mittlerer gepanzerter Mannschaftskraftwagen.

In late 1943 the design of the Sd.Kfz. 251 was improved again as the Ausf. D was introduced. The now all-welded armored body was simplified to speed construction. The large air ducts on either side of the engine compartment were eliminated, and the rear of the vehicle was completely reshaped. The complex clamshell doors were dispensed with, and the now-flat rear armor plate, set at angle, had two simple flat hinged doors in it. Integral stowage bins replaced the stowage boxes previously mounted on top of the fenders. These bins enclosed the entire space between the top of the track guards and the armored body.

The armament of the Sd.Kfz. 251 changed as well, as a pair of 7.92mm MG 42 replaced the previously used 7.92 MG 34s. Inside, the equipment layout was much the same as it had been in the Ausf. C, however, wood replaced metal and leather in many applications.

The Sd.Kfz. 251 continued to be produced throughout the war, in assorted specialized models. Not all models were produced in every (Ausf. A, B, C and D) body style, but these distinctions are made in the appropriate texts. The basic troop carrier was designated Sd.Kfz. 251/1. After WWII, the design was slightly modified to become the diesel powered, fully enclosed OT-810 used by Czechoslovakia.

National Archives and Records Administration.

Still in their shipping frames, the rockets were hung on racks mounted on the sides of the halftracks. The driver controlled the traverse of the launchers with the position of the entire vehicle.

National Archives and Records Administration.

The rockets, which were shipped in wooden or metal framework, filled the halftrack when stowed internally. This photo was taken from the very rear of the vehicle, where scarcely room for three crewmen remained.

National Archives and Records Administration.

The Sd.Kfz. 251/1 was originally armed with two 7.92mm machineguns: the MG34 and, later, the MG42. However, the vehicle often served as the basis for heavier 28 or 32 cm rockets.

Patton Museum, Fort Knox, KY

The elevation of the launchers was variable. Launchers were mounted on B through D models. This is an Ausf. D, while the others shown here are Ausf. B.

A popular modification to the Sd.Kfz. 251 was the installation of launchers for 28 or 32 cm rockets. Three launchers were installed along each side of the body. Traverse was controlled by positioning of the vehicle using aiming rods attached to the front of the vehicle. Elevation was adjustable on each launcher. The exhaust from the rockets required that the crew leave the vehicle prior to firing the rockets. The rockets were shipped in open-framed cases made of either metal or wood. These cases were hung on the launching racks and doubled launch frames. These launchers were known to have been mounted on infantry carriers and engineer halftracks, and reportedly other variants as well.

Charles Kliment collection

The back blast required that the crew leave the halftrack before firing the rockets. The accuracy of rockets left much to be desired, but was adequate for area bombardment.

Sd.Kfz. 251/1 Ausf. A, B and C similar

Length	5.8 m	Communications	FuG Spr Ger 1
Width	2.1 m		
Height	1.75	Weapon, main	2 x 7.92mm MG 34
Weight	7.81 tons	Engine make	Maybach
Fuel capacity	160 liters	Engine model	HL42 TUKRM
Maximum speed	53 km/hr (32.86 mph)		
Range, on road	300 km (186 miles)	Engine configuration	six-cylinder, liquid cooled
Range, cross country	150 km (93 miles)	Engine displacement	4.198 liters
Crew	2	Engine horsepower	100 @ 2800 rpm

Sd.Kfz. 251/1 Ausf. D

Length	5.98 m	Communications	FuG Spr Ger 1
Width	2.1 m		
Height	1.75	Weapon, main	2 x 7.92 mm MG 34
Weight	8.0 tons	Engine make	Maybach
Fuel capacity	160 liters	Engine model	HL42 TUKRM
Maximum speed	53 km/hr (32.86 mph)		
Range, on road	300 km (186 miles)	Engine configuration	six-cylinder, liquid cooled
Range, cross country	150 km (93 miles)	Engine displacement	4.198 liters
Crew	2	Engine horsepower	100 @ 2800 rpm

Sd. Kfz. 251/2

Development of a mortar carrier based on the Sd.Kfz. 251 was begun in September of 1940. A vehicle with the schwerer Granatwerfer 34 8.0 cm mortar was tested in the spring of 1941 and found to be a success. Dubbed the Sd.Kfz. 251/2, the vehicle was laid out so that the mortar could fire from inside a stationary halftrack. The flight path of the shell required the deletion of the forward machine gun. A conventional mortar base plate was carried on the outside of the halftrack, allowing the mortar to also be used as a dismounted weapon. Unlike the Sd.Kfz. 250 mortar carrier, which stowed the base plate on the rear of the vehicle, the base plate was stowed on the Sd.Kfz. 251/2's nose. While most of the mortar carriers were built in earlier bodies, some were created with the Ausf. D body. Provision was made in the 8.64-ton halftrack to stow 66 rounds of mortar ammunition, as well as transport the crew of eight.

Sd. Kfz. 251/3 Funkpanzerwagen

The next version of the 251 was the 251/3. The August 13, 1942 D-660/7 loading manual lists the 251/3 as an artillery towing vehicle. The same publication lists the /4 as an ammo carrier. Other documents dated July 6, 1943, list the Sd.Kfz. 251/3 as a Funkpanzerwagen, or communications vehicle, indicating that the designations were renumbered. The bulk of the Sd.Kfz. 251/3 production was based on the Ausf. D body, although some were built with the Ausf. C body.

Eight subvariants of the Sd.Kfz. 251/3 were built, with five of these types classified as follows:

— /3I equipped with FuG. 8, FuG. 4 and Fu.Spr. /3II equipped with FuG. 8, FuG. 4 and Fu. Spr. f, the tank formation radio. /3III equipped with FuG. 8, FuG. 5 and Fu. Spr. f

— /3IV equipped with FuG. 7, FuG. 1 and Fu. Spr. f, for air-ground co-ordination /3V equipped with Kdo. Fu. Tr. FuG. 11 and FuG. 12, command version /3VI equipped with Fu. Tr. 100 Mw (gp)

— /3VII equipped with Fu. Tr. 80 Mw (gp)

/3VIII equipped with Fu. Tr. 30 Mw (gp)

/3IX equipped with Fu. Tr. 15 Kzw. (gp)

Each version of the 8.5-ton halftrack was crewed by seven men. They were armed with two 7.92mm MG 34 or MG 42 (depending on year) with 2010 rounds of ammunition.

This view from the operator's manual shows the driver's and commander's positions.

Mittelwellenempfänger c
(Fu 4)

30 Watt Sender a
(Fu 8)

Each of the eight subtypes of the Sd.Kfz. 251/3 had a different radio installation.

Charles Kliment collection

The Sd.Kfz. 251/3 was a communications vehicle and usually had the large frame antenna and radio equipment installed inside.

Sd. Kfz. 251/4 mittlere SchützenPanzerwagen (IG)

These vehicles, constructed in the form of the Ausf. A, Ausf. B and Ausf. C, were equipped with reinforced towing pintles which allowed them to act as tow vehicles for field artillery.

Although it was intended that these vehicles would be used to tow the 7.5 cm light infantry gun 18, the 7.74-ton vehicles were also photographed towing 10.5 cm howitzers, as well as PaK 38 and PaK 40 antitank guns. The vehicle also transported 120 rounds of ammunition and the gun crew. A variation of this halftrack was used an ammunition carrier only. Production of the Sd.Kfz. 251/4 ceased in 1943.

The Sd.Kfz. 251/4 was an armored prime mover for artillery. They had pintles installed to fill this role.

Sd. Kfz. 251/5 mittlere SchützenPanzerwagen (Pi)

The Sd.Kfz. 251 began to be supplied to Pioniere, or Engineer, troops in 1939. Initially, the vehicles were standard Sd.Kfz. 251/1, but the troops installed racks inside the halftracks for the engineer equipment. Racks were attached to the upper left side of the body in order for a portable bridge to be carried. In November 1940 this type vehicle was classified Sd.Kfz. 251/5 mittlere SchützenPanzerwagen (Pi).

The crew and armament of the Engineer halftrack varied over the years, from eight to nine men, and sometimes with one, other times two machine guns. In 1943 the Sd.Kfz. 251/7 was introduced as a replacement for the Sd.Kfz. 251/5, and in January of the next year plans were made to cease production of the /5.

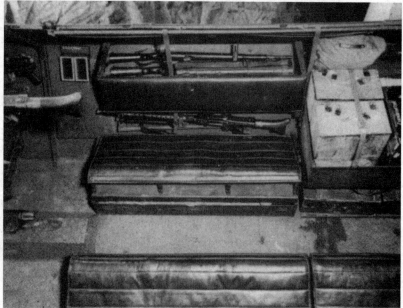

This view shows the internal stowage along the right side of the Sd.Kfz. 251/5. Notice there was no bridge panel stowed on the right side of the vehicle. Engineers of all nations were expected to fight as infantry if needed, thus weapon stowage was provided.

Sd. Kfz. 251/6 mittlere KommandoPanzerwagen

This vehicle is often confused with the similar Sd.Kfz. 251/3. However, the 8.5-ton 251/6 included additional radio equipment and operators. Also, some of these halftracks were equipped with the famous Enigma cryptographic device. Externally, the presence of markings for very senior officers was indicative of a vehicle's /6 status. The frame-type antenna was used initially, but in 1942 that began to be replaced by the star antenna and the 8-meter rod-type.

On some Ausf. A and Ausf. B-bodied versions a map table was field-installed over the driver's compartment. A-D scissors binoculars were sometimes installed on all versions.

Sd.Kfz. 251/6 assigned to Luftwaffe units were sometimes equipped with 10-meter "Flivo" pole-type antennas.

The Sd.Kfz. 251/6 closely resembled the Sd.Kfz. 251/3, but the /6 had a more extensive electronics suite and additional operators.

Patton Museum, Fort Knox, KY

The Sd.Kfz. 251/6 was used by senior commanders, and sometimes had the super-secret Enigma cryptographic device installed. This was General Guderian's vehicle.

Patton Museum, Fort Knox, KY

Sd. Kfz. 251/7 mittlere PionierePanzerwagen

An improvement on the earlier Sd.Kfz. 251/5, the 251/7 was produced using Ausf. C and Ausf. D-hulled vehicles. Like the earlier model, extensive engineer equipment was stowed in special compartments internally, but in the case of the /7, two portable bridge sections were carried, rather than the one mounted on the /5.

Introduced in late 1940, the mittlere PionierePanzerwagen remained in production by Weserhuette through March 1945. Though the vehicles were initially armed with the MG34, the eight-man crews of later models defended themselves with two MG42. Some of the earlier vehicles had no radio, while others were equipped with the Fu.Spr.Ger.f. Beginning in 1943, some 251/7 vehicles were fitted with the Fu. 5 radio set.

Normal halftrack armament was retained, despite the addition not only of the bridge sections, but a considerable amount of specialized stowage.

Patton Museum, Fort Knox, KY

These vehicles were intended to move forward with Panzer units, allowing small streams, gullies, and antitank ditches to be crossed. The bridge panels were manhandled into position.

Bundesarchiv photo

This Sd.Kfz. 251/7 was among the earliest vehicles of its type, being built on an Ausf. C hull. The pair of portable bridge sections, one stowed along either side of the hull, identify the 251/7.

Patton Museum, Fort Knox, KY

National Archives and Records Administration.

This Sd.Kfz. 251/7 has been captured by U.S. troops. Its bridge panels are missing, allowing a good view of their mounting brackets.

Patton Museum, Fort Knox, KY

When the Ausf. D hull was introduced to the Sd.Kfz. 251 line, it began to be used as a basis for the Engineer's vehicles. Note the carrying handles on the side of the bridge panels.

Bundesarchiv photo

Internal stowage of the 251/7 differed from that of the earlier 251/5, yet contained much of the same gear. Note the dogs on top of the bridge panels, used to retain them.

Sd. Kfz. 251/8 mittlere KrankenPanzerwagen

The Sd.Kfz. 251/8 was a halftrack especially outfitted for use as an armored battlefield ambulance. As such, it carried no armament. Other differences included the installation of a large water container on top of the transmission, replacing the normal seating and equipment stowage with special seats and litter racks, and the removal of the top rear connecting armor plate. The latter modification was done in order to allow litter-bearers to enter the vehicle while standing. Occasionally, conventional Sd.Kfz. 251 were pressed into service as ambulances, but these can be distinguished from the special vehicles by their upper plates, and oftentimes the weapons mounts (but not the weapons themselves). A two-man crew served the 7.47-ton vehicle.

While some ambulances were painted white with prominent red cross markings, others had their red cross markings painted on large banners.

Charles Kliment collection

In most cases red cross symbols were painted on ambulance hulls, as on this example photographed in Russia.

Patton Museum, Fort Knox, KY

In some instances, additional ambulances were converted from personnel carriers. This usually involved merely removing the guns themselves, but not the mounts, and painting red cross symbols on the hull.

Patton Museum, Fort Knox, KY

The upper portion of the rear armor on the Sd.Kfz. 251/8 ambulance was cut away in order for stretcher bearers to easily enter and leave the vehicle.

Charles Kliment collection

251/9 m Schütz Pz Wg (7.5 cm K) Kanonenwagen "Stummel"

The increasing need for a fire support vehicle based on the medium halftrack, fortunately for German, coincided with the rearming of the Panzerkampfwagen IV with long guns. The design, commissioned from Büssing-NAG in March 1942, involved mounting the 7.5cm K 51 L/24. short guns removed from the tanks as they were rearmed. These were installed in the Sd.Kfz. 251 using a mounting based on that developed for the Sturmgeschütz.

The installation required radical changes to the halftrack. As well as removal of the forward machine gun mount, a large portion of the frontal armor was cut away in the area normally used by the co-driver. This change was made so that the new gun could be mounted partially inset into the profile of the vehicle, minimizing its height. The left rear seat was removed, making room for stowage for 52 rounds of main gun ammunition. The radio was relocated to the left sidewall to accommodate the cannon and its mount. Installation of the Kw.K. pushed the vehicle's weight up to 8.53 tons, and its height to 2.07 meters.

Production of the first order for the new Sd.Kfz. 251/9 began in June of 1942 following the successful test of two trial vehicles earlier that month on the Russian Front.

During 1944 these vehicles began to be produced using the 7.5 cm K51 (sf) and a simplified mounting. This mounting did not require the major cutting away of the frontal armor as necessitated for the earlier mount. The short barrel of the Sd.Kfz. 251/9's cannon earned it the nickname "Stummel," or stump.

The Sd.Kfz. 251/9 was armed with the 7.5 cm K51 L/24 cannon. These weapons became available when they were removed from Panzerkampfwagen IV during a rearming program.

The mounting of the cannon in the halftrack required cutting away part of the superstructure on the passenger's side of the vehicle. This vehicle has lost even more of its armor through the rigors of combat.

The short gun, mounted in the halftrack, created a fire support vehicle capable of destroying machinegun nests and pill boxes, leaving heavier vehicles to deal with more threatening dangers.

Stefan De Meyer

Sd. Kfz. 251/10 mittlere SchützenPanzerwagen (3.7 cm PaK)

Production of a 3.7 cm antitank gun-armed variant of the Sd.Kfz. 251 began in 1940 and ceased in 1943. They were used as a platoon leader's vehicle and were intended to give each platoon a little heavier punch, along with integral defense against tanks and other hard targets.

A 3.7 cm PaK 36 was mounted above the driver and co-driver in lieu of the machine gun normally found in that location. A variety of gunshields were used, ranging for the standard Pak 36 shield to low-profile shields to a shield on one side only. Some even had no shield at all. The 8.01-ton halftrack transported a crew of five or six men, as well as 168 rounds of ammunition. A machine gun, either MG34 or MG42, was mounted on the rear of the vehicle. It was provided with 1,100 rounds of ammunition.

By mid-war opposing tanks were so well armored that the PaK 36 was no longer an effective weapon, and the 251/10 was rendered obsolete

As was the case with the Sd.Kfz. 250 series vehicles, a platoon leader's variant of the Sd.Kfz. 251 was created and armed with a 3.7 cm PaK. This example with a large gunshield was captured in Tunisia.

A variety of gunshields were installed on these vehicles, including the low-profile half-shield on this example.

The 3.7 cm PaK 36 had a short stint as an effective anti-tank weapon, as tank armor improved during the war. This Sd.Kfz. 251/10 was knocked out by a well-placed round penetrating the driver's compartment.

Though the utility of the 3.7 cm gun as an antitank weapon was not long-lived, it continued to be useful against many softer targets encountered by troops.

Sd. Kfz. 251/11 mittlere FernsprechPanzerwagen

This vehicle produced in the Ausf. C body was built for laying telephone cable and sometimes housed telephone exchange equipment. Delivery of the vehicles began in August of 1942.

Two versions of a telephone laying halftrack were built. One type was equipped with the leichter Feldkabelträger 6 (light field cable carrier), the other with the mittlere Feldkabelträger 10. In either case the two right-side bench seats were replaced by a cabinet with cable reels and telephone equipment. A third cable reel was mounted on the right fender. The crew of five used long staffs to hang the cable in trees and bushes.

The 8.5-ton vehicle retained the normal two-machine- gun armament found on most Sd.Kfz. 251.

A telephone cable-laying version of the Sd.Kfz. 251 was known as the Sd.Kfz. 251/11. A cable reel was mounted on the vehicle's right front fender.

The Sd.Kfz. 251/11, like the Sd.Kfz. 251/1, was armed with two 7.92mm machineguns.

Two cable reels were mounted in the bed, along with radio gear.

B2-24 Sd. Kfz. 251/12 mittlerer Messtrupp and Gerätpanzerwagen,

Sd.Kfz. 251/13 mittlerer schallaufnahmepanzer wagen,

Sd.Kfz. 251/14 mittlerer Schallauswertepanzer wagen,

Sd.Kfz. 251/15 mittlerer Lichtauswertepanzerwagen

These halftracks, which were to be equipped with various sound and flash ranging equipment for panzer divisions, are listed in the July 1943 operators manual.

However, no record, document or photograph has yet surfaced to provide evidence that any of these were actually produced.

Sd. Kfz. 251/16 mittlerer Flammpanzerwagen

The Sd.Kfz.251 was first used to mount flamethrowers beginning with the Ausf. C chassis in January 1943. When the Ausf. C body was dropped in favor of the Ausf. D, production of the flamethrower-equipped version continued. Ultimately, more than 300 were produced.

As initially configured, the flamethrowing halftrack, which was designated Sd.Kfz. 251/16, was equipped with two mounted 14mm flame projectors and a portable, but tethered, 7mm projector. The 14mm projectors were mounted on either side of the hull in a staggered manner. Their mountings allowed them to be traversed 160 degrees. Two flame oil containers, one mounted inside each rear sidewall, held a combined 700 liters of fuel. This allowed approximately 80 one-second bursts to be fired. A Koebe pumping system, powered by a separate Auto Union 28

horsepower engine, supplied the fuel to the projectors. The flamethrowers' range was 50 to 60 meters. Ignition of the 14mm flame projectors was electric, with cartridge ignition for the portable projector.

The Sd.Kfz. 251/16 was revamped in May 1944. The side-mounted flame projectors were redesigned to use cartridge, rather than electric, ignition. At the same time, the hand-held unit was deemed impractical and was discontinued.

In addition to the flame projectors, the four-man crew of the 8.62-ton halftrack had the forward MG34 at its disposal. The vehicle commander doubled as radio operator, while each mounted projector had its own operator. The fourth man drove the vehicle.

The flame projectors had a range between 50 and 60 yards. Enough fuel was carried for 80 1-second bursts.

Patton Museum, Fort Knox, KY

Originally, a benzin-Electric ignition system was used on the Sd.Kfz. 251/16, but on later models a cartridge ignition system was used.

Patton Museum, Fort Knox, KY

Fire is a feared weapon. The Sd.Kfz. 251/16 played on that by mounting two or three flamethrowers, depending upon the model.

Bundesarchiv photo

Stefan De Meyer

The earliest models included a hand-held flame projector, shown here stowed on the rear of the hull. These vehicles were built on Ausf. C chassis.

Patton Museum, Fort Knox, KY

Aside from the obvious dangers of working with flame, the crews had to wear special clothing to protect them from the flame oil, which was a strong irritant.

Bundesarchiv photo

Later Sd. Kfz. 251/16 models were built on the Ausf. D, such as this one. These vehicles did not have the handheld projector, which had limited utility.

Sd. Kfz. 251/17 mittlerer SchützenPanzerwagen (2 cm)

Although some medium halftracks had been previously modified to act as antiaircraft vehicles, the Sd.Kfz. 251/17 was the first officially manufactured one.

A 2 cm FlaK 38 was pedestal mounted in the rear of the vehicle. The gunner's seat was attached to the mount and moved along with the guns as they were traversed and elevated via hand wheels. Ammunition was fed to the weapon via 20-round magazines. A crew of four served the vehicle, which was not a total success due in part to the cramped confines of the 251's hull. The rear MG42 was retained for self defense.

Patton Museum, Fort Knox, KY

Patton Museum, Fort Knox, KY

The Sd.Kfz. 251/17 was the first series-produced anti-aircraft halftrack utilizing the Sd.Kfz. 251 chassis.

The Sd.Kfz. 251/17 was armed with a 2 cm FlaK 38 gun. There was barely enough space in the vehicle for the weapon and its crew.

Sd. Kfz. 251/18 mittlerer Beobachtungspanzerwagen

These vehicles were intended to replace the smaller Sd.Kfz. 250/5 light observation halftracks. Four variants of the new mittlerer Beobachtungspanzerwagen were introduced in August 1944. The versions differed in radio equipment. The Sd.Kfz. 251/18I was equipped with Fu 8, Fu 4, and Fu.Spr.Ger.f radio sets. The Sd.Kfz. 251/18Ia was the same, except for the deletion of the Fu.Spr.Ger.

f set. The Sd.Kfz. 251/18II mounted the Fu 5 and Fu 8 sets, while the IIa added a Fu 4 to the II's equipment ensemble.

Schichau was tasked with assembling the 8.5-ton vehicles, which carried a varying number of crewmen, depending on model and task.

Sd. Kfz. 251/19 mittlerer Fernsprechbetriebspanzerwagen

This medium halftrack was equipped as a mobile telephone exchange. It was used by signals units to provide rapid ground communications among units of advancing

armies. These vehicles were built in both the Ausf. C and Ausf. D hulls.

Sd. Kfz. 251/20 mittlerer SchützenPanzerwagen (Uhu)

Germany was very interested in developing night fighting capabilities for its Army and had begun work toward this in the late 1930s. By 1944 a night fighting system for the Panther had been developed. However, one of the shortcomings of this system was the limited range of visibility provided by the 20 cm infrared searchlight mounted on the tank. This limited the vision of the crew to only 100 to 200 meters.

The obvious solution was a bigger, better infrared searchlight. With space on and in the tank being limited, the decision was made to mount a larger searchlight on the Sd.Kfz. 251 Ausf. D halftrack. One of the 9.3-ton vehicles, classified as the Sd.Kfz. 251/20, was to be assigned for each six IR-equipped Panthers. The Sd.Kfz. 251/20 was equipped with a 60 cm IR searchlight in the rear, attached to a rotating and pivoting mount, and a smaller 20 cm IR searchlight attached to the cowl just forward of the windshield. Also installed on the vehicle were BG 1251 and FG 1252 infrared scopes, an MG 42 and radio equipment. Wumag was to assemble the halftracks with IR equipment, and it began doing just that in January

An infrared scope was mounted beneath the spotlight on the 251/20. The operator's seat pivoted with the light/scope assembly.

The Sd.Kfz. 251/20 was dubbed the "Uhu," or great horned owl. The large infrared spotlight mounted in the rear was used with an early night-vision system.

1945. The combination infrared searchlight and scope was code named "Uhu" –great horned owl.

Documentation has only surfaced to document one use of this equipment, which occurred in March 1945.

Reportedly, some of the Uhu-equipped 251s had their generators and large searchlights removed, providing a partial IR-equipped armored personnel carrier for supporting infantry. The remaining smaller searchlight, walkways, etc. remained in situ on these vehicles, and they continued to have Sd.Kfz. 251/20 stenciled on their shipping data.

Work platforms were located around the upper hull of the spotlight equipped halftracks. Inside, a generator was installed to power the searchlight.

Sd. Kfz. 251/21 mittlerer SchützenPanzerwagen (MG151S)

As Allied air supremacy continued to grow, so did the need for Germany to develop adequate mobile anti-aircraft protection for both armored and infantry units. One of the vehicles built to fill this role was the Sd.Kfz. 251/21. When production began on this medium halftrack in August 1944, it had a triple 1.5 cm machinegun mounted in its rear. The Mauser MG151 machineguns had originally been developed for use on aircraft, but had since been supplanted as aerial weapons. The pedestal mounting had been developed by the German Navy. Later, the 1.5 cm weapons were replaced with the more powerful 2 cm MG151 heavy machineguns.

The weapons were aimed manually, using optical, or later ring and bead, sights. The guns were fed ammo from chests containing 250 rounds each in the case of the outer weapons, and 400 rounds in the center chest. Spent shell casings were collected in the pedestal. The rear MG42 continued to be mounted for self defense.

As the war wore on, the need for mobile antiaircraft defenses increased. The Sd.Kfz. 251/21 was one such vehicle.

The heart of the 251/21 was this antiaircraft machinegun mount. The mount itself was originally developed for the German Navy, while the Mauser MG151 machineguns were designed for use in aircraft. *Charles Kliment collection*

The earliest versions of the 251/21 were armed with triple 1.5 cm machineguns, while later version had triple 2.0 cm guns. *Stefan De Meyer*

The Sd.Kfz. 251/21 is generally considered to be the most successful anti-aircraft variant of this chassis.

Charles Kliment collection

Initially, optical sights were provided on the Sd. 241/21, but on later versions simpler, less-expensive ring and bead sights were used.

The Sd. Kfz. 251/21 had a crew of four to six men. The rate of fire was 700 rounds per minute, and spent shell casings were collected in the pedestal mount.

In 1944, as Germany's forces were being overrun by Allied tanks, Hitler ordered antitank guns mounted on all suitable chassis. Thus, the PaK 40 was mounted in the Sd.Kfz. 251, becoming the Sd.Kfz. 251/22.

Patton Museum, Fort Knox, KY

Though sometimes used against ground targets, the 251/21 was conceived as an antiaircraft weapon. Ironically, this often garnered the vehicle unwanted attention from enemy fighter-bombers, who knocked out many of the halftracks.

Ordnance Museum, Aberdeen Proving Ground

Though it had a relatively low profile, the Sd. Kfz 241/22 halftrack was almost overburdened by the antitank gun.

Ordnance Museum, Aberdeen Proving Ground

Because of its late-war introduction, all Sd.Kfz. 251/22 were built with the Ausf. D hull.

Patton Museum, Fort Knox, KY

The PaK 40 was one of Germany's most effective antitank weapons, capable of defeating the armor on almost any Allied tank.

This very late vehicle has the one-piece engine compartment hatch, as opposed to the two-piece hatch used on most of the Sd.Kfz. 251 production.

Stefan De Meyer

The mounting used for installation of the PaK 40 in the halftrack was adapted from the mounting developed for use in the Sd.Kfz. 234/4 armored car.

Ordnance Museum, Aberdeen Proving Ground

The size of the weapon, and the heavy structural members needed to support it, made for a very cramped vehicle.

Ordnance Museum, Aberdeen Proving Ground

Sd. Kfz. 251/22 mittlerer Schützenpanzerwagen (7.5 cm PaK)

In late 1944 Hitler decreed that all suitable motor vehicle chassis were to be adapted to serve as Panzerjäger. Thus, using a mounting similar to that used on the Sd.Kfz. 234/4 armored car, the 7.5 cm PaK 40 was shoehorned into a medium halftrack.

Two heavy steel beams were installed in the rear hull, sloping from front to rear. These served as the foundation for the gun mount, which was essentially the same as used by the towed PaK 40, except for the omission of the carriage. The gun shield had to be modified, with part of the lower corners cut away to permit traverse, as did the halftrack.

A portion of the driver's compartment rough (????) was removed to allow clearance for the gun's recoil cylinder. Naturally, the interior stowage was heavily modified. The forward rear seats and rifle racks were removed, as was the commander's seat. A travel lock was added to the outside of the vehicle, and ammunition lockers to the interior.

A four-man crew served the vehicle, and they had a single MG42 with which to defend the vehicle from infantry attack. Production of the Sd.Kfz. 251/22 began in December 1944.

2 cm Flak 38 auf Schützenpanzerwagen Sd.Kfz. 251

A small group of perhaps one dozen Sd.Kfz. 251 Ausf. C were modified for the Luftwaffe to act as antiaircraft vehicles. These halftracks had a complete 2 cm FlaK 38 mount installed in the rear. In order to provide clearance for the mount, the hull side plates were extended, making the vehicle resemble the Sd.Kfz. 250 alte. However, in addition to the extension, much of the hull sides were also hinged, allowing them to fold down. This allowed the gun to traverse 360 degrees, and also allowed the weapon to

be depressed enough to engage ground targets. There was also sufficient room for the crew to serve the weapon.

These vehicles were used in field trials, but due to the complexity and expense of the conversion, they were not adopted as standard. These vehicles should not be confused with the later Sd.Kfz. 251/17, which did not have folding side armor.

Built for the Luftwaffe, the 2 cm Flak 38 auf Schützenpanzerwagen Sd.Kfz. 251 was the most elaborate conversion based on the 251 chassis.

Patton Museum, Fort Knox, KY

Patton Museum, Fort Knox, KY

These vehicles were based on the Sd.Kfz. 251 Ausf. C, with their elaborate rear clamshell doors.

Patton Museum, Fort Knox, KY

A 2 cm FlaK 38 mount was installed in the rear of the halftrack, and the forward 7.92mm machinegun mount was removed.

Patton Museum, Fort Knox, KY

The sides of the Schützenpanzerwagen Sd.Kfz. 251 hull were hinged, and could be folded down to provide room for the antiaircraft mount to traverse, as well as for the crew to serve the weapon.

The complexity and expense of these conversions precluded the vehicle from entering series production, although a few trial vehicles were fielded.

Ironically, despite the expense and complexity of the hull conversions, the command vehicles for the trial units, as seen in the foreground, had the same hull modifications made, but lacked the antiaircraft mount.

Le gep Munitionskraftwagen (Sd. Kfz. 252)

These small halftracks were designed and built specifically to provide front-line armored ammunition resupply vehicles for Sturmgeschütz units. Although these vehicles were conceived in 1936, production did not begin until mid-1940.

The chassis of the 1-ton halftrack was used as a basis, although it was shortened slightly, including reducing the road wheel stations by one, to compensate for the increased weight of the armored body. The steeply sloping rear was also designed to reduce the amount of armor, and hence weight.

The redesigned chassis was designated D7p and were produced by Demag and Büssing-NAG. The armored bodies, fabricated by Boehler, were installed on the chassis by the firms of Wegmann and Kiel. It appears that production was completed in late 1941, with a total of just under 400 being produced. It is unlikely that any of these vehicles, which were intended as shuttles between the Sturmgeschütz and ammunition trucks, survived beyond early 1944.

Le gep Munitionskraftwagen (Sd. Kfz. 252)

Length	4.70 m	Crew	2
Width	1.95 m	Communications	Fu 15
Height	1.80	Engine make	Maybach
Weight	4.73 tons	Engine model	HL 42 TRKM
Fuel capacity	140 liters	Engine configuration	six-cylinder, liquid cooled
Maximum speed	65 km/hr (40.3 mph)	Engine displacement	4.17 liters
Range, on road	320 km (198.4 miles)	Engine horsepower	100 @ 2800 rpm
Range, cross country	180 km (111.6 miles)		

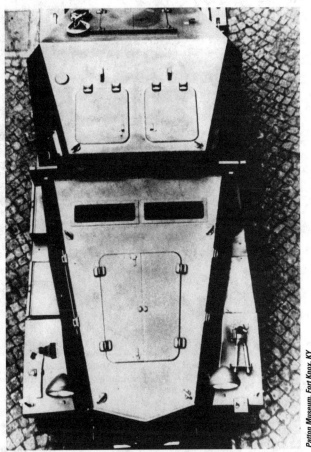

Unlike most German halftracks, the Sd.Kfz. 252 was totally enclosed. This arrangment protected the crew and its volatile cargo from small arms, grenades and shell fragments.

Like the later Sd.Kfz. 250, the Sd.Kfz. 252 was built on the D7p chassis, which was based on the Sd.Kfz. 10 chassis.

These unusually shaped halftracks were built specifically to act as armored ammunition carriers supporting Sturmgeschütz units.

Viewed from head on, the Sd.Kfz. 250, 252, and 253 look very much alike. A Maybach HL42TRKM six-cylinder engine was under the hood of each machine.

The steeply sloped rear hull not only provided excellent ballistic protection, but also reduced the amount of armor plate required, and hence the vehicle's weight.

Le gep Beobachtungskraftwagen (Sd. Kfz. 253)

With plans set for the Sturmgeschütz to play a major role in Germany's offensive operations, the need for armored ammunition re-supply and observation vehicles became apparent even in 1937. As the observation vehicle needed to have mobility characteristics equal to those of the fully tracked Sturmgeschütz, it is not surprising that attention turned to halftrack vehicles. Test vehicles were produced and tried in the fall of 1937.

Utilizing the Sd. Kfz. 10 Type D7 1-ton halftrack as a basis, a new vehicle was created. The chassis of the D7 was shortened, and one road wheel was removed to reduce weight. The new chassis was known as the D7p. A well-sloped armored body was installed that was suited to its role as an armored observation vehicle. These were designated the Leichter gepanzerter Beobachtungskraftwagen (Sd. Kfz. 253), or light armored observation vehicle. The first 25 vehicles were built in March through June 1940. These vehicles were issued in groups of five to Sturmgeschütz batteries.

Following the successful employment of these vehicles, 260 more Sd.Kfz. 253 were assembled by June 1941.

Patton Museum, Fort Knox, KY

Unlike the Sd.Kfz. 250 and 251-based observation vehicles, the top of the 253 was totally enclosed.

Le gep Beobachtungskraftwagen (Sd. Kfz. 253)

Length	4.70 m	Crew	4
Width	1.95 m	Communications	Fu 6, Fu 2
Height	1.80 m		
Weight	5.7 tons	Engine make	Maybach
Fuel capacity	140 liters	Engine model	HL42 TRKM
Maximum speed	65 km/hr (40.3 mph)	Engine configuration	six-cylinder, liquid cooled
Range, on road	320 km (198.4 miles)	Engine displacement	4.198 liters
Range, cross country	210 km (130.2 miles)	Engine horsepower	100 @ 2800 rpm

Patton Museum, Fort Knox, KY

The Sd.Kfz. 253 was an observation vehicle, or Beobachtungskraftwagen, designed specifically to accompany Sturmgeschütz units.

Patton Museum, Fort Knox, KY

Trial vehicles were tested and approved in the fall of 1937, but it would be 1940 before the first production vehicles were delivered.

Viewed from the front, the Sd.Kfz. 253 very much resembles the Sd.Kfz. 250, and 252. Only the scissors periscope protruding from its roof gives away its true purpose.

Access from the ground into the vehicle was through a single door in the rear. This door was similar to the one found on the Sd.Kfz. 250.

M gepanzerter Beobachtungskraftwagen (Sd. Kfz. 254)

This unusual vehicle equipped with both wheels and tracks was developed in 1936 by Saurer-Werke for the Austrian Army. Classified as the Raeder-Raupenfahrzeug 7, 160 of the vehicles were ordered. By the time Germany annexed Austria in March 1938, the vehicle had been renamed the M36 gg 2/2 t ZgWg.

Although it was undecided what role this vehicle would play, the German military was definitely interested in the vehicle. Three chassis were completed and shipped to Daimler-Benz, where superstructures were installed. The vehicles were then forwarded to the Kummersdorf proving ground for testing. Delivery of production vehicles began in June 1940 and continued sporadically through March 1941, until ultimately 128 were built. In March of 1940 the German Army redesignated the vehicle as gepanzerter Artillerie-Beobachtungskraftwagen auf RK7 (Sd. Kfz. 254).

The vehicles served on the Russian Front with the artillery regiments of various Panzer divisions. The operator's manual refers to the vehicle as mittlerer gepanzerter Beobachtungskraftwagen (Sd. Kfz. 254) auf Raeder-Kettenfahrgetell RK7.

M gepanzerter Beobachtungskraftwagen (Sd. Kfz. 254)

Length	4.50 m	Crew	4
Width	2.47 m	Communications	Fu 6, Fu 2, Tornister Funkgerät
Height	2.33 m		
Weight	6.4 tons	Engine make	Saurer
Fuel capacity	72 liters	Engine model	CRDv diesel
Maximum speed	75 km/hr (46.5 mph)	Engine configuration	four-cylinder, liquid cooled
Range, on road	500 km (310 miles)	Engine displacement	5.3 liters
Range, cross country	100 km (62 miles)	Engine horsepower	70 @ 2000 rpm

The Sd.Kfz. 254 was used as an artillery observation vehicle, primarily on the Eastern Front. Series production began in 1940, ending the following year.

Military History Institute, Carlisle Barracks, PA

Bundesarchiv photo

The design of the Sd.Kfz. 254 originated with the Austrian Army. Supposedly combining the best features of both tracked and wheeled vehicles, it also had the shortcomings of each, as shown by the flat tire on this vehicle.

Panzerspähwagen RK Ausf. A

This unusual vehicle was not a half track in the conventional since of the term. Though it featured both wheels and tracks, both were not in use at the same time. For on road use, the wheels were lowered to the ground, for off-road use, the wheels were raised, permitting the tracks to make contact instead.

The Panzerspähwagen RK was developed by Saurer-Werke in response to a May 1938 request from the German Army automotive design office. Intended for use as an armored reconnaissance vehicle, it had armor protection proof against 7.92mm armor-piercing rounds and turret designed by Daimler-Benz. Installed in the turret was an EW 141 7.92mm antitank rifle and a 7.92mm MG34.

A test vehicle constructed of mild steel was delivered in June 1940, which was joined by a second test machine the following August. It was anticipated that a trial series of 15 vehicles would begin production in May 1942, but it is doubtful that this occurred.

Patton Museum, Fort Knox, KY

Panzerspähwagen RK was developed by Saurer-Werke as a reconnaissance vehicle that could be operated quickly on road using tires, or lowered onto tracks for off-road use.

Mun Kw fur Nebelwerfer (Sd. Kfz. 4) and 15cm Panzerwerfer 42 auf Sf (Sd. Kfz. 4/1)

As discussed elsewhere in this volume, the Maultier came about by converting cargo trucks to halftracks to meet pressing mobility requirements on the Russian front. In 1943, Opel was asked to create a version of the Maultier with an armored body equipped for the mounting of the 15 cm Nebelwerfer. This would both increase the mobility of the Nebelwerfer battery and increase protection for the crews. This increase in protection was two-fold. Not only were they protected from enemy small arms fire, they were also protected from the launching blast, negating the time-consuming need to dig the protective trenches used by conventional Nebelwerfer batteries.

The basic Nebelwerfer vehicle shown here is an Opel 3-ton Maultier, based in turn on the Blitz truck. In 1943, an armored version of the Maultier was introduced.

Six-hundred of the armored Maultier were produced from April 1943 through March 1944. Half of these were equipped with a 10-tube 15 cm Nebelwerfer launcher.

These crews are rearming their launchers. Three hundred of the armored Maultier were built without launchers, intended to serve as ammunition re-supply vehicles for the launcher-equipped halftracks.

In addition to the 10 rockets carried in the launch racks, another 10 rockets were stowed inside each Nebelwerfer vehicle.

The Nebelwerfer was not a terribly accurate weapon, lending itself best to area use, such as bombardment prior to an assault. They were, however, quite intimidating to opposing troops.

Feürleitpanzer on 8-ton Zgkw chassis

While the dreaded "buzz-bombs" (V-1 rocket) were launched from fixed positions which were fairly easily targeted by Allied bombers, that was not the case with their big brothers. The A4, or as it is more commonly referred to, the V-2, was designed to be launched from a mobile system.

Naturally, this meant that the entire battery had to be mobile, including the launch control bunkers. To fill this need, 49 Krauss-Maffei KM m 11 8-ton halftracks were equipped with specialized armored rear bodies during 1944. The halftracks were to be oriented such that the rear faced the launcher during firing. In this way the sloping rear armor not only protected the launch control crew, but also the unarmored forward portion of the vehicle.

When the battery was being moved this vehicle also acted as a prime mover, towing additional equipment.

Patton Museum, Fort Knox, KY

The 8-ton Krauss-Maffei KM m 11 halftrack was used as the basis for the Feürleitpanzer, an armored launch control vehicle for the V-2 rockets.

When the missile battery was on the move, the Feürleitpanzer acted as a prime mover, towing the launch pad.

Patton Museum, Fort Knox, KY

Patton Museum, Fort Knox, KY

During the launch, the rear of the halftrack was oriented toward the launch, with its armored structure protecting both the crew and the unarmored cab and engine compartment.

7.5 cm Selbstfahrlafette L/40.8 Modell 1

This specialized halftrack tank destroyer was designed by Büssing-NAG in the mid-1930s. Two different trial vehicles were built, on two different chassis, both designated 7.5 cm Selbstfahrlafette L/40.8 Modell 1. The first Selbstfahrlafette, or self-propelled carriage, were on the rear-engined BNL6(H) chassis. This chassis had five roadwheels. An alternate prototype was also constructed utilizing the BN10(H) chassis, this can be distinguished by its six roadwheels.

Both vehicles had armored bodies and carried a Rheinmetall-Borsig 7.5 cm L40.8 cannon in a turret designed by the gun's maker. It is believed that three trial vehicles were produced.

Patton Museum, Fort Knox, KY

The later experimental tank destroyer was built on a longer BN10 chassis, with the engine located in the rear. The additional roadwheel is evident in comparison to the earlier vehicle.

Patton Museum, Fort Knox, KY

Another 7.5 cm-armed halftrack was built by Rheinmetall. This one, photographed in August 1938, was built on a BNL6 chassis with the engine located in the rear.

Pz Selbstfahrlafette II auf Zgkw 5t (HKP 902)

Developed as part of Germany's quest for a viable halftrack-mounted tank-destroyer, the Panzer Selbstfahrlafette II 7.5 cm Kanone L/41 auf Zugkraftwagen 5 ton (HKP 902) was rear-engine vehicle built on Büssing-NAG chassis. Its armament was a 7.5 cm Kanone L/48 mounted in a open-topped turret.

Two armored trial vehicles were assembled by Rheinmetall-Borsig in 1941 and were promptly dispatched to Libya for use by the Afrika Korps, arriving there in January of 1942. One of these was subsequently captured by British troops before May 30 that year. The fate of the second vehicle is unknown.

Though the Panzer Selbstfahrlafette II 7.5 cm Kanone L/41 auf Zugkraftwagen 5-ton (HKP 902) was credited with the destruction of several tanks, it was not ordered into series production.

The two trial models of the Panzer Selbstfahrlafette II 7.5 cm Kanone L/41 auf Zugkraftwagen 5-ton (HKP 902) were given field tests with the Afrka Korps in 1942. The vehicles did not enter series production.

3.7 cm Selbstfahrlafette L/70

This experimental halftrack was built between 1935 and 1936 by Hansa-Loyd for use as a Panzerjäger. The HL kl 3 (H) chassis was a rear-engine design with tracks extending three-quarters of the way forward. It was armed with a 3.7 cm PaK L/70 mounted in a turret, both the gun and turret being designed by Rheinmetall-Borsig. An unknown number of vehicles were built, none of which were likely used in combat.

The 3.7 cm Selbstfahrlafette L/70 was an experimental rear-engined halftrack developed in the mid-1930s. It was intended as a nimble, lightly armored, tank destroyer.

Schwerer Wehrmachtschlepper (gep Ausf.)

The sWS was envisioned to be the German Army's standard heavy towing tractor, a status that it never attained. However, its increased load-carrying capacity and mobility compared to the Maultier meant that it was natural that the military would want to use the sWS as the basis for their Nebelwerfer-armed halftracks, and in mid-1944 they did just that.

An armored body, similar to the one developed for the rocket-armed Maultier, was installed along with the 10-tube launcher. The sWS-based vehicle had the added advantage of increased ammunition stowage capacity over the Maultier vehicle.

Another armored cab was also developed along with a body with fold-down sides in order to allow the effective mounting of the 3.7 cm FlaK 43 L/89.

Both these variants saw service from mid-1944 through the end of the war.

National Archives and Records Administration.

A few of the sWS, or heavy army towing tractor, halftracks were built with armored bodies. These were supposed to be used as platforms for the mounting of 3.7 cm FlaK guns and Nebelwerfer rocket launchers.

Softskin Vehicles

The BMW R4 models purchased by the German military differed little from the civilian models. The bikes were generally considered reliable, albeit underpowered.

BMW R4

BMW was, and is, one of the most famous motorcycle builders in Germany. It was not surprising, then, that Germany's military turned to the manufacturer to supply its motorcycle troops.

The famed motorcycle units of the Wermacht were a product of an extensive training program. Much of this training took place on BMW R4 machines, which began to be delivered to the Reichswehr in 1932 in large numbers.

The military version of the R4 differed from the popular civilian model most obviously in its paint, but also by the inclusion of a skid plate and different saddlebag brackets.

The military bikes were equipped with skid pans to protect the engine, and the saddlebag mountings differed from those used on civilian bikes.

BMW R4

Wheelbase	1.32 m	Engine configuration	one-cylinder, four-stroke
Weight	137 kg		
Fuel capacity	12 liters	Engine displacement	398 cc
Maximum speed	100 km/hr (62 mph)	Engine horsepower	12 @ 3500 rpm

The BMW R12 was the successor to the R4, and was purchased in huge numbers by the military. The large, close front fenders of civilian models were a detriment to off-road applications.

BMW R12

A German military BMW with sidecar is often assumed to be an R75. This is often an incorrect assumption. The R12 was produced in far greater numbers, and had far more widespread use, this was especially so during the early stages of the war.

Production of the R12 began in 1935. The R12 had a 750 cc side-valve, two-cylinder engine, which performed remarkably with the heavy load despite its meager 18-hp rating.

The R12's lack of power, and susceptibility to damage from mud and snow, led the Wermacht to continue looking for a better bike.

The R12 was used as both a solo machine and with sidecars. This three-man crew, typical for German sidecar bikes, was photographed taking a break in front of their machine.

BMW R12			
Wheelbase	1.38 m	Engine configuration	two-cylinder, four-stroke
Weight	185 kg		
Fuel capacity	14 liters	Engine displacement	745 cc
Maximum speed	110 km/hr solo (68.2 mph)	Engine horsepower	18 @ 3400 rpm

This new R12 shows the camouflage paint scheme of the prewar era. BMW delivered 36,000 of these machines to the military by May 1941.

Military Miniatures in Review

Despite training for winter conditions, R12 crew still struggled with the harshness of the Russian front.

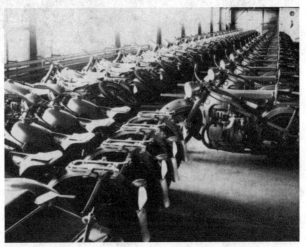

The R12 was purchased both with and without a sidecar, as evidenced by these machines queued up at the factory awaiting shipment.

The sidecar of the R12 was not driven. This weakness in off-road operation was corrected on the later R75.

Allied-Axis

The BMW R35 was a solo machine which could be identified by its telescopic front forks. This bike was used not only in training, but operationally, in large numbers.

BMW R35

The BMW R35 was a medium motorcycle purchased in large quantities to replace the R4 as a training motorcycle beginning in 1937. One of the most noticeable differences between the models is the telescopic front forks of the R35. The R35 was also used for training purposes and messenger service. Like the R12 and R4, the fuel tank of the R35 was nestled between the sides of the stamped steel frame of the motorcycle. The R61 and R75 had fuel tanks that overhung those bikes' tubular steel frames. Also like the R4 and R12, the R35 had a four-speed transmission that was shifted by hand, whereas the R75 was foot-shifted.

The R35's primary operational use was as a dispatch bike, such as this example with rider. Still, the large, civilian-style fenders remained, and were prone to becoming packed with mud.

BMW R35

Wheelbase	1.30 m	Engine configuration	One-cylinder, four-stroke
Weight	150 kg		
Fuel capacity	12 liters	Engine displacement	340 cc
Maximum speed	100 km/hr (62 mph)	Engine horsepower	14 @ 4500 rpm

www2mm.com

BMW R61

The BMW R61 was a large civilian bike that was produced from 1938 through 1941. This machine introduced rear suspension on BMW motorcycles. Less than 4,000 of these machines were built—the low number no doubt due in part to the vehicle's large size and cost.

Many of the R61 bikes, and indeed all German motorcycles (and to a certain extent, their owners), were requisitioned by the German military. Trained government employees went to dealerships and private owners, appraised the bikes, made payment to the owners for those amounts, and took the motorcycles away.

Many enthusiasts in motorcycle clubs were inducted into the service. Their experience made them excellent messengers and motorcycle infantry.

BMW R61

Wheelbase	1.40 m	Engine configuration	two-cylinder, four-stroke
Weight	184 kg	Engine displacement	597 cc
Fuel capacity	14 liters		
Maximum speed	115 km/hr (71.3 mph)	Engine horsepower	18 @ 4800 rpm

This is an early R75 (1942-1943), as evidenced by the transmission-mounted air-filter and in-tank toolbox. Both these features would be changed as a result of field conditions later.

BMW R75

The BMW R75 heavy motorcycle with sidecar is one of the most famous military motorcycles in the world. The R75 was designed from the ground up to be a military bike, with much consideration given to the combat lessons learned by the motorcycle riflemen.

Even with that, there was still room for improvement after the bike was introduced in 1941.

The BMW R75 was given a tank-mounted air filter (previously a transmission-mounted air filter had been used) starting with serial number 757201 in the first half of 1941.

Also, early bikes had metal fork covers ("gaiters" in technical terms). But when the bikes were used in North Africa and the Russian front, too much dirt and sand clogged up the working parts, so starting with serial number 762260 the factory changed to the rubber fork gaiters.

The R75's sidecar was powered, and shared many components, with that used by the Zündapp KS750. The bikes had high and low gearing ranges with a total of eight forward gears and two reverse gears.

A provision was made for hand and foot heating in cold climates. A machinegun could be installed on the sidecar.

BMW R75

Wheelbase	1.44 m	Engine configuration	two-cylinder, four-stroke, opposed piston
Weight	420 kg w/ sidecar		
Fuel capacity	24 liters	Engine displacement	745 cc
Maximum speed	92 km/hr (57 mph) with sidecar	Engine horsepower	26 @ 4400 rpm

The BMW R75 was built from the ground up as a military motorcycle. Its sidecar was powered, and often included a machinegun mount.

Even with leg protectors and handlebar heaters, operating any motorcycle, even the big R75, in these conditions was a bone-chilling experience.

On later production, the air filter was raised to a position in the tank, distancing it from the road dust. This was a result of lessons learned in Africa and Russia. The rubber boots on the front forks were also a result of combat experiences.

The Zündapp K500 model was comparable to the BMW R12. These bikes were bought by the German Army from 1934 through 1938.

Zündapp K 500 W

Though not as well known as BMW's contribution to the German war effort, Zündapp, located in Nürnberg, also was a major supplier of military motorcycles. Procurement of the K 500 W began in 1934 and continued through 1938. This was a light machine, and barely modified from the civilian model. Most of these machines were used for training purposes.

Zündapp K 500 W

Wheelbase	1.39 m	**Engine configuration**	two-cylinder, four-stroke, opposed piston
Weight	188 kg		
Fuel capacity	12.5 liters		
Maximum Speed	105 km/hr solo (65.1 mph)	**Engine displacement**	498 cc
		Engine horsepower	16 @ 4800 rpm

Some K500 bikes were used by combat units for messenger service—a task for which they were less than ideal.

The K500 had a two-cylinder, opposed-piston engine. Like most Zündapp bikes, the K500 had a pressed-steel frame.

Military Miniatures in Review

The K500 was used extensively in training the German motorcycle corps. The pressed-steel forks helped identify Zündapp bikes.

KS 600 W

Introduced in 1938, the KS 600 W was probably the Wermacht's best sidecar-equipped motorcycle prior to the advent to the KS 750 and BMW R75. It had a strong overhead-cam engine and featured Zündapp's easily repairable pressed-steel frame. Production of these machines continued until the introduction of the KS 750 in 1941 and totaled 18,000 bikes. The KS 600 W was equipped with a Type 39 sidecar.

Zündapp KS 600 W

Wheelbase	1.39 m	Engine configuration	two-cylinder, four-stroke, opposed piston
Weight	205 kg		
Fuel capacity	15 liters		
Maximum speed	135 km/hr solo (83.7 mph)	Engine displacement	587 cc
		Engine horsepower	28 @ 4800 rpm

The KS600 motorcycle-sidecar pair is believed by many to be the best combination machine fielded by the German Army prior to the advent of the very heavy R75/KS750 units. Here, a pair of motorcycle infantrymen take a break.

The KS600 was introduced in 1938 as a replacement for the K500. With a more powerful overhead-cam engine, this bike could be coupled to a sidecar.

KS 750

Work to develop the KS 750 began in April 1940. This machine was designed specifically for heavy off-road military use, and drew heavily from the evaluation of captured French and Belgian sidecar bikes. The sidecar wheel was powered, and there was provision for heating the sidecar, as well as the feet and hands of the driver. More than 18,000 of these machines were built, despite a cost that exceeded that of the VW Kübelwagen.

Zündapp KS 750

Wheelbase	1.41 m	Engine configuration	two-cylinder, four-stroke, opposed piston
Weight	400 kg with sidecar		
Fuel capacity	23 liters	Engine displacement	751 cc
Maximum speed	95 km/hr with sidecar (58.9 mph)	Engine horsepower	26 @ 4000 rpm

The KS750 used a complex, parallelogram front fork. Though it was high-maintenance, the fork provided superior riding and handling.

The Zündapp KS750 was developed concurrently with the BMW R75, and many components were interchangeable. The sidecar wheel was powered via a Zündapp-designed differential, which was also used by BMW.

K 800 W

The Zündapp K 800 W, and its sidecar-equipped stablemate, the KS 800 W, were equipped with the largest engine of any Wehrmacht motorcycle. Essentially the same bike as the civilian K 800, only painted in military gray and given a "W" suffix, this four-cylinder bike was noted for its speed and torque. In fact, it was ultimately official forbidden by the military to operate this machine sans sidecar. Approximately 5,000 of these were delivered under military contract.

Zündapp K 800 W

Wheelbase	1.405 m	Engine configuration	two-cylinder, four-stroke, opposed piston
Weight	210 kg		
Fuel capacity	12.5 liters		
Maximum speed	125 km/hr solo	Engine displacement	791 cc
		Engine horsepower	22 @ 4300 rpm

The Zündapp K800 and KS800 had the largest engine of any motorcycle ordered by the Wermacht. Operating it without the sidecar, was forbidden, although this was done occasionally.

ww2mm.com

Pkw — Personenkraftwagen (cars)

The name Light Uniform Personnel Vehicle was something of a misnomer, as very little about these cars, built by a variety of manufacturers, was uniform. What was uniform were the specifications they were built to as far as size and capability. However, makers were free to utilize the engine, transmission and other components of their choice when assembling these vehicles.

BMW, Hanomag and Stoewer all produced the Light Uniform Personnel Vehicle, oftentimes with bodies built by Ambi-Budd. In 1940 that lack of parts commonality was addressed as the Light Uniform Personnel Vehicle Type 40 was introduced. Produced only by Stoewer, these vehicles were all powered by Stoewer's own AW2 2-liter engine.

Patton Museum, Fort Knox, KY

Stoewer built the bulk of the Light Uniform Personnel Vehicles, although BMW and Hanomag also produced some of the first series units. These vehicles tended to be underpowered, and were superceded by the Kübelwagen.

Chassis for Light Uniform Personnel Vehicle Type 40			
Length	depends on body	Range, on road	350 km (217 miles)
Width	1.69 m	Engine make	Stoewer
Height	depends on body	Engine model	AW 2
Weight	1280 kg, chassis only	Engine configuration	four-cylinders, liquid cooled
Fuel capacity	60 liters	Engine displacement	1.997 liters
Maximum speed	80 km/hr (49.6 mph)	Engine horsepower	50 @ 3500 rpm

National Archives and Records Administration

The chassis of the Light Uniform vehicles was not adequate for the rigors of off-road operation, leading to frequent repairs. Conditions such as this test the endurance of any vehicle.

Daimler-Benz 170 V

Daimler-Benz introduced its compact Mercedes 170 car to the public in 1931. Its introduction coincided with the expansion of Germany's highway system, and it was also priced economically—a requirement given the depressed state of Germany's economy at the time. The German Army at the time, the Reichswehr, was expanding its mechanization. The new Mercedes was appealing to the military as a light personnel car.

With its open-top construction and bucket seats, rapid entrance and exit were possible, and a necessity for a personnel carrier. Despite its 1.7-liter engine, which should have placed it in the Medium Personnel Car class, the 170 was considered a Light Car.

Some 19,000 Mercedes 170 cars were built for the military before the VW Kübelwagen superceded it as the Army's prime light personnel car in 1942. In fact, the 170's production was second only to the Kübelwagen in this size class.

Daimler-Benz 170 V

Length	4.11 m	**Engine make**	Daimler-Benz
Width	1.58 m	**Engine model**	Daimler-Benz M 136
Height	1.80 m		
Weight	1,235 kg	**Engine configuration**	six-cylinder, liquid cooled
Fuel capacity	43 liters		
Maximum speed	90 km/hr (55.8 mph)	**Engine displacement**	1.7 liters
Range, on road	330 km (204.6 miles)	**Engine horsepower**	32 @ 3000 rpm

The compact, lightweight, fuel-efficient Mercedes 170 appealed to the military almost from its introduction on the civil market. Initially, the militarization involved little more than paint.

142.

In 1937 the Mercedes 170 VL (type W139) was introduced especially for the military. These vehicles had all-wheel drive, which produced a marked improvement in off-road operation.

More impressive than all-wheel drive, but less useful, was the 170 VL's all-wheel steering. This proved dangerous and was soon abandoned.

From 1938 through 1942 the 170 V was supplied to the German armed forces. Among its configurations was a radio car, shown here. The radio was mounted in the rear on the near side of this photo.

The radio installation in the right rear seat area resulted in these vehicles having an unusual three-seat arrangement. A canvas cover and side curtains were supplied to protect both the equipment and occupants from harsh weather.

When the weather conditions permitted, or threat of enemy attack was great, not only could the 170 V's convertible top be lowered, but the doors could be removed as well. With the doors removed, the radio equipment is easily seen.

Type 82 VW Kubelwagen

In January 1938, work began in earnest on the vehicle that would come to be popularly known as the Kübelwagen. The term Kübelwagen means "bucket car" and was actually applied to a variety of vehicles from a number of makers, but it has since come to be synonymous with the Volkswagen Type 82. Even under the skilled tutelage of Dr. Ferdinand Porsche, two years of work and testing were required before the VW took its classic form.

Its reliable, air-cooled engine and light weight made it both maneuverable and popular with the using troops. The vehicles were used from Africa to Russia, and proved successful in all theaters. Unlike the American Jeep, the Kübelwagen had only two-wheel drive, although four-wheel drive was experimented with on the Type 86 Kübelwagen. Various specialized versions of the Type 82 were built for use as radio vehicles, repair shops, ambulances and for intelligence work.

In March 1943 the original 985 cc engine was re-placed with 1131 cc unit intended for use in the amphibious Schwimmwagen. At about the same time the instrument panel was redesigned and the fenders began to be welded, rather than bolted on.

The Type 82 Kübelwagen should not be confused with the Type 181 "Thing." The Thing was a much different vehicle developed for use by Germany's postwar army. More than 50,000 of the Type 82 vehicles were built during WWII, but few survive today.

Type 82 VW Kübelwagen

Length	3.74 m	**Range, on road**	400 km (248 miles)
Width	1.60 m	**Engine make**	Volkswagen
Height	1.65 m top up, 1.10 top down	**Engine configuration**	four-cylinder, horizontally opposed, air-cooled
Weight	1.15 tons loaded	**Engine displacement**	986 cc, later 1131 cc
Fuel capacity	30 liters		
Maximum speed	80 km/hr (49.6 mph)	**Engine horsepower**	23.5, later 25 @ 3000 rpm

This is the vehicle that the German Army used in many of the same roles that U.S. forces used the Jeep. Known as the Kübelwagen, or "bucket car," this example of the versatile vehicle was captured from the Afrika Korps and returned to Aberdeen Proving Ground for testing.

A soldier, signal paddles in his hands, sits in a Kübelwagen leading a convoy of larger vehicles. The light weight of the Kübelwagen allowed it to travel many places more powerful vehicles could not negotiate.

Patton Museum, Fort Knox, KY

The driver's position in the Kübelwagen was very spartan. Wooden floorboards kept muddy feet from slipping on the steel floor, and the shift pattern for the vehicle's four-speed transmission was embossed in the instrument panel. Three different types of steering wheels were used on the Kübelwagen. This is the earliest type, made of Bakelite.

The underside of the vehicle was as simple as its interior. Note the dual exhaust outlets for the four-cylinder, air-cooled engine, and the embossed floor pan. The reduction units at the hubs allowed for increased ground clearance for the Kübelwagen—a characteristic shared with the modern HMMWV.

Any vehicle was popular with soldiers who would otherwise have to walk. These GI's have adopted this Kubel as their own. The embossments in the side panels provided rigidity, yet permitted the use of relatively thin steel.

For use in the desert, high-flotation balloon tires were installed on the Kübelwagen. The wider cross-section, rounded shoulders and lack of aggressive tread helped the vehicle stay on top of the sand.

A canvas cover was provided for the crew compartment. While the cover offered some protection from both rain and snow, it often was not fitted because of the reduced visibility.

Vehicles prepared for use in North African deserts sometimes wound up in other areas. The lack of tread is a hindrance to this vehicle on a muddy road.

Schwimmwagen (Type 166)

Rivers and other bodies of water have formed natural defenses for thousands of years. Not surprisingly, many attempts have been made to overcome that obstacle. One of the more successful devices for this purpose was the Volkswagen Type 166 Schwimmwagen.

Work began on this design, under Dr. Porsche's supervision, in July 1940 and two months later the first prototype was undergoing testing. However, it was not until February 1942 that the Schwimmwagen in its final form, the Type 166, was approved for mass production. The prototype of this version was tested in March of 1942, and production models began leaving the assembly line almost immediately. By June, 100 of the small vehicles had been completed.

The final design included a monobody made by Ambi-Budd, an improved five-speed transmission and four-wheel drive. Water propulsion was by propeller. Like the Kübelwagen, Schwimmwagen's air-cooled engine was mounted in the rear of the body. By the end of the war more than 14,000 of these machines had been delivered.

Schwimmwagen (Type 166)

Length	3.825 m	Range, on road	520 km (322.4 miles)
Width	1.48 m	Engine make	Volkswagen
Height	1.615 m top up, 1.080 m top down	Engine configuration	four-cylinder, horizontally opposed, air-cooled
Weight	1362 kg	Engine displacement	1131 cc
Fuel capacity	50 liters		
Maximum speed	80 km/hr (49.6 mph) land, 10 km/hr (6.2 mph) water	Engine horsepower	25 @ 3000 rpm

The Schwimmwagen was successful four-wheel-drive, fully amphibious vehicle. Its compact size allowed it to traverse most any terrain. This made the vehicle a hit not only with German troops, but also Allied units fortunate enough to capture the vehicles in operating condition.

National Archives and Records Administration

The Schwimmwagen was produced in large numbers. Here, a portion of the initial order waits outside Porsche's Stuttgart factory`. More than 14,000 of these machines were constructed.

The exhaust system was located on top of the Schwimmwagen's engine compartment.

The shape of the hull of the car was very streamlined and was very efficient in relatively calm waters. Four-wheel drive and a locking rear differential were beneficial for climbing up muddy shorelines.

The hinged propeller, shown here in the almost totally lowered position, was driven from the engine crankshaft. In calm water the vehicle could travel 7.5 mph.

National Archives and Records Administration

Patton Museum, Fort Knox, KY

The Schwimmwagen was well suited for its intended purpose of crossing calm lakes and rivers, but would be swamped in heavy waves.

The Type 82E Volkwagen essentially was the civilian KdF-wagen body on the military Kübelwagen chassis. Relatively few of these vehicles were made, and their use was primarily by officers.

Patrick Stansell, Military Miniatures in Review

KdF-Wagen (Type 82E) and Kommandeurswagen (Type 87)

The Volkswagen Beetle was conceived by Hitler as a political/propaganda tool. The premise was that the average citizen of Germany would be able to own their own new auto. Originally known as the KdF-Wagen, or "Strength-through-Joy-Car," the vehicle was offered for sale through the KdF (Kraft durch Freude) political organization, itself a unit of the German Labor Front (DAF). The Volkswagen, or "People's Car," supposedly would benefit the common German laborer, who could purchase one of the cars for only five-Reich mark-per-week. However, this was not a payment plan, but a layaway plan. Stamps were purchased, and placed in books. When the book was full, a car could be bought with it. Despite $67 million dollars in payments from 337,000 people, no cars were delivered to private citizens.

With the onset of war, Kdf-Wagen vehicles were earmarked for military usage. From 1938 through 1940, fewer than 100 sedan versions were produced. These cars were used for testing or assigned to Nazi party officials. Production was increased between 1942-1944, during which time 630 cars built specifically for the military left the assembly line. Originally designated as the type 92, in

May 1943 it was redesignated type 82E). These cars had the more robust Kübelwagen suspension and a very plain interior.

An obscure variant of this was the Type 87. This vehicle was a four-wheel-drive Beetle. Essentially, the body of the Type 82 was equipped with the power train of the Type 166 Schwimmwagen. They were designation the "Kommandeurswagen" (command car). Despite the vehicle's excellent performance, only a handful were built.

Kommandeurswagen (Type 82E)

Length	4.06 m	Engine make	Volkswagen
Width	1.57 m	Engine configuration	four-cylinder, horizontally opposed, air-cooled
Height	1.64 m		
Weight	755 kg		
Fuel capacity	xxxx	Engine displacement	986 cc, later 1131 cc
Maximum speed	80 km/hr (49.6 mph)	Engine horsepower	23.5, later 25 @ 3000 rpm
Range, on road	xxxx		

Medium Uniform Personnel Vehicle

Of Germany's efforts to standardize transport vehicle production in the "uniform chassis" series, only the Medium Uniform Chassis can be regarded as truly successful. Production of these vehicles began in 1937.

Vehicles in this group were initially built by Wanderer and Horch, with the latter being the more predominate of the two. In 1940 Adam Opel was also involved in production of the Medium Uniform PKW. Production of this vehicle class by all manufacturers ceased in 1943.

Different body styles were installed on these chassis, depending on the intended use. This naturally also meant that a variety of Kfz. numbers were assigned. Kfz. 12 had an open body, Kfz. 15 had four to six seats served as a communications vehicle, Kfz. 16 mounted range-finding equipment, and the Kfz. 17 was a closed-bodied communications vehicle.

One unique feature of the early vehicles were the spare tires mounted centrally on either side. These served a second purpose. The tires would rotate on their mounts, and extended beneath the lower edge of the body. The intention was that this would prevent the underside of the body from getting hung during sudden changes of gradient.

The body styles were simplified in 1940, and the newer vehicles were known as Medium Uniform Chassis Type 40. Along with this change came the elimination of the double-spare tire arrangement. From 1940 onward only a single spare tire was mounted, and it was carried internally in the vehicle. Mechanical refinements were introduced beginning in March 1942, and included stronger axles and beefed-up springs.

Medium Uniform Chassis - Horch

Length	4.695 m	Range, on road	400 km (248 miles)
Width	1.840 m	Engine make	Horch
Height	depends on body	Engine configuration	V-8, liquid-cooled
Weight	1,362 kg	Engine displacement	3.546 liters
Fuel capacity	98 liters		
Maximum speed	96 km/hr (59.52 mph)	Engine horsepower	30 @ 3600 rpm

The early Medium Uniform Personnel Vehicles are readily distinguished be their twin side-mounted spare tires. These mounts allowed the tires to rotate if the vehicle's bottom should drag.

Patton Museum, Fort Knox, KY

The Kfz. 15 was one of the more common vehicles built on the Medium Uniform Chassis. It had four to six seats and could have radio equipment installed.

A revised vehicle was built in 1940 and referred to by the military as the Medium Uniform Chassis Type 40. These vehicles had a number of mechanical refinements.

The Type 40 was given the Horch model number 901. The new models dispensed with the elaborate twin spare tire carriers. Instead, a single spare was carried inside behind the driver.

The Kfz. 17 was a closed-bodied communications vehicle built on the Medium Uniform Chassis. This vehicle has slipped off of the roadway and become mired.

Heavy Uniform Personnel Vehicles

Most of the cars in the heavy class (over a 3.0 liter engine) shared chassis with light trucks, and are discussed in the appropriate truck heading. An exception to this is the Heavy Uniform Personnel Vehicle.

The Uniform Chassis II for Heavy Personnel Vehicles were built by Auto Union at the Horch plant, and by Ford. A limited number were produced with four-wheel steering, and all had four-wheel drive. The Horch 3.5 liter and Ford 3.6 liter V-8 engines were used. Spare tires were mounted on rotating mounts on either side of the vehicles. They were positioned to prevent the bottom of the chassis from dragging in rough terrain.

In 1940 the Heavy Uniform Chassis was redesigned, becoming the Heavy Uniform Chassis-Type 40. Those vehicles built by Horch now were powered by a Horch 3.8 liter V-8. The power plant of Ford-built vehicles was unchanged. The sophisticated rotating spare tire mounts were replaced by a single internally mounted spare on the new model. Production of the improved version lasted barely a year, at which time it was phased out in favor of the Steyr 1500.

As was the case with most tactical vehicles, regardless of nation, numerous body styles were produced for this chassis. In addition to use as a personnel carrier, this chassis was put into services as a limber, searchlight power vehicle, ambulance, radio vehicle and various other special purposes.

Heavy Uniform Personnel Vehicle Horch Type 40

Length	4.76 m chassis only	Range, on road	425 km (263.5 miles)
Width	2.00 chassis width	Engine make	Horch
Height	varies with body	Engine configuration	V-8, liquid cooled
Weight	varies with body	Engine displacement	3.82 liters
Fuel capacity	120 liters	Engine horsepower	90 @ 3600 rpm
Maximum speed	90 km/hr (55.8 mph)		

The Heavy Uniform Personnel car was built by both Ford and Horch. All-wheel drive made these vehicles preferred over others of similar size.

Spare tires were mounted on both sides of the early models, on rotating mounts, to aid the car when passing over rough terrain. This vehicle has been armed with a 2 cm Flak 38 and is being used by the Afrika Korps.

This Heavy Uniform car is getting a coat of whitewash to camouflage it during the Russian winter. The harsh conditions of the war on the Russian front were a test for both men and machines.

The Type 40 Heavy Uniform chassis, introduced in 1940, eliminated the rotating spare tire mounts in favor of a single spare stowed internally. Production of the Heavy Uniform chassis ceased in 1941.

Daimler-Benz G4

While often thought of as Hitler's staff car or Limousine, the Mercedes G4 was in fact a standard heavy personnel car. Depending upon the reference consulted, between 57 and 131 of these vehicles were built. Once it became known that this type was a favorite of Hitler's, many of his underlings wanted these vehicles for their own use.

From 1934, when production began, to 1939, when production halted, three different straight eight-cylinder engines were installed in the G4. Though designed for cross-country use, and having six wheels, the G4 did not have all-wheel drive. The lack of a driven front axle, coupled with its great weight, greatly hindered its off-road mobility.

When used for parade and ceremonial purposes, the G4 was usually found painted glossy light gray with black fenders and running boards. When used as a personnel carrier, usually by very high-ranking officers in forward areas, the vehicles wore the standard matte gray military paint.

The Daimler-Benz G4 is considered by many the "classic" German staff car. While those used for parades by Hitler and the extremely high command were painted a gloss light gray with black trim, those used by lesser officials were painted in the standard Wehrmacht colors, as seen here.

The G4 could mount two 7.92mm machine guns. This was often the case for cars that formed the escort for VIPs. The front axle was not driven on the G4.

Patton Museum, Fort Knox, KY

Steyr 1500

This vehicle was the successor to the Heavy Uniform Chassis. Production of this four-wheel-drive vehicle was begun in 1941 by Steyr-Daimler-Puch in Austria. The next year Auto-Union also joined in producing this vehicle at its Wanderer plant. In 1944, the final year for this vehicle's production, the vehicles were also built in Audi's plant, although Steyr had ceased production of the vehicle the year previous.

Not surprisingly, a variety of bodies were installed on these chassis. Included were van bodies and enclosed and open cars. In total, the Austrian firm produced just over 12,000 of these chassis, while between 5,000 and 6,000 additional units were assembled in Germany.

Steyr 1500

Length	5.08 m	Range, on road	400 km (248 miles)
Width	2.00 m	Engine make	Steyr
Height	2.10 m	Engine configuration	V-8, air-cooled
Weight	2.58 tons		
Fuel capacity	100 liters	Engine displacement	3.517 liters
Maximum speed	90 km/hr (55.8 mph)	Engine horsepower	85 hp @ 3000 rpm

The Steyr 1500 was introduced in 1941. Although ungainly looking, the cars were an improvement over their predecessor, the Heavy Uniform Personnel Vehicle.

Thomas Anderson

With its unusual axle spacing, the Steyr's body seemed mismatched to the chassis. The unusual styling was due in part to the air-cooled engine. Production ceased in 1944.

This vehicle, designated an "Electric Service Car" housed a 6 KVA generator and associated equipment. It was used to provide power to A4 (aka V2) rocket controls prior to the actual launch.

Lkw—Lastkraftwagen (trucks)

Light Uniform Truck-Diesel

Along with a series of Uniform cars, the Heeres-Waffenamt ordered the development of a diesel-powered light uniform truck. While this vehicle ultimately proved to be one of the two reasonably successful "uniform" designs (the other being the Medium Car), it still fell short of the military's needs.

The trucks entered mass production in 1937, but after only 3 years were discontinued because they proved to be expensive with a number of weaknesses. However, unlike many trucks of its size in the German military at the time, this truck did have all-wheel drive.

Its diesel engine, jointly designed by M.A.N., Henschel and Humboldt-Deutz, proved to have a weak block and heads. Its frame and suspension proved inadequate for the rigorous demands of a tactical truck as well.

By the time production was discontinued, more than 12,000 of these trucks, known as the Eniheits-Diesel, had been built by M.A.N., Daimler-Benz, Faun, Hansa-Lloyd-Goliath, Henschel, Klöckner-Humboldt-Deutz/Magirus, and Vomag.

A variety of beds were installed on these chassis, ranging from basic open cargo and personnel carrier beds, to elaborate enclosed telephone and surveying equipment bodies. In most of these roles the Einheits-Diesel was replaced by the 3-ton Opel Blitz. The Blitz was classified as a medium truck, while the Einheits's had light truck rating, which meant it was more suitable for harsh wartime use.

Light Uniform Truck-Diesel-typical van-bodied Kfz. 61

Length	5.85 m	**Range, cross country**	260 km (161.2 miles)
Width	2.20 m	**Engine make**	Kämper
Height	2.53 m	**Engine model**	Hwa 526D
Weight	7.38 tons	**Engine configuration**	six-cylinder, liquid-cooled diesel
Fuel capacity	115 liters		
Maximum speed	70 km/hr (43.4 mph)	**Engine displacement**	6.23 liters
Range, on road	350 km (217 miles)	**Engine horsepower**	80 hp @ 2400 rpm

This new Uniform Light Truck-Diesel was photographed while being tested in 1938. While none of Germanys "uniform" trucks were truly uniform, nor terribly successful, the "Einhiets-Diesel" was better on most counts than the average "uniform" truck.

These trucks were built with both steel cargo beds, as shown here, and wooden cargo beds. Other specialized beds were produced for engineers, photographers, etc.

Rather than a drop-down tailgate, as used on the similarly sized American CCKW-352, the Einhiets-Diesel's bed had twin swing-open doors on the rear.

Fully enclosed beds were used for communications vehicles, mobile darkrooms, and range finding. The beds, as on this Einhiets-Diesel, were made primarily of wood.

The Büssing-NAG G31, like many tactical trucks, was outfitted with a variety of different bodies for special purposes. In this photo, a truck outfitted for telephone work moves through Poland. The double (high-low) bumper was one of the most obvious characteristics of the G31.

National Archives and Records Administration

Büssing-NAG G 31

The Büssing-NAG G 31 was one of the potpourri of trucks used prior to WWII by the Reichwehr, and later assimilated into the Wehrmacht. This 1-ton 6 x 4 truck was built with a number of different specialized beds and bodies for use as personnel carriers, limbers and maintenance vehicles. It was procured from 1931 through 1936, and used extensively in the early part of the war. This chassis was also used as the basis for some of the 6-RAD armored cars. Few survivors made it into the post-war period.

Büssing-NAG G 31 with Communications Body

Length	5.70 m	Engine model	G
Width	2.10 m	Engine configuration	four-cylinder, liquid cooled
Height	2.8 m	Engine displacement	3.92 liters
Weight	3.9 tons	Engine horsepower	65
Engine make	Büssing-NAG		

Daimler-Benz L1500 A & S

The chassis for these vehicles was conceived with two purposes in mind. One was to be a light truck; the other, to form the basis for a heavy car. Daimler-Benz also built the chassis in two versions: A, or Allrad, which had four-wheel drive; and S, or standard two-wheel drive. Those chassis completed as cars or personnel carriers always utilized the all-wheel-drive chassis. Trucks, however, were built on both two- and four-wheel-drive versions.

Daimler-Benz L1500 A & S

Length	4.93 m	Range, cross country	230 km (142.6 miles)
Width	2.05 m	Engine make	Daimler-Benz
Height	2.225 m	Engine model	M159
Weight	2.39 tons	Engine configuration	six-cylinder, liquid cooled
Fuel capacity	70 liters		
Maximum speed	84 km/hr (52.08 mph)	Engine displacement	2.594 liters
Range, on road	370 km (229.4 miles)	Engine horsepower	60 @ 3000 rpm

National Archives and Records Administration

Although the L1500 chassis was most often used for light trucks, some heavy cars, like the one shown here, were built on this platform.

This L1500 chassis arrangement worked well, as it provided units with a commonality of mobility and repair services between cars and trucks. All the chassis used to build personnel carriers were of the L1500A all-wheel-drive type.

National Archives and Records Administration

National Archives and Records Administration

Relatively few of the L1500S, standard, or two-wheel-drive trucks were completed with the open platform-type bed shown here. Production of all body types of the two-wheel-drive truck, which totaled 4,100 vehicles, continued until July 1944.

National Archives and Records Administration

All-wheel-drive vehicles were better suited to the military's needs, but were more expensive and more difficult to produce. Daimler-Benz's production of these vehicles spanned from June 1941 through July 1943, with 4,900 trucks being completed.

One of the primary jobs of the all-wheel drive L1500A chassis was to transport communications equipment. Radio was key to the German military strategy, and the communications vehicles had to be able to advance through any terrain.

National Archives and Records Administration

Daimler-Benz G 3a

The Daimler-Benz G3a was an improved version of the 1928 G3. The G3a was introduced in 1929 and featured a more powerful engine. Production of the G3a ran through 1934 and totaled about 2,000 units.

In addition to a basic open cargo and personnel body, various specialized bodies for engineer and signals units were produced. The chassis, while having three axles, did not have front-wheel drive. Few of these rugged vehicles soldiered on to the last days of the war.

Daimler-Benz G 3a			
Length	6.0 m	Range, cross country	230 km (142.6 miles)
Width	2.1 m	Engine make	Daimler-Benz
Height	2.45 m	Engine model	M 09
Weight	3.3 tons	Engine configuration	six-cylinder, liquid cooled
Fuel capacity	105 liters		
Maximum speed	65 km/hr (40.3 mph)	Engine displacement	7.41 liters
Range, on road	300 km (186 miles)	Engine horsepower	95 @ 2000 rpm

National Archives and Records Administration

This Daimler-Benz G 3a was painted in the camouflage colors of the Riechswehr. These trucks had dual rear wheels.

This Kfz. 61 radio vehicle was built on the G 3a chassis. The bed of this truck was constructed primarily of wood. Despite the size of the G 3a, it was classified as a light truck.

The G 3a was property of the German railway administration. During wartime, this administration, like many of the German government, acted as an extension of the military.

This G 3a had an elaborate body, and equally elaborate paint job, and was used by the propaganda ministry.

Krupp Typ L 2 H 43/L 2 H 143

The model designations assigned by Krupp to vehicles they produced had meaning. The code can be deciphered as follows:

— L in the first position indicates truck (Lastkraftwagen).

— D in the second position (if present) indicates it has a diesel engine.

— The first number indicates cargo capacity in tons.

— The next letter indicates frame type, H is indicative of Hochrahmen, or high frame.

The final group of numbers are more easily read right to left. The last number is the number of axles, the number to its left is the number of cylinders in the engine, and if there is a number prior to that, it indicates which modification, or series, the vehicle is.

Krupp's light truck was therefore given the model number L 2 H 43, the later L2H143, but it is more commonly known as the Protze, or "show-off." It earned this name by overwhelming the competitive trucks during the 1932 trials.

The L2 H 143 was introduced in 1936. This vehicle had a slightly longer wheelbase, as well as a slightly more powerful engine. Production of the Protze ceased in 1942. A variety of bodies were fitted, but it is most often remembered as a personnel carrier and artillery prime mover.

Krupp Typ L 2 H 143

Length	5.0 m	Engine make	Krupp
Width	1.9 m	Engine model	M 304
Height	1.8 m	Engine configuration	four-cylinder
Weight	2.7 tons	Engine displacement	3.5 liters
Fuel capacity	110 liters	Engine horsepower	65
Maximum speed	70 km/hr (43.4 mph)		

Military Miniatures in Review

The Kfz. 70 Personnel Carrier and the Kfz. 81 FlaK gun limber both had tall wooden sides on their cargo beds, making positive identification difficult.

www.2mm.com

Krupp built this style light truck for the German Army for almost a decade, ending in 1942. The truck earned the name "Protze," or show-off, for its outstanding performance.

The Krupp variant most often remembered is the Kfz. 69, which was a light artillery limber. What appeared to be sideboards on the rear of the Kfz. 69 actually were ammunition lockers, which were strapped in place.

ww2mm.com

The spare tires, one on each side, could rotate and were positioned to prevent the undercarriage from dragging. There were two standard configurations for the ammo lockers on the Kfz. 69.

Military Miniatures in Review

Despite the cessation of production in 1942, the Protze continued to serve the German armed forces until the end of the war.

Military Miniatures in Review

Large generators were mounted in the rear of some of the Protze. Vehicles such as this were designated Kfz. 83 and used to supply power to searchlights.

Allied-Axis

Opel Blitz 1.5-ton

Although nowhere near as famous as its bigger brother, the 3-ton Opel Blitz, a 1.5-ton Opel Blitz transport was built as well. Despite its lack of notoriety, 5,767 of these trucks were built, primarily for the German Army. Production ceased on this model in 1942. Like most tactical trucks, a variety of bodies were installed, including fire and ambulance, in addition to the basic cargo body shown here. These trucks were two-wheel drive.

1.5-ton Opel Blitz

Length	5.4 m	Range, on road	340 km (210.8 miles)
Width	1.94 m	Engine make	Opel
Height	2.29 m	Engine configuration	six-cylinder
Weight	1.5 tons		
Fuel capacity	57 liters	Engine displacement	2.47 liters
Maximum speed	80 km/hr (49.6 mph)	Engine horsepower	55 hp

The 1.5-ton Opel Blitz was slightly smaller than the similar, and more abundant, 3-ton Blitz. The trucks were used for many purposes. This example is a basic cargo truck.

The 1.5-ton Blitz had wheels retained with six lug nuts, whereas the military 3-ton Blitz used eight lug nuts per wheel. The trucks were built with both high and low sideboards on their beds.

The entire Blitz series of trucks, save the all-wheel-drive 3-ton, were taken over from Opel's civilian Blitz family. This is a commercial 1.5-ton Blitz.

The sideboards of the military trucks were taller, and of course military lighting and pioneer tools were installed as well. The front fenders of the 1.5-ton Blitz reach almost as far forward as the rear of the radiator shroud. This is not the case on the 3-ton version, which had a pronounced distance between the fender and shroud.

Another way to differentiate the 1.5-ton Blitz from the 3-ton is the size of the "Opel Blitz" insignia on the grille relative to the grille itself. Two "bars" are unobstructed by the logo on either side. In the case of the larger 3-ton, a third bar is unobstructed.

This Blitz, moving into Russia, has a 2.0 cm FlaK 38 mounted in its cargo bed. Such conversions were not unheard of, but sorely overtaxed the 1.5 ton-rated chassis.

Borgward B 3000

The Wehrmacht employed four versions of the Borgward B3000 series 3-ton trucks. Both 4 x 4 and 4 x 2 versions were built, as well as diesel- and gasoline engine-powered trucks

Production of the two-wheel-drive truck began in 1942 and extended into the postwar period, where it found use as a commercial truck. The all-wheel-drive version was built from 1943-45. Less than 5,000 of these vehicles were built for all markets, yet they were produced with cargo and van-type bodies.

Borgward 3000

Length	6.45 m	Engine model	D6M5
Width	2.30 m	Engine configuration	diesel
Height	2.23 m	Engine displacement	4.96 liter
Weight	3.5 tons		
Engine make	Borgward		

This gasoline-powered B 3000 was no match for the mud on the Russian front.

Borgward built their B 3000 medium trucks in both diesel and gasoline powered versions. This is diesel-powered example was photographed rolling through Russia in late 1943.

Daimler-Benz LG3000

The LG3000 was a diesel-powered 6 x 4 truck introduced by Daimler-Benz in 1934. Even though production of this model ceased in 1937, because more than 7,000 had been built at that time it is not surprising that several were used during the course of WWII. The bulk of these vehicles were equipped with a front-mounted, PTO-driven winch. Dual rear wheels were standard, although some trial vehicles were built with single rear wheels.

Daimler-Benz LG3000

Length	7.11 m	Range, cross country	240 km (148.8 miles)
Width	2.30 m	Engine make	Daimler-Benz
Height	2.80 m	Engine model	OM 67
Weight	2.80 tons	Engine configuration	six-cylinder, liquid-cooled diesel
Fuel capacity	112 liters		
Maximum speed	53 km/hr (32.86 mph)	Engine displacement	7.41 liters
Range, on road	370 km (229.4 miles)	Engine horsepower	95 @ 2000 rpm

These trucks with van bodies were built on LG3000 Daimler-Benz 6 x 4 chassis. The LG3000 was also produced with normal cargo bodies.

Daimler-Benz L3000 A & S

The German Army's primary tactical trucks were the 3-ton class of vehicles. Among these were the Daimler-Benz L3000 A & S series diesel-powered vehicles. These vehicles were produced from 1939 through 1944 (the all-wheel-drive model was dropped in 1942), when production was halted in favor of expanded production of the gasoline-powered Opel Blitz. The Blitz's gasoline engine, despite using greater quantities of a more precious fuel, started easier in cold weather and was more easily maintained by the common soldier.

Daimler-Benz L3000 A & S			
Length	6.255 m	Range, cross country	300 km (186 miles)
Width	2.350 m	Engine make	Daimler-Benz
Height	2.600 m	Engine configuration	four-cylinder, diesel, liquid cooled
Weight	4.02 tons		
Fuel capacity	90 liters	Engine displacement	4.849 liters
Maximum speed	70 km/hr (43.4 mph)		
Range, on road	450 km (279 miles)	Engine horsepower	75

The two-wheel-drive trucks like this one were more economical to build and operate, but their performance off road left much to be desired.

The 3-ton truck provided the bulk of the transportation needs, and the L3000 was Daimler-Benz's entry in this field. These diesel trucks were built in a variety of styles. This all-wheel-drive version had an open cab and a basic cargo bed.

The front driveshaft and differential distinguished the all-wheel-drive versions from the standard rear-wheel-drive trucks. This L3000 A (all-wheel drive) had a closed cab.

Daimler-Benz ceased production of the all-wheel-drive trucks in 1942, but the two-wheel-drive units were produced into 1944. Production began in 1939.

Some of the L3000 were fitted with box-type bodies for use as workshops and communications vehicles. This example has a two-wheel-drive chassis.

Ford 3-ton

Two of the largest automakers in Germany before and during WWII were General Motors (Opel), and Ford. It is not surprising that these two firms supplied many of the Wermacht's tactical vehicles. Ford established facilities in Germany in 1926, and became known as Ford-Werke AG in 1939.

Ford's biggest contribution to the German military's wheeled transport was a series of 3-ton trucks, of which about 5,000 were delivered in a variety of models, most looking alike.

Beginning in 1939, the grille of the German Fords looked much like that found on the 38 American version. The quickest differentiating characteristic was the German use of a one-piece windshield, as opposed to the American split windshield (until 1945). Through 1940, when viewed head on, the front fenders had a rounded shape; from 1941 onwards they looked flat. The 1945 model had a very boxy, metal-conserving standardized cab. While some trucks were equipped with specialized beds, the bulk of the Fords, known to the Wehrmacht as the V3000, irregardless of the factory model designation, were built as cargo trucks.

Ford V3000 4 x 2 G917TstIIIa and V3000 G918ts 41-45			
Length	6.39 m	Range, cross country	230 km (142.6 miles)
Width	2.25 m	Engine make	Ford
Height	2.18 m	Engine configuration	V-8 / V-8
Weight	2.54 tons		
Fuel capacity	105 liters	Engine displacement	3.6 liter / 3.9 liter
Maximum speed	80 km/hr (49.6 mph)	Engine horsepower	90 @ 3800 rpm / 95 @ 3500 rpm
Range, on road	330 km (204.6 miles)		

This was a familiar-looking truck to many GI's fighting the Germans. The German Ford V3000 3-ton truck had much in common with its American cousin, the 1938 Ford, including its grille. The easiest way to tell the German product from the U.S. version was the windshield. The German vehicle used the one-piece glass seen here, while the American had a split windshield.

A few of the Fords were built with open cabs, like the one shown here. The rounded contour of the front fenders, when viewed from ahead, identify this truck as a 1939 or 1940 model. Fenders on later models lacked these curves.

Henschel Type 33

Henschel & Sohn of Kassel was a heavy industrial firm that added trucks to its product line in 1928. The company's type 33 trucks were built in both gasoline- and diesel-powered versions from 1933 through 1941. More than 10,000 of these vehicles were purchased by the German military and were outfitted as cargo trucks, troop transports, range finding and a variety of other uses. Demand, in fact outstripped Henschel's production capacity, and from 1938 through 1941 Magirus license-built 3,800 copies.

These trucks were rated as "all-terrain," despite having a non-powered front axle. Most, however, did have a PTO-driven winch behind the cab, which could pull either to the front or the rear of the truck.

These trucks were well built, and many served throughout the war.

Henschel Type 33-Diesel version

Length	7.40 m	Engine model	D
Width	2.50 m	Engine configuration	six-cylinders
Height	3.20 m		
Weight	6.1 tons	Engine displacement	10.86 liters
Engine make	Henschel	Engine horsepower	100 hp

Henschel built its Type 33 trucks with either diesel or gasoline engines. As the placard on the grille proudly proclaims, this truck was a diesel-powered version.

Military Miniatures in Review

Perhaps it was due to Henschel's history of building locomotives, but the front bumper of the Type 33 was re-marked to look like that of a steam locomotive! More than 10,000 of these trucks were used by the German military.

ww2mm.com

Krupp Typ L 3 H 63/L 3 H 163

Krupp's entry into the Germany Army's medium transport market was the L 3 H 63, and its successor, the L3 H 163. Its 10-year production span reached from 1928 through 1938. Because of their age and the rigors of war, few of the vehicles survived until 1945. The front axle was non-powered, but on most vehicles a winch was mounted behind the cab, the rope from which could be played out either to the front or rear of the truck. The truck was powered by a gasoline engine. The Krupp truck model designation is described in the section of this book dealing with the famous Krupp Protze.

In 1928, the L3 H 163 was introduced as a replacement for the L3 H63. Neither of these trucks had a driven front axle, which would have been invaluable in the situation shown here.

Krupp L 3 H 163

Length	7.4 m	Engine model	M12
Width	2.5 m	Engine configuration	six-cylinder, liquid cooled
Height	3.2 m		
Weight	3.7 tons	Engine displacement	7.54 liters
Maximum speed	50 km/hr (31 mph)	Engine horsepower	110 @ 1600 rpm
Engine make	Krupp		

By the time Germany invaded Poland, the design of Krupp's L3 H 63 was already a decade old. Nevertheless, the trucks continued to be used by the German armed forces until they were destroyed, or simply wore out.

Most of these trucks were built with open-topped cabs with canvas covers. A few, however, like this Luftwaffe vehicle, had enclosed steel cabs.

In addition to use as cargo trucks, these Krupp-built vehicles also saw service as telephone maintenance trucks, flamethrower tenders. Some, like this L3 H63, were used by artillery survey troops.

Opel Blitz 3-ton

The 3-ton Opel Blitz, in both two- and four-wheel drive versions, formed the backbone of German military transport during WWII. Opel introduced the Blitz to the civilian marketplace in 1935, with the 3-ton truck added to the lineup in 1937. While the production numbers are meager compared to some U.S. vehicles produced during the period, they are nevertheless impressive.

Two-wheel-drive Blitz production was as follows: 1940: 17,605; 1941: 15,947; 1942 18,262; 1943: 23,232; 1944: 16,146. In addition, more than 20,000 four-wheel-drive versions were built, meaning more than 110,000 3-ton Blitzes were built.

Not surprisingly, the usual variety of beds were installed on these vehicles, and also not surprisingly the all-wheel-drive versions were highly desirable. So much so that they became rationed, and ultimately confined to such critical tasks as field ambulances, radio and kitchen trucks.

Demand for the 3-ton Blitz was so great that in July 1944 Daimler-Benz began producing this truck as well, adding more than 3,500 vehicles to the total. The Mercedes-produced vehicles used a simpler cab than the Opel-built trucks.

Three-ton Blitz trucks built for the military can be distinguished by the eight lug nuts retaining each wheel. Prior to 1939, Opel's civilian 3-ton Blitz used wheels retained by six lug nuts. However, the military also conscripted many 3-ton Blitzes from their civilian owners. A photograph will occasionally surface of a 3-ton truck painted in military colors and having six lug nuts per wheel.

3-ton Opel Blitz

	4x2	4x4				
Length	6.10 m	5.95 m	Range, cross country	230 km (142.6 miles)	220 km (136.4 miles)	
Width	2.26 m	2.34 m	Engine make	Opel	Opel	
Height	2.56 m	3.18 m	Engine configuration	six-cylinder, liquid cooled	six-cylinder, liquid cooled	
Weight	2.5 tons	2.5 tons	Engine displacement	3.6 liters	3.6 liters	
Fuel capacity	82 liters	92 liters	Engine horsepower	75	75	
Maximum speed	85 km/hr (52.7 mph)	80 km/hr (49.6 mph)				
Range, on road	320 km (198.4 miles)	300 km (186 miles)				

Except for the VW Kübelwagen, the 3-ton Opel Blitz is probably the most widely recognized wheeled vehicle used by the German military during WWII. Its most common use was as a basic cargo truck/personnel carrier.

The Blitz was also fitted with van bodies, including this one specially designed to transport repair parts for the A4 (aka V2) rocket. Wherever the German military went, a Blitz would be found.

Tanker trucks were also built on the Blitz chassis, including this special version built to haul "B-Stoff," a rocket propellant used by the A4. The dual rear wheels have been reduced to singles on this truck.

Another tank truck of a slightly different design was used to transport the "T-stoff," (hydrogene peroxide), a key component of the German rocket fuel.

Production of the four-wheel-drive Blitz never met demand, resulting in this type vehicle being specifically allocated. Among its permitted uses: kitchen truck, ambulance and radio truck.

The 3-ton Blitz was of enormous utility to the German military, but perhaps its most valuable version was the Alrad, or four-wheel-drive type. This four-wheel drive Blitz follows a pair of 3-ton two-wheel drive Blitz along the coast in Africa. The higher stance and visible front differential distinguished the four-wheel-drive version.

Büssing-NAG 500 & 4500 S

Heavy trucks—those rated 4.5 tons or greater—were critical to moving large quantities of supplies to the front. Most of these were used purely in the transport role, but there were a few exceptions that required the installation of specialist bodies.

Büssing-NAG of Braunschweig was Germany's oldest truck builder at the outbreak of WWII. Their contribution to heavy transport was the model 500, which was later superceded by the 4500. Both of these trucks

were powered by a 7.4-liter model LD diesel engine. The model 500 was discontinued in 1942 and replaced with the 4500. The 4500 can be distinguished by having only two louvers on each side of the hood, as well as a redesigned grille.

Both trucks were built in both two- and four-wheel-drive models. More than 15,000 of these vehicles were delivered to the Wehrmacht.

Büssing-NAG 500

		4500s		Engine make	Büssing-NAG
Length	8.14 m	8.05 m		Engine model	LD
Width	2.35 m	2.35 m		Engine configuration	six-cylinder, liquid-cooled diesel
Height	2.45 m	2.80 m			
Weight	5.35 tons	5.20 tons		Engine displacement	7.41 liters
Fuel capacity	110 liters	110 liter			
Maximum speed	62 km/hr	65 km/hr		Engine horsepower	105 @ 1800 rpm
Range, on road	440 km	440 km			

The heavily embossed lettering on the front bumper leaves no doubt who assembled this truck: Büssing-NAG. The visible front differential gives away its four-wheel drive, while the many staggered louvers alongside the hood are indicative of a model 500.

The Büssing-NAG 4500 was an improvement of the similar, earlier model 500. It had only two louvers on each engine side panel, and other refinements. These trucks were built with Büssing's own diesel engine as their power plant.

Daimler-Benz L4500 A & S

Daimler-Benz manufactured this heavy truck from 1939 through 1944. In 1944, production was transferred to Saur for the duration of the war. Built in both two- and four-wheel-drive versions, this vehicle was intended for long-range heavy hauling of supplies.

A little more than 3,000 of the 11,000 units produced were the A-type, or allrad, four-wheel drive. These were invaluable near the front lines where road conditions deteriorated rapidly. Some of these vehicles were equipped with armored cabs and had 2 or 3.7 cm anti-aircraft guns installed on their cargo beds.

The design of the Daimler-Benz 4500 was so successful that Mercedes marketed these vehicles as commercial transporters in the post-war period.

The L4500 was a heavy truck that was built from 1939 through 1944 by Daimler-Benz. Production in later 1944 and 1945 was by Saur, but postwar Daimler-Benz resumed manufacturing this heavy truck for commercial use.

Daimler-Benz 4500 S

Length	7.86 m	Range, cross country	330 km (204.6 miles))
Width	2.35 m		
Height	3.35 m	Engine make	Daimler-Benz
Weight	5.72 tons	Engine model	OM 67/4
Fuel capacity	140 liters	Engine configuration	six-cylinder, liquid-cooled, diesel
Maximum speed	43 km/hr (26.66 mph)		
Range, on road	500 km (310 miles)	Engine displacement	7.27 liters
		Engine horsepower	112 @ 2250

The Daimler-Benz 4500's large cargo capacity made it valuable for general cargo hauling, but a few trucks were built with specialized van bodies, such as this one. -

Unarmored halftracks

Kleines Kettenkraftrad (SdKfz 2) Typ HK 101

One of the most unusual, and most fascinating to the average GI, German vehicles of WWII, was the "kleines Kettenkraftrad SdKfz. 2," popularly known as the "Kettenkrad." Though some people believe this to be a tracked motorcycle, a theory reinforced by the –kraftrad in its name, in reality it was a small halftrack prime mover.

Heinrich Ernst Kniepkamp patented the concept of this vehicle in June of 1939, with the thought that the vehicle would find use moving small loads in mountainous areas. German motorcycle builder NSU Werke of Neckarsulm perfected the concept, creating the Kettenkrad. A trial series of 500 vehicles was ordered in 1940 and delivered the following year. It was June of 1941 before the Kettenkrad as accepted for troop service. The Luftwaffe was especially interested in the vehicle for use by airborne troops.

Manufacturing rates soon increased and 1,208 units were built in 1942. In 1943, production was expanded to NSU's Stoewer Werke and production totaled 2,450 machines for the year. Production peaked in 1944

with 4,490 units completed. As a result of Germany's deteriorating war position, production rates dropped during 1945. Manufacturing of the Kettenkrad continued after the war, with the vehicle being sold for agricultural use. Some of these were produced using leftover wartime stocks, while others were new production. Although the French company SIMCA produced some components for the Kettenkrad, contrary to what some sources state, SIMCA did not build or assemble complete vehicles.

There was some variation to the Kettenkrad during its production. The front forks and instrument panel, in particular, were areas of improvement. Two sub-variants were built; the Sd.Kfz. 2/1 "kleines Kettenkraftrad fur Feldfernkabel," and Sd.Kfz. 2/2 "kleines Kettenkraftrad fur schwere Feldfernkabel." Both of these were built for use by signal units for laying communications wire. The speed, small size and maneuverability of the Kettenkrad allowed it to go almost anywhere a man could walk, but at a faster pace. The Sd.Kfz. 2/1 utilized a small backpack-type wire spool, while the Sd.Kfz. 2/2 carried two larger wire spools mounted on a special framework. Additional spools could be carried on sonderanhanger–"special trailer" Sd. Anh. 1 built for that purpose.

Other trailers were also used behind the Kettenkrad. The vehicles were also used to tow small field artillery pieces.

Powered by a four-cylinder, liquid-cooled automobile engine driving through a three-speed transmission and two-speed reduction unit, the performance of the Kettenkrad was impressive. While it had a relatively high top speed (70 km/hr according to the operator's manual), it could also be driven essentially anywhere a tank would go, and could ascend a 60-percent grade. Two fuel tanks were installed, which constituted the side walls of the body. The tracks ran on four torsion bar-suspended road wheels.

Kleines Kettenkraftrad (SdKfz 2) Typ HK 101

Length	3.0 m	Communications	none
Width	1.0 m		
Height	1.2 m	Weapon	none
Weight	1.56 tons	Engine make	Opel
Fuel capacity	42 liters	Engine model	Olympia
Maximum speed	70 km/hr (43.4 mph)	Engine configuration	four-cylinder, liquid cooled
Range, on road	260 km (161.2 miles)	Engine displacement	1.478 liters
Range, cross country	190 km (117.8 miles)	Engine horsepower	36 hp @ 3400 rpm
Crew	1		

National Archives and Records Administration

Two soldiers of the 101st Infantry Division are using a captured Kettenkraftrad to transport Jerry cans from the French town of Carentan. This is a late-production vehicle as denoted by the solid rear handrails. On early vehicles these were made of metal tubing.

The idea of a lightweight, compact prime mover was appealing to the Luftwaffe, which was in charge of Germany's airborne troops. This trial vehicle was evaluated by the German Air Force in 1941.

The German military used the Kettenkraftrad as a small prime mover, and also for messenger service, particularly in areas not reachable by wheeled vehicles.

GI's couldn't help but be curious whenever they came across a captured halftrack. In this view the fuel fillers on either side of the driver are apparent.

Though its rear seat could hold two passengers, the Kettenkrad was first and foremost a prime mover, either for cargo, or for small field artillery pieces.

GI's tended to view the unusual halftrack machines more as toys than tools, and joyrides such as this were commonplace.

A specialized trailer was developed concurrently with the Kettenkrad to enhance its cargo-carrying ability. Other trailers could be used with it as well, including those developed for use with Schwimmwagen and Kubelwagen.

The inner workings of the Kettenkraftrad are revealed in this illustration from the operator's manual. The machines had torsion bar rear suspension, three-speed transmission with a two-speed reduction unit, were shaft driven and were powered by a four-cylinder, liquid-cooled automobile engine.

The Sd.Kfz. 2/1 was created to lay communication cables. A small framework was added that supported a backpack-style cable reel rack.

Patton Museum, Fort Knox, KY

The Sd.Kfz. 2/2 mounted a pair of larger reels behind the driver. The larger reels meant that cable could be laid more quickly without stopping to replace reels or splice lines.

Patton Museum, Fort Knox, KY

The Sd.Kfz. 2 was surprisingly powerful and agile. It is shown here towing a 7.5 cm field piece during trials. The weapon's crew rides the Kettenkrad.

Patton Museum, Fort Knox, KY

Sd. Kfz. 10 Type D 7 halftrack

These light halftracks, with a rated towing capacity of 1 ton, were the result of development work begun in the early 1930s. This development work came to fruition in 1934 when production began on the lighter Zugkraftwagen 1t (Sd. Kfz. 10). This vehicle was designed and originally produced by Demag AG, though during the course of the war these vehicles were also built be other firms. Among these other firms were Adler, Büssing-NAG, Saurerwerke and Mechanisehe Werke-Cottbus. By August 1944 only the latter was still producing the Sd. Kfz. 10.

The base vehicle, the Sd. Kfz. 10, was built as a light prime mover. Later production used a 100-hp Maybach NL 38 six-cylinder engine. Early versions used a 90-hp powerplant. The engine drove the rubber-padded steel rear track, but unlike American halftracks, the front wheels were unpowered. The tracks were the lubricated type.

Sd.Kfz. 10 D7

Length	4.75 m	**Communications**	none
Width	1.84 m	**Weapon**	none
Height	1.62 m	**Engine make**	Maybach
Weight	5 tons	**Engine model**	HL 42 TRKM
Fuel capacity	110 liters	**Engine configuration**	six-cylinder, liquid cooled
Maximum speed	65 km/hr (40.3 mph)	**Engine displacement**	4.199 liter
Range, on road	285 km (176.7 miles)	**Engine horsepower**	100 @ 2800 rpm
Range, cross country	150 km (93 miles)		
Crew	1		

As seen in this official portrait, the Sd. Kfz. 10 was provided with a soft top enclosure for both the driver and passenger areas of the vehicle. The flat surface of the roadwheels is indicative of an early-production vehicle.

Ordnance Museum, Aberdeen Proving Ground

The Sd. Kfz. 10 was intended to transport eight soldiers and tow a small field piece. This one appears to be filled to capacity.

The low ground pressure and high adhesion provided by the rear tracks gave the Sd. Kfz. 10 good off-road performance, although the lack of a driven front axle sometimes made steering difficult.

Even in the raised position, the hinged sideboards of the vehicle were low enough to allow troops to dismount quickly in emergency.

This halftrack is pulling a 15 cm Sturminfanteriegeschuetz 33 field gun, which is faintly visible in the background. Assigned to the SS-Totenkopf Division, the crew seems undisturbed by the May 1940 rain shower.

This light halftrack made a comfortable observation platform to observing firing trials of the Tiger I in the background.

A heavily camouflaged Sd. Kfz. 10 pulls artillery along a dry dirt road. The oversized tarp, which matches the paint scheme of the prime mover, is non-standard.

Some Panzerjäger units mounted their 3.7 cm PaK in the bed of a Sd. Kfz. 10. This allowed greater mobility for the weapon and the ability to tow another load, such as an ammunition trailer.

The crew of this Sd. Kfz. 10/4 was using semaphores to signal with. The early 2 cm Flak 30 auf Selbstfahrlafette, such as this one, lacked gun shields. These vehicles, however, did include ramps, pulleys and rope so the gun crew could mount and dismount the antiaircraft weapon.

The reliable Sd. Kfz. 10 was adapted to serve as a chassis for a 2 cm antiaircraft weapon. In this form it was designated Sd. Kfz. 10/4. Three of these vehicles roll through Krakow, Poland, in September 1939. Notice the completely reconfigured rear body, with folding mesh sides. These vehicles were armed with the 2 cm Flak 30. A total of 1,370 of these vehicles were produced.

Patton Museum, Fort Knox, KY

The Flak 30 was the standard 2 cm antiaircraft gun of the German Army and Luftwaffe when the Sd. Kfz. 10/4 was introduced. In addition to firing from the halftrack, it could be dismounted and fired from the ground. In fact, the gun was originally designed for the type of mounting shown here.

Patton Museum, Fort Knox, KY

By folding the sides down a large platform was created from which the gun crew could service the piece. Just visible behind the Sd. Kfz. 10/4 is an Sd. Anh. 51 trailer. This trailer was designed to transport the 2 cm Flak 30, the Flak 38, or an ammunition box for those weapons..

Walter J. Spielberger

Armed with a gunshield-protected 2 cm Flak 38, this vehicle was capable of almost twice the theoretical rate of fire (450 rounds per minute, rather than 280) of the Flak 30. In actual practice, the rate of fire of either of these weapons was about half that.

The rigidity of these vehicle's suspensions is evidenced in this photo, where the front wheels are lifted clear of the ground, yet there is very little deflection in the road wheels. This made for a stable firing platform. Later Flak Selbstfahrlafetten such as this one did not come with ramps, pulleys and rope for dismounting the weapon.

Walter J. Spielberger

Built by Büssing-NAG, this Sd. Kfz. 10 came equipped with 8mm-thick armor plate shielding the cab and radiator. Notice the "kill" markings on the gun shield of this Luftwaffe-operated vehicle. Though intended as an antiaircraft weapon, both the Sd. Kfz. 10 and 11 were devastating against infantry and lightly protected vehicles.

This Sd. Kfz. 10/4 was captured by troopers of the British 6th Airborne Armored Reconnaissance Regiment in early July, following the Normandy invasion. Troopers C. Davies and L. Walden, shown here, succeeded in knocking down a ME109 and a FW190.

The need for constant lookout for enemy aircraft meant that the Flak Selbstfahrlafette (motor carriages) could not have covers erected over them, meaning they had to be crewed by hearty men during winter conditions such as these.

Patton Museum, Fort Knox, KY

Sd. Kfz. 11

The Sd. Kfz. 11, or Zugkraftwagen, 3-ton halftrack was a popular and important vehicle in German military. Primarily designed as a prime mover, it was also adapted to other roles. Typical of German halftrack design, the front wheels were not powered, and the rear tracks were the lubricated pin, rubber pad type. Steering was controlled by the front wheels, but when they were turned more than 15 degrees interconnecting linkages also caused steering brakes to operate on the tracks to assist in the turns. These were initially produced by Borgward, but Hanomag took charge of the production the Sd. Kfz. 11 in 1937. In addition to these two firms, Adler and Auto-Union built various versions of the Sd. Kfz. 11.

The Sd. Kfz. 11 was originally used to tow the 10.5mm leFH 18 field howitzer, 7.5mm Pak 40 anti-tank gun, 3.7mm Flak 36 and 37 antiaircraft weapons and Nebelwerfer rocket launchers. Later in the war it was pressed into service towing larger weapons as well. The chassis of the Sd. Kfz. 11 was also the basis for the Sd. Kfz. 251 series of armored halftracks.

Sd. Kfz. 11 HL kl 6

Length	5.55 m	Communications	none
Width	2.00 m	Weapon	none
Height	2.15 m	Engine make	Maybach
Weight	7.8 tons	Engine model	HL 42 TURKM
Fuel capacity	110 liters		
Maximum speed	52.5 km/hr (32.55 mph)	Engine configuration	six-cylinder, liquid cooled
Range, on road	240 km (148.8 miles)	Engine displacement	4.199 liter
Range, cross country	140 km (86.8 miles)	Engine horsepower	100 @ 2800 rpm
Crew	1		

An opening in the rear of the bed allowed troops to board the Sd. Kfz. 11. No door was provided for personnel, although side doors were provided for the ammunition racks.

Bundesarchiv photo

The basic version of the Sd. Kfz. 11 was designed to be a prime mover for artillery pieces. Artillery ammunition was stowed in central compartments, while the gun crew rode in the rear.

This photo of an Sd. Kfz. 11 chassis cresting a hill provides a clear view of the non-powered front axle and the suspension. Non-driving front axles hampered the mobility of German halftracks.

This Sd. Kfz. 11 of the Afrika Korps is doing what it was designed for, towing artillery at high speeds—in this case a 10.5 cm leFH 18 howitzer.

"High speed" is a relative term when it comes to military vehicles. This Sd. Kfz. 11 appears to be moving along near its top speed of 25 mph.

Typical of German halftrack design, the Sd. Kfz. 11 utilized an interleaved road wheel design, as seen on this captured example. The soft top cab enclosure has been erected on this vehicle.

Walter J. Spielberger

This is the Sd.Kfz. 11/2 chemical decontamination vehicle. Germany developed quite an array of chemical warfare and counter warfare equipment.

Walter J. Spielberger

The Sd.Kfz. 11/2, or mittlerer Entgiftungskraftwagen, was developed to transport (on its central platform) 728 kilograms of calcium hypochlorite (Losantin), which the apparatus on the rear of the vehicle would distribute to neutralize chemical agents on the ground.

Photo by Hase via Thomas Anderson

This is a scarce variant of the Sd. Kfz. 11 family, fitted with a pioneer, or engineer, body. The many side doors in the rear body distinguish these from the standard Sd. Kfz. 11. In the case of this StuG Abt. 185 vehicle, soft closures cover these doors in preparation for the invasion of Russia.

Patton Museum, Fort Knox, KY

This illustration, taken from a German technical manual, shows an Sd. Kfz. 11/5 Nebelwerferkraftwagen. Similar large doors on the other side also swung down to load and unload both the rockets and the troops.

The crew of a Nebelwerferkraftwagen pauses on a grade for a photo. German halftracks, which were actually three-quarter track vehicles, easily crested sharp ridges like this that would stop U.S. halftracks with their longer gap between tracks and wheels.

Photo by Sander via Thomas Anderson

Sd. Kfz. 6

The Sd. Kfz. 6 was a 5-ton halftrack prime mover developed by Büssing-NAG beginning in 1934. It was intended to tow the 10.5 cm light field howitzer, or any of a number of different trailers.

Though initially identified as the BN1 5 (BN1 for Büssing-NAG light halftrack), there were a progression of models before the BN 9 was introduced in 1939. The 1 designation of "light" had been dropped because it conflicted with the Wehrmacht's designations. Ultimately, the Sd. Kfz. 6 was also produced by Daimler-Benz and Praga.

Various bodies were produced, including the engineer body (Sd. Kfz. 6), artillery body (Sd. Kfz. 6/1) and the Sd. Kfz. 6/2, which was a self-propelled antiaircraft weapon.

Sd.Kfz. 6 BN 9

Length	6.325 m	Communications	none
Width	2.26 m	Weapon	none
Height	2.50 m	Engine make	Maybach
Weight	10 tons	Engine model	HL 54 TUKRM
Fuel capacity	190 liters		
Maximum speed	50 km/hr (31 mph)	Engine configuration	six-cylinder, liquid cooled
Range, on road	300 km (186 miles)	Engine displacement	5.42 liter
Range, cross country	115 km (71.3 miles)	Engine horsepower	100 @ 2800 rpm
Crew	1		

An early Sd. Kfz. 6 with an engineer body moves across a floating bridge. When the later BN I 8 series was introduced, the tracks were longer, extending underneath the driver's floorboard.

Walter J. Spielberger

This early Sd. Kfz. 6 is towing a trailer laden with components for a floating bridge. Even though the front wheels are airborne, the vehicle could still be steered, as moving the steering wheel more than a few degrees engaged a steering mechanism in the track's drive.

The BN I 8 introduced the longer tracks. An Sd. Kfz. 6/1 is seen here towing a 10.5 cm light field howitzer at speed. The artillery body has one fewer row of seats than the engineer body.

Military Miniatures in Review

An Sd. Kfz. 6/1 BN 9 crosses a bridge reinforced with military treadways. When the tracks were lengthened, the front fenders were redesigned, becoming higher and loosing the skirt on the trailing edge.

The Sd. Kfz. 6/2 was armed with a 3.7 cm Flak 36 on a rotating mount. The sideboards of the halftrack folded down to provide a work area for the gun crew to serve the weapon. The shape of the rear fenders distinguished the Sd. Kfz. 6/2 from the similar early Sd. Kfz. 7/2.

Stefan De Meyer

The Sd. Kfz. 6/2 were built on the Büssing-NAG BN 9 chassis. Weight and size concerns prevented all but the most rudimentary of gun shields from being installed. Most of the Sd. Kfz. 6/2 were operated by the Luftwaffe.

This vehicle, known as the 7.62 cm FK (r) auf Panzerjäger sfl. Zgkw. 5 t, was the result of mounting captured Soviet antitank guns on BN 9 chassis. Only nine of these conversions were made.

The service life of this converted BN 9 was brief. The conversions were carried out in late 1941, and the British captured this one in the summer of 1942.

The German military wanted a standardized halftrack prime mover that was inexpensive and simple to produce. Toward this end, the Waffenamt contracted with Büssing-NAG in 1942 to design such a vehicle. Halftracks by their nature are rather complicated pieces of equipment, making development somewhat slow. However, by the fall of 1943 production had begun at Büssing-NAG's Berlin works and the Kolin works of Ringhoffer-Tatra on the new halftrack.

Never assigned an Sd.Kfz. number, Büssing's design was dubbed the shwere Wehrmacht Schlepper, or heavy army tractor. Due to its late introduction, only about 1,000 units were built. Some of these were fitted with armored bodies and antiaircraft guns.

sWS				
Length	6.68 m		Communications	none
Width	2.50 m			
Height	2.83 m		Weapon	none
Weight	xxxx		Engine make	Maybach
Fuel capacity	240 liters		Engine model	HL 42 TRKMS
Maximum speed	27 km/hr (16.74 mph)		Engine configuration	six-cylinder, liquid cooled
Range, on road	300 km (186 miles)		Engine displacement	4.19 liter
Range, cross country	100 km (62 miles)		Engine horsepower	100 @ 3000 rpm
Crew	1			

Patton Museum, Fort Knox, KY

Designed by Büssing-NAG, the sWS was supposed to become the German Army's standard halftrack prime mover in the 6-ton range. However, the design ultimately proved too complex for true mass production, and only about 1,000 were built.

German troops are on the move aboard an sWS. In addition to Büssing-NAG, these vehicles were built by Büssing-NAG and Ringhoffer-Tatra.

Stefan De Meyer

Sd. Kfz. 7 8-ton medium towing tractor

The Sd. Kfz. 7 was developed in the mid-1930s by Krauss-Maffai as an artillery prime mover. It is best known as the tow vehicle for the famed 8.8 cm Flak gun.

The initial model, the KM m 8 (Krauss-Maffai medium towing tractor), had four roadwheel stations per side. This model was also produced by Daimler-Benz and Büssing-NAG under license. These copies were designated Daimler-Benz mittlerer 8 (DB m 8) and Büssing-NAG mittlerer 8 (BN m 8), respectively.

During 1935-36, Krauss-Maffei produced an improved model: the KM m 9. Its engine, a 130-hp Maybach HL57, was an improvement over the HL 52 found in the KM m 8, which had only 115 hp.

In late 1936, the engine was upgraded again and a 140-hp Mayback HL62 TUK engine drove the halftrack, to which Krauss-Maffei assigned the model designation KM m 10. The KM m 10 was externally identical to the late KM m 9. The front fenders of the early KM m 9 had been flat, rather than the curved fenders fitted to later KM m 9 and KM m 10.

Development of the Sd. Kfz. 7 reached its pinnacle in mid-1939 when the KM m 11 and HL m 11 were introduced by Krauss-Maffei and Hansa-Lloyd-Goliath, respectively. This time the improvement was plainly visible, as the new models had two more road wheels on each side. This version of the Sd. Kfz. 7 series remained in production through 1944. By then, more than 12,000 Sd. Kfz. 7 Mittlerer Zugkraftwagen 8t had been built.

A similar vehicle was produced in Italy by Breda. Designated the Breda 61, it was a right-hand-drive vehicle powered by a 130-hp engine. Several hundred of these were built.

All models of prime mover, regardless of manufacturer, were supplied with a fold-down windshield and collapsible canvas top to protect the 12-man crew from the weather.

The Sd. Kfz. 7 also formed the basis for a pair of antiaircraft vehicles. The Sd. Kfz. 7/1 had a special body mounting a 2 cm Flak 38 in a quad mount. The Sd. Kfz. 7/1 was known as Flakvierling 38 auf Fahrgestell Zugkraftwagen 8t. The Sd. Kfz. 7/2 also had a special body, but heavier armament. Initially, the 3.7 cm FlaK 36 was mounted, ollowed by the 3.7 cm FlaK 37, and finally, near the end of 1944, the 3.7 cm FlaK 43 began to be installed. Sometime in 1943 the cab and radiator of the Sd. Kfz. 7/2 began to be protected by armor.

In both cases the body was equipped with fold-down sides that formed a platform for the gun crew while allowing 360-degree traverse of the weapon. A trailer containing ammunition was often towed.

Sd.Kfz. 7 KM m 11

Length	6.85 m	Communications	none
Width	2.40 m	Weapon	none
Height	2.62 m	Engine make	Maybach
Weight	12.7 tons	Engine model	HL 62 TUK
Fuel capacity	213 liters	Engine configuration	six-cylinder, liquid cooled
Maximum speed	50 km/hr (31 mph)	Engine displacement	6.19 liter
Range, on road	250 km (155 miles)	Engine horsepower	140 @ 2600 rpm
Range, cross country	135 km (83.7 miles)		
Crew	1		

The early versions of the Sd. Kfz. 7, up through KM m 10, including this KM m 8, can be distinguished by only having four roadwheel stations per side.

Although tank recovery is often thought of as the exclusive domain of the 18-ton Famo, the 8-ton Sd. Kfz. 7 was also used in this role, especially with smaller vehicles such as this Panzerkampfwagen II. The towing tractor is a KM m 10.

Walter J. Spielberger

The late KM m 9 and the KM m 10 looked just alike; only the engines differed. Here, one of these vehicles crosses a bridge with a field piece in tow. It appears that the entire crew is keeping a watchful eye on the vehicle's progress.

Bundesarchiv photo

Walter J. Spielberger

The final, and most common, version of the Sd. Kfz. 7 was the KM m 11. These were readily distinguished by their longer track, which necessitated the addition of two more roadwheels on each side.

Walter J. Spielberger

The basically flat fenders over the tracks, and spoked front wheels distinguish the Sd. Kfz. 7 from other similar German halftracks. Hansa-Lloyd-Goliath/Borgward built copies of the KM m 11, not surprisingly giving them the model number HL m 11.

Walter J. Spielberger

The two hinged doors in each side of the Sd. Kfz. 7 provided access to compartments housing ammunition for the towed field piece. The doors in the rear of the vehicle accessed stowage for tools.

National Archives and Records Administration

The canvas cover of the Sd. Kfz. 7 stopped short of reaching the rear of the body, while the cover of the similar Sd. Kfz. 6 reached all the way to the end. The inner and outer roadwheels are different.

Walter J. Spielberger

Beginning in April 1940, Sd. Kfz. 7/1, armed with 2 cm Flak-Vierling 38, were delivered primarily to the Luftwaffe. In spite of the relatively high rate of fire afforded by the quadruple mount, the Sd. Kfz. 7/1 was only marginally effective against aircraft, primarily as a result of the limited range of the 2 cm round.

Patton Museum, Fort Knox, KY

The sides of the Sd. Kfz. 7/1 bed folded down, forming a platform for the gun crew while providing clearance for the 360-degree traverse of the gun mount. Although of limited effect in its original antiaircraft role, the Sd. Kfz. 7/1 was devastating against infantry concentrations and soft-skinned vehicles.

Walter J. Spielberger

The earliest of the Sd. Kfz. 7/1 had the 2 cm Flak-Vierling 38 with a special mounting, as seen here. Later models utilized the standard 2 cm Flak-Vierling 38 mount attached to the bed of the halftrack.

Patton Museum, Fort Knox, KY

During 1942, an armored cab and radiator shroud began to be installed on the Sd. Kfz. 7/1 in an effort to protect the crew (and radiator) from small arms fire and shell fragments. This change resulted in a very different appearance for the vehicle.

The rear of the armored cab was open, and is visible in this photo of a vehicle captured by U.S. troops. A wartime censor has obliterated part of the image. Despite its limitations, the Sd. Kfz. 7/1 had a long production run, with the vehicles being built through 1944, and an even longer service life, remaining in use for the duration of the war. (National Archives and Records Administration.

The weight and recoil of the 3.7 cm FlaK 36 proved to be too much for the 5-ton halftrack Sd. Kfz. 6, so it was moved to the 8-ton Sd. Kfz. 7. Later, the FlaK 37 was installed on the vehicles, rather than the FlaK 36.

The FlaK 37 was virtually identical to the FlaK 37, differing only in the sight. The FlaK 36 used a Flakvisier 35 or 36, and the FlaK 37 used a Zeiss clockwork-type Flakvisier 37.

Shown here at maximum elevation, the 3.7 cm cannon was preferred over the 2.0 cm cannon due to its increased range. It was felt the greater range and heavier "punch" of the larger round more than offset the comparatively reduced rate of fire.

Beginning in 1943, the Sd. Kfz. 7/2 was fitted with an armored cab and radiator shroud. This change radically altered the appearance of the vehicle. Often, the folding sides of the bed of this type vehicle were made of wood.

The final production 7/2 was armed with the 3.7 cm FlaK 43 (not shown), which had a substantially higher rate of fire. A large, circular portion at the rear of the weapon, due to it gas-operated breech, serves as its identifying characteristic. It also uses an eight-round clip, rather than the six-round clip of the 36/37, and has an elaborate shield.

Sd. Kfz. 8

The German military authorities assigned Daimler-Benz the task of developing a 12-ton halftrack. Daimler-Benz responded with the 1934 production of the DB s 7 (Daimler-Benz heavy half-track 7), termed by the military Sd. Kfz. 8. This vehicle was powered by a 150-hp Maybach V-12 gasoline engine. There were five road wheels—three outer and two inner.

The DB s 7 was followed in 1936 with the DB s 8, which increased the number of road wheels, with an additional inner road wheel added in the leading position at each side. Simultaneously, the cowl and hood were restyled to more closely resemble other German halftracks.

In 1938, the DB 9 (the schwerer, or heavy designation being dropped) was introduced. Internally, this vehicle had a more-powerful engine. Externally, the drive and idler wheels were of a different style, and an additional step was added between the fender and mudguard.

In 1939, the final version of the Sd. Kfz. 8 went into production. Known as the DB 10, this vehicle would remain in production through 1944, with a total of 4,070 units being delivered. In addition to Daimler-Benz, the DB 10 design was built by Skoda, ELMAG and Krauss-Maffei.

Although most extensively used as it was designed as an artillery prime mover, the Sd. Kfz. 8 also saw service in engineer and armor units as a heavy towing tractor.

Sd.Kfz. 8 DB 10			
Length	7.35 m	Communications	none
Width	2.50 m		
Height	2.77 m	Weapon	none
Weight	16.5 tons	Engine make	Maybach
Fuel capacity	250 liters	Engine model	HL 85 TUKRM
Maximum speed	51 km/hr (31.62 mph)	Engine configuration	V-12, liquid cooled
Range, on road	250 km (155 miles)	Engine displacement	8.52 liter
Range, cross country	125 km (77.5 miles)	Engine horsepower	185 @ 2500 rpm
Crew	1		

Walter J. Spielberger

The solid front wheels and rise in the track fender beneath the driver's position distinguish the Sd. Kfz. 8 from similar smaller German halftracks. The shape of the louvers in the hood differentiate it from the also similar, but larger, Sd. Kfz. 9. A final identifying feature is the embossed area around the ammunition compartment door handle.

The purpose of the 12-ton halftrack was to tow large field pieces such as the 15 and 17 cm cannon, the 21 cm mortar, the 10.5 cm FlaK, and the famed 8.8 cm FlaK 41 shown here. The vehicle also provided transport of the gun's crews.

Bundesarchiv photo

Military Miniatures in Review

The crew of this Sd. Kfz. 8 relaxes and enjoys an impromptu concert. The canvas cover has been raised and completely covers the crew compartment.

Sd. Kfz. 9 18-ton halftrack

The Sd. Kfz. 9 was the largest of German's halftracks. Most commonly referred to today as a FAMO, an abbreviation of its maker Fahrzeuge-und Motorenwerke, this vehicle has attained legendary status.

Developed as a heavy prime mover, the FAMO was occasionally used to tow very large artillery pieces. However, it is most often remembered for its work in the recovery role. With or without a trailer, the Sd. Kfz. 9 was dispatched to recover mired or damaged vehicles of all sizes. As the war progressed and tanks became heavier, FAMOs were dispatched in teams of two or three to recover Panther and Tiger tanks. During the campaign against Russia, the extraordinarily large road wheels (over 3 feet in diameter) allowed it to traverse muddy terrain that immobilized many other vehicles.

A vertical-drum winch was mounted underneath the bed of the halftrack and was invaluable during recovery operations. A Maybach HL108 engine, the same one in the Panzerkampfwagen III and Panzerkampfwagen IV medium tanks, powered the massive vehicle.

Extending the Sd. Kfz. 9's recovery abilities was the Sd. Kfz. 9/1, which replaced much of the rear crew and stowage area with a 6-ton capacity crane.

Sd.Kfz. 9 F3

Length	8.32 m	Communications	none
Width	2.60 m	Weapon	none
Height	2.85 m	Engine make	Maybach
Weight	19.5 tons	Engine model	HL 108 TUKRM
Fuel capacity	290 liters		
Maximum speed	50 km/hr (31 mph)	Engine configuration	V-12, liquid cooled
Range, on road	260 km (161.2 miles)	Engine displacement	10.8 liter
Range, cross country	100 km (62 miles)	Engine horsepower	270 @ 3000 rpm
Crew	1		

The early Sd. Kfz. 9 did not have a front bumper. Shear size made visibility problematic for the driver, necessitating the corner markers on the front fenders.

Walter J. Spielberger

The Sd. Kfz. 9 shares its styling with that of many of the other German halftracks. Parked in a lineup of halftracks, the 18-ton vehicle stands out. It can be distinguished by its size and the configuration of its bed, which had only two rows of seats and no ammunition compartments.

Walter J. Spielberger

Designed as a heavy towing tractor, the FAMO was frequently used in conjunction with the 22 ton-capacity Sd.Ah.116 trailer. This combination could transport all but the largest of the armored vehicles in the German arsenal.

Patton Museum, Fort Knox, KY

Patton Museum, Fort Knox, KY

The crewmen servicing it accentuate the size of the Famo in this photo. The roadwheels stood more than 3 feet tall. This particular vehicle is an early model, as evidenced by the FAMO logo on the radiator guard.

Walter J. Spielberger

Records indicate that a single 18-ton halftrack with artillery bed was built. Perhaps it was felt that the Sd. Kfz. 9 was too valuable in the recovery role to divert production into artillery tractors, or perhaps it was simply too tall for soldiers to load and unload artillery rounds into it.

Walter J. Spielberger

Despite its high towing capacity, the rated cargo capacity of the Sd. Kfz. 9 was a rather modest 2 1/2-tons. Its bed was usually filled with various repair and recovery gear. A canvas cover could be raised to protect both the cargo and the crew.

One variation of the Sd. Kfz. 9 was the Drehkrankraftwagen Sd. Kfz. 9/1. This variant had the standard cargo replaced with a 6-ton capacity Bilstein crane. This was useful for removing power plants from vehicles, or turrets from light and medium tanks.

Patton Museum, Fort Knox, KY

Patton Museum, Fort Knox, KY

One of the 12 Sd.Kfz. 9 outfitted to carry the 8.8 cm FlaK 37. These vehicles were deployed to Italy in September 1943 with the 26th Panzer Division.

Maultier

The German Army was ill-prepared for Soviet weather. The harsh winters with deep snow and heavy ice, followed by thaws that turned the soil into soup that seemed to have no bottom, threatened to paralyze the German forces, and in some cases it did. Transport was particularly effected by these conditions, with wheeled vehicles, even those with all-wheel drive, bogging down due to inadequate flotation.

As an interim solution was to adapt 3-ton cargo trucks into halftrack vehicles by replacing the rear axle with a Carden-Lloyd type suspension assembly. Opel and Ford gasoline-powered trucks, and Klockner-Humboldt Deutz diesel-powered trucks were used as basis for these conversions, which were dubbed Maultier, or mule, regardless of builder. Due to the complexity of the work and the size of the components involved, it was decided that these conversions would take place in automotive assembly plants, rather than in military field workshops.

The rear suspension of the truck was retained and the truck's driveshaft was coupled to a differential on the leading axle of the new tracklaying drive unit. The tracks themselves were similar to those used on the Panzerkampfwagen I.

In 1942, 635 of these conversions were performed. The next year the total soared to the 13,000 range, falling again in 1944 to 7,310. During the course of the 3 years, Ford produced about 14,000 of these machines, with Opel building about 4000 and Klockner-Humboldt Deutz about 2500.

Due in part to the success of the vehicles described above, a 4.5-ton Maultier was developed by Daimler Benz. The 4.5-ton vehicle utilized the suspension units of the Panzerkampfwagen II. Beginning in May of 1943, 594 units were built, with a further 886 the next year. These vehicles were based on the Daimler-Benz DB4500 L trucks.

Gleisketten-Lastkraftwagen 2-ton offen (Maultier) Sd.Kfz. 3 Ford

Length	6.325 m	Communications	none
Width	2.245 m	Weapon	none
Height	2.773 m	Engine make	Ford
Fuel capacity	110 liters	Engine model	G39T
Maximum speed	39.6 km/hr (24.18 mph)	Engine configuration	V-8, liquid cooled
Range, on road	200 km (124 miles)	Engine displacement	3.9 liters
Range, cross country	75 km (46.5 miles)	Engine horsepower	95 @ 3500 rpm
Crew	1		

Gleisketten-Lastkraftwagen 2-ton offen (Maultier) Sd.Kfz. 3 Opel

Length	6.00 m	Communications	none
Width	2.28 m	Weapon	none
Height	2.71 m	Engine make	Opel
Fuel capacity	82 liters	Engine configuration	six-cylinder, liquid cooled
Maximum speed	38 km/hr (23.56 mph)	Engine displacement	3.6 liters
Range, on road	165 km (102.3 miles)	Engine horsepower	68 @ 3120 rpm
Range, cross country	100 km (62 miles)		
Crew	1		

Gleisketten-Lastkraftwagen 2-ton offen (Maultier) Sd.Kfz. 3 Klockner-Humboldt Deutz

Length	6.12 m	Weapon	none
Width	2.22 m	Engine make	Klockner-Humboldt Deutz
Height	2.80 m	Engine model	F4M513 diesel
Fuel capacity	70 liters		
Maximum speed	40 km/hr (24.8 mph)	Engine configuration	four-cylinder, liquid cooled
Range, on road	170 km (105.4 miles)	Engine displacement	4.94 liters
Range, cross country	80 km (49.6 miles)	Engine horsepower	80 @ 2250 rpm
Crew	1		
Communications	none		

Gleisketten-Lastkraftwagen 4.5-ton (Maultier)

Length	7.86 m	Communications	none
Width	2.36 m	Weapon	none
Height	3.22 m	Engine make	Daimler-Benz
Fuel capacity	140 liters	Engine model	OM67/4 diesel
Maximum Speed	36 km/hr	Engine configuration	six-cylinder, liquid cooled
Range, on road	220 km	Engine displacement	7.2 liters
Range, cross country	100 km	Engine horsepower	112 @ 2250 rpm
Crew	1		

The bulk of the Maultier conversions were performed by Ford, including this one. A Carden-Lloyd suspension replaced the rear axle of a 3-ton cargo truck, reducing payload capacity, but greatly increasing maneuverability.

Walter J. Spielberger

Patton Museum, Fort Knox, KY

The remainder of the Maultier drive train remained unchanged, easing the training requirements for both drivers and mechanics. Ford produced 14,000 of these vehicles.

The vast majority of the Maultiers were equipped with simple open-topped cargo beds. A handful were built with van-type bodies.

Klockner-Humboldt Deutz built only about 2,500 diesel-powered Maultiers such as this one. Germany, perpetually short on gasoline, looked towards diesel as an answer to its fuel woes.

The enclosed cabs of these vehicles were welcomed during the cold Russian winters. Note the non-driven front axle typical of German halftrack vehicles.

In addition to the normal Maultier conversions using Carden-Lloyd suspension, Opel proposed a track assembly of its own design.

Walter J. Spielberger

Most Maultiers were used for transport of troops and material. Some, like this one, however, were used as self-propelled antiaircraft guns.

Patton Museum, Fort Knox, KY

Smaller numbers of 4.5-ton Maultiers were built based on the Daimler-Benz 4500 L truck. These vehicles utilized Panzerkampfwagen II suspension assemblies.

National Archives and Records Administration

Unarmored full-tracked prime movers

Steyr RSO

As Germany's forces pushed east, and were confronted by the Russian snows and mud, they found their wheeled prime movers to be woefully inadequate. Progress was delayed by the ongoing need for tracked and halftracked vehicles to tow stranded trucks from the mire.

The Russians used STZ-5 crawler tractors, and these became prized war booty for the German forces. In 1942 the Herres Waffenamt sought to have a comparable vehicle built with which to equip the German troops.

The Austrian firm of Steyr-Daimler-Puch was directed to create such a vehicle. By utilizing the air-cooled V-8 engine taken from its 4x4 truck line, Steyr-Daimler-Puch created a new tractor. It had, at least initially, an enclosed cab, and open-topped, drop-side bed made of wood, and four road wheels on each side mounted on quarter-elliptic springs. The vehicle, intended to accompany infantry divisions, was designed with a low top speed.

After successful trials, during which Hitler personally directed that the ground clearance be raised to 600 mm, Steyr began mass production in late 1942. The vehicle was designated Raupenschlepper Ost,, or "tracked tractor for the East."

The demand for these vehicles far outstripped Steyr's ability to produce them, especially since Steyr continued to build 4x4 trucks and cars concurrently. Therefore, production contracts were also given to Gräf and Stitt, Wanderer (Auto Union) and Magirus. These later three firms built approximately 4500, 5600, and 12,500 RSO, respectively, compared to Steyr's own modest production record of 2,600 pieces. Steyr discontinued RSO production October of 1943, although it continued to be involved in the engineering.

The RSO's contoured pressed-steel cab gave way to a simplified, flat-paneled cab of composite wood and steel construction. This cab was made in both soft-top and closed versions. All Magirus-produced vehicles utilized the soft-top cab. Vehicles with the new cab were designated RSO/2, with the original version becoming RSO/1.

The third version of the RSO, the RSO/3 was built in very small numbers by Magirus, and was a considerable improvement over earlier models. Rather than the V-8 gasoline engine of earlier models, it was powered by an air-cooled diesel. The drive line of this vehicle utilized a Cletrac-type final drive, rather than the automotive differential type unit used previously.

One other interesting version of the RSO was produced—an armored vehicle mounting an antitank gun. Development of this version began in mid-1943, and trial vehicles were tested that December. Hitler, who had seen preliminary drawings, ordered a limited production run of vehicles even before the test vehicles were completed. Fifty vehicles armed with the 7.5 cm PaK40/4 were built in 1944 for testing by Army Group South, but some were instead given to Army Group Center and Army Group North.

The using troops were considerably less enthusiastic about the anti-tank RSO than Hitler was. The vehicle's high profile, slow speed, and almost total lack of armor protection for the crew were all areas of criticism.

Steyr RSO/1

Length	4.43 m	Range, cross country	150 km (93 miles)
Width	1.99 m	Engine make	Steyr
Height	2.53 m	Engine configuration	V-8, air-cooled
Weight	3.5 tons		
Fuel capacity	180 liters	Engine displacement	3.5 liters
Maximum speed	17.2 km/hr (10.66 mph)	Engine horsepower	80 hp @ 3000 rpm
Range, on road	250 km (155 miles)		

National Archives and Records Administration

The dust being stirred up and slack in the return track in this photo mask the RSO's low top speed of approximately 10 mph. A canvas cover protects its cargo.

The RSO was designed to be used as a prime mover on the Russian front, hence the name Raupenschlepper Ost (tracked tractor for the East). Nonetheless, the vehicle served on all fronts, including Normandy, where this vehicle was photographed on June 22, 1944.

The RSO/1 had an enclosed steel cab and a wooden cargo bed with hinged, drop-down sides. Though tracked vehicles are not ideally suited for towing semi-type trailers, one of the RSO's biggest drawbacks was its high profile.

The high ground clearance of the RSO is evident in this photo taken of a captured vehicle being employed by the British in Italy.

A trio of RSO/1 trucks, artillery in tow, slog through Russian mud. The enclosed cab, air-cooled engine and fully tracked design were all dictated by the conditions shown here.

This captured RSO/2 was photographed shortly after its arrival at Ft. Knox, Kentucky. This vehicle is currently undergoing restoration.

Another problem with the RSO was access to the ammunition, which was stowed in lockers beneath the deck. To gain access, clearance had to exist between the weapon, and of course the crew couldn't stand on the locker being opened.

Perhaps the most notable design flaw in the RSO was the crew's almost totally exposed position. Only the gunshield sheltered them, and the RSO's slow speed was not good for getaways.

This armored RSO with PaK40 was evaluated at Ft. Knox following its capture. Hitler was enamored with this variant, but the using troops were not.

National Archives and Records Administration

One of the primary disadvantages of the armored RSO is evident here. Even with the sides lowered, there was little room for the crew to serve the weapon.

Walter J. Spielberger

The RSO/2 had a simplified cab design, which was offered in both a hardtop style and the soft top (shown here). This cab was cheaper and easier to construct than Steyr's original semi-streamlined design.

Stefan De Meyer collection

With both the cab top and cargo cover removed, the silhouette of the RSO/2 was much smaller than that of the RSO/1. The cargo bed was basically unchanged between models.

Glossary

There are many terms used in the discussion of military vehicles that are unique to the subject matter. In the case of German vehicles, there are also some terms that don't lend themselves well to brief, direct English translation. There are also some German terms which have been taken directly into commonly used English, Panzer for example, often without the true meaning of the term being explained. Finally, some English-language publications have been produced that are liberally sprinkled with the German terms, even when English would do as well. Throughout the text of this book there are German terms incorporated, usually with a corresponding English meaning. For other times, and for general reference, we present this glossary.

A

Abteilung: a battalion with less than five companies; abbreviated Abt.

Abschnitt : Section; abbreviated Abshn

Achtradwagen: Eight-wheeled vehicle; abbreviated ARW

Achs: Axle

AFV: Abbreviation for Armored Fighting Vehicle

Als: as

Alt or alte: old

Alter: older

Amerikanisch: American; abbreviated (a)

Anhanger: Trailer; abbreviated Anh

Antenne: Antenna or radio aerial

Armee: Field army

Artillerie: Artillery, abbreviated Art

Artillerie Panzerbeobachtungswagen: Armored artillery observation vehicle; abbreviated Art Pz BeobWg

Antrieb: Drive

Auf: Upon, on

Aufbau: Vehicle superstructure

Aufklärung: Reconnaissance; abbreviated Aufkl

Aufklärer: Reconnaissance vehicle; abbreviated Aufkl

Ausbildung: Training

Ausführung: Model, design, mark; abbreviated Ausf.

B

BW: see Begleitwagen

Ballistik-Messfahrzeug: Gunnery survey vehicle

Barbarossa: Redbeard (code name for the German invasion of the Soviet Union)

Batterie: Artillery battery; plural Batterien

Befehlswagen: command vehicle; abbreviated Bef Wg

Begleitwagen: Code name assigned to Panzer IV project, abbreviated BW.

Bergegerät: Recovery devices or gear

Bergepanzer/BergePanzerwagen: Armored recovery vehicle

Beute: Booty; captured equipment

Bewaffnung: Armament

Bis: to

Brigade: A unit usually smaller than a division to which are attached groups and/or battalions and smaller units tailored to meet anticipated requirements.

Brükenleger: Bridge-laying vehicle; abbreviated bl

Brükenkampfwagen: armored bridge carrier

Brummbär: literally, Grizzly Bear, a name assigned by allied troops to the German stürmpanzer.

Bord: Intercom

C

Centimeter: 0.3937 inches; abbreviated cm

D

Deutsche: German; often denoted by (d)

Deutsche Afrika Korps: German (North) Africa Corps, abbreviated DAK

DW: see Durchbruchwagen

Doppel: Double

Drilling: Triple

Durchbruchwagen: Breakthrough vehicle (code name for Pz Kpfw V), abbreviated DW

E

Einheits: Universal (standardized); abbreviated Einh

Einheitswaffentrager: Universal weapon carrier (tracked SP carriage)

Eisenwerke: Steel works

Elefant: Elephant, name given to the SP gun formerly known as the Ferdinand

Englisch: English; denoted by (e)

Ente: Duck (code name for light tracked vehicle)

Entwicklung: Development project, abbreviated E

Ersatz: Replacement; substitute

F

Fahrerblende: Driver's visor
Fahrersehklappe: Driver's visor
Fahrgestell: Chassis; abbreviated fgst
Fahrschulefahrzeug: Driving school vehicle
Fahrschulwanne: Driving school chassis (turret removed)
Fahrzüg: Vehicle
Falke: Falcon (code name for especially equipped Sd.Kfz. 251)
Fallschirmtruppen: Airborne troops
Feldhaubitze: Field howitzer, abbreviated FH
Feldkanone: Field gun, abbreviated FK
Fernrohr: Telescope
Fernschreiber: Teletype apparatus
Fernsprechpanzerwagen: Armored telephone communications vehicle, abbreviated Fsp Wg
Fernsprechbetriebspanzerwagen Telephone exchange vehicle
Feuerleitpanzerfahrzeug: Armored fire control vehicle
FlaK : see Fliegerabwehrkanone
Flakpanzer: Armored antiaircraft vehicle
Flakpanzerwagen: Antiaircraft tank, abbreviated FlakPzWg
Flakvierling: Four-barreled antiaircraft gun, a quad mount
Flakvisier: Antiaircraft gun sight
Flakzwilling: Double-barreled antiaircraft gun
Flammenwerfer: Flamethrower, abbreviated Flw;Fl W
Flammenwerfer Anlagen: Flamethrower attachment
Flammgranate: Incendiary shell
Flammpanzer: Flamethrowing tank, denoted with (Fl)
Flammpanzerwagen: Flamethrowing AFV
Fliegerabwehr: Antiaircraft
Fliegerabwehrkanone: Antiaircraft gun; abbreviated FlaK
Flugabwehrzug: Antiaircraft platoon
Französisch: French; denoted (f)
Früher: previously
Für: for
Fu: see Funk
FuG: see Funkgerät
Funk: Radio
Funkgerät: Radio equipment
Funklenk: Radio-controlled, abbreviated Fkl
Funklenkwagen: Radio-controlled vehicle
Funkpanzerwagen: Radio-controlled AFV
Funksprechgerät: Radio-telephone equipment, abbreviated FuSpr, FuSprG
FuSpr see Funksprechgerät
FuSprG see Funksprechgerät
FuWg see Funkwagen
Funkwagen: Radio vehicle; abbreviated FuWg

G

Geheim: Secret
Gelandegängiger: Cross-country travelling ability
gepanzert: Armored; abbreviated gep
gepanzerter Lastkraftwagen: armored truck; abbreviated gep LKW

gep Mannschaft Tr Wg: see gepanzerter Mannschaftstransportwagen
gep Mun Schl: see gepanzerter Munitionsschlepper gepanzerter Mannschaftstransportwagen: Armored personnel carrier, abbreviated gep Mannschaft Tr Wg
gepanzerter Munitionsschlepper: Armored ammunition tractor, abbreviated gep Mun Schl
Gerät: Device, equipment
Geschütz: Gun
Geschützwagen: Gun motor carriage, abbreviated GW
Glacis plate: Forward sloping armor on a vehicle, usually quite strong.
Granate: Shell, abbreviated Gr
Granatwerfer: Mortar; abbreviated GrW
Grosse Panzer Befehlswagen Heavy: Armored command vehicle; abbreviated gr Pz Bef Wg
Grosstraktor: Large tractor (code name for heavy tank project)

H

Halb: Semi or half; abbreviated Hb
Halbkettenfahrzeug: Halftrack vehicle; abbreviated HK
Hängelafette: Suspended mounting for weapon
Heeres: Army
Heereswaffenamt: Army Ordnance Office
Hetzer: Literally Baiter, term properly applied to the experimental E-10 tank destroyer, usually erroneously applied to the Jagdpanzer 38.
Heuschrecke: Literally Grasshopper, name of self-propelled artillery piece with dismountable turret.
Hornisse: Literally Hornet, name given to a particular panzerjäger
Hummel: Literally Bumble Bee, name given to particular self-propelled howitzer

I

I G: see Infanteriegeschütz
Infanterie: Infantry; abbreviated Inf
Infanteriegeschütz: Infantry howitzer; abbreviated I G
Inspectorate: Inspectorate, abbreviated IN
Instandsetzungskraftwage: Maintenance vehicle
Italienisch: Italian; denoted with (i)

J

Jäger: Hunter
Jgd Pz: see Jagdpanzer
Jagdpanther: Tank destroyer built on Panther chassis.
Jagdpanzer: Tank destroyer
Jagdtiger: Tank destroyer built on Tiger chassis.

K

Karlgerät: Code name given to the heavy self-propelled siege mortar

Kpfw: see Kampfwagen

Kaliber: Caliber

Kampfwagen: Tank or armored vehicle; abbreviated kpfw or Kw

Kampfwagenkanone: Tank gun

Kampfwagen Fahrer Fernrohr: Tank driver's periscope

Kanone: Cannon

Kavallerie: Cavalry

KFF: see Kampfwagen Fahrer Fernrohr

Kilometer: 0.6214 miles, abbreviated Km

Kilometers per hour: Measurement of velocity, 0.6214 miles per hour

Kleiner: Smaller; abbreviated Kl

Kommando: Command, abbreviated Kmdo or KDO

Kommandopanzerwagen: Armored headquarters vehicle

Korps: Corps, an army unit usually consisting of two or more divisions

Kraftfahrzeug: Motor vehicle, abbreviated Kfz.

Kraftfahrlehrkommando: Driver training command

Kraftwagenwerkstattzug: Vehicle workshop Company, abbreviated Kw Werkst Z

Krankenpanzerwagen: Armored ambulance

Kugelblitz: literally Ball lightning, name given to experimental late-war antiaircraft tank

Kugelzielfehrnrohr: Ball-mounted telescope, abbreviated KZF

KwK: see Kampfwagenkanone

L

Lafette: Gun carriage, abbreviated Laf

Ladungsleger: Explosives-carrier (layer)

Ladungsträger: Explosives-carrier

Land-Wasser-Schlepper: Land and water tractor, abbreviated LWS

Landwirtschaftlicher Schlepper Agricultural tractor (code name for Pz Kpfw I and II series tanks), abbreviated LaS

Lang: Long

Lange: Length

LKW: see Lastkraftwagen

Lauf (Kaliberlange): Length of gun barrel in calibers, abbreviated L

Laufwerk: Suspension

Lastkraftwagen: Truck, abbreviated LKW

Lehr: Training

Leibstandarte: Bodyguard

Leichter SchützenPanzerwagen Light armored personnel carrier, abbreviated leSPW

leicht/leichte: Light, abbreviated le

leichte Feldhaubitze: Light field howitzer, abbreviated leFH

Leichter Geschütz: Light gun (recoilless), abbreviated LG

Leichtertraktor: Light tractor (code name for light tank project)

Leichter Wehrmacht Schlepper: Armed forces light carrier

Lichtauswertepanzerwagen: armored flash spotter vehicle

Lorraine Schlepper: Lorraine tractor, abbreviated LrS

Luftwaffe: German Air Force

Luchs: Lynx (light reconnaissance vehicle)

M

Mannschaftstransportwagen: Troop transport vehicle, abbreviated MTW

Mantlet: Moveable armored housing into which the main weapon of an AFV is installed.

Marder: literally Märten, name of tank destroyer

Maschinengewehr: Machine-gun, abbreviated MG

Maschinenkanone: Machine cannon, abbreviated MK

Maultier: literally Mule, name given to truck-based semi-track carriers.

Maus: Mouse code name given to super-heavy tank.

Messtruppanzerwagen: armored survey troop vehicle.

meter: 3.2808 feet, or 39.37 inches, abbreviated m

MG: see maschinengewehr

millemeter: 0.03937 inches

Minenräum: Mine-clearance vehicle

Minenrollern: Minerollers

Mit: With

Mitte: Middle or center

Mittlerer: Medium

MK: see maschinenkanone

Möbelwagen: Furniture van, nickname given to boxy-looking antiaircraft tank.

Mörser: Mortar

Mörserträger: mortar carrier

Munition: Ammunition, abbreviated mun

Munitionskraftwagen: Ammunition vehicle

Munitionsischlepper: Ammunition carrier

N

Nachrichten Abteilung: Communication battalion

Nahverteidigungswaffe: Close-in defence weapon

Nashorn: literally, Rhinoceros name given to tank destroyer formerly known as Hornet

Nebel: Smoke

Nebelwerfer: Rocket launcher

Neu: New

Neuer Art: New type of pattern or design; abbreviated nA

Neubaufahrzüg: New construction vehicle; abbreviated Nbfz

Notek: German automotive electrical gear manufacturer equipment, became synonymous with the style of lights on later German vehicles.

Nummer: Number

O

Oberkommando des Heeres: High Command of the Army abbreviated OKH

Oberkommando der Wehrmacht: High Command of the Armed Forces abbreviated OKW

oder: Or, other, alternatively

offen: Open

ohne: Without

Organisation Todt: Work Corps under direction of Todt abbreviated OT

Ostkette: East track, wide tracks for improved flotation on soft terrain.

Ostwind: Eastwind, name of a type of antiaircraft tank.

Östereichische: Austrian, denoted by (o)

P

PaK: see Panzerabwehrkanone

Panzer: Armor, tank

Panzerabteilung: Tank detachment, battalion, abbreviated PzAbt

Panzerabwehrabteilung: Antitank gun battalion abbreviated Pz Abw Abt

Panzerabwehrkanone: Antitank gun abbreviated PaK

Panzerartillerie: Armored artillery

Panzer Aufklärungs Abteilung: Armored reconnaissance battalion abbreviated PzAufklAbt

Panzerbefehlswagen: Command tank; abbreviated Pz Bef Wg

Panzerbeobachtungswagen: Tank used for artillery observation; abbreviated Pz Beob Wg

Panzerbrigade: Tank brigade; armored brigade

Panzerbüchse: Antitank rifle

Panzerdivision: Tank division, armored division

Panzerfähre: Armored ferry

Panzerfunkwagen: Armored radio-car abbreviated Pz Fu Wg

Panzergranate: armor-piercing Shell; abbreviated Pz Gr or Pzgr

Panzergrenadier: Private in armored infantry brigade

Panzergrenadier Division: Motorized armored infantry division

Panzerhaubitze: Howitzer adapted for fitting in armored vehicle abbreviated Pz H

Panzerjäger: Tank destroyer, tank hunter; abbreviated Pz Jag

Panzerjägerabteilung Sf: Antitank battalion (mobile (troops); abbreviated Pz Jag Abt

Panzerkampfwagen: Tank, armored fighting vehicle; abbreviated Pz. Kpfw. or Pkw

Panzerkompanie: Tank Company abbreviated Pz Kp.

Panzerkorps: Armored corps

Panzerkraftwagen: Armored vehicle, abbreviated Pz K

Panzerregiment: Tank regiment, armored regiment (mixed)

Panzer Selbstfahrlafette: Armored self-propelled mount; abbreviated Pz Sf; Pz Sfl

Panzerspähwagen: Armored scout car abbreviated Pz Sp Wg

Panzer Truppen: Armored troops; armored units; tank forces

Panzerwagen: Armored vehicle

Panzerwerfer: Armored rocket-launcher

Panzerzug: Tank platoon; abbreviated Pz Zug

Patrone: Round (ammunition)

Periskop: Periscope

Personenkraftwagen: Passenger car abbreviated PKW

PKW: see Personenkraftwagen

Pionier: Engineer, Pi

Pionierpanzerwagen: Engineers armored vehicle

Polizei Panzerwagen: Police armored vehicle

Polnisch: Polish denoted with (p)

Protectorate: Occupied Czech states öf Bohemia and Moravia

PzAbt: see Panzerabteilung

Pz Abw Abt: see Panzerabwehrabteilung

PzAufklAbt: see Panzer Aufklärungs Abteilung

Pz Bef Wg: see Panzerbefehlswagen

Pz Beob Wg: see Panzerbeobachtungswagen

Pz Fu Wg: see Panzerfunkwagen

Pz Sf; Pz Sfl: see Panzer Selbstfahrlafette

Pz Sp Wg: see Panzerspähwagen

R

Rad: Wheel

Radfahrzüg: Wheeled vehicle

Rakete Panzerbüsche: Antitank rocket launcher; abbreviated R PzB

Raketenwerfer: Rocket projector; abbreviated RW

Räumen: Clearer, usually seen as Minenräumen – minefield clearer

Raupe: Caterpillar track

Raupenschlepper Ost: Tracked carrier, East

Raupenfahrzüg: Self-propelled full tracked vehicle; abbreviated RaupFzg

Reich: Republic

Reihenwerfer: A series of mortars mounted on a frame

Ritscher: Vehicle manufacturer in Hamburg

Roadwheel: That part of a tracked vehicle's suspension that transfers the weight from the axle to the tracks.

Rot: Red

Rundblickfernrohr: Panoramic telescope; abbreviated Rblf

Russische: Russian; denoted with (r)

RSO: see Raupenschlepper Ost

S

Saukopf: literally, Boars head; postwar literature appears to have invented this term to describe a cast gun mantlet

Schachtellaufwerk: Interleaved running gear

Schallaufnahmepanzerwagen: Sound recording vehicle

Schallauswertepanzerwagen: Sound ranging vehicle

Schienen-Ketten Fahrzüg: vehicle for use on railway tracks

Schildkröte: Turtle (code name for armored car project)

Schlepper: Tractor

Schmal: Small

Schürze: Armored apron

Schützenpanzerwagen: Armored infantry vehicle abbreviated SPW

Schütz Staffein: SS (Protection Squads)

Schwadron: Troop

schwere: heavy; abbreviated s

schwere Feldhaubitze: Heavy field howitzer; abbreviated sFH

schwere Infanteriegeschütz: Heavy infantry gun; abbreviated sIG

schwere Infanteriegschütz Kompanie: Heavy infantry gun company, abbreviated sIG Kp

schwere Maschinen Karbine Heavy machine-gun (ammunition) abbreviated SMK

schwere Panzerbüchse 41: Heavy antitank rifle 41; abbreviated sPzB 41

schwere Panzerspähwagen: Heavy armored reconnaissance car; abbreviated s Pz Sp Wg

Schwere Wagen: Code name for heavy tank project

schwere Wehrmacht Schlepper: Heavy army tractor

Schwimmkampfwagen: Amphibious tank

Schwimmpanzer: Amphibious AFV

Schwimmwagen: Amphibious vehicle

Sd. Ah.: see Sonder Anhänger

Sd. Kfz.: see Sonderkraftfahrzeug

Seelöwe: literal Sealion, also code name for the invasion of Britain.

Selbstfahrlafette: Self-propelled gun mount; abbreviated Sf; Sfl

Serie: Series

sFH: see schwere Feldhaubitze

sIG: see schwere Infanteriegeschütz

Sockellafette: Pivot or pedestal mounting for gun

Sonder: Special purpose

Sonder Anhänger: Special purpose trailer; abbreviated Sd. Ah.

Sonderausführung: Special model

Sonderfahrgestell: Special purpose chassis; abbreviated Sd. Fgst.

Sondergerät: Special purpose equipment

Sonderkraftfahrzeug: Special purpose vehicle,; abbreviated **Sd. Kfz.**

SMK: see schwere Maschinen Karbine

Spähwagen: Reconnaissance vehicle

Sprengdienst Kraftfahrzeug: Demolition vehicle (Goliath)

Sprenggranate: High-explosive Shell

Sprengladung: Explosive charge

Sprgr/Spgr: see Sprenggranate

sPzB 41: see schwere Panzerbüchse 41

s Pz Sp Wg: see schwere Panzerspähwagen

SS: see Schütz Staffein

Stab: Headquarters

Stabskompanie: Headquarters Company

Starr: Rigid, gun mounted without recoil mechanism

Sturmartillerie: Assault artillery

StuG: see Sturmgeschütz

StuH: see Sturmhaubitze: Assault howitzer

StuK: see Sturmkanone

Sturmgeschütz: Assault gun; abbreviated StuG

Sturmgeschütz Abteilung: Assault gun battalion

Sturmhaubitze: Self-propelled assault howitzer

Sturm Infanterie Geschütz: self-propelled assault infantry gun

Sturmkanone: Assault cannon

Sturmmörser: Assault mortar, self-propelled

Sturmpanzer: Assault howitzer

Sturmsteg: Infantry assault footbridge

sWS: see Schwere Wehrmacht Schlepper

T

Tauchpanzer: Submersible tank

TBF: see Turmblickfernrohr

Tchechoslowakisch: Czechoslovakian: denoted with (t)

tonne: Metric ton; 0.9842 U.S. tons

Träger: Transport; carrier

Traktor: Tractor

Tropen: Tropical

Turm: Turret

Turmblickfernrohr: Turret panoramic telescope; abbreviated TBF

Turmzielfernrohr: Turret telescope

Typ: Type

TZF: see Turmzielfernrohr

U

UHU: Great Horned Owl (code name for infra-red searchlight vehicle)

ünd And

V

Versuchs: Experimental

Versuchs serie: Experimental series

Vierling: Quadruple

VK: see Vollkettenfahrzüg

Vollkettenaufklärer: Fully-tracked reconnaissance vehicle

Vollkettenfahrzüg : Fully-tracked vehicle, abbreviated VK

Vorsatz P: Device P, ball mount for curved barrel machinegun

W

Wa Prüf: see Waffenamtprüf

Waffe: Weapon

Waffen Arms; weapons; ordnance

Waffen SS: Military wing of the SS

Waffenamt: Ordnance Department; abbreviated Wa

Waffenamtprüf: Ordnance test board; abbreviated Wa Prüf

Waffenträger: Weapons carrier

Wagen: Wagon, vehicle

Wehrmacht: Armed Forces

Wehrmacht Heer: Armed Forces Army, abbreviated WH

Wehrmacht Luftwaffe: Armed Forces Air Force; abbreviated WL

Wehrmacht: Marine Armed Forces Navy; abbreviated WM

Werfer: Projector
Werkstatt Kompanie: Workshop Company
Wespe: literally Wasp, name given to a self-propelled howitzer
Winkelzielfernrohr: Angled telescope
Wirblewind: Whirlwind (antiaircraft tank)
Wurfgerät: Rocket equipment
Wurfrahmen: Rocket launcher frame
WZF: see Winkelzielfernrohr

Z

Zerstörer: Destroyer
ZF: see Zielfernrohr
Zielfernrohr: Telescope sight
Zug Platoon
Zugführerwagen: Platoon commander's vehicle (code name for the Pz III series)
Zugkraftwagen: Prime mover usually semi or half-tracked vehicle
ZW: see Zugführerwagen
Zwilling: Twin, dual
Zwillingslafette: Twin mounting

Numeric

0-serie: First series

Kfz. and Sd.Kfz. numbers

The German military assigned classification numbers to its vehicles based on the vehicle's purpose as well as the vehicle's characteristics. The Kfz. or Sd.Kfz. number was assigned regardless of chassis design. This is different from the U.S. system, which assigned a Standard Nomenclature List number according to chassis type (G-506 being a GMC CCKW, for example). The German's, in contrast, assigned the Kfz. number 1 to light off-road cars, regardless of make, model or design. The OKH Weapons Office made these number assignments. In about 1943 the assignment of numbers became somewhat sporadic. Kfz numbers above 300 were assigned to Luftwaffe vehicles.

Sd.Kfz., or sonderkraftfahrzeug, means "special purpose vehicle," while kfz., or kraftfahrzeug, is "vehicle." Minor changes in a design, such as outfitting a vehicle with special racks and equipment, were denoted by the addition of a suffix number, separated from the primary number with a slash (/). Further specific variations, such as racks for specific ammunition, or specific radio installations, were designated with yet another suffix, this time denoted with a Roman numeral.

Kfz. Number	Description
1	Light off-road personnel car
1/20	Light off-road amphibious car
2	Radio car
2/40	Small repair service car
3	Light survey troop car
4	Antiaircraft troop car
5	Medium tank truck
11	Medium off-road personnel car
12	Medium off-road personnel car
13	Machinegun car
14	Radio car
15	Cable carrier, intelligence car, radio car, telephone car
16	Medium survey car
16/1	Reconnaissance vehicle
17	Radio vehicle, survey vehicle, telephone vehicle
17/1	Radio vehicle
18	Combat vehicle
19	Telephone vehicle
21	Heavy off-road personnel car
23	Telephone vehicle
24	Support vehicle
31	Ambulance
42	Intelligence collection vehicle
43	Antiaircraft director vehicle
44	Oxygen- and nitrogen-producing vehicle

Kfz. Number	Description
51	Repair shop vehicle
61	Direction-finding vehicle, locksmith vehicle, teletype vehicle, telephone service vehicle, radio vehicle, cable measuring vehicle, support vehicle
61/1	Radio vehicle
62	Flash-measuring vehicle, light weather report-ing vehicle, print-shop vehicle, sound-receiving or measuring vehicle, staff evaluation vehicle, survey evaluation vehicle
63	Flash or sound-measuring director vehicle, flash or sound-measur-ing equip-ment vehicle, measuring equipment vehicle
64	Measuring equipment vehicle
68	Light telephone vehicle, Radio antenna vehicle
69	Limber
70	Personnel vehicle
72	Medium weather vehicle, print-shop vehicle, radio vehicle a & b, radio power or listening vehicle, support vehicle, telephone or teletype center vehicle, telephone service vehicle, teletype vehicle
72/1	Teletype vehicle
74	Antiaircraft director vehicle

Kfz. Number	Description
76	Observation balloon cable truck
77	Telephone vehicle
79	Repair-shop vehicle
81	Light antiaircraft vehicle
83	Light searchlight vehicle I & II
92	Personnel decontamination vehicle
93	Clothing decontamination vehicle
94	Water tank truck
95	Store vehicle
96	3-ton crane on 4.5-ton truck chassis, 5-ton crane on 4.5-ton truck chassis
301	Radio antenna vehicle
302	Radio vehicle
303	Radio surveillance vehicle

Kfz. Number	Description
305	Medium truck (0) with closed uniform body
317	Oxygen tank truck
343	Sprayer tank truck
344	Fire hose tender
345	Fire engine
346	Fire hose truck
384	Aircraft fuel tank truck
385	Aircraft fuel tank truck
410	Medium antiaircraft gun truck
415	Antiaircraft fire survey truck

Sd.Kfz. Number	Description
2	Motorcycle tractor
2/1	Motorcycle tractor for field cable laying
2/2	Motorcycle tractor for heavy cable laying
3a	2-ton halftrack truck (Opel)
3b	2-ton halftrack truck (Ford)
3c	2-ton halftrack diesel truck (Klockner-Humbolt-Deutz)
4	4 1/2-ton halftrack truck
4/1	2-ton halftrack truck mounting 10-barreled 15cm Nebelwerfer projector
6	5-ton halftrack tractor (Engineers' version)
6/1	5-ton halftrack tractor (Artillery version)
6/2	5-ton halftrack tractor mounting 3.7cm FlaK36
7	8-ton halftrack tractor
7/1	8-ton halftrack tractor mounting quadruple 2cm FlaK guns
7/2	8-ton halftrack tractor mounting 3.7cm FlaK36
7/6	8-ton halftrack tractor for AA range-finding
8	12-ton halftrack tractor
9	18-ton halftrack tractor

Sd.Kfz. Number	Description
9/1	18-ton halftrack tractor mounting 6-ton crane
9/2	18-ton halftrack tractor mounting 10-ton gas-electric crane
10	1-ton halftrack tractor
10/1	1-ton halftrack light gas-detector vehicle
10/2	1-ton halftrack decontamination vehicle
10/3	1-ton halftrack decontamination vehicle with spraying equipment
10/4	1-ton halftrack tractor mounting 2 cm F laK30
10/5	1-ton halftrack tractor mounting 2 cm FlaK38 and armored cab
11	3-ton halftrack tractor
11/1	3-ton halftrack smoke-generator vehicle, also used as ammunition-carrier for Nebelwerfer projectors
11/2	3-ton halftrack decontamination vehicle
11/3	3-ton halftrack decontamination vehicle with spraying equipment
11/4	3-ton halftrack smoke-generator vehicle
11/5	3-ton halftrack gas-detector vehicle
101	Pkw I, models A and B
111	Pkw I converted to ammunition carrier
121	Pkw II series

Sd.Kfz. Number	Description
122	Pkw II models D and E converted to flamethrowing tank
123	Reconnaissance vehicle, also known as Panzerspahwagen Luchs
124	10.5 cm leFH18/2 mounted on Pkw II chassis
131	7.5 cm antitank gun mounted on Pkw II chassis
132	7.62 cm Russian antitank gun mounted on Pkw II chassis D and E
135	7.5 cm antitank gun mounted on French Lorraine tractor
135/1	15 cm howitzer mounted on Lorraine tractor
138	7.5 cm PaK40 mounted on Czech tank chassis
138/1	15 cm howitzer mounted on Czech tank chassis
139	7.62 cm Russian antitank gun mounted on Czech tank hassis
140	2cm FlaK gun mounted on Czech tank chassis
140/1	Fully tracked reconnaissance vehicle based on 38(t) tank chassis
141	Pkw III series
141/1	Pkw III series — Ausf. J, L, M
141/2	Pkw III armed with 7.5cm L/24
141/3	Pkw III Ausf M converted to flamethrowing tanks
142	Assault guns based on the Pkw III chassis and armed with the short 7.5cm L/24
142/1	Assault guns based on Pkw III and armed with the 7.5cm L/43 or L/48
142/2	Assault howitzer based on Pkw III armed with 10.5cm StuH42 L/28
143	Pkw III converted to mobile observation post for artillery
161	Pkw IV series — Ausf. A through F
161/1	Pkw IV series — Ausf. G
161/2	Pkw IV series — Ausf. H through J
161/3	3.7cm FlaK43 mounted on the chassis of Pkw IV
162	Tank destroyer based on the Pkw IV chassis, armed with 7.5cm PaK39 L/48
162/1	Improved version of the Jagdpanzer IV to mount the 7.5cm L/70

Sd.Kfz. Number	Description
164	8.8cm PaK43 mounted on the Pkw III/IV chassis as a tank destroyer
165	Self-propelled carriage for field howitzer sFH 18
166	Self-propelled carriage for heavy infantry howitzer 15cm sIG33 modified and redesignated 15cm StuH43
167	Assault gun based on Pkw IV chassis and armed with the 7.5cm L/48
171	"Panther" series
172	Assault gun project based on Pkw V chassis
173	Tank destroyer based on the Pkw V chassis, armed with the 8.8cm PaK43/3 L/71
179	Armored tank-recovery vehicle based on Panther chassis
181	Tiger I model E
182	Tiger II model B
185	Tank destroyer based on the Porsche Tiger chassis, armed with the 8.8 cm PaK43/2
186	Tank destroyer based on the Tiger II chassis and armed with 12.8 cm PaK44
221	Light four-wheeled armored car (1 x 7.92mm MG)
222	Light four-wheeled armored car (2 cm gun and 7.92mm MGI
223	Light four-wheeled armored car, with radio equipment
231	Six- or eight-wheeled armored car
232	Six- or eight-wheeled armored car, with radio equipment
233	Turretless eight-wheeled armored car mounting 7.5cm KwK37
234/1	Eight-wheeled diesel-powered armored car mounting 2 cm gun
234/2	Eight-wheeled armored car mounting 5cm KwK39/ in turret
234/3	Eight-wheeled armored car mounting short 7.5cm in open turret
234/4	Eight-wheeled armored car mounting 7.5cm PaK40 L/46
247	Armored staff car on four- or six-wheeled chassis
250 and 250/1	ILight armored halftrack personnel-carrier
250/2	Telephone cable-laying vehicle

Sd.Kfz. Number	Description
250/3	Radio vehicle
250/4	Observation and fire control vehicle
250/5	Mobile armored observation post
250/6	Ammunition-carrier for Sturmgeschütz
250/7	Light armored halftrack mortar vehicle
250/8	Light armored halftrack vehicle mounting short 7.5cm K51 L/24
250/9	Light armored halftrack vehicle with 2cm KwK38 and MG34 mounted in turret
250/10	Light t armored halftrack vehicle armed with 3.7cm PaK35/36
250/11	Light armored halftrack vehicle armed with a schwere Panzerbuchse 41
250/12	Light armored halftrack survey and range-plotting vehicle
251 and 251/1	Medium armored halftrack personnel-carrier
251/2	Medium armored halftrack mortar vehicle
251/3	Radio vehicle
251/4	Ammunition-carrier and tractor for the IG 18 infantry close-support gun
251/5	Engineer vehicle
251/6	Mobile command post
251/7	Engineer vehicle
251/8	Medium halftrack armored ambulance
251/9	Medium halftrack vehicle mounting short 7.5cm K37
251/10	Medium halftrack vehicle mounting 3.7cm PaK35/36
251/11	Medium halftrack armored telephone vehicle
251/12	Medium halftrack armored survey and instrument vehicle
251/13	Medium halftrack armored artillery sound recording vehicle
251/14	Medium halftrack armored artillery sound ranging vehicle
251/15	Medium halftrack armored artillery flash spotting vehicle
251/16	Medium halftrack armored flamethrowing vehicle
251/17	Medium halftrack armored vehicle with 2 cm FlaK38

Sd.Kfz. Number	Description
251/18	Mobile armored observation post
251/19	Mobile armored telephone exchange
251/20	Medium halftrack armored vehicle with infrared searchlight
251/21	Medium halftrack antiaircraft vehicle with triple 15mm or 20mm AA MG151
251/22	Medium halftrack armored vehicle with 7.5cm PaK40 antitank gun
251/23	Medium halftrack reconnaissance vehicle
252	Light halftrack armored ammunition-carrier
253	Light halftrack armored observation vehicle
254	Medium wheel and track armored observation vehicle
260	Light four-wheeled armored car with radio equipment
261	Light four-wheeled armored car with radio equipment.
263	Six or eight-wheeled armored car with fixed turret and radio equipment
265	Pkw I converted to armored command vehicle
266	Pkw III Ausf. E through M converted to armored command vehicle
267	Pkw III Ausf D converted to armored command vehicle
267	Pkw 'Panther' with additional radio equipment Pkw
267	"Tiger" with additional radio equipment
268	Pkw III Ausf. D through M converted to armored command vehicle
268	Pkw "Panther" with additional radio equipment
268	Pkw "Tiger" with additional radio equipment
280	Ammunition carrier
300	Radio-controlled minefield-clearance vehicle
301	Demolition vehicle
302	Demolition vehicle
303	Demolition vehicle
304	Demolition vehicle

Index

Listed below are some of the most commonly referenced vehicles in this book. Additional vehicles described in the text but not listed below can be found in the appropriately headed chapters, found in the table of contents.

A

Abwurfvorrichtungen on Panzerkampfwagen I	261
Artillerie Panzerbeobachtungswagen III	45
Artillerie Schlepper 35(t)	281
Aufklärungspanzerwagen 38 (2 cm)	202

B

BMW Motorcycles	397
Bergepanzer 38	146
Bergepanzer III	148
Bergepanzer IV	148
Bergepanther	149
Bergepanzer Ferdinand	152
Borgward	443
Brückenleger II	275
Brückenleger IV	275
Brückenleger IV s	277
Büssing-NAG trucks	432, 454

D

Daimler-Benz cars	410, 426, 432
Daimler-Benz trucks	432, 444, 455

E

E-100	98
Elefant	142

F

Ferdinand	142
Flakpanzer III	155
Flamingo	244
Flammpanzer 38	251
Ford Trucks	447

G

Geschützpanzer 39 H(f) 7.5 cm PaK40(Sf) Hotchkiss	242
Geschützpanzer 39 H(f) le.F.H. 16 & 18 Hotchkiss	196
Geschützwagen IVb für 10.5 cm le.F.H. 18/1(Sf)	189
Geschützwagen Lorraine-Schlepper fuer le.F.H. 18/4	193
Goliath	263
Grille	170

H

Halftrack, armored	339
Heavy Uniform Personnel Vehicle	424
Heavy Wermacht Towing Tractor	395, 478
Henschel trucks	448
Heuschrecke Ivb	194
Hetzer	128
Hornisse	228
Hummel	182

J

Jagdpanzer 38	128
Jagdpanzer IV	133
Jagdpanther	139
Jagdtiger	144

K

Karl	199
Kettenkraftrad	456
Kommandeurswagen (Type 87)	420
Krupp trucks	436, 449
Kübelwagen Type 82 VW	413
Kugelblitz	163

L

Landwasserschlepper	277
le.F.H. 18/40/2 (Sf.) auf Geschützwagen III/IV	197
Le gep Beobachtungskraftwagen	385
Le gep Munitionskraftwagen	383
Light Uniform Personnel Vehicle	409
Light Uniform Truck-Diesel	429

M

Marder II	213
Marder III	215
Maultier	389, 493
Maus	96
Medium Uniform Personnel Vehicle	421
Minenräumgerät mit Pz.Kpfw.Antrieb	274
Minenräum-Wagen	262
Mittler Ladungsträger	273
Mobelwagen	157
Munitionsfahrzeug III/IV	285
Munitionspanzer 38(t) (Sf) Ausf. M	283
Munitionspanzer auf Fahrgestell Panzerkampfwagen III	
	284
Munitionsschlepper auf Pz Kpfw I Ausf. A	281
Munitionsschlepper fur Karlgerat	287

N

Nashorn   228

O

Opel Blitz 1.5 ton   440
Opel Blitz 3 ton   451
Ostwind   161

P

Panther   75
Panzer IV/70 (V)   136
Panzer IV/70 (A)   138
Panzer B2(F)   245
Panzerbefehlswagens III   46
Panzerfähre   280
Panzerfunkwagen   320
Panzerjäger 38(t)   215
Panzerkampfwagen I   9
Panzerkampfwagen II   17
Panzerkampfwagen II Flamm   244
Panzerkampfwagen III   29
Panzerkampfwagen III (Fl)   248
Panzerkampfwagen IV   52
Panzerkampfwagen V   75
Panzerkampfwagen 35(t)   24
Panzerkampfwagen 38(t)   27
Panzerkampfwagen 38 für 2 cm Flak 38   153
Panzerselbstfahrlafette 1a 5 cm PaK38 auf Gepanzerter
    Munitionsschlepper   237
Panzerselbstfahrlafette 1c 5 cm PaK38 auf Panzerkampf-
    wagen II Sonderfahrgestell 901   239
Panzerselbstfahrlafette 1 für 7.62 cm PaK36(r) auf fahrg-
    estell-Panzerkampfwagen II Ausf.. D   210
Panzerselbstfahrlafette II auf Zgkw 5t (HKP 902)   394
Panzerspähwagen RK Ausf. A   388
Porsche Tiger   82
Puma   327

R

RSO   497

S

Schwere Ladungsträger Ausf. C   269
Schweres Minenraumfahrzeug 'Raumer-S'   274
Schwimmwagen (Type 166)   417
Sd. Kfz. 6 5-ton halftrack   474
Sd. Kfz. 7 8-ton halftrack   479
Sd. Kfz. 8 12-ton halftrack   487
Sd. Kfz. 9 18-ton halftrack   489
Sd. Kfz. 10 1-ton halftrack   462
Sd. Kfz. 11 3-ton halftrack   469
Sd. Kfz. 250 halftrack   340
Sd. Kfz. 251 halftrack   355
Sprengladungsträger   266
Springer   272
Steyr 1500   427
Sturmgeschütz-I (Flamm)   250

Sturmgeschütz Ausf. A   100
Sturmgeschütz Ausf. B   102
Sturmgeschütz Ausf. C & D   105
Sturmgeschütz Ausf. E   108
Sturmgeschütz Ausf. F   109
Sturmgeschütz Ausf. F/8   111
Sturmgeschütz Ausf. G   113
Sturmgeschütz IV   118
Sturmhaubitze   116
Sturminfanteriegeschütz 33   120
Sturmmörserwagen   125
Sturmpanzer   122
Sturmstegpanzer   277
sWS   395, 478

T

Tiger E   85
Tiger I   85
Tiger II   91

W

Wespe   167
Wirbelwind   159

Z

Zundapp Motorcycles   404

Numeral

2 cm Flak 38 auf Schützenpanzerwagen Sd.Kfz. 251   380
2 cm Flakvierling auf Fahrgestell Panzerkampfwagen IV
    155
3.7 cm Selbstfahrlafette L/70   394
4.7cm PaK(t) (Sfl) auf Pz Kpfw I Ausf. B   206
4.7 cm PaK(t) (Sfl) auf Panzerkampfwagen 35R 731(f)- 236
7.5 cm PaK40/2 auf fahrgestell Panzerkampfwagen II   213
7.5 cm PaK40/1 auf Geschützenwagen FCM(f)   243
7.5 cm PaK40/1 auf Geschützenwagen Lorraine Schlep-
    per (f)   240
7.5 cm Selbstfahrlafette L/40.8 Modell 1   393
8.8 cm Flak auf Sonderfahrgestell (Pz.Sfl.IVc)   164
10.5cm K. Panzer Selbstfahrlafette IVa   226
10.5 cm le.F.H.16 Geschützpanzer   187
10.5 cm le.F.H. 16 auf gep.Sfl. FCM   188
10.5 cm le.F.H. 18/3 (Sf.) auf Geschützwagen B2   192
10.5 cm le.F.H. 18/6 (Sf.) auf Geschützwagen III/IV 'Heus-
    chrecke IVb'   195
12.8 cm Selbstfahrlafette L/61   233
15 cm s.I.G. (mot S) Pz Kpfw I Ausf. B   165
15 cm s.I.G. 33 auf Fgst Pz Kpfw II (Sf)   166
15 cm s.I.G. 33/2 (Sf) on Bergepanzerwagen 38   176